The handbook *of* Gardening

The handbook *of*
Gardening

A CONCISE ENCYCLOPEDIA OF PRACTICAL
TECHNIQUES FOR EVERY GARDENER

JACKIE MATTHEWS RICHARD BIRD
ANDREW MIKOLAJSKI

LORENZ BOOKS

This edition is published by Lorenz Books
Lorenz Books is an imprint of Anness Publishing Ltd

Hermes House, 88–89 Blackfriars Road, London SE1 8HA
tel. 020 7401 2077; fax 020 7633 9499
www.lorenzbooks.com; info@anness.com

© Anness Publishing Ltd 2004

UK agent: The Manning Partnership Ltd
6 The Old Dairy, Melcombe Road, Bath BA2 3LR
tel. 01225 478444; fax 01225 478440
sales@manning-partnership.co.uk

UK distributor: Grantham Book Services Ltd
Isaac Newton Way, Alma Park Industrial Estate
Grantham, Lincs NG31 9SD
tel. 01476 541080; fax 01476 541061
orders@gbs.tbs-ltd.co.uk

North American agent/distributor: National Book Network
4501 Forbes Boulevard, Suite 200, Lanham, MD 20706
tel. 301 459 3366; fax 301 429 5746
www.nbnbooks.com

Australian agent/distributor: Pan Macmillan Australia
Level 18, St Martins Tower, 31 Market St, Sydney, NSW 2000
tel. 1300 135 113; fax 1300 135 103
customer.service@macmillan.com.au

New Zealand agent/distributor: David Bateman Ltd
30 Tarndale Grove, Off Bush Road, Albany, Auckland
tel. (09) 415 7664; fax (09) 415 8892

Publisher: Joanna Lorenz
Editorial Director: Helen Sudell
Editor: Valerie Ferguson
Designer: Andrew Heath
Photographers: Peter Anderson, Sue Atkinson, Jonathan Buckley, Derek Cranch, Sarah Cuttle,
David England, John Freeman, Michelle Garrett, Jerry Hapur, Janine Hosegood, Jacqui Hurst,
Andrea Jones, Simon McBride, Peter McHoy, Andrew Mikolajski, Marie O'Hara,
David Parmiter, Debbie Patterson, Howard Rice, Derek St Romaine, Barbara Segall,
Brigitte Thomas, Juliette Wade, David Way, Jo Whitworth, Polly Wreford
Text contributors: Pattie Barron, Susan Berry, Richard Bird, Steve Bradley, Valerie Bradley,
Kathy Brown, Jo Chatterton, Joan Clifton, Ted Collins, Stephanie Donaldson, Tessa Evelegh,
Lin Hawthorne, Hazel Key, Gilly Love, Jackie Matthews, Peter McHoy, Andrew Mikolajski,
Barbara Segall
Garden designers: Declan Buckley, Lara Copley-Smith, Sally Court, Dennis Fairweather,
Jacqui Gordon, Alan Gray, Bernard Hickie, Jennifer Jones, Elsie Josland, Robert Kite,
Shari Lawrence Garden Design, Christina Oates, Antony Paul, Wendy and Michael Perry,
Ben Pike, Graham Robeson, Lucy Summers, Paul Thompson, Mrs Winkle-Howarth,
Diane Yakely

Previously published in twelve separate volumes, *Annuals for Instant Colour,*
Glorious Scent in the Garden, Hanging Baskets, Houseplant Success,
Low Maintenance Garden, Perfect Patios & Terraces, Planting for Colour Through the Year,
Planting with Perennials, Pruning Success, Right Plant, Right Place, Tasks for the Gardener
Season by Season, Window Boxes

1 3 5 7 9 10 8 6 4 2

Contents

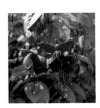

Introduction

Whatever your particular interests, this gardening handbook is designed to help you achieve your aims and enjoy your garden to the maximum. Here, you will find everything you need in order to create a lovely outdoor environment – and with the minimum of maintenance if that is your desire. The wealth of informative material has been divided into two major sections. The five chapters that comprise *Practical Planning*, will help you through gardening basics, while the latter half of the book, *Planting for*

Below: Some gardens give the appearance of blooming effortlessly.

Visual Impact & Scent, concentrates on satisfying more aesthetic considerations and also includes a chapter on growing plants indoors.

In *Right Plant, Right Place* you will learn how to assess your garden as an assemblage of mini-sites, each with its own microclimate and soil conditions that will suit certain types of plant more than others. You will also learn how to prepare soil, sow seed, plant out and then look after your plants once they are in the garden. The chapter concludes with a chart of popular plants that lists their preferred growing conditions, main season of interest and best planting time.

Perfect Patios covers everything from planning (site, size, purpose, design), through the relative merits of different construction materials, to thinking about appropriate screening and suitable plants. Style and finishing touches such as lighting, water features, arbours, furniture and even heating are also discussed.

Gardeners keen on reducing the time they spend on chores will find the chapter on *Low-maintenance Gardening* essential reading. The labour-saving tips and advice cover everything from landscaping ideas to watering, discouraging weeds, and selecting beautiful easy-care plants.

Pruning is a real worry for many people, but it does not need to be. *Pruning Success* clearly explains the basic principles, showing how you can keep all your plants the size you want and encourage them to perform superbly. General techniques and equipment are described, while helpful charts list plants (including climbers) along with the best time and method of pruning.

The last chapter of Section I, *Seasonal Tasks*, details all the gardening jobs that need to be done through the year. Each season is broken down into early, mid and late, or roughly monthly sections, to ensure that you don't miss any of the important tasks.

Above: An all-white garden can be very striking if you vary the tones of white and add in cream, silver and plenty of foliage.

Below: Colour co-ordinated borders work well in any garden.

Above: A well-tended lawn provides an attractive focal point in this garden.

The second section of the book, beginning with *Shade, Tone & Hue* explains how colour works, so that you can make choices for harmonizing your planting schemes. Advice on when particular plants are at their best and a quick-reference chart show how you can ensure glorious colour in the garden at all times of the year.

The next two chapters, *Annual Attraction* and *Perennials*, focus on those plants that are jointly responsible for so much colour in our gardens. Advice is given on how to use both types of plant effectively – temporary annuals in seasonal bedding schemes and mixed borders, perennials as permanent

planting – and which plants will do best in different situations. Useful charts provide at-a-glance information on the best choices for both groups by colour and season of interest.

Scent in the Garden shows how your garden can be filled with delightful perfume at any time of the year. Scented plants can be found in every category, so you can choose some to suit any planting and to complement any garden style. A checklist at the end of the chapter provides a seasonal reference for scented plants.

Hanging baskets are like miniature gardens. Suspended at eye-level, they can receive much scrutiny and so need to always look their best. The *Hanging Baskets* chapter lets you into all the secrets for planting up and maintaining magnificent fragrant baskets for every season of the year. A chart lists the best plants for baskets, to inspire you to experiment with your own combinations.

Before rushing out to buy a window box you need to think about the style of the container and the type of planting you want to achieve. In *Window Boxes*, you will find everything you need to know, including information on different types of container, composts and mulches as well as tips on planting and maintenance. There is also advice on keeping an arrangement looking interesting and colourful through the year. Readers with culinary interests will appreciate the section on growing herbs, fruit and vegetables. A seasonal task list plus a reference chart will help you to keep up appearances.

The *Indoor Plants* chapter completes the compendium with valuable

Below: A herb garden, complete with roses and gravel area, is a pleasant place to sit.

Above: Getting all of your flowers and shrubs to bloom at the same time and in profusion requires skill and dedication.

advice on selecting and growing plants within your home.

Finally, a list of plant names is included, giving the common and Latin names for each plant.

PRACTICAL
PLANNING

RIGHT PLANT, RIGHT PLACE

Every year thousands of plants die shortly after they are planted out in the garden simply because they have been placed in the wrong spot. A little time spent checking the ideal conditions for the plant you want to buy, or better still identifying the conditions you can offer and then seeking the right plant, will pay dividends in a better display and longer-lived, healthier plant.

Choosing the Location

EVERY PLANT HAS A PREFERENCE ABOUT ITS IDEAL GROWING
CONDITIONS, AND PUTTING A PLANT IN THE RIGHT LOCATION AND
SOIL WILL ENSURE THAT IT HAS THE BEST POSSIBLE START
AND CHANCE OF LONG-TERM HEALTH AND VIGOUR.

PERFECT PLANT ENVIRONMENTS

Many factors influence the environment in your garden and conditions can vary considerably in different parts of it. The climate, type of soil, shelter and the amount of sunlight it receives all play a role.

Fortunately, many plants can cope with a wide range of climatic variation and soil, and grow surprisingly well in conditions far removed from their natural habitat. These plants are understandably popular and deserve to be considered for inclusion in many

Above: This fuchsia and clematis look good together, and the clematis also benefits from having its roots in the shade.

schemes. But to get the very best results in the long-term, plants need to be carefully selected to suit the particular conditions that are to be found in your garden, as well as to suit the requirements of your design.

ALTERING THE ENVIRONMENT

While it is always better to work with nature, rather than against it, sometimes you may want to influence it to allow you to grow particular plants. Altering the environment within your garden allows you to create microclimates specifically for certain types of plants to enjoy.

Above: A single garden can contain dozens of environments, each of which can be exploited by growing suitable plants.

SOIL STRUCTURE

All soil consists of sand, silt, clay and humus (organic matter), and the proportions in which each is present will determine its structure – its consistency and water-retaining properties. The more large sand particles it contains, the more easily water will drain through it and the quicker it will warm up in spring, allowing earlier planting. Silt particles are smaller, so water is held for longer, but they retain little in the way of nutrients. Clay particles are the smallest of all. They hold on to nutrients and water very well, but in high percentages will produce a heavy, solid soil that is cold (slow to warm up in spring), and prone to damage if worked when too wet.

Chalky and limy soils, which overlie chalk or limestone, are shallow,

Above: Matching plants to the type of soil in your garden ensures that they will thrive and perform well.

free-draining and of moderate fertility. Loam is a perfect balance of all the elements. It is a crumbly soil, often dark in colour, which holds both moisture and nutrients well without becoming waterlogged. Unfortunately, this ideal soil is rare – most gardens have a soil that favours one particle size over the others and so needs help in the form of added organic matter.

Above: A small pond sunk into a patio allows water-loving plants to be grown in an otherwise dry situation.

GARDENER'S TIP

To find out the texture of your soil, pick up a handful of damp soil and roll it between your finger and thumb. If it feels rough and granular, but the grains don't adhere to each other, the soil is sandy. If it forms a ball when your roll it between your thumb and forefinger, it is a sandy loam. If it is rather sticky and makes a firm shape, it is a clay loam. But if you can mould it into shapes, it is a clay soil.

Above: Roses grow in most types of soil, but most prefer slightly acid conditions if they are to produce abundant blooms.

Soil pH

Whether a soil is acid or alkaline is defined by its pH level, which can vary considerably within even local areas, depending on where topsoil may have been brought in from or the nature of the underlying rock. Within a garden levels can vary depending on where manure, fertilizer, lime or even builder's rubble has been applied in the past.

Individual plants prefer different pH levels and some have quite specific requirements. It is a good idea to test the soil in your garden or border before selecting plants. You can then be sure to make an appropriate choice.

Altering pH levels

It is possible to influence the pH level in soil, although this is usually only worthwhile for growing vegetables when increasing yields is desirable. With ornamental plants it is usually more satisfactory to choose plants to suit the soil.

Raising soil pH is relatively easy and can have beneficial effects on a long-term basis, but lowering it is difficult, costly and usually only a short-term measure. If you really want to grow lime-hating plants and your soil has a pH reading of 7 or over, then the best option is probably to grow them in containers with a compost (soil mix) to suit.

Above: Foxgloves and many other cottage-garden plants are not fussy about the type of soil they grow in.

Above: Many plants, including ferns, will thrive in the moist area surrounding a fountain.

MOISTURE

Plants vary in the amount of moisture they require, and the amount of moisture available to plants in your garden will depend on a number of factors.

Rainfall can vary considerably within quite small areas depending on local topographical conditions, and even the direction in which the garden faces can affect the water it receives, depending on the prevailing wind relative to the house. Even though plenty of rain falls, it may not be falling on the soil where it is needed, but on the house, where it runs off down the drains.

How long the moisture is held within the soil, and therefore how long it is available for use by plants, is affected by the amount of sun or shade the plot receives as well as the soil type. A light, sandy soil loses its moisture quickly, while a heavy, clay soil is slower to drain, making moisture available to the plants for a longer period of time. Warmth from the sun will not only cause the soil to dry out more quickly, but will encourage plants to grow and use up more water.

Additionally, having large established specimens already in situ can mean there is less water available for newly introduced plants. An older plant will have sent roots down to the lower levels within the soil, to take advantage of all the moisture it can, leaving little for a new plant that is still reliant on water much nearer the surface. A 5-year-old tree, for example, will take up in excess of 4 litres (1 gallon) of water every day. If the garden does not receive enough rainfall to support plants with this kind of requirement you may have to consider choosing plants that need a lower intake.

Above: Ebullient yellow mimulas contrast well with the restrained foliage of hostas. Both these plants like moist soil.

Choosing the Location

SUN AND SHADE

Light is essential to plants. It provides the energy needed by the plant to manufacture food during daylight hours, a process known as photosynthesis. The length of daylight also influences the time of year when flowers and fruit are produced and leaves fall.

The amount of light individual plants require varies. Although the majority of garden plants are sun loving, there are nonetheless plenty of shade-loving plants that will also thrive in darker conditions. Many even prefer to grow in shade. Mediterranean plants and roses grow best in direct sunlight, but rhododendrons like some shade. Ivies and periwinkles like heavily shaded areas.

Above: A sun-drenched border blazes with a breathtaking display of fiery reds and yellows.

WIND AND POLLUTION

Exposure to strong winds can be a problem for some plants, especially young ones or those with fragile stems. It can damage growth and cause desiccation. Conversely a gentle wind aids the dispersal of pollen and seed, can cool plants down in hot weather, and prevents the build-up of a stagnant atmosphere round plants, which can incubate disease. Where strong wind is a regular problem, it needs to be moderated by the installation of a windbreak of some sort.

Busy urban thoroughfares can become laden with fumes and particles that can be detrimental to many plants, especially in front gardens. Finding attractive specimens that can withstand this daily onslaught will ensure that an urban garden never looks drab.

Above: Many plants enjoy shady conditions, but they tend to lack colourful flowers. Here, a garden ornament adds interest.

Above: Clever use of plant colour and shape can create stunning effects in any location within a garden.

PLANNING YOUR PLANTING

Whether you are planning an entire garden or just designing a border, you will naturally begin by visualizing the effect you want to create, and listing favourite plants that you cannot do without. Before you go any further, and without compromising your initial vision, it is essential to check all their growing requirements and be realistic about what you can grow.

Hard surfaces, including raised beds and paths, and vertical elements, in the form of climbing plants, shrubs and trees, need careful consideration. These create microclimates, extending the range of plants you can grow.

Most plants look far better when planted in largish groups. Propagation is one of the easiest and cheapest ways to increase your stock of plants. But you will need to plan when to do this

in order to have plants ready for your garden at the correct time. Most propagation is done in the autumn by taking cuttings or collecting seeds.

HOW TO USE THIS CHAPTER

This chapter explains how to successfully match plants to the conditions in your garden, to maximize good results. The first section tackles the basics of ground preparation, sowing and planting as well as offering tips on plant maintenance. In *Different Soil Conditions*, you can learn about how your soil influences the types of plants you are likely to grow most successfully. In *Planting in Different Locations* are examples of different types of site likely to exist within a garden and suggestions for planting them. Finally, there is a chart of plants with information on preferred soil type, whether they like sun or shade, and sowing, planting and flowering times.

Above: Planting in groups gives solid patches of eye-catching colour.

Getting Started

WHATEVER PLANTS YOU CHOOSE, YOU NEED TO LOOK AFTER THEM CORRECTLY. CAREFUL SOIL PREPARATION, SOWING AND PLANTING WILL PAY DIVIDENDS. REGULAR CHECKING AND MAINTENANCE ONCE ESTABLISHED WILL ENSURE THRIVING SPECIMENS.

ANALYSING YOUR SOIL

Plant nutrients are held in solution in the soil where they are absorbed by the roots. Phosphorus, potassium, magnesium, calcium and sulphur are needed in fairly large quantities for plants to thrive. Trace elements including manganese and chlorine are also needed in smaller quantities. You can test the soil for major nutrients using a special soil testing kit to see if any are lacking.

The calcium content of soil is measured on a scale of pH, which ranges from 0 to 14. The most acid is 0 and 14 is the most alkaline. The scale of pH affects the solubility of minerals and therefore their availability to plants via the roots.

Testing for pH

Before selecting plants for your garden, it is worth testing your soil to see whether it is acid, neutral or alkaline. A pH soil testing kit is easy to use and readily available from a garden centre. Alternatively, you can use a pH meter, which has a probe for inserting into the soil and is more economical in the long term.

1 Take a sample of soil from the area to be tested from about 10 cm (4 in) under the soil surface. If it is wet, allow it to dry out. Place the sample in a screw-top jar or test tube.

2 Following the manufacturer's instructions, add the indicator chemical to the soil and then the liquid. Shake vigorously and allow the contents to settle. Repeat the shaking and allow to settle again. Compare the colour of the liquid to the chart accompanying the kit to find the pH level of your soil. It is best to test several samples from different parts of the garden, as pH can vary within quite a small area. It can also alter over time, so repeat the process every few years to give you an accurate reading of current conditions.

PREPARING THE SOIL

The best results are achieved by getting the growing site in as good a condition as possible before you even purchase or propagate a plant. Once plants are in the soil, it will be difficult to dig it over or add compost in bulk. The first task is to clear the ground. Weeds will be the most likely problem, but in many new gardens there will be builder's rubbish to remove.

Weeds have to be either totally removed or killed. If the soil in your garden is light and crumbly, it is possible to remove the weeds as you dig. On heavier soils you can either cover the ground with an impermeable mulch such as thick black polythene, for several months, or use a weedkiller.

Dig the soil over, adding as much well-rotted organic matter as possible. If you can, carry out the digging in the autumn and leave the ground until spring before planting. If you do this you will see, and be able to remove, any weeds that have re-grown from roots that were missed before.

For an existing bed top-dress the soil with a good layer of well-rotted compost or farmyard manure.

GARDENER'S TIP

Never attempt to work soil when the weather is very wet. Pressure on wet soil will compact it. If you do have to get on a border when it is wet, stand on a wooden plank, which spreads the load.

DIGGING A NEW BED

1 When the ground is cleared of weeds, dig the first trench to one spade's depth across the plot. Barrow the soil to the other end of the plot.

2 Fork a layer of well-rotted compost or manure into the bottom of the trench to improve the soil structure and provide nutrients for the plants. Break it up if it is in thick clumps.

3 Dig the next trench across the plot, turning the soil on to the compost in the first trench. Add compost to the new trench and then dig the next. Continue down the border until the whole surface has been turned. Fill the final trench with the earth taken from the first.

SOWING SEED IN SOIL

For bulk growing of the more common garden plants, sowing directly into the soil is far less bother and much less expensive because you will not need to buy pots and compost (soil mix).

Like annuals, many perennials can be sown where they are to flower, but for those that will not flower until the following year it is best to sow them in a nursery bed, if you have the space.

Sow the seed in spring, as the soil begins to warm up. You can bring this forward a few weeks if you cover the soil with cloches from early spring. Mark the ends of each row with labels so you know what you have planted. Do not let the bed dry out and keep it weeded. When the seedlings have grown to a manageable size, thin them to distances of at least 15cm (6in).

Most species will be ready to plant out in their flowering position during the following autumn while the ground is still warm.

EASY SEED FOR SOWING IN
OPEN GROUND

Alcea
Aquilegia
Astrantia
Centranthus ruber
Delphinium
Foeniculum
Helleborus
Myosotis
Primula
Verbascum
Verbena
Viola

SOWING IN OPEN GROUND

1 Prepare the soil carefully, removing all weeds and breaking it down into a fine tilth with a rake.

2 Draw out a shallow drill with a corner of a hoe, about 1cm (1/2in) deep. Keep the drill straight by using a garden line as a guide. If the soil is dry, water the drill with a watering can and wait until the water has soaked in.

3 Sow the seed thinly along the drill. Larger seed can be sown at intervals to avoid the need for thinning later. Gently rake the soil back into the drill, covering over the seed. Tamp down the row with the base of the rake. Keep the drills moist until germination.

SOWING SEED IN POTS

For small quantities of seeds, and those that can be difficult to germinate, such as parsley, sow in 9cm (3¹/₂in) pots or in a tray, then place in a sheltered spot, away from direct sun. Germination will usually take from a few days to a few weeks depending on the species, although some can take longer and may even require a winter's cold weather before germination will occur. Keep the pots watered. The seedlings are ready to prick out when they have developed their first true leaves or when they are large enough to handle. Keep them covered in a cold frame for a day or so, before hardening them off by gradually opening the frame more fully each day.

Most perennials can be sown in early spring. Some, however, such as primulas and hellebores, need to be sown as soon as the seeds ripen in late summer or autumn.

SOWING SEED IN CONTAINERS

1 Fill a pot or tray with compost (soil mix). Tap firmly on the bench to settle the compost and lightly flatten the surface with the base of a pot. This will exclude air pockets which would hinder the growth of roots. Sow the seed thinly on top.

2 Cover the seed with a layer of sieved compost or fine gravel. Water the pot thoroughly either from above with a watering can fitted with a fine rose or from below by standing the pot in a tray of shallow water.

PRICKING OUT SEEDLINGS

1 Water the pot an hour before gently knocking out the seedlings. Carefully break up the rootball and split into clumps. Dealing with one clump at a time, gently ease the seedlings away, touching only the leaves.

2 Hold a seedling over a pot by one or more of its leaves and gently trickle moist compost around its roots until the pot is full. Avoid touching the fragile stem or roots. Tap the pot on the bench to exclude any air pockets, then firm down gently with your fingertips and water.

Buying Plants

Most plants are available in containers all year round. If you want good-quality plants that are accurately labelled, go to a reputable source.

Check your prospective purchase carefully and reject any plant that is diseased, looks unhealthy or is harbouring pests. If possible, knock it out of its pot and look at the roots. Again reject any that show signs of pests. Also reject any that are pot-bound, that is when the roots have wound round the inside of the pot, creating a solid mass. Such plants are difficult to establish.

If the plants are in a greenhouse or tunnel, harden them off when you get them home. Planting them straight out in the garden may put them under stress, from which they might not recover.

Above: Bulbs are invaluable for growing in borders as well as for naturalizing in grassy areas.

Planting Bulbs

Much of the interest and colour in a spring garden comes from flowering bulbs. Daffodils, tulips, snowdrops, bluebells, crocuses, *Iris reticulata*, aconites and hyacinths can be used en masse in borders or singly under trees. Daffodils, crocuses, bluebells and aconites can be naturalized in lawns. To plant in lawns remove a plug of grass and soil and replace after positioning the bulbs.

Planting Bulbs in a Border

1 Excavate a hole large enough to take a group of bulbs. If the soil is poor or impoverished fork in garden compost or well-rotted manure. You could also add a layer of grit or sand.

2 Space out the bulbs, not too evenly, planting at a depth that will leave them covered with about twice their own depth of soil.

3 To deter slugs and encourage the bulbs to flower sprinkle more grit or sand around them before returning the soil.

PLANTING SHRUBS AND PERENNIALS

When you are planting a new border put all the plants, still in their pots, in their positions according to your planting plan. Stand back to assess the result and make any necessary adjustments. When you are satisfied with the positions of the plants you can begin to plant.

Water the plants before planting out. Start planting at the back or one end of a border and move forwards. When you have finished planting, cover the soil between the plants with a layer of mulch to keep the weeds down and preserve moisture. Be prepared to water regularly in dry weather for at least the first few weeks after planting. If you are planting isolated plants in unprepared soil, add plenty of well-rotted organic matter to the soil.

If you decide that a plant is in the wrong spot you may have to leave it in place for the growing season, otherwise you might damage the roots, but in autumn or spring, you can lift it and move it to a better position.

SPRING BULBS

Crocus
Cyclamen coum
Eranthis hyemalis
Galanthus nivalis
Hyacinthoides
Hyacinthus
Iris reticulata
Narcissus
Tulipa

PLANTING OUT

1 Dig a hole with a trowel or spade, and with the plant still in its pot, check that the depth and width is right. The plant must be placed in the soil at the same depth that it was in the pot or just a little deeper.

2 Knock the plant out of its pot, tease out some of the roots, to help them become established in the ground more quickly, and place it in the planting hole. Fill around the plant with soil and then firm it with your hands or a heel to expel large pockets of air. Water thoroughly unless the weather is wet. Mulch the surface with chipped bark, gravel, leaf mould or compost.

Different Soil Conditions

SOILS VARY WIDELY IN THEIR LEVEL OF ACIDITY OR ALKALINITY AND THE STRUCTURE OF THEIR PARTICLES, WHICH RANGE FROM LIGHT SAND TO HEAVY CLAY. THESE FACTORS DETERMINE HOW MUCH MOISTURE AND NUTRIENTS THEY CONTAIN.

ACID SOIL

This type of soil can be free draining and sandy, heavy and sticky, or even organic with a high peat content. Clay soils are often acid, and peaty soils, where the organic matter has not decomposed, are almost always acid.

Some soils, even if originally alkaline, can gradually become more acid as a result of the lime being washed out of the upper layers close to the soil

Above: Azaleas are a form of rhododendron, and like them they require an acid soil to survive.

Above: Spectacular camellias prefer acid soil, where they can grow to the size of a small tree.

surface. This is because rainwater is slightly acidic, and it dissolves the lime in the soil and washes (leaches) it down through the soil. As a result, soils in high rainfall areas are more likely to be acid than alkaline.

Plants that Depend on Acid Soil

Most plants that grow naturally on acid soils (known as calcifuge) usually struggle when grown in anything else. This is because they are unable to take up enough iron from an alkaline soil.

Some excellent garden plants grow only in acid soil, so if your garden has this condition, you can look forward to growing some real treasures.

Acid soils are generally not a problem to plant because in addition to those plants that prefer them, many plants also tolerate them. If your soil is not very acid and your climate isn't too wet, there is little restriction on what you can grow, although it may be wise to avoid Mediterranean plants such as *Cistus* and lavender which thrive in dry alkaline conditions.

Many evergreen shrubs will grow on acid soil. The glossy ovate green leaves of rhododendrons, azaleas, camellias and skimmias provide

Above: Pieris thrive on acid soil. They are grown for their red-flushed young leaves and cascades of white bell-like flowers.

wonderful backdrops for their often startlingly bright blooms that provide colour from mid-spring through the early summer. Pieris has the added attraction of red-flushed young leaves.

Permanent foliage plants also include ground covers and creeping plants like gaultherias, heathers and heaths.

Deciduous trees growing on acid soils produce some stunning autumn foliage colour. Outstanding among these are the maples (*Acer*). Many of the spring- and summer-flowering deciduous shrubs also have good autumn colour.

Plenty of perennials and annuals that grow on a wide range of soils can be used to provide seasonal highlights for the border. Wake robin, Himalayan blue poppies and lupins, however, require a slightly acid soil.

Above: Lupins come in many lovely shades and have a distinctive peppery scent. They require a slightly acid soil.

29

Year-round Interest

Acid-loving shrubs are often associated with their stunning spring flowers. The showy white, pink, red or yellow flowers of camellias, rhododendrons and azaleas bloom in abundance and are deservedly much admired. The waxy beauty of magnolia blooms, in cream or blush, is breathtaking. Witch hazels produce their surprisingly frost-resistant and fragrant, spidery blooms, in yellow to dark red, from midwinter to early spring.

Many deciduous shrubs, including maples and witch hazels, are prized for their autumn foliage colour. And there are berries, too. Several species of

Above: Heather (Calluna vulgaris) *needs acid soil to surive. Most varieties flower in late summer and autumn.*

Gaultheria produce white or purple-red fruit at this time. Some shrubs also have attractive bark.

For colour through spring and summer try Wake robin, Himalayan blue poppies and lupins.

Heathers form stunning carpets of flower colour in late summer and autumn. Many varieties are grown for their foliage, which changes colour during the year.

Above: *Magnolias make splendid specimen shrubs. Many species need an acid soil.*

Above: *Spring- and summer-flowering* Wake robin (Trillium grandiflorum) *grows well in moist, shaded soil.*

Neutralizing Acid Soil

Adding lime to the soil is an easy and effective way to reduce the acidity. However, it needs to be applied to ground that is bare of plants, dug in and left to break down for several weeks at least, or preferably longer. This is only really practical on vegetable plots, which can be left bare during the winter.

Lime should never be applied at the same time as fertilizer, as the lime will cause the fertilizer to break down too quickly. It can be used when renovating or making a new border, but most ornamental plants tolerate moderately acid soil, so it is not generally worthwhile trying to neutralize acid soil in order to grow acid-hating ornamentals in your garden.

An alternative to liming is to incorporate spent mushroom compost, which is rich in lime. You may even have the benefit of a small crop of mushrooms, as there are often spores in the compost.

PLANTS FOR ACID SOIL

Acer
Amelanchier
Azalea
Calluna vulgaris
Camellia
Erica cultivars
Gaultheria procumbens
Hamamelis
Lupinus
Magnolia
Meconopsis betonicifolia
Pieris
Rhododendron
Skimmia
Trillium grandiflorum

Above: *An ornamental border should not need any application of lime for the plants to do well, even on acid soil. This colourful display of established fuchsias and dahlias will tolerate moderately acid conditions.*

31

ALKALINE SOIL

These soils are predominantly found in chalky or limestone areas or where there is builder's rubble in the soil. They are free draining with only moderate fertility.

In some areas a shallow layer of soil overlies solid chalk or limestone rock, which can make gardening problematic. The plant roots will have great difficulty penetrating the soft rock, which can lead to poor anchorage, particularly in trees. Also, during dry periods a thin soil can hold only limited reserves of water and the upper levels of the rock become extremely dry.

Once established, however, many plants will produce an extensive, deep root system that penetrates fissures, so that when rain does fall, they can absorb the maximum amount before it drains away.

High alkalinity in soil can cause various nutrient and trace elements to become locked in a form that is

Left: Many silver-leaved plants, such as Artemisia *and* Stachys, *enjoy the free-draining conditions of an alkaline soil.*

unavailable to lime-hating plants, which then grow poorly as a result and often have yellowing leaves.

Plants that Depend on Alkaline Soil

Some plants can only grow in an alkaline soil, and these are known as calcicole, or lime-loving. They have adapted to cope with the high alkalinity and cannot survive on other types of soil.

Most plants are more tolerant, but many still enjoy alkaline conditions. Among them are many Mediterranean plants, including *Santolina*, *Artemisia*, *Helianthemum*, *Cistus* and herbs, which benefit from the good drainage.

Above: Mediterranean plants, such as Cistus, *thyme and sage, cope well with alkaline conditions.*

Planning Displays

Warm and well-drained chalk and limestone soils play host to a diverse mix of plants, some with more delicate floral attributes than others, but all repaying close inspection.

A host of attractive flowering shrubs tolerate alkaline conditions, such as *Berberis, Buddleja davidii, Choisya ternata, Deutzia, Philadelphus, Sorbus* and viburnums. Many members of the pea family, including brooms, *Gleditsia* and *Robinia*, often excel on these soils.

Clematis and honeysuckle are useful climbers, the former for their long flowering period and the latter for their intoxicating scent.

Tough perennials like *Acanthus, Achillea, Eryngium* carnations, *Hypericum* and *Verbascum* are all

Above: Free-flowering mallows (Lavatera) *are tolerant of a wide range of soil conditions. They bloom throughout summer.*

useful for the middle to back of a border. Wild flowers such as cornflowers and foxgloves can be included. Smaller perennials for the foreground include *Bergenia, Doronicum*, scabious and drought-resistant thymes.

Plants with silvery-grey foliage like pinks, saxifrage and *Gypsophila* seem to have a softening effect on a sunny border, and they contribute their own attractive flowers. In shady spots you can plant stinking hellebore, wild orchids, *Iris foetidissima, Colchicum* and *Campanula*.

For filling in gaps, there are numerous annuals and biennials, including *Lavatera, Matthiola, Tagetes* and many everlasting flowers that can be dried in the autumn.

Above: Berberis is a versatile shrub that *will tolerate many soil types, including alkaline ones.*

Year-round Interest

With so many lovely plants thriving on alkaline soil, maintaining interest through the year is not a problem.

There are bulbs that flower in every season, but spring is when most of them produce their jewel-like colour. Spring flowers also come from plants as diverse as *Helleborus orientalis*, peonies, *Doronicum* and lilac. In summer *Helianthemum*, pinks, carnations, *Gypsophila*, *Verbascum* and clematis take over. Lavender and scabious continue well into autumn, when cotoneasters and firethorn flash their red, orange or yellow berries.

The Christmas rose (*Helleborus niger*) reveals its graceful white flowers through winter.

Some deciduous trees grown for autumn foliage are often described as lime-tolerant (typically *Acer davidii* and *A. rubrum*). Yet they do not always produce their foliage display on soils with a high alkaline content.

Instead, the leaves shrivel and fall, so to avoid disappointment it is better not to plant them in alkaline soil. However, *Sorbus sargentiana*, *Euonymus alatus* and *E. europaeus* will produce brilliant autumnal colour, even on poor soils over chalk.

Above: Bulbs are useful for spring colour. Here, massed tulips fill a border in late spring.

Above: French lavender (Lavandula stoechas) *thrives in the free-draining conditions of alkaline soil.*

PLANTS THAT THRIVE IN ALKALINE SOIL

Buddleja davidii
Clematis
Cotoneaster
Dianthus
Doronicum
Gypsophyla paniculata
Helianthemum nummularium
Helleborus
Lavandula
Paeonia
Pyracantha
Scabiosa
Syringa
Verbascum

Correcting Alkaline Conditions

Even though there is a wide range of plants that will tolerate high alkalinity, if you want an even richer diversity of species it will be necessary to improve the organic content of the soil. Adding copious quantities of bulky organic material, such as well-rotted farmyard manure, leaf mould, garden compost and turf, will improve moisture retention and the humus content of the soil. Incorporating organic matter is best done soon after a period of rain.

Adding dried blood and balanced artificial fertilizers can also help to improve the nutrient levels. Chalk soils tend to be lacking in potash, which must be applied for non-lime-loving plants to do well.

Sometimes, breaking up the top 60cm (24in) layer of underlying chalk with a fork or spade will help roots to develop more easily and give plants a good start.

Above: Adding well-rotted manure, garden compost or leaf mould will improve the soil structure and nutrient content.

Above: A prolific clematis scrambles over a wall. It thrives in alkaline conditions as long as its roots are protected from the sun.

SANDY SOIL

The low clay content in sandy soils (less than 8 per cent) makes them much less water-retentive than clay soils. Their particles are also larger than those of clay, making the soils light, free-draining and relatively infertile.

Sandy soils warm up quickly in spring, so planting out can start early, but they also cool down quickly.

Making the Best of a Sandy Soil

The easiest solution for coping with a sandy soil is to grow only drought-resistant plants that require few nutrients. Many of these originate in dry areas of low fertility, and you will find enough plants to create interesting displays without having to resort to wholesale enrichment of the soil.

Above: Brachyglottis *grows in sites that are too dry for many other plants, but it needs plenty of sunshine.*

Most plants that can cope with a sandy soil are deep-rooted, so that they can seek out moisture at low levels. Cacti and other succulents have fleshy leaves, stems or roots which can store water when it is available for use during dry periods.

Other plants have silvery-grey foliage to reflect sunlight or sparse, small, leathery or spiny leaves to reduce moisture loss through evaporation from the plant. Many of these plants are Mediterranean in origin.

Above: Drought-resistant plants such as thyme are perfect for growing in light sandy soil.

> MEDITERRANEAN PLANTS
> FOR SANDY SOIL
> *Brachyglottis*
> *Cistus*
> *Helianthemum*
> Lavender
> *Origanum*
> Rosemary
> Sage
> *Santolina*
> Thyme

Planning Displays

With foliage ranging from spiny yuccas to the soft feathery fronds of tamarisk, you can use all the different foliage shapes, textures and colours to good effect. Many spiny plants have architectural stature around which you can base your planting. Among these are the giant thistle (*Onopordum acanthium*) and the spiky-leaved, metallic-blue flowered *Eryngium*. *Echinops ritro* 'Veitch's Blue' has stunning blue, globular thistle flowers. Silver foliage perfectly sets off the mauve and soft hazy blue flowers that many of these plants produce. Red valerian (*Centranthus ruber*) also combines well with silvers and greys. Or you could try the yellow-green of spurges for an interesting effect.

Above: Yellow-green spurges make an interesting contrast with the silver of Elaeagnus *'Quicksilver' and a deadnettle.*

Grasses such as blue fescue (*Festuca glauca*) will add shape and movement. Allow sun-loving ground-covering plants such as *Nepeta* and rock roses to spill over from a border onto paths. In more shaded border edges encourage woodland plants.

Cornfield annuals, which grow on a wide range of soils, are useful for filling in blocks of colour. To create a meadow-like planting, which can be left semi-wild, sow seed in spring or autumn with a good mix of other wild flowers and grasses.

Above: Black-eyed Susan (Rudbeckia) *enjoys free-draining conditions, but do not let the soil dry out completely.*

SUMMER ANNUALS FOR SANDY SOIL

Calendula officinalis
Centaurea cyanus
Eschscholzia californica
Gypsophila
Lobularia maritima
Papaver rheas Shirley Series
Rudbeckia hirta
Silene alpestris

Year-round Interest

Sea buckthorn provides year-round value. It has narrow silvery leaves and tiny yellow spring flowers, which on female plants are followed in autumn by abundant orange berries. In winter, when many other plants have died, the buckthorn's shapely stems continue to provide interest.

From spring to autumn, silvery foliage provides a perfect backcloth for the bright colours of nearly all the popular summer annuals. Among the perennials, the tall spires of *Acanthus spinosus* carry white flowers and purple bracts from late spring to midsummer, red valerian blooms from late spring to the end of summer and yellow, pink or white achilleas last all summer long.

Spiny herbaceous plants like thistles, *Eryngium* and *Echinops* can be left standing after they have finished flowering, so that their intricate outlines will continue adding interest.

Above: Like other heathers, crimson-flowered Calluna vulgaris *'Darkness' enjoys sandy soil as long as it is acid.*

Above: Eryngium giganteum *thrives in the poorest of soils, as long as they are well drained and in full sun.*

On acid soils, heather flowers in pinks and white from midsummer to autumn. Its foliage comes in many shades of green or golden yellow and often changes colour in winter quite dramatically. Some varieties of heather flower in winter or spring, and these can tolerate alkaline soils.

PLANTS THAT PREFER SANDY SOIL

Acanthus spinosus
Achillea
Calluna vulgaris
Centranthus ruber
Cistus
Echinops ritro 'Veitch's Blue'
Erica
Eryngium giganteum
Euphorbia
Festuca glauca
Lavatera
Nepeta x *faassenii*
Onopordum acanthium
Papaver orientale
Phormium
Tamarix
Yucca gloriosa

Improving Sandy Soil

Adding plenty of organic matter, such as well-rotted manure, garden compost or leaf mould, will improve sandy soil. Many ornamental garden plants, however, will still need frequent and thorough watering during dry periods, and regular applications of fertilizer to increase the nutrient levels.

Creating Sandy Conditions

You may wish to grow some plants that thrive on sandy soil but find that your soil is too wet, heavy and fertile. In this case, you can create a dry sandy or gravelly garden. It does not need to be very large, but would provide the ideal spot for displaying some attractive plants.

> **GARDENER'S TIP**
>
> Heather (*Calluna vulgaris*) makes an excellent ground cover for sandy soil that is also acid. The many cultivars allow you to create a permanent carpet in a choice of shades that change according to the season.

Creating an arid-planting area will involve scraping away some of the topsoil to reduce fertility. Mix in enough sharp sand and gravel to improve drainage and create the sort of conditions you need. Adding areas of gravel or pebbles on the surface will add to the impression of a dry landscape.

If drainage is very poor, consider introducing some drainage channels filled with gravel to take away excess water fast.

Above: Potentillas are perfect plants for poor, free-draining soils. Alpine types prefer a gritty, sharply draining soil.

Above: Evening primrose and daisy-like feverfew both enjoy a sunny position on sandy soil.

Left: Yellow-flowering Berberis linearifolia *will thrive in most soils, but will benefit from improved drainage on very heavy ones.*

growth, making them very fertile. Plants growing in clay soil suffer less from the effects of drought in all but the driest of summers.

Clay soils can be acid, neutral or alkaline, which will also affect your choice of plants. Generally, however, the clay content of soil is a more important factor than its acidity or alkalinity in determining which plants will do well.

CLAY SOIL

This type of soil will consist of more than 25 per cent clay particles, which makes it moisture-retentive, heavy and sticky. It may become waterlogged in wet weather, is slow to warm up in spring, and may bake hard in summer.

Really heavy, sticky clay soils are unworkable when wet and easily compacted and must not be walked on.

Due to their moisture retention, however, clay soils also hold on to nutrients that plants need for healthy

Making the Best of Clay Soil

Grow plants with a vigorous constitution, as those are the ones likely to do best. Plants need to be resilient enough to withstand wet soil in winter

Above: Pyracantha *makes an impenetrable barrier when grown as an informal garden hedge.*

GARDENER'S TIP

Physically working clay soil is largely a matter of timing. If you try to do it when it is too wet it will form an impenetrable layer at the depth you dig down to, for plant roots and draining water alike. Leave it until it is too dry and you will be working with what feels like lumps of rock.

Left: The delightfully scented Rosa *'Zéphirine Drouhin' is thornless and is an excellent climber.*

enriched you can achieve a more or less traditional scheme with roses and herbaceous underplanting.

Generally, those reliable herbaceous perennials that tolerate a heavy clay soil are also plants that grow well in moist marginal, waterside plantings, such as *Astilbe*, *Mimulus*, *Phormium*, *Hosta*, *Houttuynia*, *Lysimachia*, *Gunnera* and *Rodgersia*. These provide plenty of striking architectural foliage and some arresting blooms.

It is possible to grow some bulbs in clay soil, but they will not survive if the soil becomes waterlogged during wet periods. Planting them on a layer of grit will help.

without rotting. But in the summer, they can take advantage of the soil's moisture-retaining properties, even when the surface is baked hard.

Planning Displays

Several resilient shrubs grow well on clay. Choose those that offer spring or summer flowers, autumn foliage or berries, or attractive coloured stems for the winter months.

Roses, too, are more tolerant of clay than many plants, and in a border that has been well prepared and

SHRUBS FOR CLAY SOIL

Berberis
Cornus
Cotoneaster
Crataegus
Philadelphus
Pyracantha
Viburnum opulus

Above: Hostas thrive in moist soils, and in time they will spread to form a large, domed clump.

Year-round Interest

As there is such a variety of plants that you can grow on all but the heaviest of clay soils, planting for interest through the year should not be a problem.

Small trees and shrubs have much to offer. The blossom of cherries, crab apples and hawthorn in spring is followed by that of guelder rose and

---

PLANTS THAT THRIVE ON
CLAY SOIL

Astilbe
Caltha palustris
Crambe cordifolia
Gunnera manicata
Hosta
Papaver somniferum
Philadelphus
Primula vulgaris
Rheum
Rodgersia
Rosa
Trollius

Left: Berberis is a good shrub to plant if you have a small garden and want year-round colour.

mock orange. *Berberis* produces bright yellow flowers in spring, and berries in autumn, adding to the colourful yellow, orange or red berries of *Cotoneaster* and *Pyracantha*. Guelder rose also has fleshy red berries and crabs have their apples.

In winter the coloured stems of dogwood and the contorted twigs of *Salix babylonica* var. *pekinensis* 'Tortuoasa' are visually arresting. Small willows are covered with silver catkins if you cut them back hard each spring to produce masses of new growth.

Above: The white flowers of Crambe cordifolia *create an ethereal haze when planted in a large group.*

Large-growing leafy perennials like *Gunnera*, *Rheum*, the giant thistles and *Crambe cordifolia* grow especially well on clay, usually to dramatic proportions.

Among flowering perennials yellow primroses and cowslips are soon followed by meadow flowers such as burnets and cranesbills. A host of summer flowers includes hollyhocks, *Mimulus*, *Phlox* and foxgloves.

Improving Clay Soil

The best way to improve clay soil is to add plenty of organic matter in early autumn or late spring, when the soil is workable. This will open up the soil and make it more balanced, allowing

Above: Roses like the moist fertility of clay soils, particularly when plenty of organic matter is added.

Above: Primroses (Primula vulgaris) *are ideal for a cottage garden or mossy bank, as long as the soil remains moist.*

nutrients and moisture to be readily absorbed by plant roots. It will also improve drainage and make the soil more workable when digging is required. Applications of fertilizer will also be more effective.

Where waterlogged soil is a problem, you can try growing bog-loving plants, or improve the drainage – either by digging in grit or, more expensively, installing drainage channels filled with shingle.

Clay soils can be quite acid, especially when they are waterlogged and moss grows on the surface. If you are making a new border it may be worth altering the pH level. You can do this by adding lime as described in the section on Acid Soils.

Planting in Different Locations

THE ASPECT OF A PLOT, THE AMOUNT OF SHELTER IT HAS, THE
DEGREE OF SHADE OR SUN IT RECEIVES AND THE MOISTURE CONTENT
OF THE SOIL ARE ALL RELEVANT WHEN CHOOSING PLANTS THAT WILL
THRIVE OVER A LONG PERIOD.

ASPECT

The direction your garden or border
faces and its relationship to your
house or adjacent buildings will influence the environment your plants will
be growing in. As the sun moves
around the house, different areas of
the garden can be thrown into shade
or receive the full glare of the sun for
various amounts of time. Shade can be
full, partial or dappled. In winter a
deeply shaded position can be very
damp and cold, whereas in summer it
can be pleasant. The sun can at times
be far too hot in summer, but of great
benefit during short cold days. And as
the seasons change, your garden may
be subjected to frost and bitter winds.

Above: Clematis montana *will grow
happily on an east-facing wall which
gives it some protection.*

All these factors should be considered
before planting, as they will have a
bearing on which plants will do well in
different parts of the garden.

Heavily Shaded Gardens

Some gardens may have shade from
the house for long stretches of the day.
In winter deep shade will make the
garden cold and damp. The winter
cold will be aggravated if the garden is
also exposed to strong, cold winds, so
a sheltering hedge may help, but in
spite of these disadvantages, there are
plants that not only tolerate these conditions but actually prefer them.

*Above: Sweet-smelling Mexican orange-
blossom* (Choisya ternata) *can survive
conditions in a shaded, cold garden.*

44

East-facing Gardens

An east wind in winter is the cruellest and when combined with a frost can spell instant death to plants that are less than hardy, and will nip tender buds. As with a shaded garden, a fence or hedge on the boundary will give some protection. However, a garden with a predominantly easterly aspect has the benefit of morning and early afternoon sun.

Gardens in Full Sun

The most sought-after aspect for most gardeners is a sunny one. With a house providing shelter against cold winds and a garden that takes full advantage of the sun's warming rays throughout the year it seems like an ideal location. At the height of summer, however, the sun can be relentlessly hot and glaring and will quickly dry out thin soil.

Some form of shading, perhaps attractive fences, screens of climbers, tall shrubs or small trees will be welcomed by many plants, as well as humans.

Sunny gardens are ideal for growing hot-climate and sun-loving plants, and exotic tender and half-hardy plants will thrive and even last well into the autumn if the garden is protected from wind.

West-facing Gardens

These gardens are likely to have some shade through the mornings, until the sun swings round at its highest point. But they then benefit for the rest of the day and in summer this can be quite late, when the low rays intensify colours. These are also warm gardens, unless they catch some of the colder winds, so you will need to assess whether some protection is needed.

Above: Blue Agapanthus *share a sunny border with vibrantly coloured summer bulbs such as lilies and* Crocosmia.

PLANTS FOR HEAVILY SHADED POSITIONS

Berberis x stenophylla
Camellia japonica
Clematis alpina
Choisya ternata
Garrya elliptica
Hydrangea petiolaris
Ilex corallina
Jasminum nudiflorum
Mahonia japonica

PLANTS FOR EAST-FACING POSITIONS

Bergenia cordifolia
Chaenomeles x superba
Cotoneaster horizontalis
Euphorbia griffithii
Hamamelis mollis
Helleborus feotidus
Lonicera periclymenum
Rosa rugosa
Vinca major

PLANTS FOR SUNNY POSITIONS

Agapanthus
Canna indica
Eccremocarpus scaber
Echinacea purpurea
Echinops ritro
Helenium
Kniphofia
Lilium lancifolium
Osteospermum
Yucca filamentosa
Zauschneria californica

PLANTS FOR WEST-FACING POSITIONS

Ceanothus
Crocosmia cultivars
Geranium 'Johnson's Blue'
Humulus lupulus 'Aureus'
Papaver orientale
Penstemon cultivars
Vitis coignetiae

Selecting Suitable Plants for Different Aspects

Before growing any new plants in your garden it is wise to establish that they will be suitable for the situation you intend them to occupy. A good local nursery will give advice on the best plants for your locality and particular situation.

Make sure, also, that you select a few plants to give some colour or interest for each season. Even if your garden faces predominantly east or is shady and cold, there should be several plants that will give pleasure even in the depths of winter.

Above: A smoke bush (Cotinus) has been planted so that the evening sun shines through its purple foliage.

WINDY SITES

Gusting wind can spoil plants in exposed areas. Light plants are at risk of being blown over. Plants with soft, tender foliage are likely to be scorched by the wind resulting in brown, withered leaves and poor growth.

Creating a windbreak will minimize the problem. One that is partly permeable to the wind is much more effective than a solid one, which can cause localized turbulence where the wind is deflected. Black windbreak netting is efficient but unsightly; depending on where you want to put it you could disguise it with trellis. A trellis clothed with climbers would slow down much of the wind, even without netting. Where there is sufficient room, a

Above: Spiraea japonica *is a tough shrub that can withstand strong wind. This one is 'Goldflame'.*

screen of tall, wind-tolerant shrubs planted along the most vulnerable side will be very effective. Many plants will tolerate this kind of exposure while providing colour and interest throughout the year. A broken windbreak would allow a good view to continue to be appreciated.

Staking vulnerable plants will also help protect them in windy areas.

Above: Helleborus orientalis *tolerates most conditions but needs shelter from strong, cold winds.*

WIND-TOLERANT PLANTS

Cornus alba 'Aurea'
Cotinus coggygria
Euonymus fortunei cultivars
Hamamelis virginiana
Hippophäe rhamnoides
Hydrangea paniculata
'Grandiflora'
Lavatera olbia
Lonicera pileata
Mahonia aquifolium
Philadelphus 'Belle Etoile'
Spiraea japonica
Tamarix tetrandra
Taxus baccata
Thuja occidentalis

SHADY MOIST SITES

Some people might regard the presence of a permanently shaded damp patch in their garden as a real problem, because many plants cannot cope with dark, wet conditions. Most bulbs, for instance, dislike very wet soil and will simply rot if waterlogged. Many ordinary garden plants will also die in persistently wet conditions.

It is these very conditions, however, that account for the lush and often large foliage of moisture-loving plants. Big leaves are nature's way of ensuring that the maximum amount of chlorophyll is exposed to the limited light to help photosynthesis (food manufacture) by the plant.

Above: Grow *lily-of-the-valley* (Convallaria majalis) *in full or partial shade in a moist location.*

Making the Best of a Shady Moist Site

The best way of coping with the area is to stop regarding it as a problem and see it as a wonderful opportunity for growing some lovely plants that would be unhappy in a drier situation.

Wetland plants have distinct preferences for the different types of wet site, so you need to match the plants to the conditions of your site. Most simply prefer permanently moist soil. Some plants can cope with particularly wet sites that are virtually permanently boggy and occasionally waterlogged. Similarly, some plants can grow in dappled or deep shade. Some, of course, can cope with all types of shade.

Above: Many plants and shrub thrive in shady gardens – choose appropriately for your soil type.

Above: A dense planting of different types of hosta keeps weeds at bay in a moist shady border.

Planning Displays

Make the most of the great variety of luxuriant foliage produced by shade- and moisture-loving plants. You can contrast the different types, colours and forms of foliage to make an interesting green tapestry of leaves. For example, place tall, strappy irises next to soft feathery ferns or the big pleated leaves of *Veratrum*.

If you work with a wide selection of different foliage forms and colours, you can create a planting that has as much interest as a colourful sunny flower border. And if you include a few evergreen shrubs as well, such as aucubas, skimmias, mahonias and fatsias, the display will last throughout the growing season, and into winter. All these shrubs have the added bonus of beautiful spring flowers, many of which are followed by colourful fruits. For foliage at ground level be sure to include hostas, bergenias and ivies.

Make the most of those perennial plants that flower in moist shade by placing them as occasional colourful highlights against the lush green foliage. The yellow spires of *Ligularia*, for instance, show up splendidly against a green backdrop. Where the planting edges are in dappled or partial shade, you have the opportunity to include more brightly coloured woodland plants than would grow in the darker shade.

Above: Delicate yellow flowers of Alchemilla mollis *contrast with lacy fern fronds in a shady damp corner.*

49

Left: Winter aconites (Eranthis hyemalis) *come through the soil before much else is stirring on the woodland floor.*

Woodland plants provide some real treasures in spring: winter aconites, primroses, snowdrops, snake's-head fritillaries and wake robin followed by lily-of-the-valley and wood anemones. Dicentras produce arching sprays of pendulous pink or white flowers.

Summer highlights are provided by many shade-loving perennials such as delicate *Astilbe*, *Astrantia major* and *Ligularia*. *Meconopsis cambrica*, *Impatiens* and pansies have long-flowering seasons. Rodgersia flowers in pinks, reds and white. The blues of monkshood (*Aconitum*) are useful from midsummer to autumn.

Helleborus niger and *H. orientale* produce white or greenish cream blooms through winter to spring. Witch hazels and sarcococcas also produce fragrant flowers in winter, in yellow and white respectively.

Year-round Interest

Even in a shady, damp spot you can guarantee some colour and interest for every season.

Aucubas have glossy green leaves and bear small red-purple flowers in mid-spring, which on female plants are followed by bright red berries in autumn. Variegated leaf forms are better in dappled shade. The scented spring flowers of skimmias are pink in bud opening to creamy white and followed by green berries usually ripening to red. The yellowish-green autumn flowers of mature ivies are followed by small black fruit, which are a good source of food for birds.

For dappled shade *Fatsia japonica* has big, glossy hand-shaped leaves. In partial shade evergreen mahonias have scented yellow spring flowers followed by blue to black berries. Rhododendrons and camellias both have showy spring blooms. *Viburnum davidii* bears tiny white flowers at this time, and on female plants these give way to turquoise fruits.

Above: The delightful flowers of Astrantia major *brighten up lightly shaded corners in summer.*

Creating Shady Damp Conditions

Even if your garden is not naturally wet, you can take advantage of a shady area to create a damp spot. Dig out a hollow, line it with black butyl liner with some drainage holes punched through, then return the soil, mixed with plenty of organic matter.

The liner will act like a layer of natural clay, helping to hold the moisture in the soil and reducing the need for watering.

However, if you do create an artificially moist site, you will have to be prepared to keep the soil moist by watering in periods of drought.

Above: The delicate flowers of Dicentra *thrive in a partially shaded border. They prefer neutral to alkaline soil.*

PLANTS THAT THRIVE IN
MOIST SHADE

Astilbe hybrids
Astrantia
Dicentra
Eranthis hyemalis
Fatsia japonica
Hamamelis mollis
Helleborus
Hosta
Rhododendron
Rodgersia
Sarcococca
Viburnum davidii

Above: Rodgersias enjoy a waterside location. They grow in full sun as well as partial shade, rather than full shade.*

SUNNY MOIST SITES

Areas around natural ponds and streams can be damp or wet, and they tend to be open and sunny. The margins of a pond are waterlogged, which means that only plants adapted to have their roots permanently or seasonally in water will survive there. The dampness of the soil decreases the further away from the pond it is. A different range of plants are adapted to each level of dampness, and there is no shortage of plants that love these type of conditions.

Making the Best of a Sunny Moist Site

The moist areas around a pond or along a stream are the ideal place to create a lush garden. Wetland foliage plants tend to be vigorous, often

---

PLANTS FOR SUNNY
MOIST SITES

Caltha palustris
Cornus alba
Darmera peltata
Filipendula
Gunnera
Iris sibirica
Ligularia
Lysimachia nummularia 'Aurea'
Lysichiton
Primula bullyeana
Primula denticulata
Rheum
Ranunculus ficaria
Rodgersia
Trollius
Salix
Zantedeschia aethiopica

---

growing to giant proportions in summer. Even in lower temperatures all the foliage plants seem to double in size daily. This is splendid for large areas, but if you only have a small site you may have to forgo the large plants and use smaller ones instead.

The water's edge provides the opportunity for growing some exquisitely flowered marginal plants. The plants must be able to cope with extremely wet conditions, and at certain times of the year to grow in water. Marginal plants create a perfect transition between the exuberant foliage on firm land and the special qualities of water.

Left: Gunnera manicata *produces some of the largest leaves seen in gardens, up to 2m (6ft) long on stalks that can be 2.5m (8ft) long.*

Planning Displays

A sunny damp garden or area is an excellent opportunity to grow some exciting large perennial foliage plants such as gunneras, rodgersias and rheums, which also thrive in more shady conditions, but they need plenty of space. In a small area, you can still create an impressive effect with the lush foliage of hostas, with the added bonus of their delicate flowers in summer. Ligularias, irises and astibles also flower well in these conditions.

Position the tallest plants either at the rear or in the centre of a moist plot, where they will not hide smaller plants. Smaller growing plants can then be planted in front of them.

Plenty of smaller perennials bear delicate, exquisitely coloured blooms above their lush, spreading foliage.

Above: The red, jagged foliage of the ornamental rhubarb, Rheum 'Ace of Hearts', is spectacular.

The bright yellows of marsh marigolds, lesser celandines and globe-flowers are counter-balanced by the hazy blues of water forget-me-nots, purple loosestrife and creamy meadow-sweet creating a country cottage effect. Many primulas come in an exciting range of colours and are invaluable for smaller settings. Once established they will spread quickly.

For permanent structure, dwarf Japanese maples and small weeping willows work well. Many have stunning autumn foliage, and some also have colourful bark that looks good in winter. Avoid larger willows as these would soon grow to a huge size, and their roots are extensive.

*Above: Creeping Jenny (*Lysimachia nummularia *'Aurea') works well as a ground cover, as long as all perennial weeds have been removed first.*

Year-round Interest

With large lush foliage and flower stems reaching for the sky, plants that thrive in the damp, sunny site make a dense and luxuriant effect from spring through to late autumn. Spring and early summer are perhaps the very best seasons, but careful inclusion of certain plants will guarantee colour later on as well.

Flower colour is available from spring to autumn, starting with the golden-yellow flowers of the marsh marigolds. *Lysichiton americanum* produces bright yellow flowers in spring. Purple drumstick primulas (*Primula denticulata*) flower in late spring, and *P. bulleyana* contributes hot colours in early summer, followed by the arum lily with its elegant white blooms.

Above: The arum lily (Zantedeschia aethiopica) *is perfect for a waterside planting. It will also grow in shallow water.*

Above: In a moist corner under dappled shade, primulas, forget-me-nots, columbines and bluebells celebrate the arrival of spring.

Perennial foliage plants last from spring to summer, but the giant leaves of *Darmera peltata* will turn red in autumn before they disappear. This plant also bears white to bright pink flowers on 2m (6ft) long stems in late spring. Do include rodgersias: their leaves turn bronze and red in autumn and their white or pink fluffy flowers are followed by dark red fruits.

Evergreen foliage plants provide year-round interest. Include *Bergenia* for edging and enjoy the added bonus of their pink blooms early in the year.

For a splash of winter colour, the bare red stems of *Cornus alba* cannot be beaten. Cut these hard back every spring to guarantee plenty of new stems. Different cultivars have variously coloured autumn leaves.

Maintaining Sunny Moist Conditions

The foliage of the vigorous plants makes excellent ground cover, which helps to conserve moisture. But even a naturally moist area may dry out during hot dry summers, as do many natural watercourses. You may need to water the area to maintain the moistness that the plants require.

Avoid planting tall trees that could eventually overshadow the site. If nearby plants threaten to encroach the area, you will have to prune them carefully to maintain their distance.

Creating a Moist Area

If you want to grow moisture-loving plants but you don't have a suitable site, you can create a damp patch quite easily by digging out soil to make a

Above: This lush summer border has been planted with a delightful combination of fresh yellows and greens.

hollow and lining it with butyl pond liner. Mix plenty of organic matter into the soil and return it to the hollow.

If you are making a pond, it is a good idea to run the liner under the soil some way from the margin of the pond in order to create a damp area. Garden ponds do not have to be large, and even a 1 x 1m (3 x 3ft) pond, with a butyl liner, will provide the correct environment for a good selection of water-loving plants. If you make the pond with more than one level, with a gradual slope towards the edge, you can grow a wide range of aquatic and marginal plants, as well as attracting a host of wildlife.

Left: The fresh, bright colours of these marginal plants create an attractive naturalistic arrangement.

SUNNY DRY SITES

Most gardens have patches where there is less moisture than elsewhere. "Rain shadows" caused by buildings or other structures, shallow or rocky soil, or disturbed sandy or gravelly subsoil can all cause dry conditions. Any of these situations combined with full sun will render any attempts to wet the soil artificially unsuccessful. Sunny gardens or borders set against a wall or next to a patio are particularly likely to be hot and dry.

On the positive side, dry soils are quick to warm up in spring, allowing you to plant out earlier than in many other sites. But you will need to keep young plants well watered.

Above: Rosemary does particularly well in a dry, sunny location as it is native to the Mediterranean.

Making the Best of a Sunny Site

A sunny dry site does not need to be a problem if you select plants that appreciate such an environment. Mediterranean plants are an obvious choice. Lavender, rosemary, sage, salvia, santolina, rock roses (*Cistus*), helichrysum and marigolds are just some of the plants that like a position in full sun and dry soil.

These plants have evolved and adapted to cope with high temperatures, low rainfall and often with poor soil. These adaptations, which include silvery, downy and sometimes succulent foliage, are often what make the plants so attractive and useful in displays for the inside as well as outside.

Above: The evergreen leaves of sage provide fragrance all year round, and they are useful in the kitchen.

Above: Geranium *'Johnson's Blue'* *produces masses of veined purple-blue flowers during the summer.*

Planning Displays

A dry planting in full sun works particularly well if it is planned with a feel for a naturally dry landscape. You can even create a dry-gravel river bed effect that will set off the drought-resistant plants beautifully. Group the plants together to make islands of flowing colour rising out of the gravel. Decide where the architectural plants will go first, then fill in with smaller plants, to make pleasing associations.

Try to blend or contrast flower colours with the foliage. Silver and grey associate well with the purples, blues and mauves that are so common among Mediterranean plants. For contrast with the silvers try the darker

green foliage of rock roses. Or use the very hot colours sparingly as eye-catchers.

Be sure to include some aromatic plants that will release their fragrances in hot sun. Mediterranean herbs are highly fragrant. Plant them where you will brush against the leaves as you walk past to release their heady aromas.

You can include grasses, too. They grow in mounds, create interesting backgrounds for borders and add movement and sound as their leaves rustle in a breeze. If you combine a variety of species you can create a stunning effect of shape, texture and colour.

Above: Grasses add form, colour and movement to a display, and they are easy to manage.

Year-round Interest

When deciding which plants to use, plan for a succession of interest, with foliage, flowers and then seedheads. Grasses are invaluable, providing interest for most of the year; from summer onwards their tall flowerheads will move gently in the wind.

Year-round foliage plants include spurges, especially *Euphorbia characias* and *E. myrsinites*, which have succulent grey-green or blue-green leaves respectively and flowers with yellow-green bracts from spring to early or midsummer. Rosemary can be grown through mild winters.

Spring is something of a famine for arid-area flowers, but some crocuses, especially the hybrids, prefer well-drained and poor soil conditions, so are worth trying, as are tulips later in the season. *Convulvus cneorum*, a leafy silvery-green evergreen, bears its funnel-shaped white flowers from late spring to summer.

For summer colour there is a wide choice. Cranesbills flower prolifically. *Lavatera* 'Barnsley' has masses of funnel-shaped white flowers ageing to soft pink throughout summer, up to 2m (6ft) high. Some types of allium do well in dry areas, and they flower profusely in summer in shades of pink, purple and white.

From late summer to early autumn, the blue and purple-blue flowers of the shrub *Caryopteris clandonensis* show prettily against its grey-green leaves. Sedums flower at this time, too, in bright pinks and ruby-reds, and are irresistible to bees.

Leave interesting seedheads after flowering to prolong the plant's features. Grey cardoons for instance develop large heads after their thistle-like, purple summer flowers are faded.

Left: The graceful plumes of Cortaderia selloana *last through the winter. The plant looks best in a prime position where it can be seen in its full glory. Cut down completely when the fronds are past their best in early spring to encourage fresh growth.*

Improving a Sunny Dry Site

Although it is usually best to accept the existing conditions and grow drought-tolerant plants, you can take some measures to increase moisture and nutrient levels in the soil. Adding garden compost or leaf mould in the autumn will help.

A mulch such as composted bark in summer will reduce evaporation and suppress weeds, or you can use a permanent mulch of gravel or pebbles, which also provide a beautiful backdrop for the plants.

Creating a Dry Planting Area

It is possible to create a dry area where you can display and enjoy plants from hot, arid areas. Choose a site that receives plenty of sunlight, and preferably one that is sheltered. You will need to scrape away some of the topsoil and use it elsewhere. In wet

Above: Massing plants together can create a lush effect in a hot, dry courtyard.

climates, digging in channels of grit will improve the drainage, allowing the soil to dry out more quickly than it normally would.

A sunny patio with planting spaces between the paving stones is an ideal setting as the area will retain heat well, especially if close to the house. Or you could build a raised bed and fill it with a fast-draining mix that could include gravel or grit.

Above: The round heads of Allium christophii *appear in early summer. Here, they are accompanied by longer flowering* Linaria purpurea.

> ### PLANTS THAT THRIVE IN A SUNNY DRY SITE
>
> *Brachyglottis* (syn. *Senecio*)
> *Calendula*
> *Caryopteris clandonensis*
> *Echinops ritro*
> *Eryngium bourgatii*
> *Euphorbia*
> *Geranium*
> *Helichrysum*
> *Iris germanica* hybrids
> *Kniphofia* hybrids
> *Lavandula*
> *Lavatera*
> *Santolina chamaecyparissus*
> *Sedum*

Above: Ivy grows well in dry shady sites, particularly against a wall, but the variegated types do like some sun.

Shady Dry Sites

Areas beneath a tree canopy or under a wall, fence or hedge often lack moisture. Trees take up an enormous amount of water from the soil, often leaving it dry. Walls and fences can interrupt driving rain, making one side drier than the other. Hedges combine both these drawbacks by interrupting rainfall and taking up moisture from the surrounding ground.

Shade can be deep, with no sun at all, or it can be partial, with some sunlight falling on the site at certain times of day. Dappled shade occurs when sunlight is filtered by leaves and branches. Some shade plants prefer particular types of shade, others can cope with a range.

Making the Best of a Shady Dry Site

This is one of the most difficult sites to contend with, but a few well chosen plants can transform even the most

unpromising of areas. Most plants that cope well with dry shade are those that naturally grow in the shadow of other vegetation.

Busy Lizzies are among the very few flowering annuals that will survive in shade, but they do prefer to be kept moist if possible. Many plants that are more naturally found growing in moist shade will tolerate dry shade conditions. These include foxgloves, *Aquilegia*, hellebores and the tall *Acanthus mollis*.

Ivies cope extremely well with dry shade, including deep shade. There are many varieties, with a whole range of different leaf formations that will grow in even the deepest shade. Variegated ivies require some light to colour well.

Above: The spurred violet, blue, pink or white flowers of granny's bonnet (Aquilegia) will tolerate a dry shady site.

Planning Displays

Heavily shaded areas will not support a bright array of flowering plants, so dry shade plantings have to rely heavily on structure and foliage. Various evergreen shrubs, such as skimmias, hollies and mahonias, can cope with a certain amount of dryness in the soil. Aucubas are invaluable for deep shade, but the variegated varieties, with beautifully yellow-mottled leaves, prefer partial shade.

Try to create contrasts in leaf colour, texture and shape. The glossy prickly leaves of hollies and mahonias, for instance, can be placed against the smooth-edged leaves of other plants. *Iris foetidissima* has long strappy leaves and seems happy in the darkest of spots.

Above: Geranium macrorrhizum *produces abundant flowers even in shade, and will spread to cover a large area.*

Ivies are unbeatable for clothing fences and walls in a variety of leaf shapes and colours. They can also be used for ground cover, as can periwinkles. Epimediums can also be grown as ground cover under trees and shrubs, where their dainty yellow, white, pink, red or purple flowers provide welcome colour.

In lightly shaded areas, resilient perennials such as monkshood, sweet violet, and some of the cranesbills are good for providing patches of colour against the green foliage.

Above: A shady area with dappled light is the romantic setting for this combination of foliage plants.

> GARDENER'S TIP
>
> Dry shady sites are the most difficult to bring bright colour into. One solution is to introduce containers of seasonal plants in flower. These will have benefited from growing in better conditions and will be able to survive a few weeks of gloom. When they finish flowering return them to a brighter situation to recover.

Year-round Interest

Plantings in shade rely heavily on ever-green foliage plants for interest, but a number of these also produce flowers, as do many of the foliage perennials.

The yellow spring flowers of maho-nias make a wonderful contrast with their glossy green foliage, and some have the bonus of being scented. Many perennials also flower in spring providing earlier colour. Pink flowers brighten up bergenias, and *Brunnera macrophylla* has blue forget-me-not-like flowers. Where it is not too dry epimediums provide a wide range of colour from spring to early summer. Periwinkles will be scattered with a carpet of violet-blue from spring to autumn.

As summer approaches, more perennial flowers appear. *Anemone x*

Above: The bright berries of a small skimmia planted among bluebells create a startling contrast.

hybrida has pink or white flowers in late summer and autumn, which is when *Liriope muscari* produces spikes packed with blue, bead-like flowers, while monkshood supports spires of blue flowers.

Autumn is the time for a superb display of berries, which can appear on aucuba and hollies, both bright red. Some skimmias bear red, black or white berries after their dainty white flowers. The large seed capsules of *Iris foetidissima* split open at this time of year to display yellow seeds. Through winter and early spring hardy cycla-men planted under trees produce their bright pink flowers and often pat-terned leaves. *Helleborus foetidus* has nodding bell-shaped green flowers. The scented blue or white flowers of sweet violet see winter out.

Above: Helleborus foetidus *prefers a site with dappled shade and a neutral to alkaline soil.*

Above: Carpet-forming Anemone blanda *will tolerate partial shade. Its flowers appear in spring.*

Improving Shady Dry Conditions

You can alter the level of shade in parts of the garden. If you have a large tree, for example, removing the lower branches allows more light to reach the ground beneath. The branches in the main canopy can also be thinned to create a dappled light. In a dark, sunless area, a fence or wall opposite the site can be painted white to reflect the available light towards the shaded bed or border.

Artificially watering a dry site will help to moisten it, but to maximize the effect, improve the soil by mixing in plenty of organic matter. Adding a mulch to the surface will impede evaporation. Many shade-loving perennials are naturally woodland plants, and so need a woodland-like soil. This should be high in organic matter.

An alternative approach, easier than trying to change the conditions, is to bring in containers temporarily, with flowering or brightly variegated plants to add interest and colour.

PLANTS THAT TOLERATE DRY SHADE

Aconitum
Anemone x hybrida
Aquilegia
Aucuba japonica
Bergenia
Digitalis purpurea
Helleborus foetidus
Epimedium
Euphorbia
Hedera
Iris foetidissima
Liriope muscari
Mahonia
Skimmia
Vinca

Above: Imported potted plants can bring temporary colour to dry and shady parts of the garden. They can be returned to more suitable areas to recover.

Airborne Pollution

Pollution can be a problem for plants in busy urban areas, especially in small front gardens. Deposits from vehicle exhausts settle on foliage throughout the year, and if the road is salted in winter the salt is splashed by cars on to the nearest plants as the traffic passes. Some plants are more tolerant of airborne pollution than others so it is worth knowing which these are if you live near a road, where traffic is constantly streaming past or snarled up in slow-moving jams.

The solution may be as simple as a hedge of plants that can tolerate this kind of treatment along the most vulnerable part of the garden. Such a

Above: Olearia x haastii *will produce a mass of snowy white blossoms, even in a polluted atmosphere.*

barrier would protect more delicate species behind it. Good hedging plants are *Berberis*, *Cotoneaster*, holly and privet. But if a hedge is not practical, you may need to concentrate on growing plants that are tolerant of these unfavourable conditions.

Pollution-tolerant Plants with Year-round Interest

A number of pollution-resistant evergreen and deciduous shrubs provide flowers and interesting foliage for the whole year.

Many of the evergreen shrubs have handsome glossy, leathery, dark green leaves, but there are also variegated varieties such as the spotted laurel to

*Above: Privet (*Ligustrum lucidum *'Excelsum Superbum') makes a colourful and useful hedge beside a busy road to act as a barrier that will protect the garden.*

Above: Silver-leaved Elaeagnus 'Quicksilver' provides year-round colour and is a useful windbreak.

PLANTS THAT TOLERATE
POLLUTED AIR

Aucuba japonica
Aquilegia vulgaris
Berberis
Bergenia cordifolia
Cotoneaster
Elaeagnus
Fatsia japonica
Forsythia
Garrya elliptica
Geranium endressii
Helleborus niger
Helleborus orientalis
Hemerocallis
Hosta
Ilex aquifolium
Iris
Lamium
Ligustrum
Olearia x haastii
Philadelphus
Pulmonaria
Rudbeckia
Symphytum
Viburnum
Weigela florida

provide extra interest. Some of the deciduous shrubs, including many of the viburnums, end their year with a flourish of vivid autumn colour. Many also produce beautiful spring, summer or even autumn flowers; the summer flowers of *Philadelphus* are delightfully fragrant. For autumn and winter, holly berries are hard to beat and from midwinter to early spring pretty catkins hang from the branches of garryas, which also make useful and effective windbreaks.

The great variety of cotoneasters makes them especially useful as ground cover, for growing up walls or hedging. Different types will bear white to deep pink flowers from spring to summer, most with autumn berries.

In addition to shrubs, there are some virtually indestructible perennials, such as *Bergenia* and *Pulmonaria*.

Above: Perennial lungwort (Pulmonaria) makes good ground cover in shade and can withstand the effects of car fumes.

Planning with Plants

USE THIS LIST OF PLANTS DESCRIBING THEIR IDEAL CONDITIONS AND
SEASON OF INTEREST TO PLAN YOUR GARDEN DESIGN.

Plants	Sow	Plant Out	Season of Interest
Acanthus spinosus (s, d)	spring	autumn	spring to midsummer
Acer (s, m)	n/a	autumn	autumn foliage
Achillea (s, d, m)	spring, in situ	n/a	summer, autumn
Aconitum (ps, s, m)	spring	autumn, spring	summer
Alcea rosea (s, d)	summer, in situ	n/a	early to midsummer
Alchemilla (s, ps, d, m)	spring	early summer	summer
Allium (s, d)	n/a	autumn	summer
Amelanchier * (s, ps, m)	n/a	autumn	spring, autumn
Anemone x hybrida (s, ps, m)	n/a	divide in spring	late summer to mid-autumn
Anemone nemorosa (ps, m, d)	n/a	divide in spring	spring to early summer
Aquilegia (s, ps, d, m)	spring	autumn, spring	late spring, early summer
Aruncus (fs, ps, m)	autumn, spring	autumn, spring	summer
Astilbe (s, m)	n/a	divide in winter	summer
Astrantia major (s, ps, m)	autumn	spring	summer
Aucuba japonica (s, ps, fs)	n/a	autumn	year-round
Azalea * (ps)	n/a	autumn	spring
Berberis (s, ps)	n/a	autumn	spring, autumn
Bergenia (s, ps, m)	n/a	divide in autumn	spring
Brachyglottis (syn. Senecio) (s, d)	n/a	autumn, spring	year-round
Brunnera macrophylla (ps, m, d)	spring	autumn, spring	spring
Buddleja davidii (s)	n/a	autumn, spring	summer
Calendula officinalis (s, ps, d)	spring, in situ	n/a	summer to autumn
Calluna vulgaris * (s, d)	n/a	autumn, spring	summer, autumn
Caltha palustris (s, m)	n/a	spring	spring

Achillea

Anemone ranunculoides

Plants	Sow	Plant Out	Season of Interest
Camellia * (ps, m)	n/a	autumn	spring
Campanula 'G.F. Wilson' (s, ps, d)	spring	autumn	summer
Canna indica (s, m)	spring, autumn	early summer	summer, autumn
Caryopteris x *clandonensis* (s, d)	n/a	autumn, spring	summer. early autumn
Ceanothus (s, d)	n/a	autumn, spring	late spring
Centaurea cyanus (s, d)	spring, in situ	n/a	spring to midsummer
Centranthus ruber ^ (s, d)	spring	autumn	late spring, summer
Chaenomeles x *superba* (s, ps, d)	n/a	autumn, spring	spring
Choisya ternata (s, d)	n/a	autumn, spring	late spring, autumn
Cistus (s, d)	spring	autumn, spring	summer
Clematis (s, ps, d)	n/a	autumn	spring, summer or autumn
Colchicum autumnale (s, d, m)	n/a	summer	autumn
Convallaria majalis (ps, fs, m)	n/a	divide, autumn	late spring
Convolvulus cneorum (s, d)	spring	autumn	spring to summer
Cornus alba (s, ps)	n/a	autumn	year-round
Cotinus coggygria (s, ps, m, d)	n/a	autumn	year-round
Cotoneaster (s, ps, d)	n/a	autumn	year-round
Crambe cordifolia (s, ps, d)	spring, autumn	spring, autumn	spring, summer
Crocosmia cultivars (s, ps, m)	n/a	spring	summer
Cynara cardunculus (s, d)	spring	autumn, spring	summer, early autumn
Daphne (s, ps, d, m)	n/a	autumn, spring	late spring
Darmera peltata (s, ps, m)	spring, autumn	autumn, spring	autumn
Dianthus (pinks) (s, d)	n/a	autumn, spring	summer
Dicentra spectabilis ñ, ^ (ps, d)	spring	autumn, spring	late spring, early summer
Digitalis purpurea (ps)	late spring	autumn	early summer
Doronicum (ps, m)	spring	autumn	spring
Eccremocarpus scaber (s, d)	early spring	autumn	late spring to autumn
Echinacea purpurea (s, d)	spring	autumn	summer, early autumn

Camellia

Crocosmia

Plants	Sow	Plant Out	Season of Interest
Echinops ritro (s, ps, d)	mid-spring	autumn	summer
Elaeagnus (s, ps, d)	n/a	autumn, spring	year-round
Epimedium (ps, m, d)	n/a	autumn	spring
Eranthis hyemalis (s, m)	spring	autumn	winter, early spring
Erica cultivars * (s, d)	n/a	autumn	winter
Eryngium (s, some d, some m)	n/a	spring, autumn	summer, autumn
Eschscholzia californica (s, d)	spring, in situ	n/a	summer
Euonymus fortunei (s, d)	n/a	autumn	year-round
Euphorbia (s, some d, some m)	spring	autumn	year-round
Fatsia japonica (s, ps, m)	n/a	autumn, spring	year-round, autumn
Festuca glauca (s, d)	autumn, winter	spring, autumn	year-round
Filipendula (s, ps, m)	autumn, spring	spring, autumn	early summer
Forsythia (s, m)	n/a	autumn	spring
Fremontodendron ñ, ^ (s, d)	n/a	autumn, spring	spring to autumn
Fritillaria imperialis (s, d)	n/a	autumn	early summer
Fuchsia magellanica (s, ps, m)	n/a	autumn, spring	summer
Galanthus nivalis (ps, m)	n/a	autumn	winter
Garrya (s, d)	n/a	autumn	winter
Gaultheria procumbens *, ñ (ps, m)	n/a	autumn, spring	year-round
Geranium (s, ps)	spring	spring, autumn	early summer
Gunnera (s, ps, m)	spring, autumn	autumn	spring to autumn
Gypsophila ^ (s, d)	spring, in situ	autumn	summer
Hamamelis (s, ps, m)	n/a	autumn	winter
Hedera (s, ps, fs)	n/a	autumn	year-round
Helenium (s, m)	spring	autumn	summer
Helianthemum ñ, ^ (s, d)	spring	autumn	late spring, summer
Helichrysum ñ, ^ (s, d)	spring	autumn	late summer, autumn
Helleborus ñ, ^ (ps, s, m)	n/a	autumn	winter, spring
Hemerocallis (s, m)	autumn, spring	autumn	summer
Hippophäe rhamnoides ñ, ^ (s, m, d)	n/a	divide in spring	spring to autumn

Euonymus fortunei

Hedera

Plants	Sow	Plant Out	Season of Interest
Hosta (fs, ps, m)	n/a	autumn	spring to autumn
Houttuynia (s, m)	n/a	autumn, spring	spring
Humulus lupulus (s, ps, m)	summer	autumn, spring	spring to autumn
Hydrangea (s, ps, m)	n/a	autumn, spring	summer, early autumn
Hypericum (s, ps, some d, some m)	n/a	autumn, spring	summer
Ilex (s, m)	n/a	autumn, spring	year-round
Impatiens (ps, m, d)	spring	early summer	summer to autumn
Iris foetidissima (s, d)	n/a	late summer	early summer
Jasminum nudiflorum (s, ps, d)	n/a	autumn, spring	winter
Kerria japonica (s, ps, d)	n/a	autumn	spring
Kniphofia hybrids (s, ps, m, d)	n/a	spring, autumn	summer, early autumn
Lavandula (s, d)	spring	autumn	summer
Lavatera (s, d)	n/a	spring	summer
Leycesteria formosa (s, ps, d)	n/a	autumn, spring	summer to early autumn
Ligularia (s, midday shade, m)	autumn, spring	spring, autumn	summer
Ligustrum (s, ps)	n/a	autumn, spring	year-round
Lilium lancifolium *, ñ (s, ps, d)	n/a	autumn	late summer, early autumn
Liriope muscari (fs, m)	n/a	summer	autumn, winter
Lonicera (s, ps)	n/a	autumn, spring	summer
Lupinus slightly * (s, ps, d)	spring, autumn	autumn, spring	summer
Lysichiton (s, ps, m)	n/a	autumn	spring
Lysimachia (s, ps, m)	spring	autumn	summer
Magnolia (s, ps, m)	n/a	autumn	spring
Mahonia (fs, m)	n/a	autumn	winter, spring
Matthiola ñ, slightly ^ (s, m)	spring, summer	spring	late spring, summer
Meconopsis betonicifolia ñ, slightly * (ps, m)	spring, autumn	spring	summer
Mimulus (s, ps, m)	autumn, spring	spring	summer
Nepeta x *faassenii* (s, ps, d)	autumn	spring	summer
Olearia x *haastii* (s, d)	autumn, spring	spring	summer
Origanum ^ (s, d)	autumn, spring	autumn, spring	summer

Hydrangea

Lonicera

Plants	Sow	Plant Out	Season of Interest
Osmanthus × *burkwoodii* (s, ps, d)	n/a	spring	summer
Osteospermum (s, d)	spring	spring	summer
Paeonia (s, ps, m)	n/a	autumn, spring	late spring to autumn
Papaver (s, d)	spring, in situ	autumn, spring	early summer
Pelargonium (s, d)	late winter	spring	summer
Penstemon cultivars (s, ps, d)	spring	autumn, spring	summer
Philadelphus (s, ps, d)	n/a	autumn	summer
Phlox annuals (s, d)	early spring	early summer	early summer
Phormium (s, m)	n/a	spring, autumn	year-round
Pieris * (s, ps, m)	n/a	autumn, spring	year-round
Primula bullyeana (ps, m)	spring	autumn, spring	summer
Primula denticulata (ps, m)	spring	early summer	mid-spring, summer
Primula vulgaris (ps, m)	spring	spring, autumn	spring
Pulmonaria (fs, ps, m)	n/a	autumn, spring	spring
Pyracantha (s, ps, d)	n/a	autumn, spring	year-round, autumn
Ranunculus ficaria (ps, fs, m)	n/a	autumn	early spring
Rheum (s, ps, m)	autumn	autumn	spring to autumn
Rhododendron * (ps, m)	n/a	autumn	spring
Rodgersia (s, ps, m)	spring	autumn, spring	spring to autumn
Rosa (s, m)	n/a	autumn	summer
Rosmarinus officinalis (s, d)	spring	spring, autumn	year-round
Rudbeckia (s, m)	spring	autumn	summer, autumn
Salix (s, most m)	n/a	autumn	year-round
Salvia officinalis (s, d)	spring	autumn, spring	year-round
Santolina (s, d)	autumn, spring	spring, autumn	year-round, summer
Sarcococca (fs, ps, m)	n/a	autumn, spring	year-round
Scabiosa ñ, slightly ^ (s, d)	spring	autumn	summer
Sedum (s, d)	autumn	spring	summer, early autumn
Sempervivum (s, d)	spring	spring	year-round

Primula

Pyracantha

Plants	Sow	Plant Out	Season of Interest
Skimmia (ps, fs, m)	n/a	autumn, spring	year-round
Spiraea (s, m)	n/a	autumn, spring	summer
Symphytum (s, ps, m)	autumn, spring	autumn, spring	spring
Syringa ñ, ^ (s, d, m)	n/a	autumn, spring	spring
Tagetes (s, d)	spring	summer	summer
Tamarix tetrandra (s, d, m)	n/a	autumn, spring	year-round
Taxus baccata (s, ps, fs, d)	n/a	autumn, spring	year-round
Thuja occidentalis (s, m)	n/a	autumn, spring	year-round
Thymus ñ, ^ (s, d)	spring	autumn, spring	year-round
Trillium grandiflorum *, ñ (s, m)	n/a	autumn, spring	spring
Trollius (s, ps, m)	spring	autumn, spring	spring
Tropaeolum speciosum ñ, ^ (s, ps, m)	n/a	autumn, spring	summer to autumn
Typha latifolia (s, in water)	n/a	spring	summer
Verbascum ^ (s, d)	n/a	autumn, spring	summer
Viburnum (s, ps, m)	n/a	autumn, spring	winter
Vinca (s, ps, m)	n/a	autumn, spring	year-round
Viola odorata (s, ps, m)	spring	autumn, spring	late winter, early spring
Vitis coignetiae ñ, ^ (s, ps, d)	n/a	autumn, spring	autumn
Weigela florida (s, ps, d)	n/a	autumn, spring	late spring, early summer
Yucca gloriosa (s, d)	n/a	spring	year-round
Zantedeschia aethiopica (s, m)	n/a	spring	late spring to summer

Trillium

Vinca

KEY

Plants marked with * require acid soil;

Plants marked with ^ prefer alkaline soil;

Plants marked with ñ prefer neutral soil.

(s) = sun

(ps) = partial shade

(fs) = full shade

(d) = free-draining soil

(m) = moist ground

PERFECT PATIOS

At its simplest a patio or terrace provides a level seating area for enjoying the garden, but to make it visually link the house and garden as well as cater for all the activities you might need it for requires a little thought and planning. Whether you are contemplating a new patio or wishing to enhance the one you already have, this chapter is packed with helpful information on style, construction materials, screening and lighting as well as effective planting ideas for year-round display.

The Garden Floor

If garden beds and borders exist for plants, a patio or terrace is conceived with people in mind. This is a dynamic part of the garden, and the style we set here is a reflection of our lifestyle as much as of our skill as gardeners.

What Is a Patio?

A garden designer might refer to the patio or terrace as an interface. Traditionally, it is the area that links the house with the garden, though in an urban setting the patio may constitute the whole of the outdoor space.

Whatever the size of the garden, a patio shares some aspects of both the indoor and the outdoor environment. Increasingly people think of such an area as an extension of the house. Paving or decking, tables and chairs, awnings and even heaters mean that it can function like an additional room,

Above: A charming, well-furnished terrace invites you to step out of the house for morning coffee, afternoon tea or alfresco meals on summer evenings.

an extra living space that is especially suitable for entertaining, eating and relaxing. But it can also be the setting for the garden's most spectacular and precious plants.

The patio now merits (and receives) as much care and thought when it comes to selecting materials and furnishings – its style, in other words – as we give to sitting rooms, bedrooms, kitchens and bathrooms.

FROM HOUSE TO GARDEN

Ideally, there should be a smooth transition from house to garden. Many people harbour the image of a beautiful house with full-length windows flung wide open and leading on to a spacious terrace which, in turn, overlooks a manicured lawn and an immaculate garden.

Something of that feeling of escape can be created in every garden, even where space is at a premium, but many gardeners have to balance the wish to have a patio or terrace with a desire for a lawn, for a herb or vegetable garden, for beds and borders for flowers and shrubs or for a greenhouse or shed. Except for the smallest courtyards, deciding how much space can be allocated to any or all of the different functions of a garden is part of the planning process, and designing and building the patio must take into account the style of the remainder of the garden, just as its surface and decoration must reflect the interior and exterior style of the house.

Patios and terraces are usually understood as adjoining the house, keeping them warm and sheltered, and within easy reach of the kitchen and other living areas. However, there is no reason why a paved area or deck cannot be created at a distance from the house, linked to it by a path. A large garden might accommodate a second patio, on which could be built a summerhouse or arbour, providing a sheltered place to sit in summer, when you can feel you are in the heart of the country rather than a mere stone's throw from your back door.

Above: A secluded corner is made more appealing by the climbers that clothe and soften the vertical surfaces.

The Garden Floor

ENJOYING YOUR PATIO

Increasingly the patio or terrace has become associated with relaxation, and it should be a peaceful place to unwind and forget the strains of modern living. Food always seems to taste better in the open air, and summer cooking outside is a pleasure even for those who show little enthusiasm in the kitchen. Nowadays, barbecues can be fitted into the smallest spaces and the patio has become a place for dining and entertaining.

Making this space a pleasant, sheltered outdoor room can be achieved by the addition of permanent structures, such as pergolas and screens, or by thoughtful planting, to create shade, colour and fragrance in summer

Above: Choose garden furniture that is in keeping with the style of your terrace. Smart enamelled metal suits the look and scale of a small urban courtyard.

but to allow all the available natural light to reach the windows of the house in winter. A sympathetic choice of materials, and furniture that is both

Above: In a small garden, a simple bench in a sheltered corner will provide a welcome sitting area, especially when it is surrounded by fragrant flowers.

comfortable and appropriate to the patio in size and scale, will increase your enjoyment. Such is the lure of the outdoors that, once you have created your perfect patio, it will be the centre of your home all summer long.

HOW TO USE THIS CHAPTER

This chapter is intended to inspire you with fresh ideas and possibilities, but whether you design and build the patio yourself or employ a garden designer and a building contractor, you will still have to define its basic function. The first section, *Planning Considerations*, explores some of the issues you need to consider when you are preparing the design. *Structural Elements* evaluates the relative merits

of the materials that are likely to be at your disposal and the impact they will make, as well as offering hints on how to shelter the area from the elements and to enhance security and privacy. *Patio Planting* describes some suitable plants for the patio.

Choosing a Style discusses some of the styles that are popular in garden design today and suggests how they can be achieved, both through the materials used in construction and through planting. Finally, *Special Features* focuses on those finishing touches that make a patio personal to its owner and that will increase your pleasure in it: choosing the appropriate furniture, lighting and heating the patio, and creating focal points.

Above: Dense planting gives this tiny patio a jungle-like lushness, while the mixed floor materials add an air of informality.

Planning Considerations

THERE ARE SEVERAL ISSUES TO CONSIDER WHEN YOU ARE PLANNING A PATIO OR TERRACE. TIME SPENT AT THE EARLY STAGES IS NEVER WASTED AND WILL ENABLE YOU TO DEVELOP A SPACE YOU WILL WANT TO RETURN TO AGAIN AND AGAIN.

SITE AND ACCESS

Consider where the patio is to be sited. Easy access from the house is important, and the position of doors leading into the garden may determine your choice. If the patio will be adjacent to the house, will it run the full length of the building? Will it be the same depth throughout or will it have a curved or angled edge to reflect other features in the garden or house?

A patio can also be sited some distance from the house, with a path leading to it, or you might prefer two

Above: *Wooden decking is an ideal material for a patio or terrace where the site is not level.*

or more linked spaces. A concealed area can be especially successful. Imagine a path that disappears among trees or shrubs, leading to a simple, open, paved circle with a single architectural plant or statue at the centre. This kind of feature can make for dynamic contrast and bring an element of surprise into the garden.

A level site poses few problems, but if the ground slopes you need to consider whether you want to construct retaining walls or raised beds so that the patio itself is level and whether you will have to build steps or a ramp so that you can easily and safely get from the patio to the garden.

Make sure that a patio that adjoins the house slopes slightly away from it toward a drain or a border, so that rainwater cannot accumulate near the house wall and cause damp problems.

SIZE MATTERS

Unless it occupies the whole of a small plot, the patio needs to be in scale with the rest of the garden. If it is too small, you are unlikely to make good use of it, but if it is too large, it might look exposed and unwelcoming. If the

Above: A zigzag path prevents the eye from leaping to the far edge of the patio, tricking you into believing that the space is larger than it is.

Above: Plants growing around the patio will soon spill over the edges of paving and steps, but at first you can use containers to soften their hard lines.

patio has to be large to link two buildings, try breaking up the expanse with changes of level or materials, a raised bed or even a small tree or fountain.

If you are using paving, make sure that the scale of the materials is in proportion to the overall area. This aspect of the design is often overlooked but will have a significant effect on the success of the area. Big patios are best paved with large slabs, and small with small. In a small area, granite setts are easier on the eye than large slabs, which seem to accentuate the restricted dimensions.

At the planning stage, be sure to allow adequate room for tables and chairs; as well as using them, you will want to walk around them, perhaps serving your guests who are sitting around the table. Make sure there is space for chairs to be pushed back – the

last thing you want is for chairs to topple backward into the neighbouring plants. Leave room for containers and remember that plants in surrounding borders will billow out in summer, further reducing the ground space.

Steps and paths must be wide enough to be safe, and if you need to include handrails or a balustrade, remember to allow for these in your ground plan. The ideal path should be wide enough to allow two people to walk along side by side in comfort, and a width of 2m (6ft) will not seem excessive once plants in adjacent borders have flopped over and softened the edges. If space is really limited, make sure that you will, at least, be able to manoeuvre a lawnmower between the borders or push a wheelbarrow through the garden with ease.

SUN OR SHADE?

Whether the patio is to be in sun or shade may already be determined by the lie of the house and elements beyond the garden, such as nearby buildings and trees. This is especially likely to be the case in town gardens.

Where you can exercise choice, your future use of the patio may well be influenced by whether it is predominantly in sun or shade and how this varies according to the season and time of day. If the far end of your garden catches the evening sun, you might use and enjoy the spot more if you created a paved area and furnished it with a table and chairs.

Above: If the patio is hot and sunny, there is nothing more refreshing than the sound of bubbling water, as the designer of this feature realized.

The idea of breakfasting on a sunny terrace is particularly appealing, and if you have a patio near the house that gets the morning sun, it is sure to get plenty of use at this time of day. By lunchtime, however, when the sun is much stronger, the same spot may be too hot for comfortable eating.

Often, it is only when the weather is really hot that we remember the need for shade, and although most of us probably dream of long days basking in the sunshine, we are continually reminded about the dangers of over-exposure to ultraviolet light. If the site you have chosen has no natural shade, consider building a pergola over which you could grow deciduous climbers or think about erecting an awning, which can be removed and stored from autumn to spring.

The solid shade cast by a building can make an area too chilly except on the warmest days, but a patio that is overhung by a deciduous tree can be enjoyed on sunny days in spring yet will offer some protection from the sun in summer when the tree is in full leaf. It is pleasant to relax with a drink on a patio or deck that is warmed by the evening sun, even if this was in shade during most of the day.

WINDY SITES

One of the worst problems to beset gardeners is swirling wind. Most small, enclosed gardens are unaffected by this problem, but if the site is relatively open, strong gusts can mar your enjoyment at any time of year. A long, narrow garden flanked by tall walls or fences may suffer from the wind-tunnel effect. You can shelter a patio with a fence, or with trees and shrubs. If you choose the latter, plant deciduous species, because they tend to filter the wind; dense evergreens can help to create even stronger currents.

On the other hand, if the patio is to do double duty as a utility space for drying washing, a certain amount of wind can only be an advantage.

Above: Planting up to the edge of the paved area is the best way of linking this shady patio with the rest of the garden.

Above: A well-maintained hedge is not only attractive but also affords maximum privacy and shelter from gusting wind.

81

CHILDREN

If there are children in the family, they will enjoy having a smooth, level patio to play on, but safety issues are paramount. Although bumps and falls are part of growing up, concrete surfaces and raised areas with no guard rails pose particular hazards. Instead of concrete or paving slabs, consider using softer materials, such as decking, bark chippings or even the rubberized tiles that are used in public play areas.

Open water should be avoided altogether in gardens where small children play. If you must have a water feature, install a small bubble fountain over cobbles, or a wall-mounted spout, and sink the reservoir into the ground.

ELDERLY AND DISABLED GARDENERS

Ease of access is a vital consideration for anyone with restricted mobility. If the garden falls steeply away from the house, rather than terracing the patio, create instead a gentle slope that can be navigated from level to level by wheelchair users. If you can install a raised bed, perhaps with a hand rail, along one side of the slope, so much the better: it will help to prevent falls and other mishaps, besides bringing any plants within reach of the gardener.

Surface materials require special consideration, too. If you opt for paving, it should be laid smoothly, with no proud edges that can trip any

Above: A well-built sandpit in a warm corner can make for hours of creative play.

Above: Raised beds surrounding a perfectly even paved surface make this patio the ideal outdoor space for a disabled or elderly gardener.

Above: Decking squares are easy to lay, and are available with a ridged surface that gives a safer footing for the very young and old than plain, smooth wood.

gardeners who are not absolutely stable on their feet. Some smooth concrete surfaces can be slippery when wet, so either roughen the surface with aggregate to prevent slips and falls or use some other material that is already rough. Grooved or ridged decking provides a better grip underfoot than plain wood and can also be laid in attractive patterns.

Older gardeners will want to avoid surfaces that are going to require constant attention and maintenance. Even paving slabs will attract moss and lichens in time (the first sign is a greenish tinge, usually around the edges) and will need to be treated. Special products are available that have to be sprayed or watered on; alternatively, the lichen has to be removed the hard way, with water and a wire brush. Softwood decking is

easy to lay, but unless it is tanalized (pressure treated) it will require regular applications of preservative.

FAMILY PETS

Cats and dogs will adore basking in the sun on smooth, warm paving stones. Extensive areas of fine gravel are best avoided if you or your neighbours have cats, which are likely to see it as a large and convenient litter tray. Chemical deterrents are available, but their effect is temporary. If you are troubled by visiting cats, it may be worth investing in sound- or motion-activated deterrents, which either emit a high-pitched whistle or spray intruders with water.

Male dogs regard almost anything as a potential urinal, and even the best-trained and exercised animals have accidents sometimes, so keep some disinfectant handy.

83

SPRINGING A SURPRISE

Although most patios and terraces will be fairly open spaces in the garden you can still introduce an element of surprise. If you have a large garden, with a patio adjoining the house, you may wish to close up the far side by means of a fence or wall so that the rest of the garden is virtually hidden, and perhaps accessible only through a gate. In this way, the patio itself becomes almost literally an outdoor room. A less extreme feeling of separation can be created by dense planting to either side of a path leading away from the patio. If the path turns a corner and disappears out of sight, the invitation to explore the garden will be well-nigh irresistible.

In a large garden, an alternative effect can be achieved by siting a patio some distance from the house and screening it, either by tall planting or by a wall or fence, so that you seem to alight on it as if by accident; the presence of a seat will encourage you to linger there. Ideally, to increase the illusion that you have really made an escape, the house should not be visible from the patio, but if this is not possible, arrange any seating to face away from the house – instead directing the eye to a pool, a statue or an especially fine architectural plant.

RELAXING AND ENTERTAINING

If you like to entertain a lot and to dine alfresco, you need to allow ample room for a table and chairs. Bear in mind that people will want to push their chairs back from the table without falling into the borders, and to be able to walk around behind them. If the table is in a sunny position, you'll

Above: Use paint to alter the atmosphere of a corner of your patio. You can easily change the colour if you tire of the effect.

Above: In a large garden you can create an element of surprise with winding paths and gateways to secret enclosed areas.

84

need to provide shade in the middle of the day. Choose a large parasol, or one that you can set at an angle, so that it shades your guests as well as the food on the table.

You might want to consider building an integral barbecue into the patio wall, but these days transportable models, which can be stored in a utility room or garage when not in use, are widely available and are not too costly. Whichever type of barbecue you prefer, safety considerations should make sure it can be used well away from any potentially flammable materials, including overhanging plants. You'll also need a level surface nearby where you can rest plates.

Privacy will be an issue for most people, especially town-dwellers. If you use the patio for sunbathing, you will probably welcome shelter from

Above: If your table is sited in the middle of a sunny terrace, a large parasol is an essential accessory in summer.

prying eyes, possibly in the form of a fence or trees, but make sure that the shadow is not cast on the patio itself or you will be defeating the object.

Above: Colourful balls signpost the path to a second paved area, tucked away out of sight of the rest of the garden.

Structural Elements

THERE IS A WIDE RANGE OF MATERIALS THAT CAN BE USED TO CREATE
A PATIO OR TERRACE, AND SOME OF THE MOST POPULAR ARE
DISCUSSED HERE, TOGETHER WITH SOME SUGGESTIONS ON HOW TO
SCREEN THE AREA AND WHICH PLANTS ARE MOST SUITABLE.

CHOOSING THE SURFACE

The siting and size of your patio will
both influence your choice of surface
material, but there are several other
factors to consider, including cost,
ease of laying, maintenance and appearance. The style needs to be appropriate to its setting, and if you have an
old property, reclamation yards are a
good source of suitable materials.

*Above: Restraint is the keynote of this
modern, elegant decked area.*

Decking

As an alternative to paving, the use of
wooden decking is now well established. It is a natural choice in areas
where wood is in abundance and the
climate is relatively dry and sunny. Its
nature makes it ideal for strong, geometric designs and it ages sympathetically. Decks are ideal if you need to
make a raised platform over sloping
ground, and a rail around the deck
will enhance the colonial feel.

Decking is laid on a framework of
timber joists, in the same way as a traditional interior wooden floor. The
joists are themselves supported on pil-
lars, and the sides of the decking are
usually covered with facing boards to
conceal the space beneath.

You can customize decking by
painting or staining it, but whatever
finish you choose will fade with age so
you may need to repeat the treatment
every year or so. The better quality the
wood, the better it ages. Hardwood is
more resistant to decay than softwood, but if economy dictates that
you must use softwood, make sure it
has been tanalized (pressure treated)
for longer life.

Above: Slabs and gravel are common enough building materials but can still have distinction if used with discretion.

Apart from traditional boards, decking is widely available in the form of square wooden tiles, which can be laid in geometric patterns to add interest to the surface. A grooved finish will provide a safer walking surface than smooth wood in damp weather.

Stone

Natural stone is beautiful to look at but is expensive and usually heavy to handle and difficult to lay, especially if the individual stones are of different thicknesses. Some stones break up easily and cannot be recommended for paving. Make sure you find a good match with the local stone, especially where this has been used as a building material.

Concrete and Artificial Stone

One of the most versatile of all building materials, concrete has become a fashionable alternative to paving, as new laying and colouring techniques give it a fresh style. You can either accept it for what it is and opt for a great sweep of unadorned concrete – perfect in a high-tech or minimalist garden – or you can use it in one of its less immediately obvious forms, as slabs, which look to all intents and purposes like natural stone and are available in a variety of shapes, colours and textures. Good-quality concrete slabs are a good imitation of real stone and are much cheaper and easy to lay.

You can make your own paving slabs from concrete, which you can tint to the exact colour you want. Either make individual slabs in a mould or just lay the concrete and groove the surface before it is fully set to suggest paving slabs (for this you will need a keen eye and a steady hand).

PATIO PLANNING AND BUILDING BASICS

• When a patio is built to adjoin the house, make sure that the final surface of the patio is not higher than the damp-proof (water-proof) course.

• Lay paving stones or concrete so that the patio slopes very slightly away from the house wall toward a drain or border, to prevent puddles forming. The drop should be about 16mm per metre (^{5}/8in per yard).

• If you have to include steps in your design to cope with changes of level, define the edges clearly with contrasting materials.

COMBINING ELEMENTS

While you might initially decide it is a good idea to stick to a single building material to keep a patio or terrace looking smart and uncluttered, it can be effective to combine different elements. In fact, it makes sense to do so. Think about how you decorate indoors: a sitting room, for instance, combines a number of textures – carpets, heavy-duty furnishing fabrics, sheer curtains – and a bathroom can unite chrome with ceramic tiling and mirrors or warm cork tiles.

If your patio is a large one, using more than one material for the surface can help to break up an expanse that

Above: A mixture of large stones and cobbles creates a natural-looking area, enhanced by informal planting and the trickle of water from a bubble fountain.

might otherwise start to seem bleak. It can also help to define different parts of the patio, such as the area around the table, or the children's play area.

Combining materials is also a good way of introducing small quantities of desirable but expensive elements into the design. A small mosaic motif or an edging strip of expensive tiles can be incorporated with more workaday materials to provide interest and focus. Alternatively, introduce areas of cobbles set in concrete. Decking

Above: This clever use of different materials, textures and colours helps define discrete areas of the patio. The gravel softens the hard edges of the bricks.

shade might be appropriate on a large patio or a specimen shrub on a smaller one. This can also be an excellent way of creating a herb garden close to the house, so that you do not need to walk far from the kitchen every time you want to pick a handful of fresh herbs for garnish or flavour. The paving will also help to contain rampant herbs such as mint.

If you have opted for gravel laid over a membrane spread directly on garden soil, a few judiciously pierced holes will allow for planting. You need to choose the plants carefully, however, because some species will actually seed themselves in the gravel and can push their roots through the membrane if this is water-permeable.

works surprisingly well with gravel, but you should be careful when combining decking squares with concrete slabs. If they are of roughly the same size, the eye gets confused and will "jump" from one to the other, which can be unsettling and discomfiting.

Water and decking work well together to create a seaside feel. An expanse of water is cooling, but where space is limited or the presence of young children rules out a pool, a vertical water feature incorporating a spout or a small bubble fountain might be considered.

In a paved area you could miss out a few slabs here and there to allow for planting – a tree that will cast light

Above: In spring, brilliant blue grape hyacinths (Muscari) will happily push their way through gravel.

Above: Brick (block) paving weathers gracefully and looks wonderful when colonized by small plants and mosses.

Brick

If your house is built of bricks (blocks), it is usually easy to find a good match for use on the patio. House bricks, whether new or reclaimed, are, however, not the best type to use as paving: they are not frostproof and tend to crack and crumble in extreme weather. For durability, look for the highest specification. Facing and engineering bricks are frost-resistant.

Bricks are eminently suitable for patterned paving. They can be laid in a variety of bonds, much as walls are built, and are also suitable for herringbone or basketweave effects.

Tiles

Terracotta tiles are beautiful, and make it possible to use the same style of flooring outdoors as you have used in the kitchen, but they are less durable than other types so are best used under cover, perhaps for a covered loggia or summerhouse. Pottery roofing tiles can be used laid on edge, either on their own or in conjunction with other materials, as a large quantity is needed to cover the ground.

Cobbles and Setts

If you can find a source – usually a reclamation yard – old street cobbles and setts are attractive, but they are not always easy to walk on, and any seating placed on cobbles will be distinctly unstable. They are best used to break up larger areas of paving, either in the form of a strip to demarcate separate areas or to highlight an edge or as decoration, in the form of swirls and spirals.

Above: Bright tiles in a formal pool are elegantly set off by a terracotta edging.

Gravel

Easy to lay and to maintain, gravel is an ideal surface material. It can be laid direct on compacted earth, ideally over a weed-suppressing membrane, or on top of another hard surface. It is available in a range of grades and colours, and it has the additional advantage of combining well with other hard surfaces. It is very useful for filling awkward corners and curved areas. The main drawbacks are that it must be contained by edging if it is not to travel, both around the garden and into the house on the soles of shoes, and it is irresistible to cats.

Railway Sleepers

Available from reclamation yards and some specialist garden suppliers, railway sleepers (ties) are usually used for edging raised beds, as low walls or as steps. Sleepers are heavy and when they are used in a single row they usually need no fixing. However, if they are used as steps or to create a raised bed several sleepers high, when there will be a considerable weight of soil behind them, they should be held together with brackets.

Sleepers can be laid directly on the ground, but if they are impregnated with preservative, lay them on plastic sheeting and line the inside with plastic to prevent the tar from leaching into the soil and harming the plants. If possible, buy untreated sleepers.

Above: *Smooth stones and pea shingle look attractive but are best used as decorative details as they may not be easy to walk on.*

Mosaics

If you are naturally creative – or have a good friend who is – you can enliven any outdoor space with a mosaic that will give pleasure throughout the year. Mosaics work especially well near water – a reminder of the Islamic concept of the paradise garden, even though your principal source of inspiration may lie elsewhere.

Experiment with patterns of broken tiles or coloured stones, even sea shells, in a dry mix of sand and cement. Once you are satisfied with the design, sprinkle with water to set the mortar or simply allow soil moisture to be drawn up by capillary action, which will do the job for you. Mosaics tend to be less durable than other forms of paving, so restrict their use to areas that will not be subjected to heavy traffic or use them to make small patterns or decorative motifs.

WALLS AND FENCES

At the most basic level, walls and fences mark the boundaries between neighbouring gardens. The need for privacy is often important, particularly in a small town garden, and a solid wall or fence will provide maximum security and privacy.

Within the garden, however, these structures may have different functions. They can be used to divide separate areas and levels or to provide shelter, and when a new patio is being designed, you may want to erect additional fences or walls at the same time.

If a windbreak is required, for example, a trellis fence will filter the strongest winds better than a solid wall. A compromise can be achieved by topping a low fence or wall with trellis panels. If you want to preserve a lovely view from the terrace, a low fence may be adequate shelter for small plants.

Walls

A new garden wall is a luxury few can afford these days owing to high labour costs, and there are, in any case, often local regulations governing the height of solid boundaries, so if you already have a wall, make the most of it.

Within a garden, however, as long as you have space to dig out the footings, walls can be used either to enhance the privacy of a patio or to create secret places and hidden corners. A wall up to 1m (3ft) tall can be built by anyone with the relevant skills, but seek professional help with anything higher.

A wall to edge a patio can be built of a material that matches the house and patio floor itself. Brick and stone are obvious choices, but concrete can be incredibly stylish, especially if the house is a modern one, and the material lends itself to abstract and innovative designs. Glass blocks are excellent in a contemporary design, and are extremely attractive in association with water features.

Brick, glass and concrete can also be used to make curved structures, but the weight and the techniques involved suggest that their construction is best left in the hands of professional contractors.

Above: Use wall-baskets and hanging baskets to bring colour to plain walls.

Above: Unusually patterned stones make an idiosyncratic boundary wall. Planting softens the effect, preventing it from becoming overpowering.

Above: Basketweave fencing is a sympathetic background for plants and is easy to erect. It requires regular varnishing to lengthen its life.

Fences

Most fencing is made of softwood, and ready-made panel fences are easy to erect, popular and effective. As a rule, the more expensive the fencing, the better the quality and the longer it is likely to last. Wherever possible, use tanalized (pressure-treated) wood to ensure a long life.

When you are using a fence within the garden to create a shelter around a patio, consider it from both points of view. For example, a fence around the edge of a sitting area might prevent you from seeing the compost heap, but if the patio is next to the house it might also pose a security problem: you might not be able to see the back of your house when you are working elsewhere in the garden.

When you are choosing fence panels, look at how they have been made. Close-board fences, made of upright timbers, look good in a woodland garden and anywhere where you want to emphasize verticals. Interwoven fences tend to stress horizontal lines and are useful when you want to exaggerate the depth of the garden. In an Oriental-style setting, a bamboo fence is entirely appropriate, but it can be too lightweight for use anywhere other than in a sheltered corner. Trellis has the advantage that it functions well as a windbreak but can be clothed with dense climbers in summer to provide maximum privacy.

All fences can be painted or stained, either to soften their impact or to help them blend in with their surroundings. Alternatively, you might want to make a strong colour statement by painting them so that they really stand out. Whatever you do, make sure that any preservative or paint you use on the fences is plant friendly.

HEDGES

A hedge can be planted either to give privacy or to mark off one part of the garden from another. Thorny hedges, such as pyracantha, can also offer increased security if they are used around the boundary, but they are not ideal near children's play areas or beside paths and sitting areas.

Deciduous or Evergreen?

If you just want a windbreak, a deciduous hedge would be a good choice, because the bare branches will filter strong winter winds but in summer the leaf cover will provide shade and help to minimize noise. For an evergreen barrier, conifers such as yew (*Taxus*), box (*Buxus*) and *Thuja* are

Above: Traditional and still best, tightly clipped box (Buxus) is a splendid choice for low hedging to surround beds in a formal garden.

traditional choices, but they need regular clipping for a sheer surface and to restrict the height.

Do not plant Leyland cypress (x *Cuprocyparis leylandii*) within the garden: it will take the nutrients from other plants and will need to be clipped three or four times a year to prevent it from taking over completely.

Bear in mind that evergreens tend to be less tolerant of urban pollution. This is an important factor in a town garden, hence the popularity of privet (*Ligustrum*), which shows outstanding resistance.

Informal Hedges

In a town or Oriental-style garden, bamboos can make an elegant screen, and the light rustle of their leaves in summer is an added delight. Make sure you choose carefully: some species are invasive, and it is a sensible precaution to restrict the root system wherever they are planted. Plant them in large tubs and sink these into the ground or surround the roots with paving slabs buried vertically.

Climbing and rambling roses make good barriers and have the bonus of summer flowers and fragrance. Alternatively, an informal evergreen hedge can be created with spotted laurel (*Aucuba japonica* 'Crotonifolia') or

HEDGING PLANTS FOR PATIOS
Aucuba
Berberis
Buxus
Cotoneaster
Escallonia
Euonymus
Fagus
Fuchsia
Griselinia
Ilex
Laurus
Lonicera nitida
Prunus (evergreen)
Rosa (some)
Rosmarinus
Santolina

Portugal laurel (*Prunus lusitanica*), while a mixed hedge of hawthorn (*Crataegus*) and holly (*Ilex*) will suit a country or cottage garden.

Above: *Hollies make good hedges, and berrying forms provide food for birds in winter.* Ilex aquifolium *'J.C. van Tol' has the advantage of almost spineless leaves.*

Above: *The cherry laurel (*Prunus laurocerasus) *makes an excellent informal evergreen hedge. This is the attractive cultivar 'Castlewellan'.*

Patio Planting

IN A LARGE GARDEN, THE PLANTING IS DESIGNED TO CONTRIBUTE TO THE OVERALL PICTURE, AND IS OFTEN SEEN FROM A DISTANCE. THE PATIO IS THE PLACE TO GROW SPECIES THAT ARE REWARDING AT CLOSE QUARTERS, SUCH AS THOSE WITH LAVISH FLOWERS OR A HEADY SCENT.

BRINGING THE PATIO TO LIFE

A beautifully designed patio or terrace with pleasing proportions may need only the minimum of plant material to decorate it. The focus of interest may be a beautiful specimen tree, or a pair of elegant containers. Most people who have a garden, however, eventually become hooked on plants, often in spite of themselves, and want to grow more unusual species. It is worth knowing which plants lend themselves especially well to this area of the garden and how they should be grown.

Above: Raised beds, generously planted with miniature roses, will be a source of colour all summer long.

Raised Beds

If you are constructing a completely new patio, you may decide to incorporate raised beds to edge the patio, in place of a balustrade or low wall. On a hard surface they must have in-built weep holes for drainage. Make sure the beds are not so wide that you cannot reach the centre (assuming there is access from both sides); this usually means limiting the width to 1.2m (4ft).

A raised bed has several advantages. It is effectively a large container, which makes it possible to grow plants that would not thrive elsewhere in the garden. Bringing in acid soil, for example, will create a suitable medium for rhododendrons and heathers, which you would not otherwise be able to grow if your soil is alkaline. If the garden soil is poor, raised beds give you the opportunity of importing new soil. Adding grit to improve drainage will open the door to a whole range of alpines and dwarf bulbs.

Combining raised beds with other borders and beds at ground level can bring a certain dynamism to the design, which is especially important if space is restricted.

Above: Ballerina apple trees are ideal patio plants. They can be trained to arch over to make a fruiting bower.

SELECTING PLANTS

What you grow in the ground adjoining the patio is obviously a matter of personal choice. The patio is often quite sheltered and if it is near the house it may benefit from the residual warmth of the walls, allowing you to grow less-hardy species.

If the patio is bounded by walls or fences on one or more sides, the rainfall will be restricted. Either be prepared to water the plants during dry weather or restrict your choice to drought-tolerant species, including bulbs and many herbs.

Planting in Sun

If your patio is sunny, you'll be spoiled for choice when planting up containers for spring and summer colour. Many fruits and vegetables are also extremely decorative, and a surprising number can be grown in containers on the patio. Ballerina apple trees were

FLOWERS FOR SUNNY PATIOS
(a = annual or biennial; p = perennial)
Argyranthemum p
Bergenia p
Felicia p
Fuchsia p
Iris stylosa p
Pelargonium p
Tropaeolum a
Verbena a and p
Viola a and p

specially bred for this purpose, but almost any cultivar is suitable provided it has been grafted on to a dwarfing rootstock. Figs thrive in containers against a warm wall, and the root restriction helps produce bigger crops earlier in the plant's life. Luscious strawberries and tomatoes also make attractive plants for a sunny corner, with the bonus that you can pick the ripe fruit from your garden chair.

Above: Well-filled borders and containers soften the severe lines of this simple paved area and create a lush feel.

97

Planting for Shade

If you want the patio to be a shady area for summer relaxation you may have to plant to create shade. Among the many widely available and reliable deciduous trees are ornamental cherries (*Prunus*) and crab apples (*Malus*), which have delightful spring flowers. The best of all shade trees are, perhaps, catalpas and paulownias, both of which have large leaves. Both respond well to pruning so can be planted even where space is limited.

Your patio may already be shaded by walls and trees, but there are plenty of plants that will flourish in cool conditions, and it is easy to create a lush, jungle-like effect with luxurious foliage plants such as hostas and hardy ferns.

Above: This small area has been designed as a cool retreat, with a pool shaded by cleverly supported ivy and a thick wall of luxuriant foliage to create a screen.

Climbers and Ramblers

House walls or fences that abut a patio cry out for the softening effect of climbers. If possible, allow space for small beds between the patio and the wall or fence. Because they are largely woodland plants, most climbers appreciate the cool root run that the paving or decking over their roots will

---

FLOWERS FOR SHADY PATIOS
(a = annual or biennial; p = perennial)
Convallaria majalis p
Dicentra p
Impatiens a
Lobelia a
Pulmonaria p

provide. Make sure that such plants receive plenty of water. Your choice of climber will depend on the aspect of the wall: some species revel in the reflected heat; others are happier in shade. Some large-flowered clematis varieties, for instance, will produce flowers of a richer colour when shielded from intense sunlight.

Climbers can also be grown in containers, either placed against a wall or trained on a support that is incorporated in the pot. Some of the weaker-growing or annual climbers are best for containers. Rampant plants, such as wisteria and bougainvillea, can be grown in pots but will need hard pruning to keep them within bounds.

If you want flowering climbers for a confined space, good choices are to be found among the large-flowered hybrid clematis and miniature climb-

> ### CLIMBERS FOR PATIOS
> (* = shade tolerant)
> *Bougainvillea* (not hardy)
> *Campsis radicans*
> *Clematis* *
> *Hedera* *
> *Humulus lupulus*
> *Hydrangea petiolaris* *
> *Jasminum officinale*
> *Plumbago auriculata* (not hardy)
> *Rosa* (miniature climbers)
> *Trachelospermum jasminoides*
> *Tropaeolum speciosum*
> *Wisteria*

ing roses. The so-called patio roses and miniature climbers have been specially bred with present needs in mind: they are compact plants that produce an abundance of flowers over a long period. They are ideal for planting in beds, borders and containers. Some of the roses bred for groundcover can also be trained upward, to cover walls and trellises.

Above: Hedera helix *'Buttercup', smaller growing than many ivies, produces its best leaf colour in a sunny position.*

Above: The annual Ipomoea tricolor *has vivid blue flowers and is perfect for guiding over a trellis.*

Patio Planting

Above: The poached-egg plant
(Limnanthes douglasii) *is a modest annual that will obligingly seed itself in the cracks of paving and in gravel.*

Perennials and Annuals

Flowering herbaceous plants put the flesh on the bones of the garden, as it were, producing an abundance of greenery and, in most cases, a spectacular show of flowers over a long period. The more compact, sturdy forms are best suited to the patio whereas tall, floppy plants, such as delphiniums and some peonies, which need to be staked, look more effective when planted in the herbaceous border.

Most valuable of all for the patio are the tender perennials, such as felicias, verbenas, pelargoniums and osteospermums, which you can grow from seed or buy as small plants in late spring. These showy plants produce a seemingly unending succession of flowers from the start of summer until the first frosts. They are ideal for all kinds of patio containers, from hanging baskets to large troughs. If you have a greenhouse, plant tender perennials in pots and tubs that can be moved under glass for the winter.

Annuals will also produce flowers all summer, although many varieties should be sown successionally for the maximum flowering period. Deadhead the plants regularly to encourage them to produce further blooms, and feed them well to maintain their flower power. While perennials and shrubs will give structure to your planting plan, growing annuals allows you to transform the look of your patio with a fresh colour scheme each year.

Above: The succulent-looking evergreen Sedum aizoon *will thrive in the heat reflected by paving.*

Low-growing Shrubs

Compact, tightly growing shrubs are ideal for patios because they are easy to control and naturally stay within bounds. Evergreens that have a pleasing shape, such as Mexican orange blossom (*Choisya ternata*), are obviously desirable, but there are others, such as box (*Buxus*), that can be clipped to shape and some, such as *Phillyrea*, that can be allowed to grow more freely. Small shrubs such as camellia, fuchsia and skimmia can be grown as specimens in containers.

Patio and groundcover roses are recently bred varieties that are quite unlike the often gangly hybrid teas and cluster-flowered roses: they are low-growing, tough and disease-resistant. They smother themselves in flowers and repeat well throughout the summer, making them perfect plants in every way for a sunny patio.

Bulbs and Corms

Many bulbs are ideal patio plants, and not just in containers. Early spring bulbs, such as crocuses and dwarf narcissi, look delightful pushing up through gravel. If you have a hot spot near a sheltering wall, include some of the late-flowering South African species, such as crinums, nerines and *Amaryllis belladonna* (the true amaryllis, not the hippeastrums sold under this name for growing indoors in winter).

SHRUBS FOR PATIOS

Buxus
Calluna
Camellia
Choisya ternata
Conifers (dwarf forms)
Erica
Fuchsia
Hebe
Ilex
Phillyrea
Rhododendron (dwarf forms)
Rosa (patio, miniature and groundcover forms)
Skimmia

BULBS FOR PATIOS

Agapanthus
Amaryllis belladonna
Crinum
Crocus
Dahlia (dwarf forms)
Iris
Lilium
Nerine

Above: *The aptly named pineapple lily (*Eucomis bicolor*) is not quite hardy but will thrive in sheltered conditions.*

Foliage Plants

Delightful as flowers are, they are present for a much shorter period in the plant's annual life cycle than leaves. Leaves are the backdrop to any planting, and once you learn to appreciate their variety of shape, colour and texture, you will come to value them as much as flowers.

Some plants are grown primarily for their foliage. In fact, some of the best – ferns – do not flower at all in the conventional sense. Mainly shade lovers, these are ideal for bringing life to cool, shady, moist corners, perhaps adjoining a basement flat. Team them with hostas for contrast, but watch out for slugs and snails, which also like shady, moist conditions.

Grasses are increasingly popular, and with good reason. They are easy to maintain, and even those that are not evergreen provide a long period of interest, since the old foliage is retained by the plant over winter. A riming of frost on a cold winter's morning only adds to their beauty. They are useful for softening a vivid planting of flowers and work surprisingly well with conifers.

*Above: A cool, shady patio with a bubble fountain to provide a moist atmosphere is the perfect environment for potted hostas and tree ferns (*Dicksonia antarctica*).*

PLANTS WITH GOOD FOLIAGE

Ajuga reptans
Aloe
Aucuba
Conifers
Eriobotrya japonica
Ferns
Grasses
Hebe
Hedera
Hosta
Ophiopogon nigrescens
Pulmonaria
Stachys olympica

Architectural Plants

Some plants are grown for their over-all impact – usually termed their habit – and they make striking shapes in the garden. If you intend to use the patio mainly in the evening and at night, it is worth including some of these in the planting: they are supremely effective

Above: Melianthus major, *with its luxuriant leaves, stately yuccas and steely blue oat grass add contrasting colour and form to a striking group of foliage plants.*

with subtle lighting, which will high-light large glossy leaves or distinctive silhouettes. Fatsias are usually grown as houseplants, but they are more or less hardy and take kindly to life out-doors in a sheltered spot. Their palm-like, evergreen leaves bring a touch of the exotic to the garden.

Above: Plant Ophiopogon planiscapus *'Nigrescens' against a light backdrop.*

ARCHITECTURAL PLANTS
FOR PATIOS

Cordyline
Cycas revoluta
Eriobotrya japonica
Fatsia japonica
Mahonia x media
Phormium
Trachycarpus fortunei
Yucca

Choosing a Style

THERE ARE AS MANY STYLES OF PATIO AS THERE ARE STYLES OF INDOOR DÉCOR. THIS SECTION EXPLORES JUST A FEW OF THE DESIGN TRENDS THAT ARE POPULAR TODAY AND SUGGESTS WAYS IN WHICH THEY CAN BE INTERPRETED ON A PATIO OR TERRACE.

DEFINING STYLE

The decorative aspects of a patio – from the plants in the borders to the cushions you place on the garden chairs – are personal, and what represents good taste to one gardener may well be anathema to another. However, factors such as proportion and scale are universals. No matter how you decorate your outdoor space, a successful patio will be in proportion to the rest of the garden and to the house, and it should be sympathetic in overall appearance to the style and materials used for the other buildings against which it is set.

Above: Foliage plants clothe the fences and screen a seat in a restful corner of the garden, providing dappled shade and shelter from the breeze.

Other aspects of design depend on your approach to life, and it is these that we tend to think of as embodying a particular "style". Fashion plays a part too, and even if you think you are not a slave to the latest trends, some become so commonplace that you can hardly avoid them. Wooden decking is now so widespread and easily available that it has become the first choice of many people who would previously have considered only

Above: Neat metal containers, filled with a phormium, ferns and clipped evergreens, give the garden an orderly air.

Above: These exuberant climbing roses ensure a private and fragrant retreat, even in a town garden.

paving. With a trend as popular as this, however, you need to consider carefully whether it is really the most appropriate material for your garden.

Some people like to give order to their spaces. Others have a more relaxed attitude and may tolerate, even prefer, a certain dishevelment. The two are not mutually exclusive, but a tendency one way or the other may well be evident in how you design and create your garden.

Like the rest of your home, the garden allows you to express your personality. It also reflects the way you choose to spend your time. If you think of the patio as a quiet retreat, you'll plan for privacy and comfort. If your garden is often the setting for parties, your priorities will be space, seating and dramatic lighting effects. If the house opens on to the patio, it is a good idea to relate the two, perhaps

using furniture in similar styles or matching colours. You could extend a tiled floor outside, or echo a wooden floor with decking.

Remember that no scheme need be for ever, and you can change the look with new planting and furniture. Many people update their gardens as often as they change their interiors.

Above: A variety of natural materials can be laid in clean, geometric designs to suit a modern setting.

COUNTRY CASUAL

Many town-dwellers would like to bring something of the countryside into their garden, so that it becomes a kind of green lung, with the same function as a park in the middle of a city. The fact that the garden (or a proportion of it) is paved does not prevent this from happening, but a bit more effort may be required to create the desired effect.

Creating the Look

The choice of materials can be critical. Instead of municipal-looking, smooth concrete slabs, look for riven paving in different sizes to create a slightly haphazard look. Decking often looks a little cosmopolitan, especially when the boards are new, but old railway sleepers (ties) have a weathered charm. As far as possible, make sure that the edges of any paved area or raised bed are softened by planting.

When it comes to garden furniture, keep an eye out for wicker or cane chairs, which will have the appropriate rustic character. Weathered pieces of wooden or metal garden furniture can often be found second-hand, and some antique dealers specialize in old garden furniture of high quality – though this can be expensive. For a seaside look, use deck chairs or steamer chairs. A hammock slung between two trees (or possibly between a tree

Above: A simple arbour made from painted wooden trellis makes a pretty backdrop for plants and an inviting place to sit a while to enjoy the garden.

Above: Billowing plants in the borders and containers create an exuberant casual effect, disguising the formal shape of a small courtyard garden.

Above: A profusion of lush plants, like Zantedeschia aethiopica 'Crowborough', creates a relaxed, unstructured cottage-garden feel.

and a house wall) makes an idyllic picture in summer and is ideal for a nap on a warm afternoon.

An eclectic mix is appropriate, and *objets trouvés* can provide just the right note. An old metal watering can or that cartwheel will give a hint of rusticity. If you cannot find old terracotta pots, paint new ones with sour milk or yoghurt to encourage mosses and lichens to take a hold.

Planting

A cottage garden is primarily one of early and high summer. Typical flowers include all kinds of roses, especially the scented ones, old-fashioned pinks (*Dianthus*) and a host of annuals. Pelargoniums are cheerful and bright and will flower for months. Lavender (*Lavandula*) is an excellent low-grow-

ing hedging plant and will provide a romantic haze of colour when in flower (as well as attracting swarms of bees).

Aim for a riotous mix of colour and don't forget the fruit and vegetables without which no true cottage gardener could survive for long.

Above: A pot overflowing with herbs epitomizes the cottage garden style.

MODERN

If you have a beautiful, architect-designed house and are a naturally neat and tidy person with an uncluttered lifestyle, this may well be the look for you.

Creating the Look

Absolutely up-to-date materials are *de rigueur* for high-tech designers, and metals and plastics are likely to be used as often as more traditional materials. Inventive finishes are important: marble and granite, for instance – surely the most desirable of all traditional building materials – can be polished to a glass-like surface or given a more frosted appearance. Crushed CDs, a recent innovation to be used in place of gravel and crushed shells, have a real sparkle.

A smart urban look can be created using a limited colour palette, in both materials and plants. While natural materials are generally left to speak for themselves, artificial ones are often dyed to shades that would never occur in nature. You can find manmade pebbles in bright blues and reds and plastic pots in a range of colours.

If you have a keen design sense (or are able to employ a designer), you might like to experiment with asymmetric shapes, but make sure that the design is not too dominant. Look beyond gardening for your inspiration: architectural magazines and the world of industry and product design may well ignite your creative fire.

A possible drawback is that a garden in this style can date quickly as new trends emerge.

Above: *Smooth tiles and mirrors create an illusion of space on a small modern terrace.*

Above: Top-dressing pots with some of the cobbles that have been used for the patio surface will help give coherence to the overall design.

Above: Colour can be used on both boundaries and containers to create a sense of unity. Even the spiral plant supports are blue.

Planting

On the green front, stick to plants that have a strong outline and architectural form. Spiky succulents, such as agaves, are perfect but will not tolerate extremes of cold and wet. Phormiums and the Chusan palm (*Trachycarpus fortunei*) are hardier and just as dramatic.

Low-growing plants with metallic-looking leaves include *Houttuynia cordata* and *Ajuga reptans* 'Burgundy Glow'. Selected forms of *Pulmonaria saccharata* Argentea Group have interestingly marbled leaves, and *Heuchera* 'Pewter Moon' makes satisfying clumps of silver-grey foliage. Many grasses are perfect for the modern look,

and they can be used on their own, either planted *en masse* or displayed for effect in matching containers.

Most flowers do not really belong in a garden of this type, but they need not be eliminated entirely, and those with a sculptural form are best. Spring-flowering hyacinths have a stiff habit and their thick, glossy leaves look positively unreal. Planted in quantity, they look (and smell) sensational. For summer interest, grow lilies, with their trumpet-like flowers. *Zantedeschia aethiopica* is a plant of unsurpassed elegance, with cool-looking, heart-shaped leaves and smooth-textured, white, arum-type flowers. It is perfect near (or even in) water.

MEDITERRANEAN

Memories of Mediterranean summers make many of us long for lazy days of outdoor living, soaking up the sun or relaxing in leafy shade, surrounded by the scents of aromatic herbs, pines and citrus. A real Mediterranean garden is usually a shady place, often a court-yard, brightened with pots of vivid flowers and sheltered by a pergola draped with fruiting vines. Walls and woodwork, often bleached and cracked by the sun, are painted in the Mediterranean palette of clear blues, dusky pinks, terracotta or white.

Above: Pale decking reflects the available light and large terracotta containers give a strongly Mediterranean feel.

Creating the Look

In cooler climates, a Mediterranean-style patio can maximize the available sunshine by using white or pale paving to reflect heat on to the plants. Another way to achieve this is through the use of gravel or, if your budget will stretch to it, dolomite chippings. If you can lay out the garden as a series of terraces that face the sun, so much the better. A brick or stone wall that faces the sun will retain the day's heat and radiate it at dusk, appreciably raising the ambient temperature. To a lesser degree, so will stone and terra-cotta pots and paving.

Your Mediterranean patio should include a shaded area to offer relief from the sun on the hottest days. Erect a simple pergola over a seat or table, and plant climbers to scramble over it.

A positive aspect of this style is that you will feel as if you are always on holiday – at least as long as the sun is shining. As soon as wet weather arrives, you may notice that gravel starts to turn green as moss and lichens take hold. Either chemical treatments or a blast with a pressure washer will solve this problem for you.

Planting

Typical plants of the Mediterranean include most of the woody herbs, including thyme, rosemary and laven-der, which thrive in gritty, well-drained soil in your sunniest spot. These,

together with rock roses (*Cistus* and *Helianthemum*), with gummy, aromatic stems, will fill the patio with evocative scents as well as attracting bees and butterflies. Oleanders (*Nerium oleander*) are also characteristic of the region, with their leathery leaves and richly coloured flowers (but they are poisonous, so treat them with care). Pelargoniums flower all summer, giving bold splashes of white, pink and red. If you need an accent plant, a fig, olive or citrus tree would be perfect.

Most of these plants respond well to being grown in containers or raised beds, making them ideal patio plants.

Mediterranean plants do not take kindly to long periods of cold, wet weather, though they will survive lower temperatures if planted in open, gritty soil. You can move delicate subjects in pots under cover in winter.

Above: Brightly painted furniture and accessories, with flowers in strong, warm colours, create a Mediterranean feel in a sunny corner of this patio.

*Above: Evergreen bay (*Laurus nobilis*) grows readily in a container and is easily clipped into decorative shapes.*

111

Above: A sheltered corner of the patio takes on a jungly character when lavishly filled with foliage plants. Although they look exotic, they are all quite hardy.

HOT AND EXOTIC

Surprisingly, it is not actually necessary to live in a hot climate to create a tropical look in your garden, and the enclosed, sheltered conditions found on many patios, which may have protecting walls on two and even three sides, often provide the ideal micro-climate for many exotic plants that would not otherwise survive.

Creating the Look

The keynote to success is to include lots of foliage plants, preferably the large-leaved kind. If you have enough greenery you will actually increase the humidity level of the garden, creating the jungle-like environment in which these plants will thrive. Bearing in mind that a lot of tropical plants have

adapted to low light levels, this style can be an effective design solution to a predominantly shady site.

A timber deck creates the appropriate colonial atmosphere, and the furnishings might be either huge wicker chairs or teak recliners. A mosquito net would provide a witty reference to the tropics, especially if there were a pool nearby.

Planting

Huge bamboos actually look extremely effective in a confined space and are hardy. Try also banana palms (*Musa basjoo*), which will require some winter protection. If the patio is shaded, you may prefer a tree fern (*Dicksonia antarctica*). Buy the biggest you can afford, because they grow at a rate of only 2.5cm (1in) a year, so if you buy

Above: Small pans of succulents will enjoy the warmth reflected from the paving.

a youngster you will have to be prepared for a long wait. Large specimens are expensive but worth the outlay when you consider the drama they bring to a garden.

An interesting and less often seen alternative is the loquat (*Eriobotrya japonica*). In a cold climate it is hardly likely to fruit, but you can enjoy it for its exotic-looking, long, pleated leaves.

Remember that if you have a lot of houseplants you can move them outdoors in summer (when there is no risk of night frosts) to enhance the tropical atmosphere.

A Desert Patio

If your patio is really hot and exposed, a desert-style planting scheme might be appropriate, concentrating on cacti and succulents. Some cacti are surprisingly tolerant of cold. What they hate is damp, muggy weather, which causes rotting, so good drainage is vital.

Above: Succulents in pots, which do duty as houseplants, will benefit from being moved outside in summer.

They will thrive in gravel beds, which can be given extra structure by the addition of rocks or pebbles.

In this kind of garden you need to avoid any suspicion of lushness. Smooth-rendered walls will enhance the desert feel and reflect sunlight and heat on to the plants, staying warm even as the temperature drops in the evening. Leave gaps for the plants among paving stones, or make larger beds by laying a weed-suppressing membrane over the soil and planting through it before topping with gravel or cobbles. On a smaller scale, fill troughs or planters with succulents.

It is possible to replicate this look even in a cold climate if you keep your exotic plants in pots for enjoying indoors in winter. Plunge them into their beds in the summer.

113

ORIENTAL

The Zen principles on which the classic gardens of Japan and China are laid out probably baffle most Westerners, but this is no reason why we should not borrow some of the ideas to create Oriental-style gardens that are places of peace and tranquillity and conducive to contemplation.

Creating the Look

The true Japanese garden usually contains only a few plants. Everything depends on the balance of a few elements: rocks, raked gravel, water and maybe a conifer or Japanese maple (*Acer*). Any tree with an interesting outline will do, however. In essence,

Above: Low, clean lines using natural materials, and the restrained use of foliage plants, create an elegant, structured look that echoes Japanese garden design.

Above: Topiarized box, trained into the traditional cloud form, is a feature of Oriental-style gardens.

the style is rather akin to the minimalist garden and will suit anyone who does not have a great deal of time on their hands, since what plants there are need little maintenance. The style also lends itself to a shady site.

Alternatively, you might like to borrow some elements of feng shui. Although this philosophy is more often thought of in relation to interior design, the principles are equally applicable outdoors. You may want to incorporate wind chimes (but think of your neighbours, who might be profoundly irritated by the tinkling sound that you find so charming) and a water feature, but it is how you place them in relation to each other that counts. Any paths should be winding, to symbolize the winding route of life.

Planting

China is often referred to as the mother of all gardens, because a huge number of the plants that are now most prized in cultivation originated there. There is therefore no shortage of plant material available to help you create an Oriental look: whether you prefer blowsy peonies or delicate grasses, you will be able to find the appropriate species.

The classic Japanese garden is predominantly green, imitating a natural landscape. Japanese maples (*Acer japonicum* and *A. palmatum*) have an elegant habit that you can enhance by wiring the stems as they grow to create an authentic gnarled appearance.

Velvety, vivid green moss is essential to the look. You can encourage it to colonize rocks by painting their shady sides with sour milk or yoghurt, but keep walkways and steps clear of moss as it can be very slippery.

If you must have flowers, some of the China roses, such as *Rosa* 'Cécile Brünner', are delightfully dainty, and many of the so-called patio roses seem to owe much to their Chinese forebears, making them ideal for an Oriental garden. Oriental lilies and chrysanthemums, such as 'Emperor of China', could complete the picture.

On a tiny patio, you might like to include some bonsai in Oriental pots.

Above: This serene Buddha would make the perfect finishing touch to an Oriental-style patio.

Above: Dainty but floriferous, Rosa 'Cécile Brünner' is ideal for a large container in a Chinese-style garden.

Special Features

Once the patio is built, finishing touches will help to bring it to life. A carefully placed pot, an unusual sculpture or intriguing items of furniture can provide the accents of colour and shape needed to tie the whole scheme together.

Furniture

The range of garden furniture available today is wide, and you can choose the type best suited to your needs. You need to consider, for instance, if the furniture is to stand outdoors all year round or if you are going to store it under cover when not in use.

Different furniture fulfils different purposes. A steamer chair is perfect for lolling in the sun with a refreshing drink and the Sunday newspaper but is less than ideal if you are eating a formal meal. If you are planning a barbecue, you might like to dispense with seating altogether, to encourage guests to mingle more freely.

Heavy furniture, such as cast iron and stone, is attractive but difficult to move once it is in place. If your patio is small and has to accommodate different activities at different times, lightweight alternatives are more convenient.

Above: A simple garden bench and fragrant flowers are all that is needed to make a delightful sanctuary.

Above: These dainty metal chairs are surprisingly comfortable and make an ideal choice for a small area, as they are in keeping with its scale.

Above: These two throne-like chairs on a raised terrace echo the curves of the patio design and have been used as its most dominant feature.

Types of Furniture

Top of the range is cast-iron furniture, which is expensive and heavy and is, in consequence, no longer made in great quantities. Antique pieces are extremely sought after and are usually highly decorative. Aluminium reproductions are much cheaper and lighter but are not always entirely convincing. Wire furniture, often painted white but more often these days coated in plastic, is highly ornate and perhaps best suited to a Victorian-style conservatory, although it is light enough to carry on to the patio in warm weather.

Wooden furniture is also expensive, especially if it is made of teak (the best wood for the purpose), but it is a sound investment and ages sympathetically. It will need treating with teak oil from time to time to stop the wood drying out and cracking. You should make sure that any teak furniture you buy is certified as having been made of wood from a sustainable source.

Deck chairs and director's chairs are convenient because they can be folded up and stored flat when they are not in use. They are also light enough to be moved from place to place as needed.

Bamboo, cane and rattan furniture is ideal for creating a colonial look, but it is not especially weatherproof. A coat of varnish can help prevent cracking, but this type of furniture is seldom long-lived.

Plastic furniture is usually cheap and readily available, but you may need to shop around to find a range that is really sympathetic. On the plus side, it is lightweight and can be painted or otherwise customized with cushions made to fit. Pre-formed plastic chairs are often stackable, which makes winter storage easy.

WATER FEATURES

A pool or fountain will add life to the patio, in more ways than one. Not only is the sound of water reviving – most people find it soothing, particularly in the evening – but water will attract a range of fauna into the garden: frogs, toads and newts as well as a host of insects.

Types of Water Feature

A patio or deck that meets or overhangs a pool looks dramatic, while even a small pool set into the paving or decking brings all the pleasures of a pool in the open garden. Formal, geometric pools work best close to a house, and they should ideally be based on the proportions of the house windows or doors and built with the same type of materials as the house.

Remember that it will be difficult (if not impossible) to excavate for a sunken pool on an existing patio. If you are building your patio from scratch and would like to include a pool, allow for the depth of the water in the height of the patio. The alternative is to build a raised pool surrounded by paving, a wooden framework or railway sleepers (ties).

If you favour an expanse of still water, try to site the pool away from trees, as leaves will rot and pollute the water. Most surface-growing water plants do best in sun, but if the pool is purely ornamental a shaded site is permissible, and you can keep the water clear with a chemical cleansing agent.

On a large patio a fountain would be the ultimate luxury, especially in a hot, dry climate. Cascades can be

Above: A well-planted raised pool is ideal on a patio because it does not involve excavating below the hard surface.

Above: When running, the wall-mounted spout will be a focal point and provide the refreshing sound of trickling water.

impressive, but for a really imposing fall of water a large reservoir and powerful submersible pump are needed. If you have a small pool in a sunny position and would like a fountain, look for one that is solar-powered. These are becoming more widely available and more attractive. Some models have separate solar panels, but increasingly they are manufactured with integral panels.

If you have small children most kinds of water feature are best avoided altogether: it is possible to drown in even the shallowest water. Installing a bubble fountain can be a good compromise because no deep water is accessible, but remember that the reservoir and pump must be housed below ground level and hidden by cobbles that sit on top of a mesh. Such

Above: A keen sense of humour is evident in the design of this water spout in a wooden half-barrel. Small raised features like this are quite simple to install.

features involve excavating below the level of the patio, so this must be taken into account during the planning process.

Many styles of ready-made water feature are available from garden suppliers, and these are simple to install. Designs such as a brimming urn or village pump are popular, and if ground space is really restricted, a wall spout that feeds into a basin just below can be delightful. Wall-mounted water features should never be fitted directly to a house wall, and it may be necessary to erect a double wall to house the pipe and pump.

Introducing the electricity needed to power a submersible pump should be considered during the planning stages. Because water and electricity are a lethal combination, seek professional advice about the appropriate switches and cables.

Above: If you choose a water feature that relies on a circulating pump, make sure you can excavate below ground for the sump.

LIGHTING

You will get the most use from your patio or terrace on summer evenings if you add some form of lighting. If the patio is some distance from the house but is visible from it, lighting it can bring an element of drama that you can also enjoy from the comfort of indoors at other seasons. Floodlighting can be spectacular when the ground is covered in snow.

All electrical lighting systems powered from the mains should be installed by a qualified electrician. Regulations stipulate how deep electric cables should be buried, and these should be adhered to. As with cabling for a pool, the lighting cables should be laid before the patio or terrace is built, but if this is not possible they should be buried where no digging that could damage the wires is likely to take place.

Remember that outdoor lighting should be designed to be seen only within your own garden. Your neighbours may prefer their gardens to be dark at night.

Types of Lighting

The simplest way to illuminate your patio is with candles or flares. Obviously, these are not permanent, and they must be supervised at all times. Both are best in still weather, but flares are much less likely to blow out than candles; you will need to

Above: This brass oil or paraffin lamp is easily portable and looks beautiful whether it is lit or not.

ensure that they can be properly supported in the ground or in stable containers. Candles can be housed in lanterns and distributed around the patio or suspended from trees.

Low-voltage lighting is cheap but is best used to edge a path, since the light shed will not be particularly strong. For safety, paths should always be lit at night if the garden is going to be used then, and solar-powered lights are now available that are ideal for this purpose.

Floodlights are much more powerful, and many dramatic effects can be achieved if they are sited with care. If

Above: Dramatic uplighting from the patio gives this delicate maple an added attraction at night.

of terracotta. These are designed as wood-burners, but you will need to substitute a non-smoking fuel if you live in a smokeless zone. They are made in a range of sizes. They need to be supervised at all times when lit and can pose a hazard if there are small children around.

Gas patio heaters are surprisingly stylish. They are usually fed by bottled gas rather than connected to the mains supply and are lit at the top, the heat being deflected downwards by a small canopy. They can look rather like municipal street lamps, but on a cool autumn evening the warmth they emit will be welcome.

there is a tree overhanging the patio, it is a charming idea to festoon it with fairy lights (coloured or not) or individual lanterns.

Underwater lamps can be used to light up a pond and will keep any fish active until well into the evening.

HEATING

Various forms of heating are available to bring a touch of warmth to those evenings when there is a chill in the air after sundown.

Perhaps the cosiest is the chiminea, a Mexican stove, which is open at the front and the top and is usually made

Above: Lighting a water feature brings drama to the patio after sundown.

SAFETY FIRST

Be sure to keep a fire extinguisher handy at all times if you are lighting or heating your patio with any form of naked flame.

MIRRORS

Not everyone appreciates the use of mirrors in a garden. There is no doubt that they increase the sense of size of a small space, but some people are unnerved by catching a glimpse of themselves. There is also the argument that birds will fly into them, although this is unlikely in an enclosed space such as a patio or terrace, since most birds prefer to keep to the trees if there is no clear runway for take-off.

If you include a mirror, site it with care for maximum impact, angling it slightly so that visitors to the garden do not merely see their own reflections. Placed at the end of a path, it will make the garden seem endless. If you have no paths, put a mirror where it will reflect a particular feature: a statue, a large container or even just a garden door. Mirrors are especially effective in association with water features, but they must be set perfectly upright if distorting effects are to be avoided. Disguise the mirror's presence by surrounding it with planting to hide the edges.

Use mirrors designed for outdoor use; those made for indoors are not particularly weatherproof and will soon begin to deteriorate.

ORNAMENTS

A well-chosen ornament can bring a touch of distinction to a patio, especially in winter when there may be a shortage of plant material to bring the

Above: An unusual metallic trellis functions as a mirror, creating the illusion that the garden is more colourful than it actually is.

Above: An arbour festooned with flowers makes a frame for a piece of classical statuary, creating a theatrical effect.

area to life. They can be given a position of some prominence or be hidden among plants or pots to make a personal or witty reference. Reflected in water or a mirror, their impact will be doubled. At best, they give a sense of permanence to the garden.

Make sure the ornament is in scale, but err on the large side if you are in doubt. Too small an ornament will look mean and lost, but one that is large will look grand and imposing and will make a considerable impact on a small patio.

Types of Ornament

Garden statuary is a matter of taste. Top of the list would be a work (possibly abstract) from a sculptor's studio, but this is likely to be beyond the purse and aspirations of most gardeners. Garden centres stock a wide range of mass-produced ornaments, and whether your preference is for stone animals or abstract designs such as obelisks or balls, you will probably find something to suit your patio.

For something a little more individual, go to a reclamation yard, where you can often find old statues and other ornaments. A rusted piece of agricultural equipment can make an appealing *objet trouvé*. Ceramics can be beautiful, though the production process limits their size. If you are naturally creative, you could try making your own abstract piece.

Above: A sombre-looking statue adds grand ornamentation to a garden. Once foliage starts to grow around it, its appearance will be less stark.

Materials

Bronze is beautiful and ages sympathetically, but the price is likely to be prohibitive. Nowadays, synthetic resins provide a convincing substitute at a much lower cost. Stone ornaments are heavy, and reconstituted stone pieces often have a tell-tale seam left from the mould that betrays their manufacture. However, they weather beautifully, acquiring an attractive covering of moss in time.

Plastic ornaments are light and tend to blow over, so they are perhaps best used among plants rather than as stand-alone features. Ceramics need to be securely placed, since they can crack or even break if they fall over.

Awnings and Shade

If the patio catches the midday sun you may find the glare and heat all but unbearable in summer. If there is no tree nearby, an awning or overhead screen can cast the necessary shade.

Types of Awning

Some awnings are designed to be attached to a house wall and are operated either manually or electronically. This restricts both their use and their design: they are an option only if the patio abuts a house wall; there must be a sufficient stretch of wall to accommodate them, and they must be rectangular or square in shape. If placed just above a sitting-room window or a pair of patio doors, they will have the dual function of shading the room. This type of awning is traditionally made of striped fabric with a scalloped or fringed edge. If you want something a little more individual, you could have a bespoke canopy made of canvas or sailcloth, to sling between poles or the patio walls.

If the patio is some distance from a suitable wall, a stand-alone awning will be required. At its simplest, this could be a large parasol; these are often designed to be used in conjunction with a table, and they have the advantage that they can be moved around as the direction of the sun changes. A rectangular gazebo, like a tent with open sides, will keep sun or rain off a larger table and chairs.

No awning is fully weatherproof. If accidentally left in the rain, they should be allowed to dry out fully then stored dry under cover.

Pergolas and Arbours

If you are building a completely new patio that is likely to be in full sun for most of the day, consider building a pergola to provide shade over part of it. A pergola is simply a framework of wooden posts with cross-pieces, but when it is clothed with climbing plants in summer it can become a shady room. A free-standing pergola constructed some distance from the house and built over a paved area will be a private, shady place.

Above: *A bespoke awning over a patio can make a bold design statement.*

A well-built pergola will be strong enough to support a large wisteria or fruiting vine, but it is also a perfect structure over which honeysuckle, roses and clematis can be trained. The deciduous hop (*Humulus lupulus*) will provide reliable summer shade but disappear in winter to admit all the available light.

An arbour is smaller in scale than a pergola but also offers opportunities to create a hideaway covered with fragrant climbers. Even a simple rustic arch, set against a hedge, will provide sufficient shelter for a table and two chairs, and a larger area, perhaps with a gazebo or summerhouse, will be a delightful retreat on a hot day.

Above: *On a small patio, a focal point can be created at ground level by using surface materials creatively.*

CREATING A FOCAL POINT

A focal point is an important aspect of any garden design, providing a resting place for the eye in much the same way as a fireplace in a sitting room, even though there may be other objects of interest present.

It need not be a permanent fixture. If, for instance, your patio is some distance from the house but visible from it, a well-positioned chair might be used to draw your attention to it.

A more permanent focal point can be provided by an ornament, a large container or an imposing plant, and other elements on the patio can be arranged to lead the eye toward it. A series of linked focal points can be useful in a large garden to draw different elements together, but they should be positioned so that they are not all visible simultaneously. Only when you arrive at one focal point will you be aware of the presence of another. Conversely, a single object can do double duty at the axis of two paths, providing the focal point for both. There is no limit to the number of visual games you can play.

Mark out the position of focal points with string stretched between pegs, and move them around until you find the right spot for the object. If the intended focal point already exists – for instance a garden door or a tree – use the string to determine the lie of the paths.

LOW-MAINTENANCE
GARDENING

If you want a lovely garden but don't have the time or energy to do a lot of work in it, help is at hand. There are countless ways you can minimize the amount of maintenance your garden requires, while still keeping it looking beautiful. This chapter offers suggestions for designing an easy-care garden, as well as tips on reducing routine tasks and a wide range of plants that can be happily left to take care of themselves.

Making Less Work

CREATING AND MAINTAINING A BEAUTIFUL GARDEN DOESN'T HAVE TO
BE TIME-CONSUMING. THERE ARE DOZENS OF WAYS IN WHICH THE
VARIOUS COMPONENTS OF THE GARDEN AND THE PLANTING METHODS
CAN BE ADAPTED TO MAKE MAINTENANCE EASIER.

Gardens should give pleasure and be places to enjoy. If yours takes up so much of your time in routine maintenance that you have little left in which to really appreciate it, you need to think about how to reduce the labour, without losing out on its beauty.

WHAT IS LOW MAINTENANCE?

Low maintenance does not simply mean cutting down on the number of plants that you grow. The choice of specimens and how you use them is more important – many plants

Above: Ground-cover plants like this prostrate cotoneaster look better than bare soil, and they won't give weeds a chance to grow once they are established.

require hardly any attention from one year to the next. You can also greatly reduce your workload with imaginative design and landscaping.

THE BENEFITS

A modestly sized, low-maintenance garden may require only half an hour a week to keep it looking good. But a truly low-maintenance garden, in which many labour-intensive components such as the lawn or difficult plants have been dispensed with, could require so little work that even if you took several weeks' holiday, it would have little effect on the appearance.

Left: Heathers and dwarf conifers are attractive all year round and need only occasional attention.

Assessing Your Garden

You need to assess which jobs you enjoy and which you dislike, then set about modifying your garden in the order of your priorities and how much time you want to save. If you enjoy propagating but hate weeding, for instance, you need to eliminate the weeds, and if you don't have time to mow the lawn you need to install other surfaces.

Take into account the style of your house and the existing shape and design of the garden itself to make sure that any new feature will fit in and not look out of place.

Check that new plants will grow happily in the soil and position. Some low-maintenance plants such as heathers and conifers have distinct soil preferences for you to consider.

How to Use This Chapter

Take from this chapter those ideas that will combine the plants and features you like with the amount of time you want to spend maintaining your garden. In *Easy Garden Maintenance* find out how to make routine jobs less of a chore. *Easy-care Gardens* contains ideas on how different features can be combined to create an attractive garden design needing minimal attention. *Low-maintenance Landscaping* explains how hard and soft surfaces can be used to reduce your workload. *Low-maintenance Plants* provides information on easy-to-grow plants. There is also a section showing how special features, such as a kitchen garden, can be made less time-consuming, as well as a chart to help you select and grow easy-care plants.

Above: Containers with low-maintenance plants can be used to add interest to areas of paving which also require minimal attention.

Easy Garden Maintenance

NO MATTER HOW WELL DESIGNED A GARDEN IS, A SMALL AMOUNT OF
ROUTINE MAINTENANCE WILL ALWAYS BE NECESSARY, BUT THERE ARE
VARIOUS WAYS OF MAKING MANY OF THE REGULAR TASKS MUCH LESS
TIME-CONSUMING AND EASIER TO DO.

LABOUR-SAVING TOOLS

Using the right tools can save you time
and effort, and will make the difference between a job being a pleasure or
a chore. Good tools, especially power
tools, can be expensive and take up
space, so decide which ones will really
reduce the time you spend gardening.

Nylon Line Trimmers

These useful
tools will cut
down long
grass around
trees, against fences
and along edges in no time
at all. Many can also produce a trim edge for the
lawn much more quickly
than traditional shears.

Lawnmowers

If you want to retain a lawn but wish
to reduce mowing time, consider buying a mower with a wider cutting width.
Rotary mowers are light and easy to
use, but unless you are happy to leave
the clippings on the lawn, or rake
them up, buy one with a clippings col-
lector. The same applies to wheeled

rotaries, which many people prefer.
For a striped effect a cylinder mower
with a rear roller is the best choice,
although some other types now have
rollers fitted to create a similar effect.

Hedge Trimmers

A powered hedge trimmer will save a
lot of time on what is a dusty and
unpleasant job if your garden has a lot

of hedge. A mains electric trimmer is
the best choice for most small gardens
where the hedge is within easy reach
of a power supply, but for a large
garden a petrol model may be more
practical. Battery-powered trimmers
are useful for small hedges.

Compression Sprayers

A large-capacity com-
pression sprayer with
a   long   lance
makes   all
kinds   of

spraying work easy, whether you are applying foliar feeds, pesticides and fungicides, or growth inhibitors to reduce the frequency with which you have to cut your hedge. Keep a separate watering can fitted with a dribble bar and shield for weedkiller.

BASIC GROUNDWORK

Time spent preparing soil before planting will pay dividends in the long term in a low-maintenance garden. Soil that is in good condition provides the best start for new plants, which will then grow well and be better equipped to withstand pest and disease attacks.

Eliminating weeds

If your soil is light, weeds can easily be removed by digging. On heavier soil it may be easier to kill the weeds, which you can do by either covering the ground for several months with an impermeable mulch, such as a thick black polythene sheet, or applying a weedkiller.

After digging and hand weeding an area, leave the soil for a few weeks to allow seeds brought to the surface to germinate. You can then hoe off the weed seedlings before planting and so reduce the amount of weeding you will need to do later on.

Improving the soil

The best way to improve soil structure and fertility is to add plenty of organic matter such as homemade garden compost or well-rotted farmyard manure. When added to existing soil, it will improve drainage in heavy soils and water and nutrient retention in light ones. The traditional way to add it is by digging, but this is now widely regarded as unnecessary and even undesirable, except perhaps for initial preparation of very heavy soil. In most cases, simply applying a good layer of organic material to the surface is the best method, since worms will take it down into the soil.

Above: Eliminating weeds before planting has long-term benefits for the garden.

Above: Digging in organic matter improves the quality of the soil.

AUTOMATIC WATERING

A system that automatically delivers water when it is required will save hours of time every year, and it is better for plants, as they are less likely to suffer from water stress. There are many systems available, so you need to look at several to see which one will be best for your situation.

Most automatic watering systems are fitted with a suitable control system to reduce the pressure, and act as a filter.

Some systems are controlled by the moisture level in the soil, but most operate on a continuous drip basis. Drip feed systems are versatile enough to be used for plants in beds, borders or in containers. Use a T-joint to run branches or tubes for individual drip heads. A timing device will turn your watering system on and off automatically, yet can easily be deactivated if the weather is wet.

Above: Leaky pipe and perforated hose systems are suitable for beds and borders where they can be hidden.

Unless your garden is very small, it is best to install a pipeline buried just beneath the ground surface, then you can "plug in" various watering devices as necessary.

Leaky pipe and perforated hose systems are suitable for beds and borders or the kitchen garden. You can bury them beneath the surface or lay them on top of the soil.

Above: A pop-up sprinkler can be set into the lawn. The head is pushed up out of the ground by the water pressure when the tap is turned on.

Above: A drip feed system is ideal for hanging baskets and window boxes. It will eliminate the daily chore of watering by hand.

Above: Apply a slow- or controlled-release fertilizer to established plants in spring or early summer.

LOW-MAINTENANCE FEEDING

This really does pay dividends. If you see a garden with particularly lush and healthy-looking plants, the chances are they have been well fed.

Slow- and Controlled-release Fertilizers

If you use modern slow- or controlled-release fertilizers, you can feed your plants just a couple of times a year. Both allow the nutrients to seep out into the soil over a period of months but controlled-release fertilizers are affected by soil temperature. Nutrients are only released when the soil is warm enough for growth. Use a hose-end dilutor for applying a soluble fertilizer.

Feeding Beds and Borders

Most established plants, but especially demanding ones like roses, benefit from an annual feeding. Apply a slow- or controlled-release fertilizer in spring or early summer, sprinkling it around the bushes. Keep it away from the stem, sprinkling it further out where most of the active root growth occurs. Hoe it into the surface then water it in, unless rain is expected, to make the fertilizer active more quickly.

Feeding the Lawn

The quickest way to feed your lawn is with a wheeled spreader. Individual models vary, but you can usually adjust the delivery rate. Test the rate on a measured area of path first, then sweep up the fertilizer and weigh it to ensure the application rate is correct.

Feeding Container Plants

Plants grown in containers require supplementary nutrients to keep them healthy. You can mix controlled- or slow-release fertilizer granules into the potting soil when you plant, or slip sachets or pellets beneath individual plants as you plant them.

Above: Container plants need additional feeding such as this slow-release pellet.

REDUCE WEEDING

It is entirely possible to have a beautiful garden where weeds are seldom a problem. The trick is to not allow any space where they can gain a major hold. Reducing the amount of bare earth in your garden and introducing more hard landscaping will reduce the area that weeds can grow in.

In beds and borders dense planting and ground cover will blanket the ground so well that weeds are unlikely to gain a foothold. Where young plants have not yet reached their maximum spread, applying a mulch to patches of bare earth will ensure that weeds cannot grow.

Using Weedkillers

Pulling up perennial weeds by hand is time-consuming and often ineffective as they usually grow again unless you remove every piece of root. Digging

Above: A contact weedkiller applied through a dribble bar will be useful for clearing a large area that has been overrun by perennial weeds. You may need to shield adjacent plants from the spray.

Above: Difficult and perennial weeds, like this ground elder, can be killed by painting on a translocated weedkiller.

them up may not be possible in an established bed or border, and you may have to resort to a contact weedkiller. Beware, as most weedkillers will kill or damage whatever they come into contact with.

Deep-rooted perennial weeds, such as bindweed, can be very difficult to eradicate and are best treated by painting on a translocated weedkiller, such as one based on glyphosate. Other contact weedkillers may not kill all the roots, but this chemical moves to all parts of the plant.

GARDENER'S TIP

Paths can easily be kept weed-free for a season by using products sold for the purpose. A single application will quickly kill existing weeds and prevent the growth of new ones for many months. Use an improvised shield to prevent the weedkiller being blown on to the flowerbeds.

Above: Gravel makes an attractive surface, and can be weed-free with very little effort.

MULCHES FOR GROUND COVER

A mulch is a layer of material that will cover the ground completely to suppress weeds and conserve moisture in the soil by preventing loss of water through evaporation. It can be purely functional or it can be decorative, and it can be organic or not. Always prepare the ground thoroughly before applying a mulch, taking care to eliminate perennial weeds and work in plenty of organic material such as well rotted manure or garden compost. Make sure the ground is wet before applying a mulch; soak it first if necessary.

Loose Mulches

Most loose mulches, such as chipped bark, cocoa shells, gravel, garden compost and rotted manure, are more visually appealing than sheets, and the organic ones rot down to improve the soil's structure and fertility. They need to be applied about 5cm (2in) thick.

Sheet Mulches

Woven plastic mulching sheets are effective and economical, but unattractive. However, they can be used in combination with a decorative loose mulch, which can then be applied more thinly than the recommended depth. Sheet mulches are useful for low-maintenance shrub beds and newly planted trees, both of which can be left undisturbed for several years, and are best used when the bed or border is to be newly planted.

PLANTING THROUGH SHEET MULCH

1 Make a slit around the edge of the bed with a spade, and push the sheet into this.

2 At each planting position make a cross-shaped slit in the sheet. Fold the flaps open to plant, then fold back in place. Small plants can be planted using a trowel, but for shrubs you will need to use a spade.

135

Easy-care Gardens

SOME GARDEN STYLES LEND THEMSELVES PARTICULARLY WELL TO LOW-MAINTENANCE GARDENING. THEY OFTEN RELY ON A VISUALLY PLEASING USE OF HARD LANDSCAPING ELEMENTS COMBINED WITH A MINIMUM OF WELL-CHOSEN PLANTING.

A MINIMALIST GARDEN

It is possible to create a striking garden using very little at all. The garden elements can be pared down to the absolute minimum and anything fussy, distracting or unnecessary can be excluded from the scheme.

A garden that relies on minimal planting will be the most labour-saving of all, but you need to choose carefully. The few plants used must work hard to earn their place there.

Using Space

Form and space are what matter in a minimal design. Anyone embarking on such a totally labour-saving design will need an eye for shape and contrast, so that the garden is pleasing to the eye, yet uncluttered.

The design will rely on the clever use of space, defined by a few strategically placed features, such as pots, stones, statues or plants, or a bold architectural feature such as a wall.

Above: The painted wall and gravel act as a foil to the carefully selected foliage plants in this striking area.

Left: Strong architectural features, such as the brick wall, unadorned pergola and symmetrical oblong planter, are typical elements of a modern garden.

Simple dramatic juxtapositions can create sufficient interest. For instance, a paved or gravelled area can become a visually pleasing space with the addition of just a few carefully sited large pots containing some architectural plants, or perhaps a raised bed or pool. Pebbles or boulders can be used to add extra texture, and perhaps some flowering annuals will add a splash of summer colour.

Adding Colour

Colour in the form of painted surfaces can also be used for impact in a minimalist garden, perhaps on a large wall or the edges of a raised bed. It can be used to complement planted gravel or an expanse of paving.

Above: A striking individual plant such as this easy-care bamboo in a pot is complemented by the adjacent pebbles.

Positioning Plants and Pebbles

A few good plants can go a long way if they are carefully positioned to create form in an open space. They need to be dramatic in shape or colour so that they make an impact on the design. Architectural plants such as phormium, yucca, bamboo clumps or even small trees all work well, especially when used in isolation.

Pebbles are also a good way to introduce additional texture. They work particularly well in areas of paving or with potted plants.

Left: Form is paramount in this dramatic garden comprising a series of integrated islands.

GRAVEL AND PAVED GARDENS

Gardens that rely heavily on paving or gravel instead of lawn can be virtually maintenance-free. They need to be well planned, however, to avoid them looking oppressive and harsh. The solution is to include a variety of materials to create contrasting shapes and textures, and to complement this with the planting. Even the simplest of designs can be transformed into a garden full of charm and character.

Designing with Hard Materials

Different materials can be used effectively to divide a large area into smaller sections, creating interest through changes of texture, and even height if you introduce features such as raised beds.

Formal structures usually work best for paving, especially in a space bounded by walls. Bricks can be laid in attractive patterns, adding colour and warmth to a design. The small dimensions of bricks will create satisfying contrasts when juxtaposed with large paving slabs. Granite setts, cobbles and brick or clay pavers can also be laid in interesting patterns.

Gravel, which has a softer texture than hard paving, adds another type of contrast. It works with both formal lines and informal designs as it lends itself to curves. There are lots of different gravels available in many colours and grades. Choose one, or several, that will suit your design.

Above: Gravel is a sensible alternative to grass and will look good when used with the right plants and accessories.

Left: A raised central planting area and water features in this paved garden have been constructed from contrasting materials.

Additional Features

Including other features in paving or gravel gardens adds yet more interest. Ponds or fountains introduce the element of water. Statues, large containers and even benches all make excellent focal points.

Incorporating Plants

Beds and borders can easily be incorporated into gravel and paved gardens. If you do not want to be bothered with maintaining large planting areas, you can create small filled spaces within the gravel or paving.

Beds can be filled with some low-maintenance ground-cover plants, but focal plants may also be desirable to draw the eye, especially during winter. Architectural plants, such as

Above: Even the tiniest area can become a gravel garden.

Cordyline australis (for warmer winters) or *Yucca gloriosa* (for cooler areas), work well as focal plants. Clipped box (*Buxus sempervirens*) is useful for formal designs. Two or three clips during the growing season are sufficient to keep it in shape.

Containers are another option, but they will require daily watering in summer unless you install an automatic watering system.

Above: Paving constructed in an interesting design becomes an extra feature in the garden.

GARDENER'S TIP

The pattern to which bricks and pavers are laid alters the overall impression created when viewed en masse. The stretcher bond is most effective for smaller areas and for paths. Herringbone is suitable for both large and small areas. Basket weave needs a reasonably large expanse for the pattern to be appreciated.

A JAPANESE GARDEN

True Japanese gardens require very little maintenance as the components are mainly easy-care features such as gravel, pebbles, stones, wood, water and occasional, carefully-chosen and well-positioned shrubs or small trees.

Designing the Garden

A sense of tranquillity and areas for contemplation are important elements in a Japanese garden. The design must be kept simple and uncluttered, concentrating on outline, shape and contrasting surface textures, while the use of plants is restrained, resulting in a garden that satisfies the senses but requires mimimum aftercare.

Focal Points

Rocks and stones have a special importance in many Japanese gardens. They can be set in an area covered with fine pebbles, which are an ideal labour-saving ground cover. When wet, they change colour and catch the light.

Choose some special stones of varying size, colour and character, and arrange them asymmetrically in one or two areas in uneven numbers. Traditionally, the pebbles are raked into variations of parallel lines and snaking spirals centralized on the main rock features. Gravel can be substituted for pebbles as a cheaper option.

Above: *Strategically placed large stones are an intrinsic and symbolic feature of a traditional Japanese garden. They are said to focus the mind for contemplation.*

Left: *A classic Japanese-style garden is simple and uncluttered with various harmonious focal points.*

PLANTS FOR A JAPANESE
GARDEN
Acer palmatum
Azalea
bonsai trees
camellias
dwarf bamboos
Iris ensata
moss
small pines

You can inset a walkway of large paving slabs or sawn tree-trunk pieces in the gravel.

Minimal Planting

In an authentic Japanese stone garden the only plants might be mounds of green moss providing a softening contrast with the stones and rocks, but other types of Japanese-inspired garden include a few more plants, chosen for their interesting form or grace. These can be planted through the pebbles or in large simple containers.

If mosses, which thrive in moist conditions out of direct sun, cannot be encouraged to grow, try moss-like plants as an alternative, such as *Sagina subulata*, *S. procumbens*, or, in mild areas, the ground-hugging carpeter *Soleirolia soleirii*.

A Water Feature

Water, the essence of life, should always be present. In a real Japanese garden, it would be fresh running water, but for the low-maintenance gardener even a bowl filled with water is calming in a garden and offers birds the opportunity to drink. A bubble fountain washing over pebbles or a running stream effect would be ideal.

Traditional Ornaments

In eastern philosophy, traditional garden features have their own significance within the strict rules and special meanings of the garden design. Bamboo wind chimes create soothing sounds, while a rounded lantern and a linear bridge are pretty, and useful for introducing contrasting shapes. You could introduce different ornamentation to suit your own preferences, with the purpose of providing contrasting shapes and colours.

Above: *Bamboo, smooth pebbles and rounded water features are ornamental and require little attention.*

A HOT AND COLOURFUL GARDEN

The kind of garden that is inspired by the Mediterranean countryside is packed with tough, self-sufficient plants that are colourful, attractive to bees and butterflies and wonderfully scented. It may also stock many aromatic edible plants that are useful for the kitchen. You might start off with a small patch or bed, but the benefits of this style of labour-saving garden are such that you may consider converting a larger area.

Mediterranean plants are resilient and drought-resistant. Their constant adaptations for survival in hot, arid areas – aromatic vapour, shimmering foliage, tough or spiny leaves and silvery hairs – also make them unappealing to pests, and their tough constitutions help them to resist disease.

Basic Groundwork

All the above make Mediterranean plants ideal candidates for a low-maintenance garden, as long as the ground is prepared so that they will thrive in temperate climates.

You will need to add plenty of grit or gravel to the soil to give it sharp drainage so that the plants do not have to struggle to survive in wet, compacted

Above: The graceful spring flowers of Tulipa sylvestris *and grape hyacinth grow amongst rosemary and lavender, just as they would in the wild.*

Left: Lavender, Cistus, Euphorbia and asphodels make their distinctive mark on a gravel bed in summer.

Left: This herb garden is full of leaf and vibrant colour a mere 15 months after planting.

There is no need to add fertilizer or manure when planting. Most Mediterranean plants are adapted to grow in poor soil, and if it is too rich they will produce weak, sappy growth. In poor soil they will generally grow tougher and flower more freely.

Simply cover the surface of the soil with gravel and water the plants well until they establish themselves. After their first season, you will not need to water them. In severe summer drought, you can revive any stressed plants by dousing them with water; if watering is impractical, cut back the plants severely and they should revive.

ground, where they would inevitably rot as their roots need dry conditions.

A top layer of gravel or stones will work as moisture-retaining mulch that also keeps foliage crowns dry and absorbs heat for the benefit of the plants.

Designing the Garden

This kind of garden requires no planning to ensure the colours and textures complement one another. The plants naturally team well, forming a magical tapestry of wonderful partnerships.

The predominant shrubs and sub-shrubs are evergreen, with grey and silver tones, sustaining the garden through the quieter winter months. In spring, flowering bulbs pop up in bright reds and yellows. Summer explodes with foliage and flower.

Suitable Planting

Select only those types of plant that will survive with minimal attention and enjoy the sharp draining conditions of your garden.

Containers

Following the age-old Mediterranean tradition of growing special plants in pots you can grow a few brightly coloured geraniums against a white-washed wall, or perhaps a fig tree if you have a very sunny, sheltered corner in the garden.

MEDITERRANEAN PLANTS

Artemisia absinthium
Cistus
Cytisus
Eryngium
Euphorbia
Lavandula
Rosemarinus
Salvia officinalis
Thymus

A Wildflower Garden

An established wildflower garden requires much less maintenance than a conventional one. Making one, however, can initially be quite demanding as there is some basic preparation of the soil required and the garden takes time to become established. Creating a large meadow will need much more effort, so it is advisable for the time-pressed gardener to concentrate on a small wildlife swathe.

Planting a Border

The simplest way to grow wildflowers is in an existing border, either on their own or with some other herbaceous plants and shrubs. This can work especially well if you combine wildflowers with the many garden plants that are forms of wild flowers, such as carpeting *Ajuga reptans* and self-seeding poppies and forget-me-nots.

Wildflowers can be sown or planted in the same way as other plants, but they will not thrive in ground that is fertilized.

Above: *Once a threatened species, yellow cowslips* (Primula veris) *are now quite widely seen in wild areas.*

On cultivated ground the ranker weeds tend to take over and smother the plants you want to encourage, so it is worth clearing the area of weeds first. Then you can sow the wildflower mixture or plant out perennials in the spring.

Colonizing a Lawn

You can scatter the wildflower seed directly over the area, but the competition from the grass will be intense. For better results, sow the seed in trays, prick out and grow the plants in pots first. Plant them out in spring, when the perennials are strong enough to compete with the existing grass.

Once the perennials are established, they will self-sow, which is always more successful than simply scattering seed yourself.

PERENNIALS FOR WILD-
FLOWER PLANTINGS

Achillea millefolium
Ajuga reptans
Campanula rotundifolia
Cardamine pratensis
Centaurea scabiosa
Fritillaria meleagris
Geranium pratense
Monarda fistulosa
Primula veris
Ranunculus acris

Converting a Field

If you are lucky enough to have a field and want to turn it into a wildflower meadow, your task is much harder. Before you can start sowing or planting wildflowers you will need to spend a whole year mowing the grass at regular intervals to keep it short. This will kill off most of the more invasive grasses, and leave only the finer ones. When the grass is under control, you can proceed as for a lawn.

Clearing New Ground

For those with a smaller area to convert, another effective method for establishing a wildflower area is to clear it completely, removing all traces of perennial weeds. Then sow a wildflower and grass seed mixture formulated for your area, as for a border. There are several suppliers for this type of seed.

Above: Cornflowers are a delightful addition to a wildflower garden with their intense lavender colouring.

Maintaining Wildflowers in Grass

Wildflowers growing in grass should be cut once or twice a year. The best time is in summer once the main flush of plants have seeded. Remove the cuttings to prevent feeding the soil.

Above: Create a tranquil summer haven within the informal splendour of a wildflower garden filled with colourful plants.

Low-maintenance Landscaping

YOU CAN ARRANGE YOUR GARDEN AND MODIFY THE WAY YOU PLANT BEDS AND BORDERS SO THAT VERY LITTLE REGULAR MAINTENANCE WILL BE REQUIRED. YOU CAN ALSO MAKE YOUR GARDEN MUCH MORE INTERESTING IN THE PROCESS.

Above: Mixing hard landscaping materials and plants makes an attractive alternative to a large area of lawn.

THE GARDEN FLOOR

The greater part of most traditional gardens is given over to a large expanse of lawn, which is often edged by a path or a small area of paving. Lawns are time-consuming and expensive to maintain in good condition, and they can be boring. There are ways of keeping mowing to a minimum, but anyone wishing to cut down drastically on the labour involved should consider alternative surfaces such as gravel or paving for at least part of the area normally covered by the lawn.

SIMPLER LAWN MAINTENANCE

If you want to keep a lawn there is a lot you can do to reduce mowing time to a minimum. Upgrading your lawnmower to a more powerful or wider cutting one is the most obvious, but

Above: This garden has been mainly planted with large shrubs that require miminal attention, leaving only a small central area of lawn that will not take long to mow.

eliminating fussy beds and curved edges to borders might speed things up by allowing you to mow in straight lines. There are also other approaches to try. Alternatively, keep just a small area of lawn, and plant ornamental grasses, ground-cover plants or shrubs over the remaining area.

Trimming Edges

Unsightly untrimmed edges can make a garden look untidy, but trimming with shears, long-handled or ordinary, is tedious and time-consuming. If you have a lot of these to trim, invest in a powered lawn edge or nylon line trimmer with a swivel head, which can be

Above: Replacing lawn with low-maintenance plants will reduce mowing time.

used for this job as well as scything down persistent weeds. It is best to buy the sturdiest you can afford as the lighter versions can prove less economical in the long term.

Multi-level Mowing

Another way to reduce the amount of time spent mowing is to cut different parts of the lawn at different intervals, leaving some areas to grow longer. This involves cutting broad "pathways" regularly, and mowing other areas every second or third time with the mower blade set higher giving a more natural appearance. You can leave some grass uncut except for a couple of cuts a season, but it will probably need to be cut with a nylon line trimmer instead of a lawnmower.

Above: A nylon line trimmer will enable you to trim lawn edges with considerable speed.

147

MAKING A MOWING EDGE

Edging the lawn with brick or paving, so that the mower can run over it saving time and evergy, means that the only trimming you will need to do will be occasionally cutting back any long stems of grass that grow over the paving.

1 Lay paving slabs or bricks on the grass for positioning, and use a half-moon edger (edging iron) to cut an edge.

2 Slice off the grass with a spade and remove soil to the depth of the pavers, plus several centimetres (a couple of inches). Lay a sub-base of sand and gravel mix, and consolidate it using a piece of wood and a mallet.

3 For paving slabs, use five blobs of mortar for each slab, and lay them on top, then tap them hard, using a mallet. Bricks will just need a small blob of mortar under each.

4 Make sure the slabs are flush with the lawn, and use a spirit level to check that the slabs are laid evenly. Mortar the joints for a neat finish, otherwise unsightly weeds will grow in them.

> **GARDENER'S TIP**
> Choose a paving or brick colour that will blend well with the adjacent border. Creeping plants will soon extend over the surface to soften the effect.

ALTERNATIVES TO GRASS

If you like a green lawn, but don't enjoy or have time for regular mowing, you could consider a grass substitute. Those mentioned here are fine for occasional foot traffic and as a visual focal point, but they won't stand up to the hard wear of a children's play area like grass will.

There are other drawbacks to using grass substitutes for lawns. You won't be able to use selective lawn weed-killers on them, so you will have to hand weed as necessary for a season or two, until the plants have knitted together. Beware of common stone-crop (*Sedum acre*), an attractive yellow-flowered carpeter sometimes sold as a grass-substitute. It may become a serious weed in your garden.

Thyme

A quick spreader with attractive foliage and flowers, thyme makes a good grass substitute and is aromatic

Above: Romantic and unusual, chamomile is quite hardy and will last for many years.

when crushed. Culinary thyme (*Thymus vulgaris*) is too tall, so use a carpeter like *T. pseudolanuginosus* or *T. serpyllum*.

Chamomile

Another aromatic plant for lawns is chamomile (*Chamaemelum nobile*, syn. *Anthemis nobilis*). Look for the variety 'Treneague', which is compact and does not normally flower.

Clover

If clover is a problem in your lawn, it may make a good grass substitute. Once established it will keep green for most of the year and will tolerate dry soils. You'll only have to mow a couple of times a year, after the flowers appear, to keep it looking smart.

Above: Swathes of thyme make an eyecatching and fragrant alternative to a lawn.

149

GRAVEL

Decorative gravel is an excellent, inexpensive but practical garden surface. It is attractive, trouble-free, easy to lay and harmonizes well with plants. It will conform to irregular outlines, and it can be effective in a large or small area. Whole gardens can be turned over to gravel with some judicious use of complementary paving and attractive planting. An edging is a good idea, otherwise the gravel will become scattered into surrounding areas.

Many garden centres and stone or builders' merchants sell a wide range of gravels in different sizes and colours. You will find the appearance changes according to the light and whether the stones are wet or dry.

Above: Gravel makes an attractive background for plants and needs minimal maintenance.

Above: Curves present no problems for gravel. Using edging will keep the gravel in the right place.

Making a Gravel Bed

You can set a gravel bed in a lawn or within an area of paving. In a large lawn a winding ribbon of gravel, designed to imitate a dry river-bed, can look very effective. If the garden is smaller, a more compact shape, perhaps oval or kidney-shaped, may be more appropriate.

Cut out a shape using a half-moon edger (edging iron) and remove the turf about 10cm (4in) deep with a spade. If you want to grow drought-loving plants, dig in plenty of coarse grit. For growing more hungry plants, add well-rotted manure or compost. The gravel needs to be about 5cm (2in) deep. Keep the gravel well below the surface of the lawn, otherwise it will spill on to the surface of the lawn and damage the mower. Choose a size that will be noticeable if it does stray.

Large Gravel Areas

For anything larger than a small island bed, consider laying a plastic sheet over the area to suppress weed growth. If the gravel garden is low-lying or in a hollow, provide a sump for excess water to drain into. Ensure that the surface is quite smooth before laying the sheet, and overlap the joints. Tip gravel over the plastic sheet and rake it level to make a 5cm (2in) layer.

Planting in Gravel

Many plants will grow well in a gravel bed, but for a low-maintenance garden choose drought-resistant plants that won't need watering, even in dry spells. Scoop back the gravel and plant normally, but avoid planting too

deeply and keep the gravel away from the immediate area around the stem.

If planting through a plastic sheet, scoop back the gravel then make cross-slits through the plastic. Enrich the soil with garden compost or fertilizer and plant normally. Fold back the sheet and replace the gravel, taking care not to cover the crown of the plant.

Above right: A recently planted gravel bed within a lawn is already showing plenty of colour. The plants will soon spread to cover much of the gravel.

Right: Soft mounds of thyme planted in a gravel area soften the effect, adding colour and contrasting textures.

PAVING

A paved area needs practically no maintenance, just an occasional brush and every few years a blast with a high-pressure water jet. As well as being labour-saving it should contribute positively to your garden design, linking and complementing other elements of the garden.

Creating Effects

Builders' merchants and many garden centres stock a variety of attractive paving materials to suit most tastes and styles, and these can be laid to create all sorts of patterns, formal or informal. As well as different materials, surfaces can vary in texture. Big slabs are suitable for large areas, while bricks and pavers are better for small areas. A mixture of different paving materials will introduce variety and interest to a scheme.

Above: This crazy-paved area is softened by the addition of container-grown plants.

Above: Builders' merchants stock a variety of paving materials. Choose those that will complement other elements in the garden.

Concrete Paving Slabs

Large slabs made from concrete are a popular choice for patios, paths and drives. They come in a range of sizes, textures and colours, and are easy to lay once a solid foundation has been prepared. Slabs, especially circular ones, are suitable for use as stepping stones set in a lawn or in gravel.

Natural Stone

Although this looks splendid, it is very expensive and difficult to lay. It can be dressed, that is cut into regular shapes with smooth edges, or random, with irregular outline and thickness. The latter is suitable for crazy paving and looks much better than broken concrete fragments.

Bricks and Pavers

Concrete or clay pavers and bricks are very striking when they are laid in small areas. They are especially suitable for visually linking the garden to a brick house. They can be laid in

to be only 5–10cm (2–4in) thick for foot traffic but about 15cm (6in) if vehicles are to be driven over it. Concrete and brick paving slabs can be bedded on mortar, but clay pavers must be bedded on sharp sand using a plate compactor.

Plants and Paving

A few strategically placed plants will greatly improve the appearance of the paved garden without requiring too much extra work.

Plants in beds alongside the paving can be encouraged to fall on to the paving to soften the hard edges. Containers are useful, too, to break up a large expanse, or to introduce colour where there is no bed for planting in. But if you design the paving with integral planting areas or raised beds, the plants will need less watering than they would in containers.

intricate designs. Pavers come in a wide range of sizes, colours and thicknesses and have different finishes.

Laying Paving

Paving needs to be laid on to a firm base. The area will have to be excavated to a depth that allows for hardcore, mortar and paving. Hardcore needs

Above left: You can create planting spaces in paving by removing slabs to expose the soil below. A stone mulch disguises the soil and prevents it splashing on to the paving.

Left: Combining different types of paving will add considerably to the visual impact and interest.

153

BEDS AND BORDERS

Attractive, well-filled beds and borders bring a garden to life, but they are potentially time-consuming. You can reduce the amount of work involved simply by choosing low-maintenance plants and keeping them weed-free by mulching, perhaps with a decorative chipped bark, or with chemical controls. Whatever planting style you choose avoid using plants that grow rampantly, need constant cutting back or frequent pruning, and any with lots of seeds that germinate readily where you don't want them to.

Above: Foliage plants create colour and interest but require very little attention through the year.

Foliage

Interesting foliage often acts as a backdrop to flowers, but it can also be used on its own. The enormous range of greens as well as purples, bronzes, silvers and striking variegations makes it entirely possible to create unusual effects using foliage alone.

Evergreens are especially useful because they don't shed leaves like deciduous shrubs do or die down leaving dead matter to be cleared away as do perennials. However, deciduous shrubs produce some stunning autumn effects, which are particularly useful when the number of flowers is declining in your border.

Incorporating Flowers

However attractive foliage may be, for most people a garden would not be complete without flowers. Happily, many will perform well with little attention, and there are a number of different types of flowering plants to choose from.

Above: Packed borders require little weeding once established.

Above: If you want to include summer bedding plants in your border choose a long-flowering type, such as geraniums.

Traditional seasonal borders are replanted twice a year with bedding plants to take full advantage of spring and summer flower colour. They are packed with colour but require most work and are best avoided if you have limited time. Using more permanent plants instead will involve less time.

Annuals are less work for the gardener as many can be sown in situ. They are invaluable for filling gaps with bright summer colour. You sow them in late spring and they flower in summer, and many will self-seed for years. Pot marigolds, nasturtiums, love-in-a-mist, and different types of poppy, including Californian and common field poppies, are all good self-seeders. Any seedlings that appear in the wrong place can simply be pulled up. When the plants have finished flowering they can be removed.

With many different growth habits, sizes and flower shapes and colours, herbaceous perennials bring an extra dimension into a garden. Choose those that you can plant and forget, at least for a few years. They will flower year after year.

Shrubs are among the best plants for borders. Most will grow for years without any attention, but those that grow too vigorously (such as budd-lejas and many roses) or that are tall and difficult to manage (such as lilacs) are best avoided. Fortunately, there are so many well-behaved shrubs, that a low-maintenance border is easy to achieve. Potentillas flower for months, as do hardy fuchsias, though these may be partly cut down in cold winter. Mahonia and hebe are also reliable.

Above: Papaver somniferum will self-seed on to any bare patches of soil in a border.

155

Herbaceous Borders

Whole borders devoted to herbaceous perennials look stunning during the summer months and well into autumn. Plants like astilbes, dicentras and bergenias, which need no staking, spread relatively slowly and are easy to pull up when necessary, are ideal. If you are in doubt about a plant's suitability, always find out whether it needs staking, how fast it spreads and whether it is prone to pests and diseases. Phlox and perennial asters are prone to mildew, for example.

Mixed Borders

These contain a mixture of shrubs for structure and foliage and perennial plants, perhaps supplemented by annuals. Generally, they require less maintenance than herbaceous borders, especially if the emphasis is on low-maintenance shrubs, with some easy perennials to add colour.

When you plant the border, you will need to leave gaps to allow shrubs and perennials to grow. The gaps can be temporarily filled with annuals such as marigolds, poppies or nasturtiums, or bedding plants such as geraniums or begonias. This will keep down the weeds and look good.

Above: Self-sufficient spurge, purple sage, lavender and iris pack a mixed border with colour.

Left: Attractive, low-maintenance perennials in a border can provide years of interest with their colourful flowers and variety of foliage.

PLANTING A BORDER

After initial planting, you will need to water the border regularly in dry periods until the plants are established, but thereafer they should need little attention to keep them looking good over a long period.

1 Water the plants, then arrange the pots in their planting places. Try to visualize the plants at their final height and spread, then adjust their positions, allowing room for growth. Dig the first hole, and add some well-rotted compost, farmyard manure or slow-release fertilizer.

RELIABLE AND EASY
HERBACEOUS PERENNIALS
Anemone x *hybrida*
Anthemis tinctoria
Astilbe
Bergenia
Dianthus
Dicentra spectabilis
Echinops ritro
Erigeron
Hemerocallis
Kniphofia
Liriope muscari
Rudbeckia
Schizostylis coccinea
Sedum spectabile
Tradescantia
Veronica spicata

2 When you are ready to plant, knock a plant out of its pot and tease out some of the roots. Start at the back, or at one end of the border.

3 Return the soil and make sure the plant is at its original depth or just a little deeper. Firm it with your hands or a heel to expel large pockets of air in the soil and prevent wind rock. Water thoroughly unless the weather is wet.

Above: *The several varieties of* Sedum *provide pinks and reds in autumn. They require practically no attention and do not need staking.*

157

Low-maintenance Plants

PLANTS THAT REQUIRE LITTLE ATTENTION THROUGH THE YEAR AND ARE GENERALLY DISEASE- AND PEST-RESISTANT ARE THE ONES TO INCLUDE IN A LOW-MAINTENANCE GARDEN. THERE IS ENOUGH CHOICE TO ENSURE INTEREST AND PLENTY OF COLOUR AT ALL TIMES.

Left: Stipa tenuifolia *produces silky flowerheads that sway sensuously in summer breezes.*

GRACEFUL GRASSES FOR YEAR-ROUND INTEREST

Perennial grasses are easy plants. Once planted, they require very little attention, except occasional removal of dead foliage and old flower heads if they offend. Cutting back the dead foliage to ground level in early spring will encourage lots of new growth.

There are many types to grow, from compact dwarfs to huge plants that reach 2.4m (8ft) or more. They can be used in beds, either on their own or in mixed plantings, to stunning effect.

Be cautious about mixing grasses among other plants, however, as some are difficult to control, and rampant species will soon take over a bed and become inextricably entwined with other plants, so clump-forming types are best. The more spreading grasses are better grown in an isolated spot, but the smaller ones will work in a border if you plant them in a large container sunk into the ground, with the rim flush with the surrounding soil. Annual grasses will self-seed unless you deadhead them after flowering.

GRASSES

Andropogon
Carex
Cortaderia selloana
Deschampsia
Festuca glauca
Hakonechloa
Miscanthus sinensis
Stipa arundinacea
Stipa tenuifolia

FERNS FOR MOIST SHADE

The intricate foliage of ferns makes these fascinating plants essential for moist, shady corners of any low-maintenance garden, where they will thrive without any intervention. Many die down in winter, but there are also plenty of evergreen species, and they are varied enough in shape and size to make an interesting planting despite the lack of flowers.

Above: *Ferns can be used effectively in many areas of the garden. There are so many varieties, there will be plenty to suit the situation of any garden.*

FERNS

Adiantum (some evergreen)
Asplenium ceterach (evergreen)
Asplenium scolopendrium
(evergreen)
Blechnum capense (evergreen)
Dryopteris affinis 'Cristata'
(evergreen)
Polypodium (some evergreen)
Polystichum setiferum (evergreen)

PLANTING FERNS

Most ferns prefer a moist, shady or partially shaded position, and will do especially well if you take time to prepare the soil by incorporating plenty of organic material. This is very important in an area shaded by a tree or wall, where soil is usually dry. If the soil is impoverished, rake a balanced fertilizer into the surface of the soil when you plant. If planting in late summer, autumn or winter do not use a quick-acting fertilizer.

1 Water the fern thoroughly about half an hour before planting. It is very important that ferns do not dry out, especially when newly planted.

2 Make a hole large enough to take the rootball. Firm the fern in carefully. Then water thoroughly so that the surrounding soil is moist down to the depth of the rootball.

3 To help conserve moisture and maintain a high level of organic material in the soil, mulch thickly. Top up the mulch each spring.

159

HEATHERS FOR CARPETS OF COLOUR

Robust heathers make excellent low-maintenance beds in open sunny positions. There are varieties to provide year-round colour and most have attractive foliage, which often changes colour according to the season.

If you have space, heathers look best planted in bold drifts. Depending on the size of the bed, plant them in groups of perhaps ten or twenty of each variety. If you make your selection with care, you can have some in flower in virtually every season of the year. They can also be used in combination with conifers to create striking effects.

Limited Maintenance

The only attention heathers need is an annual trim in mid-spring; cut out old flowerheads as well as any dead, diseased or damaged shoots. Apply a slow-release fertilizer after pruning.

Heathers can become woody with time and may require replacing after some years.

Above: A carpet of heathers is a glorious sight. Mix varieties that flower at different times for year-round interest.

PLANTING HEATHERS

Make sure you choose the correct type of heathers for your soil. Winter-flowering *Erica carnea* varieties, which are more correctly known as heaths, will grow on neutral or even slightly alkaline soil. True heathers, such as *Erica cinerea* and *Calluna vulgaris* varieties, need an acid soil. When planting, it is important to prepare the soil thoroughly, and adding peat to the planting area will benefit all types. Plant through a sheet of black plastic or a plastic mulching sheet to keep weeding down to the absolute minimum. Then you can mulch on top of the sheet with a more attractive material such as chipped bark or gravel.

2 Start planting at one end or at the back of the bed. Space the plants about 30–45cm (12–18in) apart. The planting distance will vary according to the species and even variety, so check first. Plant with a trowel and press the soil down firmly with your hands to exclude any air pockets.

1 Prepare the soil thoroughly before planting. Add plenty of organic material such as compost or well-rotted manure, especially if the soil is dry or impoverished of nutrients. If planting in spring or summer, rake in a balanced general fertilizer. If planting in autumn or winter, wait until spring to apply fertilizer to avoid scorching tender roots.

3 Use a mulch of peat or composted chipped bark to suppress weeds, conserve moisture, and improve the appearance of the soil while the plants are still young. Over time this will rot down and provide nutrients for the growing plants and may need topping up every few years.

HEATHERS

Calluna vulgaris
Daboecia cantabrica
Erica carnea
Erica ciliaris
Erica cinerea
Erica x darleyensis
Erica erigena
Erica mackaiana
Erica tetralix
Erica vagans

ARCHITECTURAL CONIFERS

Slow-growing conifers need little attention after their first year, as long as they are given a good start with careful site preparation and planting.

Dwarf and slow-growing conifers can be columnar, rounded, oval or prostrate in outline, and to look effective they are best grown as a group with contrasting shapes, sizes and colours. They are ideal for small beds or borders where they will soon provide year-round interest.

Planting Conifers

If you find it difficult to plan beds and borders on paper, stand the pots where you think the plants will look good and be prepared to shuffle them around until they look right. Bear in mind the eventual height and spread.

Dig a hole larger and deeper than the rootball, and fork in rotted manure, garden compost or planting mixture, especially on dry soils, then work in a controlled- or slow-release fertilizer. Mulch with a decorative material at least 5cm (2in) thick.

Above: Slow-growing conifers provide year-round colour.

Left: Dwarf conifers look good in a group. Before planting check how they will look together and make any necessary adjustments to their positions.

Above: Surround newly planted conifers and heathers with decorative organic mulch such as chipped bark.

HEATHER AND CONIFER BEDS

Dwarf conifers combine especially well with heathers, their foliage providing fascinating contrasts of texture and colour. There are hundreds of suitable heathers and conifers so you can design exactly what you want. Remember to choose varieties that are suitable for your soil type. The initial outlay may seem expensive, but the bed should last for a long time without the need for replanting and will require minimal maintenance.

DWARF CONIFERS

Abies cephalonica
'Meyer's Dwarf'
Chamaecyparis obtusa
'Nana Gracilis'
Picea abies 'Gregoryana'
Taxus baccata 'Standishii'
Thuja picata 'Irish Gold'

Planting a Mixed Bed

Arrange and plant all the conifers first, making sure they look pleasing from all angles. Space the heathers around the conifers, then plant them in groups or drifts of one variety at a time. Avoid planting the heathers too close to the conifers as all the plants will spread and merge into each other within a year or two. Meanwhile cover the bare soil with chipped bark or gravel.

Above: Conifers and heathers make a natural combination in this setting.

163

TIME-SAVING BEDDING PLANTS

Traditional summer bedding involves a lot of time and work. Even if you buy all the plants from a nursery to avoid the annual rituals of sowing, labelling and potting on, they still have to be planted out in the garden. However, if you like the instant cheerful brightness of seasonal bedding rather than the predictable show from shrubs and border plants, you can compromise by mixing a temporary selection of seasonal bedding with established planting. The bedding plants will add splashes of bright, long-lasting summer colour among the more permanent plants. A low-growing perennial, such as sedum, can be used as a neat year-round edging that requires at the most an annual trim to keep it looking tidy. The centre of the bed can then be filled with spring bulbs and summer bedding plants.

TROUBLE-FREE SUMMER
BEDDING PLANTS
Begonia semperflorens
Impatiens
Lavatera trimestris
Osteospermum
Pelargonium
Petunia
Tagetes patula

If you choose bedding plants such as begonias or petunias that flower prolifically over a long period without much attention, you will further cut down on the amount of work involved. The plants listed above will continue to flower for many months without requiring deadheading, regular attention or watering. They are some of the most trouble-free and spectacular bedding plants you can use.

Below: Impatiens *and* Begonia *'White Devil' (right) are two long-flowering and reliable summer bedding plants.*

PLANTING A PERMANENT EDGING

If you want to add small permanent plants at the front of a border that will give seasonal splashes of colour rather than temporary bedding plants choose from the wide range of miniature bulbs or creeping plants.

1 Dig over the ground at the front of the border and clear it of weeds. Rake in a general fertilizer if planting in spring to encourage vigorous early growth and help the plants to knit together. (Wait until spring to do this if planting in autumn or winter.)

Above: Cyclamen *form a clump of variegated leaves, with bright flowers in late winter. They are particularly suited to the front of a shady border.*

2 Space the plants out in their pots and adjust them to go evenly around the bed. About 15cm (6in) apart is suitable for most plants if you want quick cover, further apart if you don't mind waiting a little longer. Plant using a trowel.

3 Firm in to remove large pockets of air, then water thoroughly. The bed may be planted immediately with bulbs or spring or summer bedding plants as appropriate.

PLANTS AND BULBS FOR
PERMANENT EDGING

Creeping willow
Cyclamen
Dianthus
Grape hyacinth
Lavandula 'Munstead Dwarf'
Miniature box
Salvia officinalis

Above: Creeping willow *is an excellent plant for permanent edging with its delicate, glossy green foliage and attractive yellow flowers.*

165

SELF-SUFFICIENT SHRUBS

Some of the most popular shrubs, like roses and buddlejas, require a lot of attention. Regular pruning is necessary for many of them to remain looking good, and others may be prone to pests and diseases, which require time and effort to prevent or eliminate. Fortunately, there are many low-maintenance shrubs that are just as attractive and almost trouble-free.

You can choose from hundreds of well-behaved compact shrubs that will not require frequent pruning or hacking back. Check with your local garden centre to make sure the shrubs you select won't need regular pruning, won't become bare and leggy at the base with all the flowers at the top, and aren't susceptible to diseases.

Viburnum tinus is useful for its autumn and winter flowers, but it can

Above: Easy to grow Elaeagnus *is an ideal low-maintenance shrub. Its silvery foliage is set off by* Erysimum.

grow tall and require pruning to keep it compact. Many hebes are naturally compact and so require little pruning; most have pretty flowers, but some need protection during cold winters.

Above: Compact and evergreen hebes need protection where winters are severe.

LOW-MAINTENANCE SHRUBS

Flowering
Cistus
Escallonia
Hibiscus syriacus
Hypericum
Mahonia
Olearia x *hastii*
Yucca

Foliage
Aucuba japonica
Berberis thunbergii
Choisya ternata
Elaeagnus pungens 'Maculata'
Euonymus fortunei
Ruscus aculeatus
Viburnum davidii

Above: Choisya ternata *has the benefit of a strong shape, pale green foliage and delightfully scented white flowers.*

Planting Shrubs

Your choice of shrubs will be in position for many years, so plant them carefully and take time to prepare the ground thoroughly.

Water the pots and let them drain. Position them where you think they should be in the border. Check the likely size on the label or in a book, then revise your spacing if necessary. If the spacing seems excessive initially, leaving large gaps, you can always plant a few extra inexpensive shrubs between them to discard when they become crowded.

If planting in spring or summer, apply a balanced fertilizer according to the manufacturer's instructions; if planting at any other time, wait until spring to apply. Hoe or rake it into the surface then water thoroughly.

1 Dig a hole large enough to take the rootball. Stand the plant in the hole and use a cane or stick to check that the plant will be at the same depth as it was in the pot. Add or remove soil as necessary.

2 Carefully tease out some of the roots if they are tightly wound round the inside of the pot. This will encourage them to grow out into the surrounding soil and become quickly established.

3 Return the soil and firm it well around the roots to steady the shrub in wind and to eliminate large pockets of air that might allow the roots to dry out. Keep it watered during dry periods to begin with; once established, it should rarely require watering.

LOW-MAINTENANCE BULBS

Producing flower colour for virtually any time of the year, bulbs make a valuable contribution to the low-maintenance garden. Many bulbs will flower reliably year after year, with the clumps improving all the time, and once they have been planted they need very little attention.

Most summer-flowering bulbs, such as alliums and lilies, are best planted in groups in a border, but the easiest way to grow many spring- and autumn-flowering bulbs is to natural-ize them in grass. This eliminates the need for annual replanting and means that you don't have to cut that part of the lawn until the leaves have died down naturally. It is better to keep naturalized bulbs to one small area of the lawn so that the rest can be cut normally and it won't look too untidy.

Caring for Bulbs

Naturalized bulbs and those left in a border for many years will eventually need dividing to prevent overcrowd-ing, which would lead to deteriorating results. Lift large clumps when the leaves have just died back, or any time when the bulbs are dormant. Separate the clump into smaller pieces and replant. You do not have to separate into individual bulbs.

Above: A sunny border aglow with yellow tulips will give pleasure year after year.

Left: Daffodils naturalized in a small area of lawn look charming in the early spring.

168

NATURALIZING LARGE BULBS

1 To create a natural effect, scatter the bulbs on the grass and plant them where they fall. Make a hole for each, roughly three times their own depth, using either a trowel or a bulb planter, which pulls out a neat plug of grass and soil. Insertion will be easier if the ground is moist rather than dry.

2 Place a bulb in the hole. Crumble some soil from the bottom of the plug and let it fall around the bulb to make sure it will not be left in a pocket of air. Press the plug back into position.

Above: *Autumn-flowering* Colchicum *extend the interest in a bulb-filled lawn.*

EASY BULBS
Allium
Colchicum
Crocus
Cyclamen
Galanthus nivalis
Lilium
Muscari
Narcissus
Tulipa

NATURALIZING SMALL BULBS

1 For small bulbs and corms it is sometimes easier to lift and then replace the grass. Use a spade to slice beneath the grass, then roll it back for planting.

2 Loosen the soil with a fork, and work in a slow-acting fertilizer such as bonemeal. Scatter the bulbs randomly as a uniform pattern will look unnatural in grass. Small ones can be left on the surface; larger ones are best buried slightly.

3 Aim to cover the bulbs with twice their own depth of soil under the grass. Roll back the grass, firm it well with your hands and water thoroughly.

TIME-SAVING GROUND COVER

Plants that cover bare ground with a carpet of colour are invaluable in the low-maintenance garden, not least for their ability to suppress weeds. They are ideal for softening the hard edges of a path or the front of borders and for filling in gaps.

Ground-cover plants usually grow no more than 45cm (18in) in height, but many shrubs and sub-shrubs are compact enough to be used as ground cover as well. Heathers and conifers make pleasing ground cover, although the latter may be slow growing. Prostrate cotoneasters make excellent ground-hugging cover in front of other shrubs. Many prostrate thymes are also good ground covers.

Some herbaceous plants make a carpet of lush foliage in summer, as well as flowers in many cases. Hostas, for instance, have a wide range of leaf

Above: Hostas make excellent ground cover in moist, shady areas.

colour and delicate spears of pale lilac or white flowers, while cranesbills bloom for a long period.

Some ground-covering shrubs, such as *Hypericum calycinum*, are normally too aggressive for a small garden and will quickly take over. But this hypericum is ideal for a sloping bank that is difficult to cultivate. (If you plant it elsewhere you will need to contain it with paving.)

Left: Euonymus fortunei 'Emerald 'n' Gold' makes a striking ground cover in sun or shade. Its brightly variegated leaves will provide winter colour.

Left: Lamium maculatum *is quick to become established and makes an effective and colourful ground cover in spring.*

GROUND-COVERING PLANTS

Ajuga reptans
Alchemilla mollis
Bergenia
Cerastium tomentosum
Convallaria majalis
Geranium endressii
Hypericum calycinum
Lamium maculatum
Pulmonaria
Tiarella cordifolia
Vinca minor

Filling Shady Locations

Fast-growing ivy is excellent for all types of shade, and *Pachysandra terminalis* 'Variegata' makes a green-and-white carpet in dry shade. Lily-of-the-valley, *Liriope muscari* and periwinkle also grow well below trees.

Maintenance of Ground Cover

Many ground-cover plants are quite tough, and once planted require little attention other than an annual feed. Heathers need an annual trim with shears after flowering to keep them looking neat. And plants like *Hypericum calycinum* can be clipped annually with shears or a nylon line trimmer to reduce their height and encourage bushiness.

Planting Ground-cover Plants

Ground cover will eventually suppress weeds, but initially needs protection from them. Before you start planting, clear the ground thoroughly of existing weeds.

Unless you are planting a ground cover that spreads by underground stems or rooting prostrate stems on the surface, it is best to plant through a mulching sheet to control weeds while the plants are becoming established. If you are planting large ground-cover plants, you may need to dig holes with a spade before laying the mulching sheet.

Above: Evergreen ivy is a fast-growing plant for ground cover.

171

MAKING THE MOST OF TREES

Trees make attractive features as specimens set in a lawn, or planted towards the back of a shrub border. Once they are established, most trees require no maintenance. Those in a border are generally less trouble because falling leaves drop almost unnoticed onto the soil, where they are quickly recycled.

Make your selection to suit the size of your garden and to give as much long-term interest as possible. Many small ornamental trees bear spring blossom, or have bright autumn foliage such as *Acer palmatum*, or they may have berries or fruit, including many varieties of *Malus*. Some have interestingly coloured or textured bark, which stands out in winter; the peeling bark of *Acer griseum*, for instance, is cinnamon-coloured.

SMALL GARDEN TREES

Acer palmatum
Crataegus
Malus
Prunus
Sorbus vilmorinii

Trees in Lawns

Leaves on a lawn usually have to be raked up, but a way around this problem could be to choose a tree with small leaves or an evergreen one. Mowing beneath a low-hanging tree or up to a trunk can also cause difficulties. Lawn trees are generally better planted in a bed cut into the grass, which can either be planted with attractive ground cover or covered with a decorative mulch to suppress weeds and retain moisture.

Trees in Borders

The best way to cover the ground beneath trees in a border is with ground-cover plants that will tolerate shade and dry soil. If the tree is very large or has large leaves you may have to rake the leaves off the plants when they fall, but most of them usually work their way between the plants and soon rot down. If you use a ground cover that dies down in winter, falling leaves will not matter.

Left: Mulch around the base of a specimen tree to prevent weed growth. Large pebbles have been used here but you could also choose chipped bark or gravel.

Planting a Lawn Tree

1 Mark a circle on the grass about 90–120cm (3–4ft) across. Lift the grass with a spade, and remove about 5cm (6in) of soil with it. Dig a planting hole, and fork in plenty of garden compost or well-rotted manure.

3 Place the tree in the hole and use a cane to check that the final soil level – about 5cm (2in) below the grass – will be the same as in the container (or with bare-root trees the soil mark on the stem).

2 Insert a short but sturdy wooden stake before you plant the tree, placing it on the side of the prevailing wind. Place it off-centre, to allow space for the large rootball.

4 With bare-root trees, spread out the roots; with container-grown ones, gently tease some out. Return the soil, and firm in well. Water thoroughly, secure with a tree-tie, and mulch the bed.

Above: This magnificent magnolia is underplanted with grape hyacinths. The colours look stunning when both are in flower.

Ideas for Special Features

SOME OF THE MOST POPULAR GARDEN FEATURES CAN ALSO BE LOW-
MAINTENANCE IF SELECTED WISELY AND CAREFULLY ESTABLISHED.
HERE ARE SOME SUGGESTIONS FOR INSTALLING AND MAINTAINING A
SELECTION OF ATTRACTIVE ADDITIONS TO YOUR GARDEN.

EASY-CARE CONTAINERS

The main task with containers is
watering, which in summer often
needs to be done more than once a
day. However, an automatic watering
system can take care of this.

Alternatively, choose tough plants
such as shrubs, rather than bedding
plants. They will still need watering,
but will survive limited periods of
neglect. There are also perennial
plants that can remain in their containers for several years. These will
provide less of a summer show than
brightly coloured bedding plants, but
can be successful as focal points.

Mixed Collections

Try a mixed planting of perhaps three
small shrubs, with different foliage
shapes and colours. If you really want
the brightness of bedding plants, plant
just a couple of these and have permanent plants in other containers.

Decorative Containers

Some flowering evergreens can look a
bit boring when not in bloom. A frost-
proof decorative pot will make sure
such plants always remain a feature.

**EASY-CARE PLANTS
FOR CONTAINERS**

Azalea
Bergenia
Dwarf conifers
Erica hyemalis
Euonymus fortunei
'Emerald 'n' Gold'
Fatsia japonica
Gaultheria
Hebe
Phormium
Rhododendron
Santolina chamaecyparissus
Skimmia

Left: *A collection of shrubs, conifers and
bergenia has plenty of impact. They won't
die if left unwatered for a day or two.*

WATER FEATURES

If you like water features, installing a fountain or pond are simple ways to create an interesting low-maintenance garden. A large pond may be less demanding than a flowerbed.

How to Make a Pond

Make your pond as large as possible. Fish and wildlife will be happier, and the water will stay clearer. You can dig out a pond and line it in a weekend, but you may prefer to get someone else to excavate it for you. Leave a shallow ledge 23cm (9in) down around part of the pond for marginal plants, and to allow wildlife access.

Planting a Pond

The best time to plant aquatics is spring and early summer, so that they

can become established. Use a planting basket designed for aquatic plants, line it with a special basket liner and use aquatic soil.

Maintenance

Overcrowded plants benefit from division and replanting in spring, and in autumn it's best to cut down dead foliage that might pollute the water, and to rake out the leaves. Every few years the pond should be emptied and cleaned – the only big task.

> TROUBLE-FREE PLANTS
> FOR PONDS
> *Acorus graminens* 'Variegatus'
> *Aponegeton distachysos*
> *Iris laevigata* (Japanese iris)
> *Myriphyllum aquaticum*
> *Pontederia cordata*

Above: A pond can become a strong focal point, yet the amount of maintenance required is modest.

175

HEDGES

Well-clipped hedges are excellent plants for defining and giving structure to a garden, and for many gardeners a hedge is preferable to a fence or wall. However, hedges can be tedious and time-consuming to trim. Nonetheless with imagination you may be able to overcome some of the problems.

Down-sizing

Many established hedges will respond well to quite severe height or width reduction, which will cut down considerably on the amount of trimming required. Cut back to about 30cm (12in) lower or in from the final height or width, to allow for new growth. Improving the shape of a straight-sided hedge by sloping the sides will marginally reduce the amount to be cut and make pruning easier.

LOW-MAINTENANCE HEDGES
Beech
Carpinus betulus
Ilex
Laurel
Ligistrum
Taxus Baccata

Alternative Plants

Think about using low-maintenance plants if you are planting a new hedge. It may even be worth replacing a rather boring or very formal hedge with a more easily maintained and attractive alternative. Informal flowering hedges only need cutting back once a year after flowering, whereas formal hedges usually require clipping two or three times a year to look good. A beech or hornbeam hedge requires only one clip a year, in late summer.

Above: A mature beech hedge will need trimming only once a year.

Above: A Clematis 'Bees' Jubilee' scrambling over a rhododendron will flower after its host has finished.

CLIMBERS

Although climbers are popular for softening walls and fences, many require regular pruning, training or tying which can be time-consuming. However, many climbers are self-clinging or twining, so do not need tying in. Roses do need regular pruning to flower well, and many plants benefit from dead-heading, but most

---

SELF-CLINGING AND TWINING CLIMBERS

Ceropegia sandersonii
Clematis
Hedera
Lonicera periclymenum
Manettia leuteorubra
Parthenocissus quinquefolia
Tropaeolum
Wisteria sinensis

---

climbers will perform well if simply pruned when they outgrow their allotted space.

Planting a Climber

1 Make the planting hole at least 45cm (1½ft) away from a wall or fence, to avoid the "rain shadow" that will prevent moisture reaching young roots. Work plenty of moisture-holding material such as garden compost or manure into the soil.

2 Plant at an angle so that the stems grow towards the wall. Leave in any cane that was used as a support while in the pot, but if there are several stems untie them and spread them out.

3 To help start off newly planted self-clinging plants, use small ties that you can fix to the wall by suction or a special adhesive.

4 Water thoroughly after planting and whenever the ground is dry during the first season. Once the plant is well established, watering should seldom be necessary.

A SIMPLIFIED KITCHEN GARDEN

Kitchen gardens are usually labour-intensive, with many hours spent digging, watering, feeding and weeding. If you want to grow fruit and vegetables in a low-maintenance garden, choose those that demand the least attention and try some of the techniques described here.

Watering Edible Plants

Vegetables and salads need plenty of water, so a sprinkler will be essential. To save more time, you could add a time switch to make the system automatic. Seep hoses are ideal for rows of vegetables as the water goes directly to where it is needed at the roots (see Easy Garden Maintenance).

Above: Planting fruit and vegetable seedlings through a mulching sheet will avoid the need for weeding.

Eliminate Weeding

By using a mulching sheet that will keep out light yet let through water, you can almost eliminate weeding on beds. Always make sure the soil is enriched with well-rotted manure or garden compost and fertilizers before you lay the mulching sheet. Secure the sheet edges, then cut crosses in the sheet with a knife and plant through the holes, folding the sheet back after planting. Water thoroughly. Later, feeding is best done by applying a liquid fertilizer, rather than compost, so that it will penetrate the mulch to reach the plant roots.

Above: French beans need a rich soil but require little after-care, apart from regular harvesting to maintain production.

> **GARDENER'S TIP**
> If you find spacing seeds by hand difficult, one of the proprietary seed-sowers might help. These are available for both seed trays and drills. For sowing in the ground, you can choose a long-handled version, to avoid the need for bending.

178

GROWING FRUIT

Concentrate on soft fruit such as blackcurrants and raspberries. Gooseberries are trouble-free in themselves but are prone to pests and diseases. Rhubarb is completely trouble-free. You can leave it for years, to flourish without any attention at all.

Avoid troublesome fruit such as apricots, which are demanding, and apples and pears, which are prone to problems and require careful pruning if trained to one of the systems popular in small gardens.

If you really want to grow apples, try one of the flagpoles that grow upright and form the fruit on natural short spurs along the upright stem. Apart from cutting out the odd wayward shoot, pruning is not required.

Above: This eye-catching herb and salad garden is easy to maintain.

GROWING VEGETABLES AND SALAD

There are many vegetables and salads that are easy to grow and are not overly troubled by pests and diseases. Many can now be bought as plugs from the garden centre if you do not want to sow them from seed. Try courgettes, French beans, sweetcorn, perpetual spinach, lettuces and rocket. If you enjoy the taste of home-grown new potatoes, but do not want all the hard work of earthing up several times and heavy digging to harvest, you can grow them beneath black polythene.

Above: Potatoes grown under black polythene are easy to cultivate and harvest as they do not require earthing up.

GROWING HERBS

After the initial soil preparation to provide well-drained conditions, many herbs are easy to grow. If you stick to perennials such as chives, sage, rosemary, thyme, French tarragon and winter savory, the only maintenance required is regular picking to prevent flowering and cutting down in the autumn or early spring to encourage new growth.

179

Easy-care Plants

USE THIS LIST OF EASY-CARE PLANTS TO PLAN YOUR GARDEN SO THAT
IT REQUIRES MINIMUM MAINTENANCE.

Plant Name	When to Plant	Season of Interest
Acer palmatum (s)	autumn	autumn foliage
Ajuga reptans (ps, fs)	autumn, spring	year-round
Allium (s)	autumn	summer, autumn
Anemone x *hybrida* (s, ps)	spring	late summer to mid-autumn
Anthemis tinctoria (s)	autumn, spring	summer
Aquilegia (s, ps)	autumn, spring	late spring, early summer
Artemisia absinthium (s)	autumn, spring	late summer
Astilbe (s)	autumn, spring	summer
Aucuba japonica (s, ps, fs)	autumn	year-round
Azalea * (ps)	autumn	spring
Begonia semperflorens ñ (ps)	late spring	summer
Berberis (s, ps)	autumn	spring, autumn
Bergenia (s, ps)	autumn, spring	spring
Buxus sempervirens (ps)	autumn	year-round
Calendula officinalis (s, ps)	sow in situ, spring	summer to autumn
Calluna vulgaris * (s)	autumn, spring	summer, autumn
Carex (s, ps)	autumn, spring	year-round
Chamaecyparis, dwarf cultivars ñ to slightly ^ (s)	autumn, spring	year-round
Chamaemelum nobile 'Treneague' (s)	sow in situ or divide in spring	year-round
Choisya ternata (s)	autumn, spring	year-round
Cistus (s)	autumn, spring	summer

Allium

Calendula

Colchicum autumnale (s)	summer	autumn
Cortaderia selloana (s)	autumn, spring	late summer
Cotoneaster (s, ps)	autumn	year-round, autumn berries
Crataegus (s, ps)	autumn	spring flowers, autumn fruits
Crocus (s)	autumn, summer	spring, autumn
Cyclamen (ps)	late summer	autumn, winter, early spring
Cytisus (s)	autumn	summer
Deschampsia ñ to * (s, ps)	autumn, spring	late spring, early summer
Dianthus ñ to ^ (s)	autumn, spring	summer
Dicentra spectabilis ñ to ^ (ps)	autumn, spring	summer
Digitalis purpurea (ps)	autumn	late spring, early summer
Echinops ritro (s, ps)	autumn	early summer
Elaeagnus pungens (s, ps)	autumn	summer
Erica cultivars * (s)	autumn	winter, spring
Erigeron (ps)	autumn	spring, summer
Eryngium (s)	spring, autumn	summer
Eschscholzia californica (s)	sow in situ, spring	summer to autumn
Euonymus fortunei (s)	autumn	year-round
Euphorbia (s)	autumn	summer
Fatsia japonica (s, ps)	autumn	year-round
Festuca glauca (s)	autumn, winter	year-round
Galanthus nivalis (ps)	autumn	late winter, early spring
Gaultheria (syn. *Pernettya*) * to ñ (ps)	autumn	year-round
Geranium (s, ps)	spring, autumn	summer
Hakonechloa (s, ps)	spring, autumn	year-round
Hebe (s, ps)	autumn	year-round, summer flowers
Hedera (s, ps, fs)	autumn	year-round
Helichrysum ñ to ^ (s)	autumn	summer, autumn
Hemerocallis (s)	autumn	summer
Hosta (ps, fs)	autumn	summer

Deschampsia

Erica *cultivars*

Houttuynia cordata (s)	autumn, spring	spring, summer
Hypericum calycinum (s, ps)	autumn	summer
Ilex aquifolium (s)	autumn, spring	year-round, autumn berries
Impatiens (ps)	autumn, spring	spring to autumn
Juniperus horizontalis (s)	autumn	year-round
Kniphofia hybrids (s, ps)	autumn, spring	summer
Lamium maculatum (ps, s)	spring, autumn	summer to autumn
Lavandula (s)	autumn	summer, early autumn
Lavatera trimestris (s)	autumn, spring	summer
Laurus nobilis (s, ps)	autumn	year-round
Lilium * (s, ps)	autumn, spring	summer
Limnanthes (s)	sow in situ, spring	summer
Liriope muscari (fs)	autumn	autumn
Lonicera periclymenum (s, ps)	autumn	summer
Lupinus slightly * (s, ps)	autumn, spring	summer
Mahonia (fs)	autumn, spring	autumn, winter, spring
Malus (s, ps)	autumn	spring, autumn fruits
Miscanthus sinensis (s)	autumn	spring to autumn
Muscari (s)	autumn	spring
Narcissus (s)	autumn	spring
Olearia x *haastii* (s)	autumn	year-round, summer flowers
Origanum vulgare ^ (s)	autumn	summer
Osteospermum (s)	spring	summer
Parthenocissus quinquefolia (s, fs)	autumn, spring	spring to autumn
Pelargonium (s)	spring	summer
Persicaria affinis (s, ps)	spring	summer to autumn
Petunia (s)	spring	summer to autumn
Phormium (s)	autumn, spring	year-round
Pyracantha (s, ps)	spring, autumn	autumn berries
Rhododendron *(ps)	autumn, spring	late spring
Rosmarinus officinalis (s)	autumn	year-round

Lavandula   Juniperus horizontalis

Rudbeckia (s)	autumn, spring	summer to autumn
Salvia officinalis (s)	autumn	year-round
Santolina chamaecyparissus (s)	autumn, spring	year-round, summer flowers
Schizostylis coccinea (s)	spring, autumn	summer, autumn
Sedum spectabile (s)	autumn	late summer
Sorbus vilmorinii (s)	autumn	autumn berries
Stipa (s)	autumn	year-round
Tagetes patula (s)	autumn, spring	summer to early autumn
Taxus baccata (s, ps, fs)	autumn	year-round, autumn berries
Thuja orientalis 'Aurea Nana' (s)	autumn, spring	year-round
Thymus ñ to ^ (s)	autumn, spring	year-round
Tropaeolum speciosum ñ to ^ (s, ps)	autumn	summer
Tulipa (s)	autumn	spring
Veronica spicata (s, ps)	autumn, spring	summer
Viburnum davidii (s, ps)	autumn	year-round
Vinca minor (s, ps)	autumn, spring	year-round
Waldsteinia ternata (ps, fs)	spring	mid- to late spring
Wisteria sinensis (s, ps)	autumn	summer
Yucca gloriosa (s)	spring	year-round

Stipa

Tulipa

Symbols

Plants marked with * require acid soil;

Plants marked with ^ prefer alkaline soil;

Plants marked with ñ prefer neutral soil.

(S) = sun

(PS) = partial shade

(FS) = full shade

PRUNING SUCCESS

Many plants benefit from some form
of regular pruning, either to keep them
to size or to increase the amount of
flowers. Knowing which plants benefit
from the treatment and how and when
to prune is the key. The pruning notes
in this chapter cover general
techniques and details for all the main
types of plant, while a seasonal chart
enables you to identify exactly when
and how to prune particular plants.
Different types of hedging plants
are included.

What is Pruning?

PRUNING IS A TECHNIQUE USED TO RESTRICT THE GROWTH OF PLANTS, INCREASE THE YIELD OF FLOWERS AND FRUIT AND GENERALLY KEEP PLANTS IN GOOD HEALTH. IT CAN ALSO BE USED TO ENHANCE THE DECORATIVE EFFECT OF LEAVES AND STEMS.

PRUNING CONCERNS

Amateur gardeners are often more baffled by pruning than by any other aspect of gardening; this may be partly due to conflicting advice in publications, and on television and radio pro-

grammes. Even many experienced gardeners approach the subject with caution. The main concerns are that pruning incorrectly will result in the failure of plants to flower or fruit, or that the shape will be spoilt or, in the worst scenario, that the plant will be killed. However, take comfort from the knowledge that you are unlikely to kill a plant by pruning it, as plants are surprisingly resilient. The worst that can happen is that you may lose a season's flowers or fruit,

and even then, you will probably find that the plant will perform better than ever the following year.

Once you have learned a few basic principles, it's a good idea to watch your plants to discover how they grow and flower. Different techniques will yield different results, so adopt the approach that best suits you and your style of gardening.

Some gardeners like the garden to look tidy with everything tightly controlled and clipped to shape. This can be

Above: Shrub roses are usually quite large and bushy but they still benefit from pruning.

Right: Clematis 'Barbara Dibley' needs selective pruning in early spring for a flush of flowers in late spring and summer.

rewarding but is also time-consuming. Others take a more relaxed approach, often through necessity. The overall appearance of their gardens may be less regimented, but the plants will still be healthy and will perform well.

BUILDING CONFIDENCE

The best way to learn to prune is to do it, then to observe the results. You will soon discover which methods produce the effect you want. You can then apply the same technique to other similar plants.

Always remember that pruning is not always strictly necessary. If a plant pleases you exactly the way it is, you can often leave it alone as long as it remains healthy and productive. However, this does not mean that you

should allow your plants to grow unchecked for years, and then attack them with the shears only when they have got out of hand.

Prune a plant indiscriminately at the wrong time and in the wrong way and it may well regrow with redoubled vigour, making it much more of a problem than it was in the first place. If you have any serious doubts, prune lightly; you can always do a little more trimming later if the plant responds well. Alternatively, prune the plant in stages, perhaps a quarter of the growth one year, then, after checking the response, tackling the remainder in the following year.

Above: Pruning climbing roses in spring will encourage stronger growth.

Left: A healthy camellia at its peak.

187

What is Pruning?

WHY WE NEED TO PRUNE

We prune plants for a variety of reasons: one is to control size and shape. This is especially important in a small garden where space is at a premium. However, the number of plants that you can control in this way is relatively small.

It is better to think of pruning as a means of refreshing the plant, so that it will produce a large proportion of young growth. Young wood flowers and fruits better, provides good, strong material for taking cuttings, and is healthier than the old.

If allowed to build up, old, dead wood can harbour disease. Thinning stems is also a good means of improving air circulation within the body of the plant. If the growth is dense and congested, damp air tends to settle

Left: Pruning a late-flowering clematis in late winter produces abundant blooms.

> **GARDENER'S TIP**
>
> To help a plant recover speedily after pruning, give it a dose of fertilizer, preferably as a root drench or foliar feed. This is especially important if you are dealing with a sickening or weak specimen.

around the stems, encouraging mildew and other fungal diseases which can only be eliminated with fungicides. These days, gardeners try to keep their use of chemicals in the garden to the absolute minimum, and correct pruning can mean you will not need them.

You can also prune to enhance a particular decorative effect, for example, to give larger leaves, or to encourage a mass of brilliantly coloured young stems. Remember, however, that these techniques usually bring some losses as well as gains. Prune a dogwood hard for its vivid winter stem effect, and you will lose that summer's flowers, because the plant does not have time to grow and ripen sufficiently for flowering. The choice is yours.

Fruit trees and bushes usually have quite specific needs, in order to help them produce the biggest crop. Turn to any pruning manual and you will find a number of complicated procedures, most of which have been developed by professional fruit-growers whose livelihood depends on a large crop. There is no need to worry about those methods as you can easily achieve yields good enough for the average family using the simplified methods described in this book.

When to Prune

The important thing to remember is that pruning always stimulates new growth, from the point at which you cut. For this reason, it is unwise to prune after midsummer and into autumn. The plant will put on a spurt of fresh, sappy growth that will not have time to harden before the onset of winter, and will probably die back.

New Wood or Old?

The first rule in pruning is to make the cut on the correct part of the stem, so it is important to be able to recognize new and old wood. Sometimes also called the current season's growth new wood is supple and bright green in colour, gradually turning brown in summer as it becomes progressively less pliable. One-year-old wood is usually brown. Older wood tends to be grey.

Making the Cuts

Depending on the plant, growth buds either lie opposite each other on the stem or are arranged alternately.

In both cases, you need to cut back to just above a growth bud. In the case of plants with opposite buds, two new shoots will grow, making a bushier

Right: Rambling roses flower once on old wood.

This year's growth – greener and flexible

Last summer's growth – darker and less flexible

Two-year-old wood – darker, thicker and more rigid

plant. With alternate buds, a new shoot will emerge growing in the direction the bud was pointing. This is why you often hear about cutting back to an outward-facing bud, a method that creates a vase-shaped plant with an open centre through which air can circulate freely.

189

MAKING A GOOD CUT

1 Cut about 5mm (¼in) above a bud, angled so that moisure runs away from the bud and not into it. If the plant has buds lying opposite one another, cut straight across the stem, just above a strong pair of buds.

2 Avoid leaving a long stump as this will be starved of sap and may rot back.

3 Avoid cutting too close to the bud as this may allow infection to enter.

4 Blunt secateurs (pruning shears) or careless use may bruise or tear the stem instead of cutting through it cleanly. This is an invitation for disease spores to enter. The stump is also too long.

5 If the cut slopes downwards towards the bud, the excessive moisture that may collect in the area could cause the stem to rot.

6 Shrubs with opposite leaves should be treated in a different way to those with leaves that form an alternate leaf arrangement. Cut straight across the stem, just above a strong pair of buds.

HOW TO USE THIS CHAPTER

The chapter is arranged so that the basic principles of pruning various well-known and popular plants are explained in detail. Drawings are included for each pruning method showing clearly how the cuts should be made. Read the chapter through and you will soon discover that many of the techniques are similar – because the principles of pruning remain the same whatever type of plant you are dealing with.

Roses and clematis have specific needs depending on the variety. Use a good rose catalogue if you are unsure which type of rose you have. Clematis are divided into three groups, and this information is usually stated on the plant label when you buy your plant. If in doubt, the section on clematis will help you ascertain to which group your plant belongs.

The chapter begins with details of basic pruning equipment that you will need. At the end of the chapter, a quick reference chart provides appropriate pruning methods for each plant, with the exception of roses, clematis and fruits, which have specific needs. The chart also gives the time of year that each plant should be pruned.

This book does not deal with tree pruning. If you have a large tree that needs attention, it is best to contact a qualified professional. Ask at your local nursery or garden centre for their recommendations.

Saws & Power Tools

GRECIAN SAW

This is a good general-purpose pruning saw. It has a curved blade that narrows towards the tip, making it easy to use among congested branches. It is also easy to use above head height, because the backward-pointing teeth cut on the pull stroke.

STRAIGHT PRUNING SAW

This is a general-purpose tool for cutting through thicker branches. Choose one with teeth on just one side of the blade.

BOW SAW

Because this saw is designed to cut on both the pull and push strokes, it cuts fast and is useful for making horizontal cuts low down on a plant. However, it is difficult to use in a confined space.

POWERED HEDGE TRIMMERS

Electrically powered models are suitable for most gardens. They can be mains or battery powered, but mains-driven types can be used for longer periods of time. Always carry the cable over your shoulder to avoid accidents. Battery-driven models are useful for a small or remote hedges, where access is difficult with a cable; the charge may not last long enough for a long hedge without recharging. If you have a long stretch of hedge to cut, use a petrol- (gasoline-) driven model, which can be be hired.

SAFETY TIPS

• Electrically powered tools must be used with a circuit breaker.

• Wear goggles to protect your eyes and (if necessary) ear defenders to protect your ears.

• Take extra care with power tools when standing on a stepladder as your balance will be affected.

• Do not use electrical equipment during or just after rain.

Small Hand Tools

ALTHOUGH MOST OF US CAN MANAGE WITH A GOOD PAIR OF
SECATEURS (PRUNING SHEARS OR PRUNERS), LONG-HANDLED PRUNERS
(LOPPERS OR LOPPING SHEARS) AND HAND SHEARS, THERE ARE TIMES
WHEN MORE SPECIALIST TOOLS ARE REQUIRED.

BYPASS SECATEURS
(Pruning shears)
Good secateurs (pruning shears) are
suitable for a range of pruning jobs.
Bypass secateurs have a broad concave or square blade that cuts against
a narrower, hooked blade that holds
the branch while the cut is made.

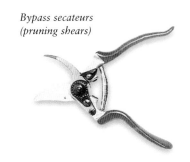

*Bypass secateurs
(pruning shears)*

ANVIL SECATEURS
(Pruning shears)
These have a straight blade that cuts
against a flat anvil, often with a
groove cut in it through which sap can
drain away. Ensure that the blade is
sharp to avoid crushing the stems.

If you have a weak grip, ratchet
shears may be more appropriate. The
ratchet device enables you to cut
through the stem in several small
movements that require less effort.

Most secateurs will cut stems up to
1cm (½ in) thick.

*Anvil secateurs
(pruning shears)*

LONG-HANDLED PRUNERS
(Loppers or lopping shears)
These can be used to cut through
stems that are too thick to be cut with
secateurs. They are useful for reaching
high or low, congested branches.

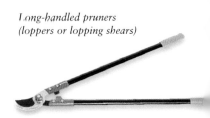

*Long-handled pruners
(loppers or lopping shears)*

Pruning knife

Hand shears with a straight blade

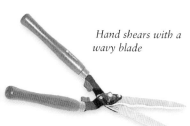

Hand shears with a wavy blade

TREE PRUNERS

(Tree loppers or pole pruners)
For tall shrubs, these will make the job easier. Long-handled pruners do not reach as high and can be tiring to use above shoulder level.

The mechanism by which these work varies with the make: they may be operated by rope, metal rods, or fixed or telescopic handles. The small lever mechanism in the handle transfers the cutting action to the cutting head. The hooked end makes it easier to position and steadies the tool.

PRUNING KNIFE

These knives have a curved, folding blade that ensures the blade cuts into the shoot as you cut towards yourself with a slicing motion.

Because of the temptation to use the thumb as an anvil, such knives must be used with great care.

SHEARS

Mainly used for hedge trimming, shears can also be used for cutting through branches on shrubs and trees that are too thick for secateurs or loppers, provided there is a notch at the base of the blades. They can also be used to trim low-growing shrubs. Some models have blades with wavy edges that help trap and hold the shoots while cutting.

Choose shears of a weight you feel comfortable with; cutting a hedge by hand can be tiring work.

Coppicing & Pollarding

THESE METHODS, CARRIED OUT IN EARLY SPRING TO DOGWOODS AND
SOME WILLOWS, ARE USED TO ENHANCE THE COLOUR OF ORNAMEN-
TAL STEMS OR THE LEAVES, OR TO RESTRICT TREE SIZE.

Left: *To coppice, cut back all the recent growth in late winter to early spring, leaving a low woody mound (or 'stool').*

Below: Rubus cockburnianus, *coppiced for winter effect.*

PLANTS TO TRY

Catalpa bignonioides
Cornus sibirica
Cornus stolonifera
Eucalyptus gunnii
Paulownia tomentosa
Rubus cockburnianus
Salix alba vitellina

1 For coppicing, pruning is severe. Cut back stems to near ground level leaving a low, woody framework. Do this early every spring or every other spring if the plant is still young.

2 A coppiced shrub will look like this at the start of the growing season. The technique is a useful means of restricting the size of plants that could otherwise grow too big.

194

Above: The stems of a pollarded Salix alba vitelina *'Britzensis' in full winter glory.*

1 For pollarding, allow the plant to grow until the trunk has reached the desired height.

2 In late winter or spring, cut the stems back hard near to the top of the trunk to leave short stubs. The new shoots produced over the summer will create a colourful winter effect.

PLANTS TO TRY

Catalpa bignonioides
Eucalyptus gunnii
Paulownia tomentosa
Robinia pseudoacacia
Tilia

3 Over time the pollarded head becomes more stubby and will produce fine colourful stems annually.

4 If possible, feed immediately after pruning to give the plant a boost and to achieve the desired growth.

195

Cutting Back to a Framework

SHRUBS THAT FLOWER ON SHOOTS PRODUCED IN THE CURRENT YEAR
WILL BECOME INCREASINGLY STRAGGLY UNLESS THEY ARE PRUNED
ANNUALLY. PRUNING WILL PROMOTE BLOOMS CLOSER TO THE GROUND.

Left: Prune hard annually to a low framework of old, darker wood to encourage a mass of new shoots and a bushy habit.

Below: Buddleja davidii *produces masses of flowers when pruned this way.*

PLANTS TO TRY

Buddleja davidii
Caryopteris
Hydrangea paniculata
Sambucus racemosa

1 In late winter to early spring, before new growth starts, cut back to a low framework no higher than 90cm (3ft).

2 You can also prune harder, cutting the thicker stems flush with the ground. If you delay pruning until early spring, new growth from the base of the plant will be clearly visible.

Cutting to the Ground

THIS TECHNIQUE IS OFTEN USED ON LATE-FLOWERING SHRUBS OF
BORDERLINE HARDINESS THAT TEND TO DIE BACK IN WINTER. LEAVE
THE STEMS OVER WINTER TO PROVIDE FROST PROTECTION.

Left: Cut back all the previous year's growth just above the ground each spring.

Below: Fuchsia 'Tom Thumb' benefits from a pruned framework after the winter.

PLANTS TO TRY

Ceratostigma willmottianum
Cestrum parqui
Fuchsia (hardy varieties)
Perovskia atriplicifolia

1 In spring, as soon as new growth is visible, cut the old stems back hard, flush with the ground or close to it.

2 The plant will grow strongly, having more access to the light. This will create a bushy, compact plant.

Deadheading with Shears

REMOVING FADED FLOWERS IS A FORM OF PRUNING. IN THE CASE OF HEATHERS (*CALLUNA*, *DABOECIA* AND *ERICA*) IT IS EASIEST TO SHEAR THEM OFF IN ONE GO.

Above: *Trim back heathers as the flowers begin to fade, being careful not to cut back into the darker, old wood.*

Above: *Pruning to keep heathers compact will give you a neat heather bed.*

1 Shear over your plants, cutting just below the flower spike. Heathers will not regenerate from cuts made into old, bare wood. Prune winter-flowering heather in spring to ensure you do not damage tender growth.

2 Some heathers are grown for their coloured foliage, not their flowers. In winter, lightly trim back the developing flowers before they have the chance to open. This will encourage further leaf growth.

198

Clipping

MANY EVERGREENS RESPOND WELL TO BEING CLIPPED TO SHAPE,
EITHER WITH SHEARS OR (IF THE LEAVES ARE LARGE) WITH SECATEURS
(PRUNERS). WITH PRACTICE YOU CAN CREATE UNUSUAL TOPIARY.

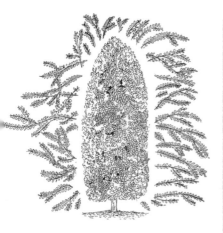

*Above: Trim new growth to shape in
spring and midsummer.*

*Above: Yew is the classic shrub to clip
into interesting shapes.*

1 Trim off the new growth as necessary, but avoid cutting into old wood.
Shear the plants twice in the growing
season to produce a smooth surface.
Practise on quick-growing plants such
as *Ligustrum vulgare* before progress-
ing to ambitious schemes.

PLANTS TO TRY
Berberis
Buxus sempervirens
Ligustrum vulgare
Lonicera nitida
Osmanthus decorus
Phillyrea angustifolia
Prunus lusitanica
Taxus baccata

Large-leaved Evergreens

MOST EVERGREEN SHRUBS GROW HAPPILY WITHOUT ROUTINE PRUN-
ING, BUT IF YOU HAVE A SMALL GARDEN YOU MAY WANT TO RESTRICT
THE SIZE OF LARGER SHRUBS.

Above: Prune out awkwardly placed stems and some of the older growth. You can also shorten stems that have flowered, cutting back just above a growth bud.

Above: Most larger leaved evergreens only need pruning when they need restricting.

1 If a shrub produces a shoot that spoils the outline of the plant, cut it back to its point of origin, reaching right into the plant if necessary. This will restore its uniform shape.

Variegated evergreens sometimes pro-duce plain green shoots. These are always more vigorous than the typical growth and should be cut out entirely as soon as you spot them.

The 'One-third' Method

THIS SIMPLE TECHNIQUE WORKS ON A WIDE VARIETY OF ORNAMENTAL FLOWERING SHRUBS. IT IS A GOOD WAY TO KEEP THEM COMPACT AND FRESH, AND IT ENCOURAGES HEALTHY BLOOMS.

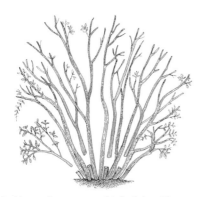

Above: Cut out one-third of the oldest stems close to ground level.

PLANTS TO TRY

Cornus (grown for foliage effect, e.g. *C. alba* 'Elegantissima' and 'Spaethii')
Cotinus coggygria
Forsythia
Hypericum
Kerria japonica 'Pleniflora'
Kolkwitzia
Leycesteria
Philadelphus
Potentilla (shrubby types)
Ribes sanguineum
Spiraea

1 Immediately after flowering, cut back a third of the oldest stems, cutting some back to strong buds low down and removing others at or near ground level. Remove any weak or badly placed branches and shorten any damaged stems. Use this technique for established plants, not for any under three years old.

Above: Kolkwitzia amabilis *pruned by one-third will stay compact.*

201

Shortening New Growth

A LIGHT TRIMMING WILL ENCOURAGE A BUSHIER HABIT ON PLANTS SUCH AS *CYSTISUS* AND *GENISTA* THAT OTHERWISE CAN EASILY BECOME GAUNT WITH LONG, BARE BRANCHES.

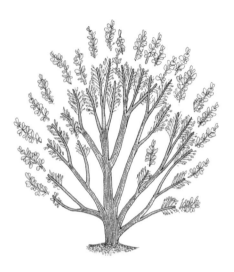

> ### GARDENER'S TIP
> Use this method on young plants only. Old, neglected plants will not respond well and are best replaced.

Below: *This* Genista lydia *is covered with flowers the year following pruning.*

Above: *Trim back the new growth by half after flowering. Be careful not to cut back into older wood.*

1 Immediately after flowering, shorten last season's growth, which will be pale and supple, by about half. Take care not to cut back into old wood.

2 A light trimming is all that will be necessary on some of the stems. Ensure that you cut recent growth only, that made last summer.

202

Shortening Side Shoots

SHRUBS THAT FLOWER ON THE PREVIOUS YEAR'S SHOOTS OFTEN BENE-
FIT FROM A LIGHT PRUNING AFTER FLOWERING. THIS WILL ENCOUR-
AGE MORE BLOOMS THE FOLLOWING YEAR.

Above: *Trim back shoots that have flowered (shown here in yellow) by between a half and two-thirds of their length.*

PLANTS TO TRY
Cistus
Convolvulus cneorum
Helianthemum
Kalmia latifolia

Below: *A* Cistus *in full flower.*

1 Immediately after flowering, trim back only the shoots that have flowered. Shorten the current season's growth, which will still be soft and pliable, by up to two-thirds. Do not cut into older, darker wood.

Plants in this category keep a good shape whether you prune or not, but a trimming results in more shoots which will all be flower-bearers.

203

Grey-leaved Foliage Plants

MANY GREY-LEAVED PLANTS LOOK UNATTRACTIVE IF ALLOWED TO
BECOME STRAGGLY. ANNUAL PRUNING WILL KEEP THEM LOOKING
FRESH AND WELL-CLOTHED WITH FOLIAGE.

Above: *Cut back grey-leaved plants to as low down on the stem as possible, just above a new growth bud.*

PLANTS TO TRY

Artemisia (shrubby types)
Helichrysum italicum
Lavandula
Santolina chamaecyparissus

Above: *A* Santolina chamaecyparissus *that has become leggy.*

1 In early spring, as the new growth emerges, prune back last year's growth, cutting just above a new shoot or a developing bud. The plant will look sparse.

2 The plant will soon be well-clothed with new leaves. Start this regime early in the life of the plant: most grey-leaved plants will not regenerate well if you cut into very old wood.

Rejuvenating the Neglected

OLD AND NEGLECTED SHRUBS OFTEN NEED TO BE REPLACED, BUT IT IS
WORTH TRYING SOME DRASTIC PRUNING FIRST. IF THE SHRUB DOESN'T
RESPOND, THEN REPLACE IT.

Above: Staggering drastic pruning is often effective. Here, the central stem has been left unpruned. Two stems pruned hard last year have produced fresh growth, so it is safe to cut back the two old branches as shown to encourage further growth.

Above: New shoots will soon appear.

1 In late winter to early spring, cut back all the stems to just above ground level. Alternatively, cut the shrub back in stages. Prune back one-third of the stems in the first year, a second third in the next. Cut back the remainder the following year.

2 Trim any ragged edges with a pruning knife or rasp to prevent infection entering the wound. If the shrub shows no sign of life in the first year after pruning, dig it up and replace it.

Floribunda Roses

SOMETIMES CALLED CLUSTER-FLOWERED ROSES, FLORIBUNDAS ARE
NOTED FOR THEIR PROLIFIC BLOOMING.

*Above: Cut out damaged, badly placed,
and weak shoots, then shorten the
remainder by between a half and two-
thirds of their length.*

Above: Rosa 'Sexy Rexy'.

1 In early spring, cut back all dead,
diseased and damaged stems, cutting
them back to their point of origin,
if necessary.

2 Remove any crossing or awkwardly
placed shoots that are growing into
the centre of the bush.

3 Shorten the remaining stems by up
to two-thirds of their length, cutting
back to healthy buds that are pointing
outwards. Prune vigorous varieties
lightly, weaker-growing plants harder.

4 During the flowering season,
remove spent flower trusses to encourage the plant to flower further.

Hybrid Tea Roses

ALSO KNOWN AS LARGE-FLOWERED ROSES, HYBRID TEAS HAVE LARGE, FULLY DOUBLE FLOWERS WITH A HIGH CENTRE. THEIR BEAUTIFUL BLOOMS ARE PERFECT FOR FLORAL DISPLAYS.

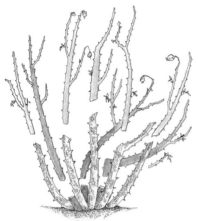

Above: Cut out badly placed, diseased or dead wood to the base. Shorten all other stems by about half.

Above: Rosa 'Savoy Hotel'.

1 In early spring, cut out any diseased or dead shoots, as well as any stems that are badly placed. Most of these can be cut back to their point of origin, but if growth is sparse, cut to just above a healthy bud.

2 Prune the remaining stems to within 20–25cm (8–10in) of the ground. Always cut to an outward-facing bud.

3 During the flowering season, remove spent flowers to prolong the display.

207

Shrub Roses

WILD ROSES AND OLD-FASHIONED VARIETIES OF ROSES THAT
PRE-DATE HYBRID TEAS AND FLORIBUNDAS ARE KNOWN AS SHRUB
ROSES. THEY GENERALLY FLOWER FOR A FAIRLY SHORT PERIOD.

Above: *Shorten main stems by about a
quarter to a half, side shoots by up to
two-thirds. Cut out weak and badly
placed stems entirely.*

Above: Rosa *'Frühlingsgold'*.

1 Pruning prevents congestion,
improves the shrub's appearance and
increases the number of blooms. In
early spring, thin congested growth by
cutting back old stems at ground level.

2 Shorten main shoots by up to a half.
Some need only light trimming.

3 Side shoots can be shortened by up
to two-thirds.

208

Standard Roses

PRUNE STANDARD ROSES IN EARLY SPRING TO FORM AN ATTRACTIVE, ROUNDED HEAD. WEEPING STANDARDS ARE PRUNED IN SUMMER TO RETAIN THEIR FLOWING APPEARANCE.

Above: Shorten the previous season's growth by about a half (left). On a weeping standard, cut back the trailing shoots to new buds in the crown when flowering has finished (right).

Above: Standard roses need staking to keep them upright.

1 In early spring, shorten the previous year's main stems to about six buds from the base, cutting to outward-facing buds. Aim for a balanced shape, but do not prune too hard or new shoots may spoil the shape.

2 Shorten side shoots to a couple of buds. To prevent congestion cut back dead or diseased wood.

3 Remove the flowers as they fade to prolong the display.

209

Climbing Roses

PROLIFIC CLIMBING ROSES ARE USUALLY REPEAT-FLOWERING, OFTEN ON A COMBINATION OF THE OLD AND NEW WOOD. THEY ARE FREQUENTLY HIGHLY SCENTED AS WELL AS IMPRESSIVE TO LOOK AT.

Above: *Cut some of the oldest stems back to strong new shoots near the base or where there is a suitable replacement. Shorten laterals by up to two-thirds.*

Above: *The magnificent wall-mounted* Rosa *'Climbing Iceberg'.*

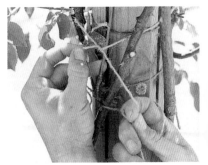

1 In the first few years after planting, the aim is to build up a framework of branches. In spring, cut back any unproductive shoots, but not more than one-third of the stems or flowering will suffer next year.

2 In summer, tie in vigorous shoots as they grow, using soft string. Do not tie too tightly – you may chafe the stems.

3 Cut back the faded flowers to encourage further flowering.

Rambling Roses

THESE ROSES FLOWER ONCE, ON THE OLD WOOD. THEY THEN PRODUCE A MASS OF NEW GROWTH NEAR TO THE BASE.

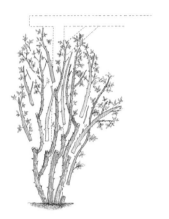

Above: Remove very old or diseased stems entirely. Cut back old canes that have flowered to a point where there is vigorous replacement growth.

Above: Ramblers, such as Rosa 'Rambling Rector', should be pruned after flowering.

1 In late summer, after flowering, cut out all dead or damaged shoots, as well as any that are weak and spindly.

2 Shorten older canes that have flowered to vigorous new shoots. You will be able to leave some unpruned.

3 Tie in the new shoots to the support. Try to pull them to the horizontal – they will produce more flower-bearing laterals for next year.

4 On the canes that remain, shorten the side shoots to two or three leaves.

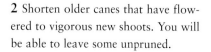

211

Clematis

THESE POPULAR CLIMBERS ARE DIVIDED INTO THREE GROUPS, EACH
FLOWERING AT DIFFERENT TIMES OF THE YEAR. THE GROUPS ALSO
HAVE DIFFERENT PRUNING REQUIREMENTS.

Clematis climb by curling leaf stalks, and are attractive against walls or on fences (fitted with trellis supports), over pergolas, or growing through other plants. Vigorous species look spectacular growing through trees.

For pruning purposes, clematis are divided into three groups, depending on when they flower. Most clematis on sale will state on the label to which group they belong.

Group 1 clematis flower from late winter to spring on wood made the previous year. Usually small-flowered, several of this group are species.

Group 2 consists of large-flowered hybrids that flower in late spring and early summer, on wood made the previous year, then again in mid- to late summer on the new wood. The group includes some species with double flowers. However, the flowers in the second flush are always single.

Group 3 clematis flower from midsummer to autumn on the current season's growth. The group includes many large-flowered hybrids, as well as texensis and viticella types. There are also several notable species: the yellow-flowered *C. tibetana* subsp. *vernayi*, and *C. flammula* and *C. rehderiana*.

Above: C. 'Fireworks' is one of the most spectacular clematis with large luminous violet flowers.

GARDENER'S TIP

Training is vital and should begin
early. Tie the stems to the horizontal
as far as is possible as they grow,
but take great care: the stems are
brittle and are easily broken.

Group 1 Clematis

THIS GROUP COMPRISES THOSE CLEMATIS THAT FLOWER BEFORE MID-SUMMER, ON SHOOTS PRODUCED THE PREVIOUS YEAR. PRUNE ONLY TO KEEP THE PLANT WITHIN BOUNDS.

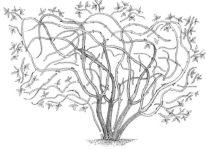

Left: Shorten only those stems that have outgrown their allotted space and cut out a proportion of the remainder to relieve congestion. Otherwise, this group can be left unpruned.

Above: C. montana *var.* rubens 'Continuity' *requires only light pruning.*

1 Immediately after flowering, when necessary, cut back to their point of origin any stems that have outgrown their allotted space.

2 Thin congested growth if necessary. After pruning, the plant will look neater at the edges but overall few shoots will have been removed.

Group 2 Clematis

THESE CLEMATIS FLOWER TWICE: IN LATE SPRING OR EARLY
SUMMER ON WOOD MADE THE PREVIOUS YEAR, AND IN MID- TO LATE
SUMMER ON THE CURRENT SEASON'S GROWTH.

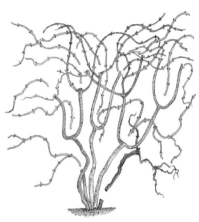

Above: Prune selectively in early spring.
Cut out old, damaged and weak shoots,
thin tangled growth, but leave a good
proportion unpruned.

GARDENER'S TIP

You can also prune group 2 clematis
as for group 3. You will lose the first
crop of flowers, but the second will
be more spectacular. Double-
flowered types will only produce
single flowers, however.

---

1 Cut back any dead or damaged
stems to near ground level. Shorten
any that have outgrown their space.

2 Leave some of the growth
unpruned, respacing the shoots. These
will carry the first crop of flowers.

Above: Group 2 Clematis 'Royalty'
produces glorious, rich purple flowers
twice each year.

Group 3 Clematis

THESE CLEMATIS FLOWER FROM MIDSUMMER TO AUTUMN. THE GROUP INCLUDES SEVERAL SPECIES, MANY LARGE-FLOWERED HYBRIDS AND THE TEXENSIS AND VITICELLA TYPES.

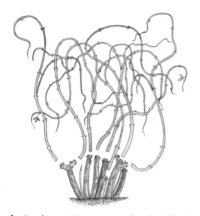

Left: *Pruning a group 3 clematis is basically a matter of renovation. In late winter, cut back all the previous year's growth to the lowest set of strong buds on each stem to leave a woody framework.*

> **GARDENER'S TIP**
> For a late crop of flowers, delay pruning until mid-spring.

1 In late winter, cut back all the growth to a pair of strong buds low down on the stem. Any dead stems can be cut off at ground level.

2 If you want the flowers high up the plant, for example to cover the top of a pergola, cut back higher on the stem. This method particularly suits vigorous species and the stunning yellow-flowered C. 'Bill MacKenzie'.

Above: *The enduringly popular C. 'Jackmanii Superba'.*

215

Honeysuckle

LONICERA (HONEYSUCKLES) NEED LITTLE PRUNING WHEN YOUNG, BUT WITH AGE CAN EASILY DEVELOP A TANGLE OF UNPRODUCTIVE STEMS THAT FLOWER ONLY ABOVE EYE LEVEL.

Above: *Shortening congested stems will control the spread of a honeysuckle.*

Right: *Regular pruning of honeysuckles will ensure an even distribution of flowers.*

1 In late winter to early spring, when the stems are bare and you can see what you are doing, shear back dead and congested stems, cutting just above strong buds. You can be brutal. Honeysuckles are vigorous plants that seem to thrive on rough treatment.

2 If the plant is badly tangled, cut back all stems to a height of 30–60cm (1–2ft) from the ground. Flowering in the next season will not be prolific, but the plant will soon return to its full glory. You can train the new shoots to a support as they appear.

Wisteria

THIS IS A VIGOROUS PLANT THAT PRODUCES A VAST QUANTITY OF LEAFY STEMS ANNUALLY. CAREFUL PRUNING DIVERTS ITS ENERGIES INTO FLOWER PRODUCTION.

Above: After flowering, wisterias suddenly produce a mass of new stems. Cut back any that are not needed to extend the framework. Shorten this growth further in winter.

Above: A wisteria in full flower.

1 Throughout the growing season, train in the new stems that are needed to extend the framework. Once this is established, in late summer shorten the new growth to between four and six leaves to restrict the plant's spread.

2 In late winter, shorten the pruned stems further to two or three buds. This usually means reducing the summer's growth to 7.5–10cm (3–4in). Over time the plant develops a system of spurs that carry the flowers.

217

Other Climbers

MANY CLIMBERS ARE VIGOROUS PLANTS THAT CAN EASILY BECOME CONGESTED. PRUNING IS EASIEST TO DO WHEN THE STEMS ARE BARE IN WINTER AND YOU CAN SEE WHAT YOU ARE DOING.

Above: When pruning climbers, cut out older, unproductive stems to the base and shorten other stems as necessary.

Right: Solanum crispum 'Glasnevin'.

1 In winter cut out old, dead wood completely. You may need to shorten long stems bit by bit if they are very congested. Shorten any overlong but otherwise healthy and supple stems.

2 Tie in the remaining shoots to create a balanced framework. Although the plant will probably occupy a similar area, the growth should look less congested and more evenly balanced.

Wall-trained Chaenomeles

SOMETIMES KNOWN AS ORNAMENTAL QUINCES OR JAPONICA, *CHAENOMELES* ARE VALUED FOR THEIR ATTRACTIVE FLOWERS IN LATE WINTER. WALL-TRAINED SPECIMENS NEED ANNUAL TRIMMING.

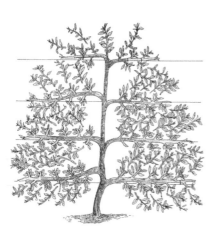

Above: Chaenomeles *should be trained espalier-fashion as shown. Once the shape of the espalier is established, shortening the side shoots in summer will help display the flowers.*

Above: The bright, waxy flowers of Chaenomeles speciosa *'Cardinalis'.*

1 As they grow, tie in strong shoots to the horizontal to extend the framework. This will help maintain a neat and controlled shape.

2 In summer, shorten sideshoots growing away from the main stem to five leaves. Remove any that are growing towards the wall.

Wall-trained Pyracanthas

PYRACANTHAS ARE POPULAR AS WALL-SHRUBS, EITHER TRAINED AS ESPALIERS OR MORE INFORMALLY TIED BACK, DEPENDING ON THE EFFECT YOU WISH TO CREATE.

Above: On wall-trained pyracanthas, shorten side shoots in midsummer to expose the berries.

Right: Pyracanthas are grown mainly for their brilliantly coloured berries.

1 Tie in new shoots to the wall to create an espalier or fan shape, or pin back the strongest shoots and let the others billow forward.

2 In midsummer, remove any awkwardly placed shoots as these will induce spur-like shoots. Shorten other side shoots to expose the berries.

Ornamental Vines

VINES, SUCH AS *VITIS COIGNETIAE* AND *V. VINIFERA* 'PURPUREA', ARE OFTEN GROWN OVER A FRAMEWORK. UNLESS YOU ADOPT A METHODICAL APPROACH TO PRUNING, THEY WILL BECOME TANGLED.

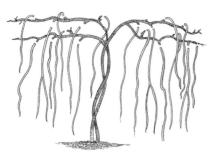

Above: A vine that has been trained over a pergola or similar support will produce stems that cascade downwards. Prune these back close to the main stem when the plant is dormant.

Right: A well-pruned ornamental vine provides neat and even coverage.

1 Train the stems horizontally over the support as required. Once established, each winter cut back the previous season's growth to within one or two buds of its point of origin, to keep the plant tidy.

2 Over the years, short spurs (stubs) will form along the main framework of branches. Cut new growth back to these each winter to produce a fresh curtain of new shoots each summer that is free of tangles.

Conifers

GENERALLY, CONIFERS ARE TROUBLE-FREE PLANTS THAT THRIVE
WITHOUT REGULAR PRUNING. HOWEVER, YOU MAY OCCASIONALLY
EXPERIENCE THE PROBLEMS DESCRIBED HERE.

Above: *Conifers with a spreading habit
may grow so wide that they begin to
encroach on a path or surrounding plants.
Cut back offending branches to a point
where the cuts are hidden by other
branches that cover them.*

Right: *A group of dwarf conifers.*

REMOVING A COMPETING LEADER

1 To ensure a straight, single stem,
where two or more leaders have
formed, leave the strongest unpruned.
Cut the other back to its point of origin to prevent further competition.

2 If the remaining leader is not growing strongly upright, tie a cane to the
main stem. Tie the leader to the cane
to encourage vertical growth. Once
established, remove the cane.

Cutting Back Uncharacteristic Growth

Conifers have two types of foliage: juvenile and adult. Sometimes a conifer retains its juvenile form but may produce adult shoots. If the conifer throws out a stem that is uncharacteristic, it will spoil the overall appearance of the plant. Cut back the stem to its point of origin, reaching into the heart of the plant if necessary.

Below: This Cedrus atlantica *'Glauca Pendula' has a naturally arching habit. Removing the leader has encouraged it to spread far and wide. The horizontal branches will need support as they age.*

Shaping Conifers

Though most conifers achieve a pleasing profile unaided, you can clip them, provided you do this regularly and do not cut back into old wood. In spring or summer, lightly trim the conifer with shears or secateurs (pruners).

Removing Dead Patches

Dead patches occasionally appear on conifers, sometimes as the result of drought or very cold winds. Prune out the dead growth, cutting back to live wood. If this results in an unsightly gap, loosely tie in some of the surrounding stems to cover the gap.

New Hedges

IF THEY ARE TO PROVIDE A THICK, EVEN BARRIER, HEDGES NEED
PRUNING FROM THE VERY START. CUT THEM BACK WHEN YOU PLANT
THEM TO ENSURE THEY BRANCH NEAR TO THE BASE.

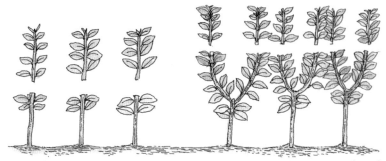

*Above: Shorten the stems on newly planted hedges by up to a half to encourage branching
close to the base (left). Once the new growth appears, shorten this as well, to make
bushier plants (right).*

GARDENER'S TIP
When buying hedging material,
young plants make sense. They are
not only very cheap, but also
establish much more quickly than
the more expensive larger ones.

---

1 Hedges are best planted in spring or
autumn. They are usually purchased
as young plants with a single straight
stem. To ensure they bush out properly, cut them back by up to one-half of
their length when you plant them.

2 The following summer, trim the new
shoots back by about a half to encourage further branching from near to the
base of the plant. This will encourage
a thick, bushy habit.

Above: Box is an excellent hedging plant.

224

Formal Hedges

CLASSIC FORMAL HEDGES GIVE STYLE AND ELEGANCE TO A GARDEN. THE SIMPLE TECHNIQUES DESCRIBED HERE WILL KEEP THEM LOOKING WELL SHAPED AND SMART.

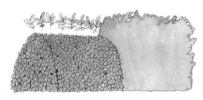

Above: Cut the sides so that they slope towards the top. A flat top is easier to clip than a curved one (top). A rounded top is attractive, but you need a good eye to keep it even (bottom).

<table>
<tr><td>

PLANTS TO TRY

Buxus sempervirens
Buxus sempervirens 'Suffruticosa'
x *Cupressocyparis leylandii*
Taxus baccata

</td></tr>
</table>

Above: A carefully clipped yew.

1 Clip established hedges twice a year, in mid-spring and midsummer. To cut the top straight, run a string between two uprights and check the level with a spirit level. Hold the shears flat and horizontal when trimming the top.

2 Shear over the surface of the hedge, holding the blades flat against the surface. Using power tools (see inset) can speed up the job considerably. Use an even, wide, sweeping motion, keeping the blade parallel to the hedge.

225

Informal Flowering Hedges

FLOWERING HEDGES NEED PRUNING AT THE RIGHT TIME IF THE FLOW-
ERS ARE NOT TO BE LOST. A CRISP OUTLINE IS NOT EXPECTED, SO
PRUNING IS AIMED MAINLY AT RESTRICTING SIZE.

Above: *Restrict pruning to shortening the
shoots that have grown since the last
prune to maintain a reasonably compact
habit. Prune early-flowering hedges
immediately after flowering and late-
flowering hedges in early spring.*

Above: *Fuchsia makes a delightful informal
hedge when it flowers in late summer.*

A hedge of rugosa roses will not need
extensive pruning like those used in
rose beds, but it is worth cutting damaged, old, tired and woody shoots
back to ground level periodically. This
will avoid congested growth occurring.

An early-flowering hedge, such as this
spiky berberis, can be lightly trimmed
immediately after flowering. Shear
back the flowered growth. The aim is
to keep the plants compact and dense
rather than to create a formal outline.

226

Rejuvenating a Neglected Hedge

IT IS SOMETIMES WORTH SALVAGING A NEGLECTED HEDGE THAT WOULD TAKE YEARS TO REPLACE, BUT CONIFER HEDGES (APART FROM YEW) WILL NOT RESPOND WELL TO THIS TECHNIQUE.

Above: Cut back all the growth on one side of the hedge to near the base of the shoots. Leave the other side uncut (left). The following year, once new growth has appeared on the cut stems, cut back the other side (right).

Above: A neglected hedge after pruning.

1 This hedge has been neglected and is a mass of tangled shoots. In winter, cut back the top of the hedge by up to 1m (3ft) below the desired height.

GARDENER'S TIP
If individual plants within the hedge do not regenerate well, dig them up and replace with young specimens.

2 Trim back all the shoots to one side of the hedge, using loppers or a pruning saw, if necessary.

3 Lightly trim new growth that arises from the cut stems once it has reached about 15cm (6in) in length to encourage bushiness. Tackle the other side of the hedge the following year.

227

Dwarf Bush Apple

FOR A SMALL GARDEN, A DWARF BUSH IS USUALLY THE MOST POPULAR OPTION. THIS GIVES YOU A TREE WITH BRANCHES CLOSE TO GROUND LEVEL, MAKING IT EASY TO HARVEST AND PRUNE.

Left: *Cut out completely any badly placed or crossing branches close to the point of origin. Then shorten all side shoots to leave a couple of buds on each.*

Below: *A well-pruned bush apple.*

> **GARDENER'S TIP**
> It is best to buy a tree ready trained that has been grafted onto a dwarfing rootstock.

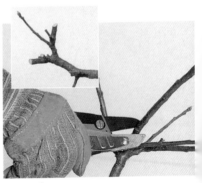

1 Young trees may not need pruning. Only prune if they begin to look congested or bear less fruit. In winter, when the tree is dormant, remove any congested or crossing branches to keep the centre of the bush open.

2 Cut the previous year's growth by two-thirds. On mature specimens, you can cut some back harder to within one or two buds. Shorten any side shoots on the pruned branches to leave just a couple of buds (see inset).

228

Espalier Apple

COMPACT ESPALIER APPLES ARE PRACTICAL IN CONFINED SPACES AND
CAN BE TRAINED ON HORIZONTAL WIRES AGAINST WALLS OR FENCES.
THEY CAN BE BOUGHT READY TRAINED.

Above: Espalier apples need pruning
towards the end of the growing season to
control their shape. Cut back side shoots
from the main stems to about three leaves
above the basal cluster. Side shoots growing from shoots pruned the previous year
can be cut back to just one leaf.

Above: A productive espalier apple.

1 Once the main stem has reached the
desired height, cut it back to a bud
just above the top wire. Growth is
directed into the horizontal branches.

2 In summer, cut shoots from the main
branches that are over 23cm (9in) to
three leaves above the basal cluster.

3 In winter, when the tree is dormant,
cut back any shoots that have grown
since the summer prune to about 5cm
(2in), to develop a system of short
spurs (see inset). Shorten all other long
shoots to buds close to the main stem,
cutting back to one or two buds.
These will bear the next crop of fruit.

Cordon Apple

ANGLED CORDONS ALLOW YOU TO GROW A NUMBER OF DIFFERENT
VARIETIES IN A LIMITED SPACE, BUT REGULAR PRUNING IS ESSENTIAL
TO STOP THEM OVERLAPPING EACH OTHER.

GARDENER'S TIP
Prune cordon pears in the
same way as apples.

Above: *Prune cordons in summer by
cutting the current season's growth back
to two or three leaves above the basal
cluster of leaves (and side shoots on these
back to one leaf).*

Right: *Cordons are economic with space.*

1 Between late spring and midsummer, prune back the main stem if it has outgrown its allotted space, to within 1–2.5cm (½–1in) of the old wood. Repeat annually with any new leaders that form to prevent leggy growth.

2 In mid- to late summer, shorten side shoots from the main stem that are over 23cm (9in) long, so that only three leaves remain above the basal cluster. Cordons can also be pruned in winter in the same way as espaliers.

Raspberries

PRUNING RASPBERRIES DEPENDS ON WHETHER THEY FRUIT ON SHOOTS PRODUCED THE PREVIOUS YEAR (SUMMER-FRUITING) OR IN THE CURRENT YEAR (AUTUMN-FRUITING).

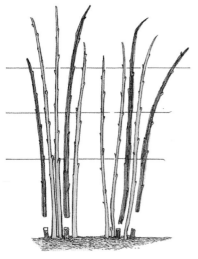

> **PLANTS TO TRY**
> Summer-fruiting raspberries:
> 'Glen Coe'
> 'Glen Moy'
> 'Leo'
> 'Malling Admiral'
> 'Malling Delight'
> 'Malling Jewel'
> 'Malling Promise'
> Autumn-fruiting raspberries:
> 'Autumn Bliss'
> 'Heritage'
> 'September'
> 'Zeva Herbsternte'

Above: *On summer-fruiters, cut out the shoots that fruited the previous summer and tie in the new canes to replace them.*

SUMMER-FRUITING VARIETIES

1 In spring, prune back the old canes, which are darker than the new ones, cutting right back to the base.

2 Tie the new canes to the support. If the clump is very congested, thin the new canes to 7.5cm (3in) apart.

AUTUMN-FRUITING VARIETIES

When dormant in winter, cut all the stems back to just above soil level.

Right: *The autumn-fruiting 'Zeva Herbsternte'.*

Gooseberries

THESE FRUITING PLANTS ARE USUALLY GROWN ON A SHORT LEG OR AS
BUSHES. THE MAIN PRUNING IS IN WINTER, BUT YOU CAN THIN THE
GROWTH IN SUMMER TO KEEP THE BUSHES OPEN.

Above: Shorten the summer's growth at the ends of the main stems by between one-third and a half, then shorten side shoots growing from the main stems to two buds.

Right: A gooseberry bush after pruning.

1 Gooseberries are thorny plants. Wearing gloves, reduce last season's growth at the end of each main shoot by between one-third and a half. You should also cut out any low, weak, badly placed or crossing branches.

2 Shorten side shoots arising from the main stems, cutting them back to two buds from the old wood. This makes the plant less congested. After fruiting, thin the new growth to improve air circulation and prevent mildew.

Black, Red & White Currants

PROLIFIC BLACKCURRANTS FRUIT BEST ON YEAR-OLD BRANCHES. RED AND WHITE CURRANTS FRUIT ON SHOOTS THAT ARE AT LEAST TWO YEARS OLD. ALL ARE PRUNED IN WINTER.

Below: White currants ready for picking.

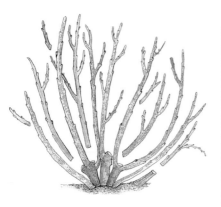

Above: On blackcurrants, cut out some of the oldest wood each year, close to the base where there is a younger shoot to replace it. Also prune any damaged or badly placed branches.

2 For red and white currants, remove one old stem only, pruning just above a bud near ground level.

1 For blackcurrants, remove branches that are too low or growing inwards. Cut back some of the oldest branches (usually the thickest and darkest) close to the base. Aim to remove one-third.

3 Shorten the wood produced the previous summer by half its length. Trim back overlong branches, cutting back to a replacement side shoot.

233

Blackberries & Hybrid Berries

THESE BERRIES (INCLUDING TAYBERRIES AND LOGANBERRIES) ARE
EASY TO PRUNE, SINCE MOST FRUIT ON YEAR-OLD CANES.

*Left: In winter or early spring, cut back
the older shoots that have previously
fruited. Tie in the greener shoots made
the previous summer.*

Below: Ripening blackberries.

PLANTS TO TRY

Blackberries:
'Bedford Giant'
'Himalaya Giant'
'John Innes'
'Smoothstem'
'No Thorn'

Hybrid berries:
Boysenberry
Loganberry
Sunberry
Tayberry
Veitchberry

1 Prune out the darker, fruited canes,
which grew the previous year, cutting
as close to the ground as possible.

2 Untie the one-year-old canes that
have yet to fruit and reposition them
in an evenly spaced fan shape. Tie in
new shoots as they grow.

Blueberries

THESE ARE SLOW-GROWING PLANTS THAT FRUIT ON BRANCHES TWO TO THREE YEARS OLD. START PRUNING THEM LIGHTLY WHEN THEY ARE THREE OR FOUR YEARS OLD.

Above: On established plants, prune out older, unproductive wood in spring, cutting back to a vigorous side shoot.

Above: Blueberries when ripe have a whitish bloom which is safe to eat. It is better not to wash berries before eating them.

1 Cut back any unproductive shoots, either to a strong replacement shoot or to the ground. Do not remove more than one-quarter of the branches.

2 Remove any weak, spindly growth.

PLANTS TO TRY
'Berkeley'
'Bluecrop'
'Bluetta'
'Coville'
'Darrow'
'Earliblue'
'Goldtraube'
'Herbert'
'Ivanhoe'
'Jersey'
'Patriot'

235

Pruning Methods & Timing

Name of plant	Type of pruning	Time to prune
Abeliophyllum	no routine pruning	
Abutilon	shorten side shoots	summer
Actinidia	as for ornamental vines Winter	
Akebia	no routine pruning	
Artemisia	cut back hard, if necessary	early spring
Aucuba	clip to shape	spring, summer
Berberis	one-third method	winter (deciduous); spring (evergreen)
Brachyglottis	prune to a framework	early spring
Buddleja	prune to a framework	early spring
Buxus	clip to shape	spring, summer
Callicarpa	no routine pruning	
Calluna	deadhead with shears	after flowering
Camellia	no routine pruning	
Campsis	no routine pruning	
Carpenteria	one-third method	early spring
Caryopteris	prune to a framework	early spring
Catalpa bignioides	coppicing	early spring
Ceanothus, deciduous	trim previous year's shoots	spring
Ceanothus, evergreen	shorten side shoots	after flowering
Ceratostigma	prune to a framework	early spring
Cestrum parqui	prune to the base	early spring
Chaenomeles, wall-trained	trim previous year's shoots	after flowering
Chimonanthus	one-third method	spring
Choisya	no routine pruning	

Berberis

Erica

Cistus	shorten side shoots	after flowering
Clematis	see clematis section	
Clerodendrum	no routine pruning	
Clethra	no routine pruning	
Colutea	one-third method	early spring
Convolvulus	shorten side shoots	late summer
Cornus alba (most cvs)	one-third method	mid-spring
C. alba 'Sibirica'	prune hard	early spring
C. controversa, C. florida	no routine pruning	
C. kousa	no routine pruning	
C. stolonifera 'Flaviramea'	prune hard	early spring
Corylopsis	no routine pruning	
Corylus	one-third method	spring
Cotinus	one-third method	spring
Cotoneaster	one-third method	winter (deciduous); spring (evergreen)
Cytisus	shorten new growth	after flowering
Daboecia	deadhead with shears	after flowering
Daphne	no routine pruning	
Deutzia	one-third method	after flowering
Elaeagnus	no routine pruning	
Enkianthus	no routine pruning	
Erica	deadhead with shears	after flowering
Escallonia	one-third method	late spring
Eucalyptus	prune to a framework	early spring
Euonymus	no routine pruning	
Fallopia	one-third method	spring
Fatsia	no routine pruning	
Forsythia	one-third method	after flowering
Fothergilla	no routine pruning	
Fremontodendron	shorten side shoots	spring
Fruits	see individual sections	
Fuchsia, hardy	prune to the base	early spring
Garrya	one-third method	spring
Gaultheria	one-third method	spring
Genista	shorten new growth	late summer
Griselinia	no routine pruning	
x *Halimiocistus*	shorten side shoots	late summer
Hebe	no routine pruning	
Hedera	clip to shape	summer
Helianthemum	shorten new shoots	after flowering
Helichrysum	cut back close to old wood	early spring
Hibiscus	prune out old wood	early spring
Hippophae	one-third method	spring

Hydrangea macrophylla	cut back thin shoots;	
	shorten flowered stem	spring
H. paniculata	prune back to a framework	early spring
H. petiolaris	no routine pruning	
Hypericum	one-third method	spring
Ilex	clip to shape	spring, summer
Indigofera	cut back to a framework	late summer
Jasminum nudiflorum	one-third method	after flowering
J. officinale	thin, as necessary	after flowering
Kalmia	one-third method	after flowering
Kerria	one-third method	early summer
Kolkwitzia	one-third method	after flowering
Laurus	clip to shape	spring, summer
Lavandula	trim previous year's growth	early to mid-spring
Lavatera	prune to a framework	spring
Leycesteria	one-third method	after flowering
Ligustrum	clip to shape	spring, summer
Lonicera, climbing	thin tangled stems	after flowering
Lonicera, shrubby	no routine pruning	
L. nitida	clip to shape	spring, summer
Mahonia, bushy	one-third method	early summer
Mahonia, groundcover	cut to 15–30cm (6–12in)	spring, alternate years
	above ground level	
Mahonia, tall	shorten flowered stems	after flowering
Olearia	one-third method	after flowering
Osmanthus	no routine pruning	
Paeonia	cut out dead wood	early summer
Parthenocissus	as for vines	winter
Passiflora	thin tangled stems	spring
Paulownia	no pruning necessary,	early spring
	but can be cut back to	
	a framework	
Perovskia	prune to the base	early spring

Convolvulus

Fuchsia

Philadelphus	one-third method	after flowering
Phlomis	cut back side shoots	spring
Phormium	remove dead leaves	late spring
Potentilla	one-third method	after flowering
Pyracantha, wall trained	shorten side shoots	midsummer
Ribes	one-third method	after flowering
Robinia pseudoacacia	pollarding	late winter
Rosa	see rose section	
Rosmarinus	clip to shape	spring, summer
Rubus (most)	one-third method	midsummer
R. cockburnianus,		
R. thibetanus	cut back to ground level	early spring
Ruta	trim previous year's growth	spring
Salix	no pruning necessary, but	
	some can be cut back hard	
Sambucus	one-third method,	mid-spring
	or cut back to a framework	early spring
Santolina	trim previous year's growth	mid-spring
Skimmia	no routine pruning	
Sorbaria	one-third method	late winter to mid-spring
Spiraea, spring-flowering	one-third method	after flowering
Spiraea, summer-flowering	trim previous year's growth	mid-spring
Symphoricarpos	one-third method	midsummer
Syringa	remove a quarter of the	
	oldest stems	winter
Tamarix	no routine pruning	
Tilia	pollarding	late winter
Ulex	clip to shape	early summer
Viburnum	no routine pruning	
Vinca	shear back to near ground level	early spring
Vitis	shorten to stubs	winter
Weigela	one-third method	midsummer
Wisteria	cut back new growth	after flowering

Syringa

Peony

SEASONAL TASKS

Keeping up with the gardening year is essential if you want to get the most out of your garden; running a few weeks behind in some cases could mean missing a whole season's results. To help you keep on track, this chapter divides the year into 12 time frames; refer to it regularly to see what you should be doing and when.

Jobs for Each Season

KEEPING A GARDEN LOOKING GOOD ALL YEAR ROUND SHOULD NEVER BECOME A BURDEN. SPREADING ESSENTIAL TASKS THROUGHOUT THE SEASONS, SO THAT THE GARDEN IS ALWAYS UNDER CONTROL, WILL ENSURE THAT IT REMAINS A PLEASURE EVEN AT THE BUSIEST TIMES.

Good gardeners are always thinking about the future, and forward planning is important if the garden is always to look its best. However, with the busy lives that most of us lead these days, it is easy to overlook some of the simple gardening tasks that will save time in the long run – hence the value of a mini season-by-season guide to gardening activities.

No gardening calendar can ever be followed rigidly, of course, because not only does the climate vary from one place to another, but the weather is never the same two years running. In one year a bumper crop of slugs will wreak havoc on your young plants, but in another you may hardly be troubled by them; and disease attacks vary considerably from year to year, also largely depending on the weather. Fruit crops may be delayed to early or mid-autumn by late spring frosts or may be ready for harvesting in late summer. Nevertheless, even given the vagaries of the weather, it is

Above: *Successional sowing of vegetables in spring will ensure that your kitchen garden plots are well filled and productive all summer long.*

242

possible to list the main tasks in the general order in which they should be done so that you can complete them when you have time and when the weather permits you to get into the garden to carry them out.

WORKING WITH THE SEASONS

Fortunately, many plants are forgiving and allow you a certain amount of leeway if certain tasks are mis-timed. A mild, damp winter, for example, might mean that your roses burst into growth, persuading you that they need pruning early. If a sudden cold spell kills off the resulting new growth, you can simply prune them again and reconcile yourself to the fact that flowering may be a bit later than usual. The plants don't seem to mind.

It's a good idea to make staggered sowings of vegetables or summer bedding plants, so that you always have reserve stock should any early sowings fail. If you do not have a greenhouse, you can make use of your kitchen windowsill to start seeds into growth several weeks earlier than if you wait to sow them outdoors.

HOW TO USE THIS CHAPTER

This chapter is organized by season, with each season further subdivided into early, mid and late to coincide broadly with the months of the year. Within each mini-season, tasks for the ornamental garden, kitchen garden

Above: Give a summer hanging basket a head-start by planting it in spring and keeping it in a greenhouse until there is no more fear of late frosts.

and greenhouse or conservatory are described, with handy, at-a-glance checklists of the main jobs to be done. The more important tasks are dealt with in greater depth, with pictures showing the correct techniques.

Below: A good crop of apples is largely dependent on the weather.

Early Spring

THE BEGINNING OF THE NATURAL YEAR IS AN EXCITING TIME IN THE GARDEN, EVEN IF WINTER CANNOT YET BE ENTIRELY FORGOTTEN. MANY PLANTS ARE BEGINNING TO WAKE UP FROM THEIR WINTER DORMANCY AND TO PUT OUT FRESH GREEN SHOOTS.

THE ORNAMENTAL GARDEN

Despite the cold, early spring is a good time to make a start on many outdoor jobs. The soil is starting to warm up and spring rains will help plants establish well and get off to a good start.

Planting

As long as the soil is not waterlogged or frozen, early spring is one of the best times to plant new shrubs and

Above: A welcome sight in early spring, Muscari armeniacum *'Blue Spike' forms clumps that can be divided in summer.*

perennials. Prepare the ground first, digging over the whole area thoroughly and removing any perennial weeds, such as couch grass and bindweed. Fork in plenty of well-rotted garden compost or farmyard manure and add a handful of a slow-release granular fertilizer or some bonemeal. Dig a hole twice the width of the plant's container, slide the plant out of the pot, carefully tease out its roots and set it in the centre of the hole. Backfill with the excavated soil, firming it in well, and water thoroughly.

Sowing Hardy Annuals

Hardy annual seeds, such as hawksbeard (*Crepis rubra*), poached-egg plant (*Limnanthes douglasii*) and love-in-a-mist (*Nigella damsascena*), can be sown where the plants are to flower. Weed the ground and rake it level, then sow the seeds in rows (which makes weeding easier) or by sprinkling (broadcasting) it over the ground. Cover the seed lightly and water in dry weather. When the seedlings are large enough to handle, thin them to the distances recommended on the seed packets.

Laying Turf

Early spring is a good time to make a new lawn, either by sowing grass seed or by laying turf. Although turf is the more expensive option, it does provide an instant result. However, after a few years you will not be able to tell the difference between a seed-raised lawn and bought-in turfs.

2 Place a plank on top of the first strip of turf and stand on this when positioning subsequent rows, moving it as necessary. Place the second row of turfs tight against the first, but stagger any joints between the strips like the bonds in brickwork.

1 Mark out the area of the new lawn. Dig over the area, removing any large stones and all traces of perennial weeds. Taking very small steps, tread over the area to consolidate the soil, then rake the surface level. Lay the first strip of turf along a straight edge.

3 Tamp down each row of turf using the back of a rake. Trim the edges, after the turf is laid, using a half-moon edger. In dry weather, water the new lawn frequently until it is established.

THE KITCHEN GARDEN

Now is your best opportunity to improve the soil in the kitchen garden, which can become impoverished over time. To improve its structure and moisture-retentiveness, dig in plenty of organic matter such as well-rotted farmyard manure or garden compost. A general fertilizer such as bonemeal, or a granular fertilizer, will break down gradually as the crops grow. Use organic or chemical formulations as you wish, but follow the quantities recommended by the manufacturer.

Above: Space onion sets about 15cm (6in) apart and cover with soil, leaving just the tips of the bulbs protruding.

This is also a good time to plant onion sets in a shallow drill, made with the corner of a hoe or rake. If birds disturb the sets, simply push them back into the ground.

Keeping Seedlings Warm

Sowing seed can be a gamble, because a sudden cold snap can cause vulnerable seedlings to rot or run to seed, but if you cannot wait to get busy, cover the seeds with horticultural fleece, which is a virtually foolproof way of ensuring a good crop. It will warm up the soil as well as providing protection from frost and pests. It allows light and moisture through to keep plants growing but will not squash them.

Perforated plastic film is an alternative to fleece. A cloche – a sheet of film stretched over wire supports – can be used to protect larger seedlings.

Above: With careful planning, even a small border can accommodate both ornamental plants and vegetables.

THINGS TO DO
IN THE KITCHEN GARDEN

Apply fertilizers
Warm up the soil with cloches or fleece
Plant new strawberries
Chit seed potatoes
Plant onion sets or shallots
Sow vegetable seeds (in mild areas only)

The Greenhouse

You can steal a march on other gardeners by raising new plants from seed under glass before the weather has really warmed up. Even if your greenhouse is not heated, the extra shelter will make it possible for you to sow the seed of half-hardy annuals and tender vegetables, which can be potted up as they germinate. Don't forget, however, that a bright windowsill can be just as useful.

Using a Propagator

You can speed up the germination of early sowings using a propagator. A heated propagator will give you even more options, especially if it is thermostatically controlled.

1 Use different containers for different seeds. Square or oblong seed trays that fit snugly into the propagator make the most economical use of the space. The modules on the right are useful for small seedlings, or for seeds that are large enough to sow individually.

> ### THINGS TO DO IN THE GREENHOUSE
> Start begonias and gloxinias into growth
> Pot on cuttings of
> pelargoniums and fuchsias
> Prick out tender seedlings
> Ventilate the greenhouse on warm days

2 An unheated propagator should be placed in a warm position in the greenhouse. Adjust the ventilation as soon as the seeds have germinated.

Keeping Hippeastrums

If you have grown hippeastrum bulbs for winter flowers, instead of discarding the bulbs when the flowers are over, you can try building them up for flowering next year.

Keep the plants growing in a warm, bright spot and feed and water them regularly as long as the leaves are growing strongly. Stop watering as the leaves start to turn yellow and die back, and store the bulbs in dry potting mix until the winter. Flowering cannot be guaranteed, but it is worth the attempt.

Starting off Begonias

Tuberous begonias can be started into growth now. Set the tubers on the surface of the potting mix, in either individual pots or trays. Look for emerging shoots or place the concave surface of each tuber uppermost. Keep them in a warm, light place and water as the shoots develop.

Mid-spring

THE GARDEN WILL BEGIN TO FILL WITH COLOUR AS THE WEATHER
WARMS UP AND THE DAYS LENGTHEN. MID-SPRING IS THE BEST TIME
FOR MOVING AND DIVIDING PLANTS AND FOR SOWING SEEDS IN
READINESS FOR THE JOYS OF SUMMER DISPLAYS TO COME.

THE ORNAMENTAL GARDEN

As the sap rises with the warmer
weather, work in the garden can begin
in earnest. This is a great time for
pruning shrubs, either to revive
neglected specimens or to keep vigorous species within bounds. You also
need to plan for the big events of
summer in the herbaceous border by
setting stakes and ties in position.

Pruning Bush Roses

The old, rather rigorous rules for rose
pruning have been reappraised and
relaxed in recent years, but some long-

*Above: This old rose needs little more
than a general tidy up. Old wood should
be cut out completely.*

established principles remain. Cut out
any damaged and diseased wood completely, then assess the rest of the
bush. Spindly shoots are unlikely to
bear flowers, so cut them back hard to
stimulate stronger growth. Shoots that
are already growing strongly need cutting back only lightly, if at all. If the
centre of the bush is overcrowded,
with lots of crossing branches, thin
these out. Feed the rose with a special
rose fertilizer and water it in, then
apply a generous mulch of well-rotted
organic matter.

Supporting Summer Climbers

Climbing plants, such as sweet peas
(*Lathyrus odoratus*), look sensational
rising above smaller plants in summer
borders. Although you can buy ready-
made obelisks and tripods, it is easy to
make your own using bamboo canes,

THINGS TO DO
IN THE ORNAMENTAL GARDEN

Plant aquatic plants
Sow sweet peas and other annuals
Stake border plants
Take softwood cuttings
Prune early-flowering shrubs
Trim winter-flowering heathers

Above: *Make a support for sweet peas by driving bamboo canes into the soil in a circle. Bind at the top with wire or string.*

Above: *Plants with large flowers, such as Paeonia lactiflora 'Bowl of Beauty', will benefit from staking.*

held together at the top with garden twine. You can also buy special plastic grips, which are designed to hold the canes securely at the top. Put one plant at the base of each cane.

Staking Plants

Some border plants that have large, heavy flowers, such as peonies and delphiniums, need staking if the weight of the flower is not to bring the stem crashing down. Stakes should be set in position before the stems grow too tall, so that new growth can be fastened to the supports as it develops.

There are a number of ways of supporting plants, depending on their habit. In an informal, cottage garden border, twigs can be pushed into the ground around the plants; they will soon be hidden by the leafy growth.

Bamboo canes are best for tall, single-stemmed plants like delphiniums, but shorter, clump-forming plants, such as some peonies, can be effectively supported with a ring stake, which can be raised as the stems grow.

Above: *Set up proprietary supports early so that herbaceous plants can grow up through the framework.*

The Kitchen Garden

Although the weather is still unpredictable, the soil should be warming up sufficiently for you to consider planting out seedlings of cabbages, broccoli and cauliflower when they have been hardened off. You should also make further sowings of onion sets and shallots to give a longer cropping season.

Remember, however, that late frosts can kill tender young shoots, so be prepared to cover vulnerable plants with horticultural fleece, cloches or even sheets of newspaper if frosty weather is forecast.

Protecting Blossom

A spell of warm spring weather will encourage fruit trees to produce blossom, but an air frost at this time can do untold harm. This occurs when the temperature of the air about 1.2m (4ft) above ground level falls below freezing point at night, freezing the moisture in the blossom and in other tender shoots. When the temperature rises in the morning, the cell walls of the plant tissue often burst, damaging the blossom so that it never sets fruit. Pears are particularly badly affected by this problem, as they tend to flower early.

**THINGS TO DO
IN THE VEGETABLE GARDEN**
Sow maincrop vegetables
Plant potatoes
Transplant cabbages and cauliflowers
Apply a mulch of well-rotted compost to
fruit bushes
Protect early strawberries
Protect blossom on fruit trees

Above: Sowing vegetables in rows makes subsequent weeding of the plot easier, as it allows annual weeds to be quickly removed with a hoe.

Wall-trained fruit trees can be protected most easily by draping sheets of plastic or even fine netting over a framework. Free-standing standard trees are more difficult to protect, although horticultural fleece can be used. If you use plastic sheeting, make sure it is held above the plant and cannot touch the young shoots, which might otherwise rot. Remove the protection during the day so that insects can pollinate the blossom.

PLANTING POTATOES

You will get the best results if you chit the potatoes before planting. Chitted potatoes get off to a quicker start than unchitted tubers, and this is a useful method of staggering crops. Chitted tubers are those that have begun to sprout, and to encourage this you should place the tubers in a light, frost-free position – a windowsill indoors is ideal.

Potatoes can be planted through a heavy-duty black plastic sheet, which saves the trouble of having to earth (hill) them up. Cultivate the soil, then cover the area with the sheet, holding it down around the edges with soil. Cut X-shaped slits in the sheet at regular intervals and plant the tubers through these.

If you prefer to plant your potatoes in the traditional way, cover the soil with a cloche for a week or two before planting to warm it up.

1 In prepared soil, make broad drills 10–13cm (4–5in) deep and 50–75cm (20–30in) apart, using a draw hoe.

2 Space the tubers 30–45cm (12–18in) apart in the drill, making sure that the buds (eyes) or shoots face upward.

3 Cover the tubers with the excavated soil or use a sheet of heavy-duty black plastic, held down in the soil.

> **GARDENER'S TIP**
> If you want larger potatoes, once you have chitted the tubers rub off all but three of the shoots before planting.

Mid-spring

THE GREENHOUSE

This is the time of year when most gardeners wish they had a larger greenhouse. Not only are all the seedlings from earlier sowings now ready to be pricked out or potted up, but tender vegetables, including outdoor tomatoes and runner beans, can be sown under glass now.

PLANTING A HANGING BASKET

Hanging baskets are associated with high summer and are planted up in late spring, usually at the time when it is safe to put tender plants outdoors. However, if you have a greenhouse or conservatory that provides protection from frost, or, better still, one that is heated, you can get your baskets off to a flying start now and have a mature display earlier in the season.

Above: The trailing habit of the tender fuchsia 'Dark Eyes' makes it an ideal subject for a hanging basket.

1 Rest the basket in a bucket or large pot to keep it steady and line it with moss or a hanging basket liner. Half-fill with a suitable potting mix.

2 Set trailing plants around the sides of the basket. Add more potting mix to cover the rootballs.

3 Place larger plants in the centre, fill any gaps with potting mix and water well. Hang in a light, sheltered place.

> **GARDENER'S TIP**
> Use water-retaining crystals in hanging baskets to reduce the likelihood of the contents drying out in summer.

Sowing Tender Vegetables

For early crops of tender vegetables, such as marrows, courgettes (zucchini) and outdoor cucumbers, sow now in small pots, filled with seed potting mix to within about 2.5cm (1in) of the rim. Water the potting mix and allow it to drain before sowing the seed, which should be lightly covered with sieved potting mix. Keep in a warm, light place until the seeds germinate, then grow them on under cover until

Above: Courgette (zucchini) plants germinated in the greenhouse need to be hardened off in a cold frame before they can be planted outside.

all risk of frost has passed. Transfer them to a cold frame to acclimatize before planting them out in their final positions in the garden.

Above: Sow two or three seeds of outdoor cucumbers in each pot, setting them on edge, and lightly cover with potting mix.

**THINGS TO DO
IN THE GREENHOUSE**

Sow tender vegetables
Prick out or pot up seedlings
Take leaf cuttings of flowering houseplants, such as *Saintpaulia* and *Streptocarpus*
Decrease the water given to cyclamen
Take cuttings of tender perennials
Check for vine weevil grubs when repotting plants

253

Late Spring

THIS IS MANY PEOPLE'S FAVOURITE SEASON IN THE GARDEN, WHEN
PLANTS ARE GROWING STRONGLY BUT WITH ALL THE FRESHNESS OF
YOUTH STILL UPON THEM. YOU SHOULD STILL BE ALERT FOR LATE
FROSTS AND GIVE ANY FROST-PRONE PLANTS ADEQUATE PROTECTION.

THE ORNAMENTAL GARDEN

Unseasonal weather, in the form of
late frosts or extremely wet or windy
weather, can still cause problems, so
keep an eye on forecasts and be ready
to protect vulnerable plants. After
especially strong winds, check that all
newly planted shrubs and perennials
are still firmly bedded into the soil and
have not been affected by wind rock.

Bedding Plants

Half-hardy annuals that you have
raised under glass can now be hardened off – that is, acclimatized to outdoor conditions. Place them outdoors
in a spot that is sheltered from strong

*Above: Many gardeners regard waterlilies,
such as this Nymphaea 'Attraction', as the
most desirable of all water plants.*

sun and wind for increasingly longer
periods during the day. Move them
back under cover at night, either
indoors or into a cold frame. They can
be planted out in their final positions
once all danger of frost has passed.

THINGS TO DO
IN THE ORNAMENTAL GARDEN

Plant hanging baskets
Harden off bedding plants
Clip evergreen hedges
Prune *Clematis montana* after flowering,
if necessary
Deadhead flowered bulbs

254

PLANTING A WATERLILY

This is the best time of year to plant waterlilies, which should now be producing signs of fresh growth. Waterlilies should be planted as soon as possible after purchase to ensure that the rhizomes do not dry out. Plant them in baskets specially designed for aquatic plants; those with a fine mesh do not need lining, but open-sided baskets should be lined with coarse hessian (burlap).

1 If necessary, line the aquatic planting basket and half-fill with garden soil or specially formulated potting mix. Place the waterlily rhizome on top and cover with more soil, leaving the buds exposed.

2 Place a layer of stones or gravel on top so that soil does not float out of the basket. Hold under the surface of the pool to flood it with water, then lower it to the appropriate depth, depending on the variety of waterlily. Support it on bricks if necessary.

Above: If necessary, prune the vigorous Clematis montana *'Elizabeth' when it has finished flowering.*

Hedges

Evergreen hedges should be given their first trim about now. To make sure the top is level, run a string between two uprights as a guide. If you are using power tools (possibly on loan from a hire shop), make sure you follow any safety advice and remember to wear gloves, goggles and ear protectors.

Above: As well as clipping hedges, now is the time to neaten up topiary specimens, such as this spiral bay (Laurus nobilis).

255

THE KITCHEN GARDEN

When you are planting out in the kitchen garden, remember that successional sowing and planting will reduce gluts and give you a continuous supply of vegetables and fruit over a longer period.

Intercropping

One of the best ways of making good use of every available scrap of ground is to grow some quick-growing plants, such as cut-and-come-again lettuces or radishes, in the spaces between larger, slower-growing plants, such as Brussels sprouts and parsnips. Not only will this give you two crops in the space of one, but it will also help to keep down weeds by covering what would otherwise be bare soil. Do not overcrowd plants, however, or they will compete with each other for available light, air and nutrients, and all the crops will suffer.

Although combining a variety of different plants in your vegetable plot can minimize the incidence of pests and diseases, there are some crops that should not be grown close together. Onions and garlic, for example, do not grow well alongside beans and peas, and potatoes should not be combined with cucumbers, marrows and courgettes (zucchini).

There are also some herbs that can be invasive. Mint is the most notorious but you might also consider growing tansy *(Tanacetum vulgare)* and woodruff *(Asperula odorata* syn. *Galium odoratum)* in pots too.

*Above: Mints, including the variegated applemint (*Mentha suaveolens *'Variegata'), are vigorous plants that can be divided now. Restricting the roots by growing them in containers or a separate bed will stop them becoming too invasive.*

THINGS TO DO
IN THE KITCHEN GARDEN
Sow sweetcorn (corn)
Sow root crops such as beetroot (beets),
carrots and parsnips
Plant outdoor tomatoes
Plant runner (green) and pole beans
Lift and divide mint
Hoe around vegetables to keep
weeds down

PLANTING RUNNER BEANS

Runner (green) beans are twining climbers that need support, and a wigwam of canes works well in a small space. In warm areas, simply plant a seed at the base of each cane. In cold districts, it is better to raise seed-lings under cover and delay planting out until the threat of frosts has gone.

1 Crossing pairs of canes in rows is a good method of supporting beans if your plot is rectangular.

2 Plant one bean plant at the base of each support and water in well. As they grow, twine the stems around the canes.

Growing Outdoor Tomatoes

Many gardeners find outdoor tomatoes an easier proposition than indoor ones, because they need less maintenance, although the crops will be smaller and the season is shorter. The plants must still be raised from seed under cover. If you don't want to sow seed, you can usually buy small plants for growing on from garden centres. Harden them off first, before planting them out in containers or growing bags. Wait until all risk of frost has passed before planting them out.

Above: *Outdoor tomatoes are often tastier than those grown under glass, particularly if the summer has been hot and the fruit is able to ripen well.*

THE GREENHOUSE

It is not too late to sow tomatoes, marrows, melons, ridge cucumbers, courgettes (zucchini), pumpkins, sweetcorn (corn) and half-hardy annuals.

On warm, sunny days make sure that the greenhouse is well ventilated. Humid, still air will encourage fungal diseases, and seedlings will die. A common problem in a poorly ventilated, overcrowded greenhouse is damping off, a disease that causes seedlings to collapse at soil level. Use sterile pots and new potting mix for seeds and do not overwater. If you do not mind using chemicals in the greenhouse, apply a fungicidal drench to the potting mix before sowing.

Above: Melons need a sturdy framework to support the growing plants. Nets slung above the containers hold the fruit.

GROWING INDOOR TOMATOES

Indoor tomatoes, either raised from seed or bought in as young plants, can now be planted. Because tomatoes cannot be grown in the same soil year after year, it is best to use growing bags or large containers. To support the growing plants (unless you are growing the bush or dwarf types), erect a cane next to each of the plants or train them on strings.

1 Cut holes in the growing bags according to the instructions on the bag. Most growing bags will accommodate three plants, but make sure that when you plant the tomatoes they are the recommended distance apart.

2 Fix a horizontal wire across the greenhouse, as high above the plants as possible. Fix a second length of wire parallel to the first but near ground level. Tie a length of string between the wires in line with each plant. Loop the string around the growing tip of each plant.

Biological Controls

The warm, humid atmosphere of a greenhouse is the perfect environment for insect pests, but increasing numbers of these can be controlled with other insects so that you do not have to use chemicals. The beneficial insects are released on to the susceptible plants in order to attack the pest.

Whitefly, spider mites, soft scale insects and thrips can be controlled by

Above: Control greenhouse pests by introducing natural predators such as parasitic wasps, effective against whitefly.

this method. Remember that once a biological control has been introduced, you should not use pesticides of any kind (or you will also kill the predators) and you should also remove any sticky traps that you put up earlier in the year.

Above: Peppers are increasingly popular as a greenhouse crop. They appreciate the extra heat and humidity that the enclosed environment provides.

Early Summer

EVERY TIME YOU STEP INTO THE GARDEN AT THIS TIME OF YEAR YOU
ARE GREETED BY A MASS OF FRESH NEW FOLIAGE AND FLOWERS. THE
KITCHEN GARDEN IS COMING INTO ITS OWN NOW, PROVIDING A FEAST
OF HOME-GROWN PRODUCE FOR THE TABLE.

THE ORNAMENTAL GARDEN

Early summer is a transitional period
in the flower garden, and there may be
a week or two between the spring-
flowering plants and bulbs dying
down and the summer bedding coming into flower. Focus attention on the
patio and create an instant display by
planting up pots and troughs that will
provide colour and interest now and
for the rest of the summer.

PLANTING A CONTAINER

By now it is safe to leave tender plants
outdoors, and because these are usually long-flowering, they make ideal
subjects for a container planting.

2 Place a feature plant in the centre of
the arrangement. An osteospermum
will carry on flowering until well into
the autumn.

3 Position other flowering plants and
trailers around the container to soften
the edge, then fill the gaps with more
potting mix. Water well.

1 Line a large container with crocks
and half-fill with potting mix.

Pruning Shrubs

Now is the time to tidy up any early-flowering shrubs, which will be putting on rapid growth. Remove all faded flowers, then cut back any damaged branches and remove the thick, old growth entirely, reaching into the base of the plant with loppers if necessary. Shorten the remaining stems to

Above: Inspect lilies, such as these Asiatic hybrids, for signs of the bright red lily beetle, a serious pest of lilies and fritillaries.

produce an open, well-balanced plant, cutting back thin shoots hard but trimming vigorous ones only lightly.

Above: As soon as lilacs finish flowering, deadhead them by cutting back to the first pair of leaves below the flowerhead.

**THINGS TO DO
IN THE ORNAMENTAL GARDEN**

Sow hardy annuals for late flowers
Move hanging baskets outdoors
Check lilies for signs of lily beetle
Plant containers for summer interest
Layer climbers to increase your stock
Prune early-flowering shrubs
Feed lawns
Deadhead rhododendrons

GARDENER'S TIP

Choose containers that are as large as possible. Not only will they dry out more slowly, but they will also provide the most impressive display. Move the container into position before filling it with potting mix and plants: it will be too heavy to move when it is full.

261

THE KITCHEN GARDEN

Keep an eye on newly planted-out seedlings so that you can take prompt action to prevent pests and diseases from building up and becoming a serious problem.

Earthing up Potatoes

An important aspect of potato growing, earthing (hilling) up protects potato tubers that are near the soil surface. If they are exposed to light, the tubers turn green and become inedible. When the green shoots are about 15cm (6in) tall, draw the soil up with a hoe on either side of the plants. Continue to do this as the potatoes grow, until the soil is mounded up to about 15cm (6in).

> **GARDENER'S TIP**
> Spray cuttings in a propagator with a fungicide to prevent mould.

> **THINGS TO DO**
> **IN THE KITCHEN GARDEN**
> Thin the fruit on gooseberry bushes
> Check gooseberry foliage for
> sawfly caterpillars
> Check strawberries for grey mould
> (botrytis)
> Feed asparagus plants after harvesting

Thinning Seedlings

Unless they are thinned now, vegetable seedlings will crowd each other out and crop poorly. The recommended distance for each crop will vary depending on the variety; check the seed packet for details. The uprooted seedlings of some crops can be used in salads.

Thin the emerging crops in stages. The first thinning should leave the plants twice as close as the final recommended spacing. Simply pull up the surplus plants with your finger and thumb and discard.

Above: Use a hoe to draw soil up around the developing potatoes without damaging the delicate root system.

Above: Thin seedlings to the distance recommended on the seed packet to give them space to develop properly.

262

THE GREENHOUSE

Summer is a time when you need to keep a watchful eye on your greenhouse and conservatory plants, which can easily overheat as the temperature rises outdoors.

If you have time and if there is space in the greenhouse, this is a good time to take softwood cuttings of shrubs from the open garden.

TAKING SOFTWOOD CUTTINGS

Softwood cuttings usually root readily, but need the warm, protected environment that glass provides. The method is suitable for many garden shrubs as well as conservatory plants.

2 Insert up to two-thirds of the stem in a pot of cuttings potting mix.

3 Place a clear plastic tent over the pot supported on canes. Keep in shade, in the warmth of a heated propagator. Softwood cuttings root in 4–6 weeks.

1 Cut a sideshoot just above a bud. Trim just below a leaf joint, and trim the tip leaving a stem 10cm (4in) long.

THINGS TO DO
IN THE GREENHOUSE

Feed and water pot plants
Use biological controls to eliminate pests
Divide congested pot plants

SHRUBS TO INCREASE BY
SOFTWOOD CUTTINGS

Abutilon
Aloysia
Cotoneaster
Cytisus
Daphne
Fuchsia
Hydrangea
Philadelphus

Midsummer

FOR MOST GARDENERS THIS IS THE PEAK OF THE GARDENING YEAR, WHEN ALL YOUR EARLIER EFFORTS ARE REWARDED. THE FLOWER BORDERS ARE A RIOT OF COLOUR AND SCENT AND THE VEGETABLE PLOT IS FILLED TO OVERFLOWING WITH FRESH YOUNG CROPS.

THE ORNAMENTAL GARDEN

On the hottest days of summer you will want to sit back and relax and enjoy your garden, but there are still plenty of jobs to be done if the garden is to continue looking good.

Above: Iris *'Blue Eyed Brunette' is one of the large number of rhizomatous irises that can be divided in midsummer.*

THINGS TO DO
IN THE ORNAMENTAL GARDEN

Divide flag irises
Take semi-ripe cuttings
Plant hardy cyclamen
Prune wisteria
Watch for and treat roses
for disease
Top up ponds in hot weather
Thin oxygenating plants in ponds

PLANTING AUTUMN CROCUSES

Corms of autumn crocus (*Colchicum autumnale*) can be planted in lawns, borders or even in the light shade of a deciduous tree. They will flower after two or three months, but the leaves will not appear until the following spring.

1 For an informal look, scatter the bulbs over grass and plant them where they land.

2 Use a bulb planter to take out a plug of soil. Place a corm in the base of each hole. Remove a little soil from the bottom of the plug. Replace the plug and firm in.

Above: Autumn crocuses, such as Colchicum *'The Giant', are not in fact crocuses, but resemble the spring flowers.*

264

DIVIDING IRISES

Rhizomatous irises can be divided immediately after they have flowered.

1 Lift the clump and cut away the old, unproductive parts of the rhizome. Sections for replanting should have at least one growing point.

2 Replant the cut sections, ensuring the upper surface of the rhizome is above the surface. Trim the topgrowth into a V-shape to minimize wind rock.

PLANTS TO INCREASE BY LAYERING

Aucuba
Campsis
Chaenomeles
Clematis
Erica
Humulus
Laurus
Lonicera
Magnolia
Rhododendron
Skimmia
Solanum
Wisteria

LAYERING

Woody shrubs and climbers with flexible stems can be increased by layering. This is a reliable method because the new plant remains attached to the parent while rooting takes place, but it is not usually practicable for producing more than a couple of plants. Layers can take up to a year to root, after which they can be severed from the parent plant.

1 Bring a flexible, low-growing branch down to ground level about 15–30cm (6–12in) from the tip.

2 Dig a shallow hole where the stem meets the ground and peg the stem in place. Cover with soil. Bend the tip of the stem as near to the vertical as possible and tie loosely to a supporting cane, to encourage upright growth.

GARDENER'S TIP
Conserve water by installing water butts and mulch around plants to reduce evaporation from the soil surface.

THE KITCHEN GARDEN

This is a busy time in the kitchen garden. Plants must be watered regularly so that their growth is not checked, and weeds, which will compete for nutrients, must be removed as soon as they are noticed. If you are an organic gardener, this is a good time to apply a dilute seaweed foliar feed as a spray.

CONTROLLING WEEDS

Effective weed control is important throughout the growing season, but especially so now, when any weeds missed earlier on will be growing strongly, flowering and setting seed. Once you have got on top of the problem, use mulches to prevent weed seeds blown in from neighbouring gardens from germinating.

1 Chemical weedkillers are useful for clearing a large area quickly. Choose a still day to prevent them blowing on to neighbouring ornamental plants. Repeated applications may be necessary for tough weeds.

2 To remove deep-rooted weeds by hand, loosen the soil around the weed with a fork first. With perennial weeds, make sure you remove every piece of root, or they will regrow.

3 Covering the soil around vegetable crops with black plastic is unsightly, but it will suppress weeds.

4 A layer of bark chippings or crushed cocoa shells is easier on the eye and can be spread around plants once all the weeds have been eliminated. Any weeds that germinate in the mulch itself should be removed promptly.

**THINGS TO DO
IN THE KITCHEN GARDEN**

Pinch out tips of runner beans when
they reach the required height
Cut back foliage on
fruited strawberries
Sow autumn and winter salads
Earth (hill) up celery
Harvest onions, garlic and shallots
Water vegetables during
dry weather

THE GREENHOUSE

As the temperature rises in the greenhouse, you may need to provide shade, either in the form of purpose-made blinds or by applying a special wash to the glass. On hot, sunny days, damping down by spraying the floor and staging first thing in the morning will improve the atmosphere.

CULTIVATING INDOOR TOMATOES

As they come into flower, the tomatoes growing in the greenhouse need regular attention if they are to produce the best crop. Look out, too, for early signs of pests and diseases and deal with these promptly.

1 If you are growing tall varieties, snap off any sideshoots as soon as they appear. Do not remove sideshoots from bush varieties.

2 To ensure pollination in the greenhouse, shake the tomato plants each day or spray the flowers regularly with water to disperse the pollen.

3 Remove any yellowing leaves from the base of the plants.

4 After the plant has set between four and seven fruit trusses, stop the top of the plant by removing the growing tip. (The warmer the environment, the more trusses you can allow to ripen.)

Other Indoor Crops

Pinch out the growing tips on aubergine (eggplant) plants once they are about 30cm (12in) tall. Allow only one fruit to develop on each shoot. Count three leaves beyond the fruit then pinch out the tip of each shoot. Keep the atmosphere around the plants humid by regular misting.

Train the sideshoots of melon plants on to horizontal wires. To pollinate the flowers, transfer the pollen from the male to the female flowers using a small paintbrush. Pinch back the sideshoots to two leaves beyond each fruit that develops.

Pinch out male flowers on cucumbers to prevent pollination (which affects the flavour of the fruits). Many modern varieties have exclusively female flowers.

> **THINGS TO DO
> IN THE GREENHOUSE**
> Care for tomato plants and other crops
> under glass
> Damp down the floor on hot days
> Ventilate on hot days

Late Summer

SUMMER TRAVELS MAY MEAN THAT YOU HAVE TO BE AWAY FROM THE GARDEN WHEN IT NEEDS DAILY CARE. IT'S WORTH ASKING A NEIGHBOUR TO TAKE ON SOME OF THE LIGHTER TASKS, ESPECIALLY WATERING, AND OFFERING TO RETURN THE FAVOUR.

THE ORNAMENTAL GARDEN

This is often the hottest time of year, and you won't want to tackle a heavy workload. Above a certain temperature, plant growth stops anyway, and this year's growth on woody plants is now starting to firm up.

You need to keep a close eye on containers and hanging baskets, which can dry out all too quickly. Water them every day – twice a day if necessary – and remember that an evening watering is more economical, since the moisture will evaporate more slowly. You might also consider moving the containers to a position that is shaded at midday, to avoid leaf scorch.

Plants are rapidly forming seeds at this time, so remember to remove faded flowers promptly to keep up the flower power in containers and hanging baskets. In the open garden, however, this is a good time of year to harvest seed from any perennials and bulbs that you wish to increase. Cut off the flowerheads as soon as the seeds ripen but before they fall, and shake them into a paper bag for storage. Species are easily raised from seed (*Lilium regale* is especially rewarding) but hybrids will not come true.

Above: Grouping containers together helps to shade the pots, keeping them cooler and conserving moisture.

THINGS TO DO
IN THE ORNAMENTAL GARDEN

Collect seed from annuals and perennials
Take cuttings of tender perennials
Dig up spent annuals
Layer carnations and pinks
Remove shed leaves from roses
Prune rambling roses
Trim hedges

Above: Collect seed by shaking it off the seedhead (here of an allium) into a paper bag. Store in a cool, dry place.

The garden can easily start to look tired after a prolonged hot spell. Cutting back flopping foliage on perennial plants such as artemisias and achilleas will usually promote a flush of new leaves, restoring freshness to your borders.

Rambling Roses

By now, rambling roses will have finished flowering and there should be plenty of vigorous shoots appearing near the base. Cut out the older stems and tie in the new ones while they are still flexible, training them horizontally to promote plenty of sideshoots.

This is a time of year when ramblers often fall victim to mildew and other fungal diseases, caused by poor air circulation through the plant and dryness at the roots. Keep plants well watered, especially if they are next to a wall where the soil may be dry.

PRUNING RAMBLERS

Opening up the topgrowth by pruning can help to revive congested ramblers and prevent disease.

1 Cut old flowered stems back to near ground level, reaching in to the base of the plant with loppers if necessary.

2 Tie in new shoots close to the horizontal, for flowering next year.

> ### GARDENER'S TIP
> Stop feeding roses and other shrubs, as a rush of new, lush growth will be susceptible to frost damage.

THE KITCHEN GARDEN

Regular watering and weeding will ensure that all your fruit and vegetables produce good crops.

Watering Systems

Although they can seem expensive luxuries, automatic watering systems that deliver water to the ground rather than spraying it around indiscriminately can save time, money and effort. They are especially useful if your vegetable plot is any distance from your outdoor tap and if your water is metered.

A simple seep or drip hose, which can be laid along a row of plants, will water the ground immediately under it and supply water to the roots of nearby plants. More sophisticated systems allow you to attach T-junctions so that several rows can be watered. Attaching a water timer or even a computer to the tap will give a completely automatic system.

**THINGS TO DO
IN THE KITCHEN GARDEN**

Summer-prune fruit trees
Support heavily laden fruit tree branches
Watch for viral diseases
Lift ripening marrows, pumpkins and squashes on to straw
Pinch out tops of tomato plants

GARDENER'S TIP

Don't store damaged or thick-necked onions – use them straight away.

HARVESTING ONIONS

When the foliage on onion plants has withered, the bulbs can be lifted. Choose a warm spell of weather and allow the onions to ripen for a few days in the sun. They will harden and store better.

1 Allow the foliage to die back naturally; do not bend it over as this can lead to disease in storage.

2 Gently ease the onions out of the ground, and place them on racks until the skins are completely dry. In wet weather, bring them under cover.

3 Onions can be hung up to dry through. Store good specimens in a dry, frost-free place.

THE GREENHOUSE

As you empty plant pots and seed pans, make a point of washing them thoroughly before you store them. It is all too easy to put the used containers to one side and then to forget about them: they will be an ideal breeding ground for pests and diseases.

Bringing Cyclamen into Growth

Tender cyclamen (hybrids of *Cyclamen persicum*) that have been resting over summer can now be brought back into growth. Gently remove the tuber from its pot and rub off the old potting mix. Using fresh potting mix, pot the tuber on, so that the top is just above the potting mix surface. Put the pot in a well-lit position (but out of direct sunlight) no warmer than around 16°C (61°F). Water sparingly around the tuber, increasing the amounts as the plant comes into growth.

Above: The many unnamed hybrids of Cyclamen persicum *can be started into growth now to give a good winter display.*

PLANTING HYACINTHS FOR FORCING

Specially prepared hyacinth bulbs that will flower indoors in winter should now be appearing for sale. They will have been kept in controlled conditions that persuade the plants that winter is already well advanced. Plant them in specially formulated bulb fibre, which contains extra bark.

1 Plant the bulbs in a shallow container, close together but not touching.

2 Pack potting mix around the bulbs, leaving the tops exposed. Water gently. Keep in a cool, dark place and water just to keep the potting mix moist until the shoots are about 5cm (2in) high. Then bring them into a light position, out of direct sunlight.

THINGS TO DO
IN THE GREENHOUSE
Bring cyclamen into growth
Sow seed for flowering pot
plants, such as *Calceolaria*
and *Schizanthus*

Early Autumn

AUTUMN IS THE SEASON FOR HARVESTING FRUITS FROM THE GARDEN. THE DAYS ARE GETTING COOLER AND SHORTER NOW, AND THIS IS A TIME TO PRESS ON WITH SEVERAL IMPORTANT TASKS.

Above: The autumn display of Rosa *'Buff Beauty' is often even better than the summer one.*

THE ORNAMENTAL GARDEN

Traditionally, autumn is the time to plant hardy shrubs and trees, and conditions are usually ideal. The soil is still warm, but the days are shorter and cooler, making plants less likely to dry out. And the first frosts are still some weeks away.

THINGS TO DO
IN THE ORNAMENTAL GARDEN

Take cuttings of tender perennials
Sow hardy annuals for spring flowers
Clear summer bedding
Disbud dahlias and chrysanthemums
Lift gladioli and other tender bulbs

Planning for Spring

Good gardeners are always looking ahead, and as soon as one group of plants starts to die back, they begin to think about what is going to replace them. Spent summer bedding plants can now make way for fresh plantings in preparation for the following spring. The soil is likely to be exhausted, so once the bed is cleared work in some general fertilizer and some organic matter to improve structure.

PLANTING SPRING BEDDING

Early-flowering bedding plants such as wallflowers (*Erysimum*) and forget-me-nots (*Myosotis*) can be interplanted with bulbs such as tulips for a colourful spring display.

1 Spring bedding plants are often sold at this time of year in modules, or you may have grown your own. Space them evenly across the bed.

2 Once all the bedding plants are in, drop the bulbs among them and plant them, using a trowel, so that they are covered with twice their own depth of soil.

Lifting Gladioli

In mild areas gladioli may still be flowering in early autumn, but in colder districts you will need to lift the corms for storage over the winter before they can be nipped by the first hard frosts.

As the topgrowth starts to die back, lift the corms with a fork. Trim off most of the foliage to leave just a stub. Dry the corms off for a few days in a well-ventilated place.

Snap off the tiny new corms that you will find around the base of the main corm. You can either discard these or keep them for growing on (they will take several years to reach flowering size). Dust the large corms with fungicide and store them in paper bags in a dry, frost-free environment for re-planting next spring.

Above: *After flowering, lift gladioli corms and store in a dry, frost-free place. This is* Gladiolus *'Charming Beauty'.*

273

THE KITCHEN GARDEN

There are a number of leafy vegetables that can be sown now for winter crops. Look for lettuce varieties that have been bred for autumn sowing, and try sowing lamb's lettuce (mâche), rocket (arugula) and winter purslane as cold month crops. Spring cabbages sown now will provide spring greens early next year. Cover seedlings with a cloche if the weather turns cold.

Lifting Root Vegetables

Beetroot (beets), carrots and turnips can be lifted now for storing over winter. Only undamaged roots are suitable for storing. Twist off the leaves and pack the roots in wooden boxes filled with sand. Keep the root vegeta-

Above: Beetroot, here grown in a raised bed, is best harvested while still quite small, about seven weeks after sowing.

bles in a cool, frost-free place. Parsnips and swedes (rutabagas) should be left in the ground until after the first frosts, as this improves their flavour.

Above: Globe artichokes will be ready for harvesting in early autumn of the second year after planting. They should be eaten as soon as possible after cutting.

274

PROTECTING OUTDOOR TOMATOES

It is likely that outdoor tomatoes will still be ripening. Green fruits can be picked and ripened indoors provided they are reasonably mature, but for the best flavour it makes sense to ripen as many as possible on the plant. They will benefit from some protection, particularly if frosts are forecast. Plants trained to vertical stakes can be tented with horticultural fleece. Alternatively, the plants can be untied and rested on the ground.

2 Cover the tomatoes with a rigid plastic cloche, which will warm the air around them – thus speeding up ripening – as well as keeping off frost.

1 Untie the plants from their stakes. To avoid damaging the fruit and provide a little extra insulation, spread a layer of dry straw on the ground and gently lower the plants on to this.

3 Alternatively, cover the plants loosely with horticultural fleece. This protects against frost but will not warm up the air as a rigid cloche does.

THINGS TO DO
IN THE KITCHEN GARDEN

Protect outdoor tomatoes
against frost
Plant strawberries
Stake Brussels sprouts
Divide herbaceous herbs

GARDENER'S TIP

Sow a crop of green manure (such as mustard) to use up nutrients left in vacant ground after harvesting. It will be recycled when the crop is dug in.

THE GREENHOUSE

Before the first autumn frosts, take time to make sure that any heating system in your greenhouse is in good working order. Check that all extension leads are in good condition and take any heaters to be serviced if you are not confident of your own abilities to look after them.

Plants now need all the light they can get, so remove greenhouse blinds or shading. If you applied a shading wash earlier in the year, it can usually be rubbed off with a cloth when the glass is dry.

Sowing Hardy Annuals

If you want an early display of flowers next season, hardy annuals can be sown now for planting out next

Above: Continue to keep the greenhouse well ventilated. Even in autumn the temperature under the glass will rise sharply on a sunny day.

spring. They can also be grown on in pots to provide flowering pot plants for the conservatory. Compact forms of pot marigolds (*Calendula*) are easy and rewarding, or try cornflowers, godetias or stocks (*Matthiola*).

Protecting Early-flowering Shrubs

If you grow early-flowering shrubs, such as daphnes, skimmias or camellias, in pots, move them under cover for earlier, perfectly formed flowers. Keep them well-watered and in good light, but check that they do not scorch on the odd sunny day when the temperature can rise dramatically.

Bringing in Houseplants

Many winter- and spring-flowering houseplants, such as zygocactus, solanums grown for their winter berries and even orchids, benefit from spending the summer outdoors, but they must be brought inside before the first frost threatens. Remove any fallen leaves and debris from the soil surface and clean the pots carefully to avoid contaminating the greenhouse. Check for any signs of disease and look under the leaves for snails and other pests before bringing them in.

REPOTTING CACTI

Cacti and succulents can be repotted at any time of year, but it is often convenient to do so either in spring or autumn. Cacti benefit from a specially formulated potting mix that allows very free drainage while supplying the correct nutrients. They also demand special handling.

1 Wrap the cactus in thick paper to protect your hands from the spines. Ease it from the container.

2 Centre the plant in the new container and fill with cactus potting mix.

3 Top-dress with grit to improve drainage and to protect the collar of the plant from excess damp. Withhold water for several days to allow any damaged roots to form calluses.

**THINGS TO DO
IN THE GREENHOUSE**

Bring in houseplants that have spent
the summer outdoors
Sow seed of spring-flowering
tender perennials
Clean off summer shading washes
Pot up and pot on seedlings of pot
plants as necessary
Check greenhouse heating system

Mid-autumn

At this time of year sudden changes in the weather can affect the garden. In a balmy spell, plants will continue to grow, but a cold night will have an immediate effect.

The Ornamental Garden

If you need to lay a new lawn and did not do so in spring, consider ordering turfs or sowing seed now. The soil will still be warm enough to encourage the roots to grow strongly and there will be plenty of autumn rain.

If your established lawn is looking rather tired and bedraggled, autumn is the time for tasks such as scarifying, to remove an accumulation of clippings, and spiking, to aerate the soil. Sweep up all fallen leaves, which can damage the lawn. They should be collected to make leaf mould, a precious organic substance that can be used either as a mulch or as a general soil improver.

Pond Care

Garden ponds – especially informal and wildlife ones – generally look after themselves, but most repay a little extra attention at this time of year. There is always the danger that leaves shed by deciduous shrubs and trees, as well as other plant debris, will find their way into the water. If left there, they will rot and create poisonous gases. Either net the pond to catch any debris, or rake the surface to collect any fallen leaves.

Above: Osteospermums are not reliably hardy, but they have a long flowering season and will bloom until the first frosts. This is Osteospermum 'Lady Leitrim'.

Pruning Deciduous Shrubs

Although hard pruning should be left until spring, you can cut back whippy growth on tall deciduous shrubs, such as buddleias and some roses, to prevent wind rock. Reduce the topgrowth by up to one third.

Beds and Borders

Plants of doubtful hardiness, such as fuchsias, osteospermums, busy Lizzies and *Begonia semperflorens*, can be dug up now for storage over winter. Fuchsias should be kept dry, but the others can be kept growing in a warm, light place, where they will continue to flower for a few more weeks.

LIFTING AND STORING DAHLIAS

Dahlias are not hardy, but they should be left in the ground until a hard frost has blackened the topgrowth. The tubers can then be lifted for storage over winter.

1 When the foliage turns black, cut back the topgrowth to about 15cm (6in) above the ground and remove any stakes. Lift the tubers with a fork.

2 Carefully rub off as much soil as possible. Leave the tubers to dry off in an airy place such as a shed or unheated greenhouse. Store in paper bags in a cool but frost-free place over winter.

Planting a Root-balled Conifer

Root-balled conifers are lifted from the nursery field in autumn, and should be planted as soon as possible. Prepare a planting hole of the correct depth and width to accommodate the roots (check the depth with a cane) and remove the covering from the roots. Backfill with the excavated soil and firm in well. Keep the conifer well watered during dry spells and shelter it from winter gales, which could dry out the foliage.

Above: Place a cane across the hole to make sure that trees and shrubs are planted to their original depth.

**THINGS TO DO
IN THE ORNAMENTAL GARDEN**

Plant spring bulbs (except tulips)
Plant bare-root roses and other shrubs
Lift and store dahlias
Plant spring bedding
Divide herbaceous plants
Bring tender perennials under cover
Plant new hedging
Scarify and spike established lawns

The Kitchen Garden

Taking steps to protect your plants from frost will keep them in good condition in case it turns cold before you are ready to harvest them. The stems of vegetables such as celery and beetroot (beets) can be protected with straw. Bend the surrounding leaves over the heads of late cauliflowers. Other vulnerable vegetables can be sheltered under cloches.

Lifting and Storing Potatoes

Late potatoes are mainly grown for use during the winter, and should now be ready for harvesting and storing. Small crops can be kept indoors, but if space is at a premium, consider making a potato clamp in a sheltered spot in the garden.

2 Sort the potatoes by size, as the largest tubers are the most suitable for winter storage. The tiniest potatoes should be used immediately, otherwise they can be discarded. You should be able to sort the remainder into three groups: small, for early consumption, medium and large, for storing indoors or in a potato clamp in the garden.

1 Once the foliage has died down, lift the potatoes with a fork – they can be left longer if there is no frost. Leave on the soil surface for a few hours to harden off the outer skins.

3 Place in sacks and store them in a dark, cool, frost-free place. Paper sacks are best, but if you cannot obtain these, use plastic sacks, making slits to provide some ventilation.

THINGS TO DO
IN THE KITCHEN GARDEN
Plant spring cabbages
Earth (hill) up celery and leek plants
Lift and store potatoes
Protect vulnerable vegetables
with cloches
Pot up herbs for winter use
Harvest and store apples
Cut spent canes of summer-fruiting
raspberries to the ground
Protect late-fruiting strawberries
from frost
Apply grease bands to apple trees

4 To make a potato clamp, excavate a shallow depression in bare soil and line it with a thick layer of dry straw. Pile the potatoes on top. Heap another layer of straw over the top of the potatoes to provide good insulation. Mound the excavated earth over the straw, but leave a few tufts protruding to ensure adequate ventilation in the clamp. The tubers will be protected from all but the most severe weather.

Caring for Fruit Trees

Pick apples when they are ripe, which is usually when the fruit comes away easily with a quick twist. Store unblemished fruit in a cool, dark place, ensuring the fruits do not touch.

Clear away fallen fruit and leaves from around fruit trees. If it is left on the ground it tends to harbour pests and diseases ready to attack the trees next spring. Fasten grease bands around the trunks of fruit trees so that wingless female codling moths cannot climb up the trunks to lay eggs.

Protecting Herbs

You can keep some of your herbs, including parsley, cropping throughout the winter if you protect them from frosts with a rigid plastic cloche. Make sure the end pieces are tightly secured to keep out the cold, but remove the cloche on warm, dry days.

Above: Rigid plastic cloches are ideal for protecting herbs such as parsley throughout winter.

THE GREENHOUSE

As the weather turns damper, you need to keep a look out for fungal problems, such as grey mould (botrytis). Good ventilation should minimize the risk, but this becomes less easy as the outdoor temperature drops. Remove dead, faded or diseased-looking leaves from plants and burn them. Spray the plants with copper fungicide solution. If you decide to use fumigation to control any pests and diseases that are lingering, read the manufacturer's instructions before use because some types can be used only in completely empty greenhouses.

Above: *If you can empty the greenhouse completely, you can make sure that you rid it of all lurking pests and diseases by fumigating it.*

Below: *Good ventilation, particularly in the warmer months will ensure that greenhouse crops don't suffer the effects of intense heat.*

Forcing Lily-of-the-valley

For fragrant early flowers, force some lily-of-the-valley (*Convallaria majalis*) under glass. Dig up or buy a few rhizomes (sometimes known as pips) and pot them up. The more heat you can provide, the earlier they will flower. Although they can be planted out after flowering, they may take a season or two to regain their vigour and to flower as usual. Do not try to force the same rhizomes again.

STORING PELARGONIUMS

Pelargoniums that have flowered their hearts out in summer borders will now be performing less well. They can be lifted from the ground this month and stored over winter, either for replanting next year or to provide material for early cuttings.

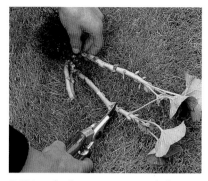

2 Trim the longest roots and shorten the shoots to about 10cm (4in).

3 Pot up the plants in 15cm (6in) deep trays or pots of sowing compost. Water well initially, but sparingly over winter, just to prevent the soil from drying out. New shoots will emerge in spring, from which you can take cuttings.

1 Lift the pelargoniums from the ground before the first frost – they will often survive a light frost if you take them in promptly afterwards. Shake off the soil from the roots.

> ### THINGS TO DO
> ### IN THE GREENHOUSE
> Continue to ventilate in mild weather
> Install a thermometer to check minimum temperatures at night
> Remove and burn any dead or diseased leaves from plants
> Clean and disinfect work areas

Late Autumn

THIS TIME OF YEAR OFTEN SPRINGS A SURPRISE: ALTHOUGH COLD, THE DAYS CAN BE CLEAR AND SUNNY. TAKE A STROLL ROUND THE GARDEN AND NOTE ANY DESIGN FEATURES THAT NEED IMPROVEMENT. NOW IS THE TIME TO GET THE GARDEN READY FOR WINTER.

THE ORNAMENTAL GARDEN

If you like a tidy garden, begin to cut back herbaceous perennials to about 15cm (6in) above the ground as the foliage and flowers die back.

Some gardeners prefer to leave the dead topgrowth in place until spring because it protects the crowns from winter cold. In addition, many plants, especially grasses, look attractive when their dry leaves and flowerheads are touched with frost. Seedheads left on plants such as teasels (*Dipsacus fullonum*) provide valuable winter food for birds, as do the insects that overwinter inside dead stems. However, garden pests, including slugs and snails, will also overwinter among the dead plant material, and it can be difficult to avoid damaging the tender new growth when you are cutting back the old topgrowth in spring.

Bulbs in Beds and Borders

As nerines start to die back after flowering, mulch them with straw or some other dry material if you live in a cold area. This is a good time to divide congested clumps, but do this only if the plants have ceased to flower well.

Above: Spiraea japonica 'Goldflame' is one of the shrubs that can be propagated from hardwood cuttings taken about now.

Nerines are best left well alone as far as possible, but some other tender bulbs, such as gladioli, should be lifted so that they can be stored in a dry, frost-free place until next spring. There is still time to plant spring-flowering bulbs, including tulips.

GARDENER'S TIP

If you plan a bonfire, either warn your neighbours or light it in the evening when you are least likely to cause inconvenience.

TAKING HARDWOOD CUTTINGS

You can increase your stock of a wide range of trees and shrubs by taking hardwood cuttings. They occupy little space, and aftercare is minimal, though they take up to a year to root.

1 Dig a narrow trench about 20cm (8in) deep. If the soil is heavy, line the base with a 2.5cm (1in) layer of grit. Take cuttings from the plant, each with four or more buds. Trim the base of each cutting just below a bud and the top just above a bud.

2 Insert the cuttings in the trench. Two or three buds should protrude above the ground, although if you are taking cuttings from a single-stemmed tree, you should insert them to their full length so that the topmost bud is just below the soil surface.

3 Firm in the cuttings, label them and water them in well. Leave them undisturbed until the following autumn, by which time they should have rooted.

SHRUBS TO INCREASE BY HARDWOOD CUTTINGS
Aucuba
Berberis
Buddleja
Buxus
Cornus
Cotoneaster
Escallonia
Forsythia
Kerria
Philadelphus
Rosa
Salix
Spiraea
Weigela

Above: *Plant tulip bulbs to a depth of 8–15cm (3–6in). Tulipa praestans 'Fusilier' has up to six flowers on each stem.*

THINGS TO DO IN THE ORNAMENTAL GARDEN
Cut back perennials
Burn woody garden debris
Plant bare-root roses and other shrubs
Plant tulip bulbs
Take hardwood cuttings
Plant hedges
Collect and compost fallen leaves
Protect vulnerable plants by packing around them with straw

The Kitchen Garden

As you clear the vegetable plot of the last of the summer crops, dig over the soil and leave it so that winter frosts can break down large clods. This is especially important if your soil is heavy. Continue to protect vulnerable plants with cloches or straw.

Planting Soft Fruit

Traditionally, soft fruit bushes are sold at this time of year as bare-root plants, and they should be planted as soon after purchase as possible, while they are dormant. Container-grown plants can be planted at any time of year when the weather is suitable and the ground is not waterlogged or frozen, although these, too, are best planted at this time of year.

1 Dig a large hole for each plant and work organic matter into the base. Soak the plant roots in a water for an hour and then place them in the centre of the hole. Use a cane to make sure you are planting at the original depth.

2 Backfill with the excavated soil and firm in well with your foot to eliminate pockets of air. Hoe around the plant, then water the plant well.

3 Soft fruits that grow on stems that sprout from the base are pruned hard. Cut back the topgrowth to 23–30cm (9–12in) from ground level to stimulate new shoots from the base.

> **THINGS TO DO
> IN THE KITCHEN GARDEN**
> Protect vulnerable vegetables
> with cloches
> Plant bare-root fruit bushes and trees
> Prune soft fruit bushes
> Pot up herbs for winter use

Pruning Soft Fruit

Once established, soft fruit bushes need pruning while dormant to maintain their vigour. Blackcurrants should be pruned only once they are fruiting reliably. Cut back one third of the shoots to the base, choosing the oldest. Red and white currants fruit on wood that is two or more years old, so pruning should concentrate on removing overcrowded shoots. Shorten sideshoots to one or two buds, and on main shoots cut back last summer's growth by half. Gooseberries also benefit from annual pruning to keep an open shape.

Autumn-fruiting raspberries bear fruit on the new season's canes, so all canes can be cut to ground level during the dormant season. On summer-fruiting varieties, the old canes that have fruited should be removed and the new shoots tied in to replace them.

Planting Garlic

To grow successfully, garlic needs a period of cold and can be planted throughout the autumn until early winter. Although it is possible to grow garlic from cloves bought for cooking, you will get better results from specially produced bulbs.

Snap each bulb into its component cloves and plant them in a row in a sunny spot, up to 10cm (4in) apart and with the tips of the cloves just below the soil surface.

Above: When frost is forecast, protect crops such as strawberries with a portable plastic cloche.

> **GARDENER'S TIP**
> Pot up herbs such as mint, chives and marjoram and keep them in the greenhouse or kitchen to ensure a supply of fresh leaves throughout the winter.

Above: Use a dibber to make holes for garlic cloves, spacing them about 10cm (4in) apart along the row.

287

THE GREENHOUSE

As the temperature drops, you need to start thinking about heating and insulation. Most conservatories are heated by means of the domestic system, but if your greenhouse is free-standing and has no power supply, you may consider installing a small gas or paraffin heater. These can be used only in a properly ventilated environment, however, because of the risk of fire or a build-up of noxious fumes.

Good insulation will help save on fuel bills. Bubble plastic is cheap and can be fixed to the greenhouse roof with clips. If you installed blinds or netting for shade in summer, you may be able to use the same fixings to hold the insulation in place.

If you have a large greenhouse that would be costly to heat, you may be

Above: An electric fan heater, especially if it is fitted with a thermostat, is an efficient way of heating a greenhouse.

able to group all the most tender plants together at one end and close this section off with a curtain of bubble plastic. Heat this area only.

Hygiene

If you have not already done so, take the opportunity to give the greenhouse a thorough clean before putting the insulation in place. If you used blinds or netting to shade the greenhouse during the summer, wash them before storing them away.

Clear away all dead and dying foliage and flowers so that grey mould (botrytis) cannot overwinter on the debris. Use hot water and a garden disinfectant or non-toxic detergent to clean the glass inside and out, taking particular care to clean between overlapping panes of glass, where algal growths tend to form. Also scrub down all wooden or metal frames and clean the staging.

Above: Insulate the greenhouse with sheets of bubble plastic fixed against the glass on the inside.

Before storing all your containers, plant pots and drip saucers over the winter, make sure they are clean, and wipe the outside of all containers used for long-term plants with a dilute solution of garden disinfectant.

Cold Frames

Although a cold frame is usually designed to store hardy plants, bear in mind that the plants will be young – and therefore more vulnerable than mature ones – and that their roots are above ground level: potting mix in pots can easily freeze in severe weather. On

Above: Clean the greenhouse glass inside and out to maximize light levels and prevent the build-up of algae.

the coldest nights, cover the frame with old carpet to protect from frost. Keep the carpet on in the daytime if the temperature stays below freezing. Excluding the light in very cold weather will do the plants no harm.

Above: Scrub all your plant pots and containers when not in use, so that they do not harbour disease.

THINGS TO DO
IN THE GREENHOUSE

Clean all surfaces
Clean greenhouse glass
Insulate, if necessary
Ventilate on mild days
Check on indoor cyclamen and remove
any dead leaves

Early Winter

THERE ARE STILL SOME ESSENTIAL GARDEN TASKS TO BE DONE IN WINTER, BUT THERE IS MUCH TO ENJOY AS WELL. AT THIS TIME OF YEAR THE VALUE OF EVERGREENS AND CONIFERS AS THE BACKBONE OF THE GARDEN CAN BE FULLY APPRECIATED.

THE ORNAMENTAL GARDEN

Continue to sweep up fallen leaves, especially from the lawn, and use them to make leaf mould.

One of the few perennials to be in flower at this time of year, the Christmas rose (*Helleborus niger*) can be difficult to keep looking its best. It often flowers during the worst of the winter weather, and it is worth protecting the emerging flower buds from rain and mud splashes. Alpines will also appreciate protection from winter wet, which is more likely to kill them than cold weather.

THE KITCHEN GARDEN

There will still be plenty of tidying up to do, as you clear away the last of this year's crops and dig over vacant beds to prepare for next season.

Pruning Apple and Pear Trees

Give some attention to apple and pear trees now that they are dormant. Pruning is largely a matter of tidying them up. Thin older branches to open up the crown and cut back any damaged branches entirely. If any growth shows signs of fungal disease such as mildew, cut back to firm, healthy

Above: *A sheet of glass placed over* Helleborus niger *will keep mud splashes off the pure white flowers.*

Above: *Established apple cordons should be pruned in both winter and summer, but standards can be pruned in winter only.*

wood and burn the prunings. Use a pruning saw with a serrated edge to deal with thicker branches. Take care that you do not prune too many branches too hard, as this will result in an excess of thin, sappy growth the following spring.

THE GREENHOUSE

On mild days make a point of opening the door or the roof lights to ventilate the greenhouse, and remove any fallen leaves or flowers. Reduce the water you give to plants that are being over-wintered in the greenhouse.

CHECKING STORED BULBS

If you are storing the dried bulbs, corms, tubers and rhizomes of such plants as freesias, gladioli, dahlias and begonias, it is worth checking up on them from time to time to make sure they are not showing any signs of rot.

1 About once a month, gently squeeze the bulbs (these are begonia tubers) to make sure they are still firm. Any that feel soft, or are showing signs of mould, should be discarded at once.

2 For extra protection, dust the healthy bulbs or tubers with a fungicidal powder, following the safety measures stipulated on the product label.

THINGS TO DO

Ornamental Garden
Sow seed of alpines
Put cloches over *Helleborus niger*
Protect alpines from winter wet
Install a pond heater

Kitchen Garden
Prune apple and pear trees
Force whitloof chicory

Greenhouse
Inspect bulbs in storage
Prune grape vines
Sow seed of pelargoniums

GARDENER'S TIP

Clean and oil your lawn mower now, as you are unlikely to have time when it is in regular use in summer, or take it to be professionally serviced before the busy spring season.

Midwinter

At this time of year you need to start looking forward. No matter how cold the weather, spring is only just around the corner. Now is the time to plan your planting schemes, order seeds and check that your tools are in good repair.

The Ornamental Garden

A job that is easily overlooked at this time of year is to knock off snow from the tops of hedges and specimen conifers. Evergreen hedges are usually trimmed so that the top slopes slightly, encouraging snow to slide off. Sometimes, however, heavy snowfall can lie on branches, causing permanent damage.

Taking Root Cuttings

Root cuttings are an excellent way of increasing stocks of a number of perennials, but the plant must be fully dormant for the technique to be successful. Keep the cuttings in a cold frame or unheated greenhouse. New growth should appear in spring, when the young plants can be potted up individually and grown on for a season.

> ### PLANTS TO INCREASE BY ROOT CUTTINGS
>
> *Acanthus*
> *Echinops*
> *Gaillardia*
> *Phlox maculata*
> *Phlox paniculata*
> *Pulsatilla vulgaris*
> *Romneya coulteri*

1 Dig up the plant when dormant, cut off some of the thicker roots close to the crown. Replant the crown.

2 Cut the roots into 5cm (2in) sections. Angle the cut at the base of each one to show the correct way up. Insert vertically in cuttings potting mix.

3 For plants with thin roots, such as border phlox, lay 5cm (2in) lengths of root in pots of potting mix. Cover with a fairly thin layer of potting mix.

> ### THINGS TO DO IN THE ORNAMENTAL GARDEN
>
> Firm in new plantings lifted by frost
> Check the stakes on trees
> Prune wisteria
> Aerate lawns
> Melt ice on ponds

THE KITCHEN GARDEN

While most of the vegetable plot is bare, take the opportunity to test the soil. Most vegetables do best in slightly alkaline soil, so if necessary apply lime, in the form of calcium carbonate or calcium hydroxide (slaked lime), following the supplier's directions precisely.

Forcing Rhubarb

If you grow rhubarb, cover some of the crowns with a large bucket or a special rhubarb forcer that excludes light. This will encourage early growth that is pale, thin and tender – excellent for pies and fools in spring.

For a really early crop of rhubarb, lift the crown to expose the roots and leave it on the soil surface for a few weeks. This will persuade the plant that winter is more advanced than it really is and bring it into growth earlier. Replant the crown and cover the emerging shoots.

Above: Check stored apples regularly and promptly remove any fruits that show signs of rot.

Forcing Chicory

Chicory roots are sometimes sold at this time of year for forcing to produce chicons. Leave the roots on the soil surface for a few days to retard growth. Trim back the tops to leave stumps 2.5–5cm (1–2in) long and pot them up in threes, leaving the crowns exposed (trim the roots if necessary to fit in the pot). Cover with a second pot with the holes blocked to exclude light and keep at a temperature of 10–18°C (50–65°F). The chicons will be ready to cut in about three weeks.

> ### THINGS TO DO IN THE KITCHEN GARDEN
> Net fruit bushes to protect emerging buds from birds
> Force rhubarb and chicory
> Sow broad (fava) beans and peas (mild areas only)

293

The Greenhouse

If you have a heated greenhouse or a heated propagator, it is not too soon to sow some summer bedding plants that need a long growing period, such as fibrous-rooted begonias *(Begonia semperflorens)*. Check seed packets to see if early sowings are needed.

It can be tempting to make early sowings of all half-hardy annuals and summer vegetables. However, remember that you will need plenty of space to keep the pricked-out and potted-on seedlings warm and well lit before they can be planted out. Seedlings that are kept in overcrowded, poorly ventilated conditions are susceptible to damping off, so in a small greenhouse it is more sensible to put off most early sowings for a few weeks.

Above: Now is the time to plan for next summer's chrysanthemum display. This is the early-flowering 'Primrose Allouise'.

Propagating Chrysanthemums

Chrysanthemums that are overwintered in a greenhouse or cold frame are generally used to produce new plants once they start into growth. In order to ensure large, robust plants for summer flowering, take cuttings from your stock plants now, once the new shoots reach about 5cm (2in).

1 Cut shoots growing from the base of the plant. Pull off the lower leaves and trim the base of each cutting.

2 Insert the stems in a pot containing a mixture suitable for cuttings.

3 Water and cover with a plastic bag, making sure it does not touch the leaves, or place the pot in a propagator.

Bringing Hippeastrums into Growth

Bulbs of hippeastrums, which are often, incorrectly, sold as amaryllis, can be obtained at this time of year for indoor display. Plant the bulbs in pots of bulb fibre or potting mix with the top half of the bulb above the surface. If the bulb is slow to start into growth, place the pot in a propagator for a week or so until the first green shoots appear.

> ### GARDENER'S TIP
> To make tiny seed like begonia easier to handle and see, mix it with a small quantity of silver sand and sprinkle the sand and seed mix over the surface of the tray.

> ### THINGS TO DO
> ### IN THE GREENHOUSE
> Pick off and burn dead leaves from pot plants
> Check stored corms and tubers for signs of rot
> Continue to ventilate on mild days
> Sow seed of annuals for early flowers

Above: Exotic-looking hippeastrums, such as this variety called 'Christmas Star', grow with phenomenal speed indoors and bloom in the depths of winter.

295

Late Winter

THIS IS OFTEN WHEN THE WORST OF THE WINTER WEATHER STRIKES, BUT THE DAYS ARE BECOMING PERCEPTIBLY LONGER AND MANY OF THE SPRING BULBS ARE BEGINNING TO SHOOT FROM BELOW GROUND. THE AIR OF ANTICIPATION IS ALMOST PALPABLE.

THE ORNAMENTAL GARDEN

There is plenty to do in the garden at this time of year – and plenty to enjoy. Magnolia buds are fattening up, and many winter-flowering shrubs are at their best. Several have bewitching fragrances, and a few cut stems will scent the whole house.

Prune late-flowering clematis hard back to a pair of strong, healthy buds. Thinner stems that show no signs of shooting can be cut down completely.

Above: When you prune a clematis, cut each stem back to a pair of strong buds near ground level.

Summer bulbs will be appearing for sale. If you are buying lilies, look for firm, plump bulbs that show no sign of disease and plant them as soon as possible, adding grit or sharp sand to the soil to ensure good drainage. Dahlia tubers should be stored until the weather warms up in late spring.

Above: One of the first bulbs to appear, Crocus tommasinianus *is ideal for naturalizing in grass.*

THINGS TO DO
IN THE ORNAMENTAL GARDEN

Sow sweet peas
Plant snowdrops and winter aconites immediately after flowering
Prune clematis
Divide overcrowded snowdrops
Take root cuttings of perennials with thick, fleshy roots
Prepare ground for new lawns

THE KITCHEN GARDEN

Unless the soil is waterlogged or frozen, continue to dig over the vegetable plot, but take care that you do not compact wet soil by standing on it. Apply a mulch of well-rotted compost or manure to prevent weeds from germinating in the bare soil.

SOWING EARLY CROPS

If you have a cold frame erected directly over garden soil, take advantage of the few extra degrees of warmth it provides to sow some early crops. In the open garden, you can warm up patches of soil for early sowings with cloches of various kinds.

2 Rigid cloches made of polycarbon are useful for warming up small areas of the garden. Butt the sections close together and firmly fix them in the ground. Close the ends with further sections of polycarbon to prevent the cloche becoming a wind tunnel.

1 If your cold frame stands on bare soil, prepare the ground by forking it over and adding as much organic matter as possible. Well-rotted farmyard manure is useful for enriching the soil for early crops. Powerful artificial fertilizers are not recommended. Rake the soil level and sow the seed thinly in shallow drills.

3 You can warm up a larger area of soil with plastic sheeting stretched over hoops – an ambitious tunnel will have enough headroom to allow you to walk in and out of it. Pull the sheeting taut and secure it firmly at each end. Anchor the edges of the plastic to the ground by heaping soil over them.

> ### THINGS TO DO
> ### IN THE KITCHEN GARDEN
> Continue winter digging
> Force young strawberry plants for an early crop
> Sprout early potatoes
> Feed asparagus beds
> Plant out Jerusalem artichokes
> Sow vegetables under cloches for early crops

THE GREENHOUSE

Make the most of your greenhouse, conservatory or kitchen windowsill to begin sowing seed of early vegetables and half-hardy annuals. To maximize the light that gets to your seedlings, make sure that the glass is clean. Don't forget to ventilate the greenhouse on warm days.

If you have stored dahlia tubers over winter, they can now be coaxed out of their dormancy. A good way of increasing your stock is to take cuttings from the emerging shoots. Provided you give them the appropriate care and attention, they should flower the same year.

For flowers in early summer, press on and sow seeds of annuals. A propagator can speed up germination, which is especially useful for half-hardy plants. To produce sturdy, healthy plants, prick them out as they grow. Early sowings can also be used to provide flowering pot plants for indoor displays.

Have a look at tender perennials you have overwintered, which will be mostly woody plants, such as fuchsias, pelargoniums, argyranthemums and felicias. Spraying them with water can help encourage them to push out fresh shoots. If the plants are old and straggly, any such shoots can be used as cuttings, if you didn't take cuttings the previous autumn.

Young plants need tender loving care. Keep them warm, in good light and out of draughts, and make sure they never dry out. If you need to keep

Above: Dahlia tubers that have been stored over the winter should be showing signs of growth now, and you can take cuttings to increase your stocks.

them in a closed environment such as a propagator, check regularly for signs of fungal disease, usually the result of excessive moisture.

Check that you have good supplies of clean pots and seed trays, potting mix for both seed and cuttings, and plant labels. You can save time later by stocking up now. Days that are too cold or wet for you to venture outside will be well spent washing old pots and sorting out seed packets.

Growing Cacti from Seed

As a change, try growing cacti from seed, which is a gratifyingly easy way of producing large numbers of these fascinating plants. Use a heated propagator to start them off, then grow them on under normal greenhouse conditions but maintaining a minimum temperature of 10°C (50°F).

2 Top-dress with a thin layer of fine gravel, water the pots or trays and stand them in a place that is warm and bright but out of direct sunlight.

3 Prick the seedlings out when they are large enough and pot them up. Most cacti do best in pots that are small in proportion to their topgrowth.

1 Fill small pots or a seed tray with potting mix specially formulated for cacti. Scatter the seed evenly and thinly over the surface.

THINGS TO DO
IN THE GREENHOUSE
Take cuttings of dahlias
Bring overwintered tender perennials
back into growth
Sow tomatoes
Ventilate on mild days
Sow cacti

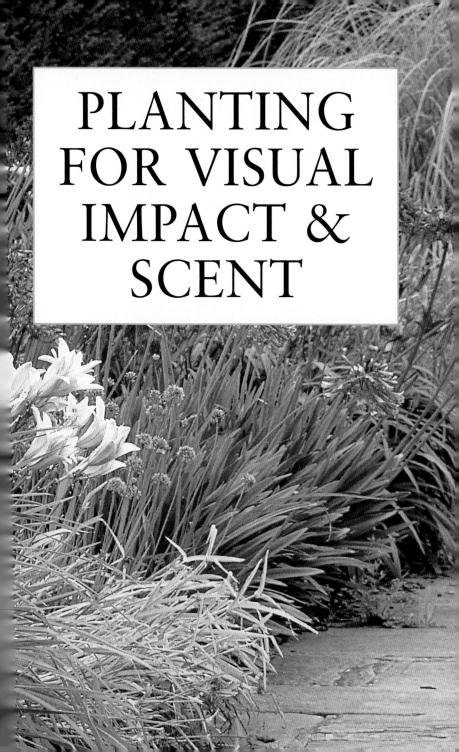

PLANTING FOR VISUAL IMPACT & SCENT

SHADE, TONE
& HUE

Knowing how colour works and how
to match hues to create visual
harmony or eye-catching contrasts is
fundamental to planning a successful
scheme for any garden, no matter
what its size. This chapter includes
information on year-round plants as
well as more seasonal performers that
will enable you to sustain or subtly
alter a scheme as the year progresses.

Visual Delight

We expect to find colour in our gardens, but to create stunning effects and ensure a continuous show throughout the year will require some understanding of how colour behaves and when plants are at their best. With planning, even the smallest gardens can provide year-round colour.

Year-round Colour

As the year progresses, different types of plant come into their own. Using the right mix of plants and blends of colour will ensure that a garden has plenty of colour the year round. In mixed borders, shrubs provide the basis of any planting, giving it structure as well as colour. These can be in-filled with a multitude of other types of plants, mostly herbaceous perennials, bulbs, and annuals, their seasonal time and

Above: Yellows and creams blend to create a restful feel to this summer border.

colour chosen to complement the more permanent plants. Beds devoted to particular types of plants can be planted up on a rotation basis.

Borders

Spring-flowering bulbs can be planted in borders used for summer bedding, providing colour early in the year. Herbaceous and mixed borders also benefit from a generous scattering of bulbs to help provide colour and interest until the late spring, when the early summer plants take over.

Left: Irises and primulas dominate this late-spring border for a striking effect.

Certainly, the flowers of some bulbs are short-lived compared with summer flowers (often no more than a couple of weeks at their peak), but this shortcoming is easily rectified by inter-planting with spring bedding plants such as winter-flowering pansies, forget-me-nots and polyanthus. They ensure a superb display for more than a month, by which time the beds will probably have to be cleared when the ground is prepared for summer flowers. They also help to fill in around the base of tall bulbs such as tulips that can otherwise look rather stalky.

Make sure that mixed borders include shrubs that flower at different times of the year.

The planting schemes used by your local parks department can provide some useful ideas for successful colours and plants, especially if your plant knowledge is limited.

Above: The colourful bark of Salix *is at its best in the winter months.*

CONTAINERS

An ideal way to ensure a display of plants at their peak is to plant them in containers. This allows plants to be moved about as they come into flower and fade. Tubs, troughs, window boxes, and even hanging baskets can all be replanted for spring colour.

PERMANENT COLOUR

Annuals and perennials are wonderful for providing successional colour, but growing them does involve work – sowing, potting on, planting out, deadheading, dividing and clearing away dead matter. So some gardeners prefer to create most of their colour using more permanent plants such as heathers and evergreen shrubs, including conifers and ivies which require less maintenance.

Left: Dahlias provide strong colours for the autumn border.

THE EFFECTS OF COLOUR

Colour has a strong influence on mood and you can use it in your garden to create different effects. Reds are restless and passionate, blues can be calming, yellows are cheerful. Colours also affect the tones of other colours next to them, creating slight changes in their appearance. The way colours work is explored in more detail later in the chapter.

Nothing in a garden is static and whatever effect you create will undergo changes through the day and according to the season. The colour of a flower or leaf will change as it develops, from bud to fall.

LIGHT

Each season has a different type of light, and this affects the hues of plants. Light also changes throughout the

Above: The copper-tinted leaves of the Phormium *make an interesting contrast with small, vivid geranium flowers.*

day. Pale flowers stand out in shade and at dusk, while bright ones seem to bleach out in the midday sun.

USING FOLIAGE

Most foliage is green, but the number of different greens is almost infinite. Careful arrangement of these various greens will enhance the display, but even more can be achieved by incorporating into the garden the large number of plants, especially shrubs, that have foliage in other colours, including yellow, gold, silver, white, purple and blue.

To enjoy coloured foliage at its best, remember that purple and silver-leaved plants need the sun to retain their colour; golden and yellow foliage, however, often need a dappled shade

Left: The various smoke bushes (Cotinus) *all have excellent purple foliage. They look especially effective when they are planted so that the evening sun shines through the leaves.*

Above: *The variegated* Hosta *'Golden Tiara', with its creamy-edged leaves, brightens a shaded corner.*

as too much sun can scorch the leaves and too much shade causes them to turn greener.

VARIEGATED FOLIAGE

Some plants have leaves in two or more colours, known as "variegated" foliage. There are many different types of variegation. In shrubs most variagations are gold, followed closely by cream and white. These have the effect of lightening any group of plants they are near. Green-on-green variegations also have a lightening effect, but variegations involving purples often introduce a more sombre mood.

Variegated plants should be used with discretion. They can become too "busy", and if several are planted together they tend to clash. Reserve them for use as accent plants, to draw the eye. They are useful in shade or in

Right: *The purple foliage of* Canna *'Roi Humber' is eyecatching against red, yellow and green.*

a dark corner because they shine out and create interest in an otherwise unpromising or dull situation.

Although many variegated shrubs will tolerate full sun, many prefer a light, dappled shade, out of hot sun.

HOW TO USE THIS CHAPTER

Begin by reading *Choosing a Colour Scheme* which explains how colours work together. It is possible to install permanent colour in the garden, which remains constant through the changing seasons. The section entitled *Year-round Plants* describes the plants to use for this effect.

The following sections are each devoted to a season of the year. They explore successful seasonal colour combinations and catalogue the main jobs that need to be done in the garden.

To plan for colour through the year, you can refer to the plant charts in this book.

Choosing a Colour Scheme

PLANTS ARE AVAILABLE IN A WONDERFUL RANGE OF COLOURS, WHICH
GIVES GARDENERS TREMENDOUS SCOPE WHEN DESIGNING AN AREA.
START BY PLANNING YOUR COLOUR SCHEME ON GRAPH PAPER USING
COLOURED PENCILS, TO GIVE YOU A BETTER IDEA OF THE END RESULT.

USING COLOUR

There is such vast choice of colour in
plants, that with a little imagination it
is possible to paint any picture you
like and create any mood you desire.

Not all colours mix well, so rather
than randomly scattering colours, it is
better to use them in drifts, placing
plants so that each has a harmonious
relationship with its neighbour. When
this is done, the eye can move effortlessly along a border, enjoying inher-
ent subtleties as it passes over a
thoughtfully blended whole.

If in doubt about colour combinations, bear in mind that white or blue
will go with almost any other colour,
and look good. Pastel shades are forgiving colours. The ones to be careful
with are brilliant orange and strong
magenta, which could look discon-
certing when placed together.

BLENDING COLOURS

Unless you want a monochromatic
scheme, the basic principle is to blend
colours. If you want to use two different colours that oppose each other on
the colour wheel in close proximity,
you can sometimes find another
colour that will link them. Blue and
red are in stark contrast to each other,
and you may prefer to keep them apart
by placing a purple plant between
them, which will greatly improve the
appearance of the flower border.
Incorporating areas of interesting
foliage in suitable colours is often an
excellent way of linking and separating
blocks of colour.

*Left: Silver leaves, a dusty pink and the
crimson flowers of* Digitalis *are unified
by the purple* Aquilegia *and* Ajuga *which
both stimulate and please the eye.*

and white imparts a general sense of purity and tranquillity. Each colour has many tones and shades and all of these can be found in flowers and the many varieties of foliage.

Pastel colours have a romantic quality, and are often suitable for a dull, grey climate. However, a garden devoted entirely to pale colours such as these can be rather boring.

Above: The hot yellow and reds of the primulas contrast perfectly with the blue Myosotis.

LEAF COLOUR

Foliage plays an important part in any colour scheme and wonderful effects can be created by placing a stunningly different coloured flower against an interesting leaf colour. For instance the delicate pink of an opium poppy *(Papaver somniferum)* is beautifully set off against silver-grey leaves.

HOT AND COOL COLOURS

When you are decorating the whole mood of a room can change depending on whether you are using hot or cool colours. It is exactly the same when you are designing and planning a garden.

Hot colours – the flame reds and oranges – are lively and will bring a dash of excitement to a border. Intense blues will definitely cool things down,

THE COLOUR WHEEL

Artists and designers use what is known as a colour wheel, in which colours that are situated next to each other on the wheel have a sympathetic bond and will work well together. Purple and blue as well as blue and green, for example, look good together. Colours on opposite sides of the wheel are contrasting and may clash with each other. Orange, for instance, will stand out quite starkly against blue.

There are occasions, however, when combining opposing colours can be used to create a focal point or to add life in an otherwise bland scheme.

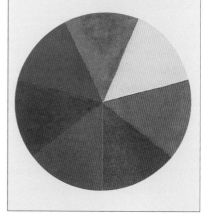

Colour in the Garden

As you plan for colour in the garden, decide which effect you wish to achieve. You can use calming, soft colours or include a bright, vibrant focal point or a hot border. You may even choose to create peace and tranquillity with a completely white border.

Using Hot Colours

Confine hot colours to one border, possibly as a centrepiece, but use softer colours in the other beds to ring in

Above: Kniphofias have several alternative names, of which "red-hot poker" aptly describes the colour of many of them. These shafts of hot colours are useful not only for their brightness, but also for their shape.

the changes and to provide a more tranquil planting area. It is possible to create a border containing nothing but red flowers, but it is always more interesting to have one that incorporates other hot colours as well. However, many people prefer to use a limited number of hot-coloured perennials in a cooler-coloured border, where they will act as a strong focal

point and make a dramatic statement. Red or yellow flowers are the strongest colours for impact.

Hot colours have a tendency to "advance" – that is, they seem much closer than they really are – so if you want to make a long border appear shorter than it is, plant the hot colours at the far end.

Use the different hues of foliage to link the hot colours with cool colours in the border.

Above: The glorious ruby-red flowers of Rhododendron 'Dopey'.

Using Cool Colours

Although blues are, in theory, cool colours, those blues that are tinged with red are warm. Combined with the warm pinks, the overall effect is

Above: The cool colours of Nemophilia menziesii *(Californian bluebell).*

one of cool calm. Use blues, purples and pinks, including many of the pastel shades, to achieve this effect.

Pastel colours create a misty effect, which means that they can be mixed together or dotted around. An even better effect can be achieved by using drifts of colour, merging the drifts.

Above: Use bright-red plants, such as Dahlia *'Bishop of Llandaff', as a bold focal point.*

RED FLOWERS

Amaranthus caudatus
Antirrhinum 'Scarlet Giant'
Begonia semperflorens 'Volcano'
Canna
Cleome hassleriana 'Cherry Queen'
Crocosmia 'Lucifer'
Dahlia
Geum "Mrs. J. Bradshaw'
Impatiens (various varieties)
Kniphofia (red hot poker)
Lobelia erinus 'Red Cascade'
Monarda 'Cambridge Scarlet'
Paeonia
Papaver rhoeas
Pelargonium (various varieties)
Penstemon barbatus
Petunia 'Red Star'; P. 'Scarlet'
Tropaeolum majus 'Empress of India'
Verbena (various varieties)

RED

The fiery reds are hot, exciting colours. They combine well with oranges, and golden and orange-yellows, but don't generally mix well with blue-reds, which are more sub-dued. Use them wherever you want to inject some vibrancy into your garden designs – in beds and borders or in hanging baskets and other containers. But remember that too much of a good thing can become monotonous, so use these strong colours sparingly.

Hot reds can be found in many perennials, but are especially well rep-resented in summer annuals, which are so useful for adding dramatic patches of colour between other plants.

311

Above: This brilliant bright orange Osteospermum *makes a strong contrast against green foliage.*

ORANGE FLOWERS

Antirrhinum
Canna 'Orange Perfection'
Crocosmia
Dahlia
Eccremocarpus scaber
Erysimum
Euphorbia griffithii
Geum 'Borisii'
Hemerocallis
Kniphofia
Ligularia
Papaver orientale
Potentilla 'William Robinson'
Primula bulleyana
Rudbeckia hirta
Tagetes erecta
Tropaeolum
Trollius
Zauschneria californica

ORANGE

A warm, friendly colour, orange has quite a wide range of shades. At the deeper end of the spectrum it is quite definitely a hot colour, exciting and vibrant, but at the golden end it is warm rather than hot and can be used more freely.

Orange mixes well with most colours although the redder shades are not so complementary with the bluer reds, including purple and pink, unless you like to combine colours that clash. It shows up well against green foliage and can be picked out at a distance.

Autumn gardens often display orange tones, not only in flowers, such as chrysanthemums, but in trees and shrubs with coloured foliage and brightly coloured berries.

Above: This Calceolaria, *with its flame-orange flowers, is a striking annual to use in the border.*

Many annuals and biennials can add a vibrant orange note throughout the year, including winter-flowering pansies followed by wallflowers (*Erysimum*), snapdragons (*Antirrhinum*) and pot marigolds (*Calendula*). During summer, nasturtiums (*Tropaeolum*) and African marigolds (*Tagetes erecta*) will follow.

YELLOW

There are three distinct yellows within this part of the spectrum, all exhibiting different qualities in a planting scheme. One side is tinged with green and may be described as a cool colour, while the other side is tinged with orange, making it very much a hot colour. These hot yellows have a warm, cosy feeling about them, and go well with flame-reds, oranges and creams. In

Above: *The yellow heads of* Achillea *'Coronation Gold' float above its delicate foliage.*

between the two yellows are pure clear yellows. These will blend happily with most other colours.

The green or lemon yellows look much better when associated with greens blues and white. They can be bright, but create a fresher effect than the warmer yellows.

Above: *The stately yellow spires of* Verbascum *add height to a traditional summer border.*

YELLOW FLOWERS

Achillea
Aurinia saxatilis
(syn. *Alyssum saxatile*)
Canna
Centaurea macrocephala
Chrysanthemum
Coreopsis verticillata
Dahlia
Erysimum 'Jubilee Gold'
Geum 'Lady Statheden'
Helianthus
Heliopsis
Hemerocallis
Inula
Ligularia
Primula
Rudbeckia

GREEN

Foliage can provide an effective link in borders and beds. Dark green is good used with hot colours, whereas soft green and silver suit cool colours, especially pink, pale blue and pale, greeny yellow. Blue foliage, which can be found in some grasses and hostas, can also be useful in linking or separating blocks of colour.

BLUE

The different shades of blue can be bright, clean-cut colours with a great intensity, or softened to such an extent that they only have a whisper of colour left, creating a very soft, hazy image. Intense blues can be used in a bold way in the garden, but the softer blues are good for romantic container arrangements, especially those in large stone pots or urns.

Above: *Use the delicate* Nigella damascena, *with its blue flowers and feathery fronds, in a cool border.*

Blues are versatile and can be combined with most colours. They create a rather rich, luxurious combination with purple-reds, but avoid mixing them with orange-reds. With orange, however, the effects can be startling, so use this combination sparingly.

Blue and yellow is another exciting combination, giving a fresh, clean-looking contrast. The pale blues and yellows, however, are more hazy and have a soft, romantic image, but still retain a distinctive, fresh quality.

Blues set against silver or grey foliage create an interesting combination that is distinct yet soft.

PURPLE AND VIOLET

Even a patch of purple appears as a strong block of colour, never as a misty haze. Over-use of this solid colour can have a deadening effect. As purple

---

BLUE FLOWERS

Agapanthus praecoc x subsp *orientalis*
Ageratum houstonianum
Brachyscome iberidifolia
Campanula medium
Centaurea cyanus
Consolida ambigua
Eryngium x *oliverianum*
Felicia bergeriana
Lathyrus odoratus
Limonium sinuatum 'Blue Bonnet'
Lobelia erinus
Myosotis
Nigella damascena
Nolana paradoxa 'Blue Bird'
Salvia farinacea 'Victoria'

Above: Digitalis *creates wonderfully elegant spires of flowers, bringing height to a planting scheme. These flowers vary in colour from a light pink to purple.*

too much, creating a leaden effect. Lime-green flowers such as lime zinnias and the lime foliage of *Helychrysum petiolare* 'Limelight' make excellent border companions.

Lavenders combined with pinks are a delightfully romantic combination and have the bonus of a delightful scent. When used with creamy-yellow they have a soothing effect.

PINK

This colour can be quite bright, even startling and brash, particularly when tinged with purple and moving towards cerise and magenta shades. On the other hand it can be very soft and romantic. You have to be careful

tends to sink back into green foliage, it is better to contrast it with foliage that is silver or grey.

Violet is a more lively colour, and has still more vibrancy when on the dark side. Nonetheless, it should still be used with care and discretion.

Both purple and violet can be used more extensively if they are mixed with other colours. Lighter colours, such as yellows and whites, contrast with and stand out against purple. Purple also harmonizes well with purple-reds and purple-blues, but if these are too dark, the colours tend to blend

Above: The delicate pink flowers of Oenothera speciosa rosea *have creamy white centres.*

Above: Cream blended with soft mauve and gently variegated foliage creates a soothing effect.

in choosing the right colour for the effect you want to achieve. Pinks tend to mix best with lavenders and soft blues. But they can be used with reds to tone them down slightly. Pinks do not mix harmoniously with bright yellows and oranges.

CREAM

White mixed with a little yellow makes the sensuous and luxurious shade of cream. It goes well with most colours, adding a slightly mellow hue and often blending in sympathetically with hot colours.

WHITE

Long associated with purity, peace and tranquillity, white flowers add sophistication to a scheme. White goes well with most other colours, and it can be used to lighten a colour scheme. Used with hot oranges and reds, pure white can create a dramatic effect. White and blue is always a popular combination and it can be particularly effective to combine different shades of white with a mixture of pastel colours.

White is visible until well after dark, and so it is a good colour to plant where you eat evening meals. It also can be used to illuminate dark

Left: The large pompom heads of creamy yellow Marigold 'French Vanilla'.

corners of the garden. White busy Lizzies (*Impatiens*), for example, in a hanging basket against a dark background or in shade, will shine out.

A disadvantage with white flowers is that they often look unsightly when they die. To keep such displays at their best, deadhead once a day.

Some gardeners devote whole borders, even whole gardens, to white flowers. Although these are referred to as white gardens, there are usually at least two colours present, because most white-flowered plants have green leaves. A third colour, in the form of grey or silver foliage, is also often added.

There are many different shades of white, and they do not always mix sympathetically. On the whole, therefore, it is better to plant pure whites since the creamier ones tend to "muddy" the picture. Many white and cream flowers have bright yellow centres, and it is best to avoid these if you are planning a white border.

Above: The tiny flowers of Gypsophila elegans *make a delicate display in any summer border.*

WHITE FLOWERS

Alcea rosea
Anaphalis margaritacea
Clarkia pulchella 'Snowflake'
Cosmos bipinnatus 'Purity'
Gypsophila elegans 'Giant White'
Impatiens 'Super Elfin White'
Lathyrus odoratus
Lobelia erinus 'Snowball'
Lobularia maritima
(syn. Alyssum maritimum)
Matthiola (white varieties)
Nicotiana alata
Osteospermum 'Glistening White'
Pelargonium (various white forms)
Petunia (various white forms)
Viola x *wittrockiana* (white varieties)

Left: This white Osteospermum *will lighten any scheme, from hot oranges to misty blues.*

Year-round Plants

<small>BY SELECTING PLANTS WITH YEAR-ROUND INTEREST, IT IS POSSIBLE TO ACHIEVE CONTINUOUS COLOUR WITH MINIMUM EFFORT. HEATHERS, GRASSES AND EVERGREENS, INCLUDING CONIFERS AND IVIES, ARE ALL INVALUABLE SOURCES OF RICH COLOUR.</small>

Above: *The genus* Calluna *consists of one species,* C. vulgaris, *but this has over 500 cultivars in a wide range of colours.*

HEATHERS

Multi-coloured heathers are enduring garden performers. Tough and hardy, most can withstand extreme conditions, and some even put on their finest performance when the weather is at its most severe. One of the many advantages of heathers is that they provide year-round colour. Not only is there a heather in flower every month of the year, but some have coloured foliage that can itself be a strong, year-round feature, the leaf colour often changing with the seasons. For gardens without acid soil, many heathers need to be grown in raised beds or containers with the correct acidity.

Heathers are most highly rated as plants for the winter garden. Choose from varieties of *Erica carnea* and *E. x darleyensis*, perhaps mixing in selections of *Calluna vulgaris*.

COLOURFUL HEATHERS

Calluna vulgaris:
'Beoley Gold', golden-yellow
'Golden Feather', gold/orange red
'Multicolor', yellowish green, orange and coral tips
'Red Fred', dark green/vivid red tips
'Roland Haagen', gold/orange-red
'Sister Anne', grey-green/bronze
'Sunset', golden-yellow/orange/red

Erica:
E. carnea 'Ann Sparkes',
golden-yellow, bronze tips
'Foxhollow', yellow/slightly orange
'Golden Starlet', lime-green/yellow
'Westwood Yellow', yellow
E. cinerea 'Fiddler's Gold', golden-yellow/red
'Lime Soda', lime green
'Windlebrooke', golden yellow/orange-red
E. x darleyensis
'J.W. Porter', red and cream tips
E. vagans 'Valerie Proudley',
bright yellow

In summer, varieties of *Calluna vulgaris*, *Erica cinerea* and *E. vagans* dominate the scene, and are all effective with other acid-loving plants.

As an edging to a shrub border, heathers provide a softer line than the more conventional *Buxus sempervirens*.

GRASSES

A wide variety of ornamental grasses is available, ensuring that there is usually at least one type for every garden situation. Grasses look good when grouped together, or used as single specimens. They often work particularly well when associated with other plants. Their airy form and movement contrast effectively with larger-leaved plants, and their vertical accent lifts and lightens dense groupings. They are particuarly useful for adding winter interest.

Above: A collection of grasses in containers makes a versatile display for a small garden terrace or balcony.

In shady areas, the variegated foliage of *Carex hachijoensis* 'Evergold' will shine out all year round. Other shade-tolerant variegated grasses include *Molinia caerulea* ssp. *caerula* 'Variegata', *Hakonechloa macra* 'Alboaurea' and 'Aureola' and *Phalaris arundinacea* var. *picta* 'Picta'. They complement other shade-loving plants such as hostas, ferns and hydrangeas.

Areas of dry shade are difficult to plant successfully but *Stipa arundinacea* copes with these inhospitable conditions. Shady woodland areas can be carpeted with the golden foliage of *Milium effusum* 'Aureum', or with varieties of *Deschampsia cespitosa*, which have elegant flower spikes that catch the light beautifully.

Left: Use grasses, such as this Stipa calamagrostis, *as architectural plants in your scheme.*

EVERGREENS

Brachyglottis (Dunedin Group)
'Sunshine'
Choisya
Daphne tangutica
Euonymus fortunei
Hebe cupressoides
Ligustrum lucidum
Pieris japonica
Rhododendron
Santolina chamaecyparis
Vinca

Above: Many of the hebes are evergreen. This one, H. cupressoides, has striking violet flowers and small leaves.

EVERGREENS

The great feature of evergreens is that they hold on to their leaves throughout the year. They can be used as a permanent part of the structure of any border or garden. Unless they are carefully sited, however, evergreens can become a bit dull, so plan your planting with care.

Many evergreens have dark green leaves, but using plants with variegated leaves, or clever planting combinations, will add colour and interest. Try *Eleagnus pungens* 'Maculata' with its yellow-centred leaves or *Ligustrum lucidum* 'Excelsior Superbum', which has a golden variegation in the open, although in shade it glows with a bright yellowish green.

Lots of evergreens have the bonus of glorious flowers. Rhododendrons and azaleas in particular, many of the evergreen hebes and camellias, are prized for their gorgeously coloured blooms. *Choisya* is a good example.

The shiny leaves catch the sun and it produces masses of fragrant white flowers in spring and often again later in the year.

CONIFERS

Dwarf conifers are especially useful for providing year-round interest. Planted close together they will grow into each other, assuming a sculptural quality, besides making excellent ground cover. Some form dense mats,

DWARF CONIFERS

Abies Cephalonica 'Meyer's Dwarf'
Chamaecyparis lawsoniana
'Minima Aurea'
Juniperus communis 'Compressa'
Taxus baccuta 'Elegantissima'
Thuja orientalis 'Aurea Nana'
Thuja plicata 'Irish Gold'
Picea glauca var. albertiana 'Conica'
Picea pungens 'Globosa'

Above: Conifers provide a wonderful selection of shapes and textures. This juniper produces an attractive "sea of waves" effect that can never become boring.

particularly the prostrate junipers such as *Juniperus horizontalis*, *J squamata* and *J. procumbens*.

Most dwarf conifers are suitable for rock gardens and containers, and also look good planted with heathers. Choose upright conifers, to provide height.

IVIES

One of the great features of ivies is their ability to cover and conceal unsightly structures or eyesores. They will thrive in different locations.

The classic situation for ivy is growing up a wall. *Hedera helix* 'Buttercup' is spectacular against a sunny wall. *H. h.* 'Goldheart', which has green-

IVIES
Hedera 'Bruder Ingobert'
Hedera helix 'Goldheart'
Hedera hibernica
Hedera 'Merion Beauty'

edged, gold-centred leaves, retains its colour on a shaded wall. Don't grow different ivies too closely together on walls or they will cover each other.

Some designers use mixed ivies for mass bedding, but these do require pruning once or twice a year. Ivy also makes excellent edging to a flower border. It can be grown along the edge of a garden path or planted on a terrace garden to great effect.

Ivies make excellent ground cover and can completely cover large areas quickly. One of the best for this is *Hedera hibernica*. Many *Hedera helix* cultivars are also suitable, especially the dark green 'Ivalace' or 'Shamrock'.

Above: Here a golden ivy rambles happily over a wall intermingled with a rose and underplanted with complementary flowers.

321

Spring

FRESHNESS AND VITALITY ARE THE KEYNOTES OF SPRING. FOLIAGE AND FLOWERS ARE BRIGHTLY COLOURED, WITH SUNNY YELLOW ONE OF THE MOST PREVALENT COLOURS.

PLANTS AT THEIR BEST

After the short, dark days of winter, spring begins tentatively with a few jewel-coloured bulbs and occasional perennial flowers. Flower buds on trees and shrubs begin to open. Before long plants are bursting into colour all around. The spring light makes everything in the garden look new and fresh.

Bulbs

This is a wonderful season for bulbs and corms of all kinds. There is a multitude of crocuses, daffodils, tulips, hyacinths, fritillaries, dog's tooth violet (*Erythronium*), irises, snowflake (*Leucojum*), grape hyacinths and trilliums, coming into flower in grass, borders and containers. These are all hardy plants, unharmed by frosts.

Above: Spring in the cottage garden is a glorious jumble of colours with primulas, Myosotis *(forget-me-nots) and* Dicentra.

Perennials

Some herbaceous plants have been around all winter. Lungworts (*Pulmonaria*), for example, have been in full leaf constantly, but now produce masses of blue, red, pink or white flowers. Hellebores are flowering as are primulas, of which the primrose is perhaps the best loved. As the days continue to lengthen and the air and ground become warmer, early flowers move into the background as other herbaceous perennials begin to emerge. Among the next phase are bleeding hearts (*Dicentra spectabilis*) and other dicentras, which need light shade and

Left: Hyacinthus orientalis *'Pink Pearl' interspersed with* Viola *makes a beautiful, scented display.*

will grow happily under trees that have yet to open their leaves. Wood anemones (*Anemone nemorosa*), in a range of white and delicate blues, pinks and yellow, also make use of the temporary light under deciduous trees and shrubs. Among the brightest flowers are the brilliant golden daisies of leopard's bane (*Doronicum*), and buttery kingcup (*Caltha*) flowers, which are essential for any bog or waterside planting. *Paeonia mlokosewitschii*, one of the earliest peonies to flower, has delicate yellow flowers.

Shrubs

Many shrubs flower early in the year. Rhododendrons, azaleas, magnolias, pieris, camellias and many others provide outstanding spring colour.

Spiraea 'Arguta' is among the earliest to flower, producing frothy pure white flowers over quite a long period. One of the best-loved shrubs is *Magnolia stellata* with its mass of delicate, star-like flowers in glistening

Above: Euphorbia polychroma *creates a perfect dome which is effective in any spring border.*

white or tinged with pink. The effect is enhanced because the flowers appear before the leaves develop. *Exochorda* x *macrantha* 'The Bride' is so covered in pure white flowers that the leaves are barely visible.

Forsythia creates one of the biggest splashes of spring colour. It should be cut back immediately after flowering to ensure that new flowering shoots grow in time for next season. Lilac (*Syringa*), prized for its colour and perfume, flowers late in the season. The white forms especially can look untidy when the flowers die, so they should be removed.

Rhododendrons and azaleas, especially, have such a vast range of glorious colours and flower sizes, that perhaps the best way to make a choice for your own garden is to see as many as you can in flower and then discover the names of the ones you like.

Left: Rhododendrons *grow into large shrubs which burst into colour in late spring.*

323

COLOUR COMBINATIONS

In lawns and under shrubs and trees, naturalized bulbs flower in cheerful multi-coloured carpets without constraint. In many spring borders, however, regularity and uniformity of planting are often preferred. Spring light has a softening effect and so strong opposing colours, such as primary red and blue, seem to go together better at this time of year.

Formal Beds

In formal beds you can interplant spring bulbs with bushy bedding plants, for example late-flowering tulips with pansies, forget-me-nots, polyanthus, double daisies *(Bellis perennis)* or dwarf wallflowers. These bedding plants hide the bare soil and make tall-stemmed bulbs like tulips less ungainly and vulnerable to wind damage. Pink tulips with blue forget-me-nots is a classic combination that can be enlivened by the occasional dot of a red tulip.

Such schemes offer scope for colour coordination and combinations that vary from the subtle to the gaudy. For example, pale pink hyacinths and white or pale yellow *Polyanthus* make a restful, receding combination, while deep yellow *Polyanthus* makes an arresting sight. Try planting two different kinds of spring bulbs together, such as bright blue *Scilla siberica* among 'Pink Pearl' hyacinths.

Such a border, recreated at the home of Monet in Giverny, France, combines a number of favourites – tall bearded blue-and-white iris fronting masses of Siberian wallflowers (*Erysimum hieracaciifolium*), scented wallflowers and *Hesperis matronalis*. All of this display could be edged with purple-flowered *Lobularia maritima* 'Royal Carpet'.

Informal Borders

Planting an informal border is easier. Generally, bold clumps of a single variety work best in a border, and if the clumps or drifts are used to fill gaps they will probably be well spaced out with little risk of colour clashes. It is often possible to plant bulbs between perennials that will hide the dying foliage as they emerge.

Above: *The variegated* Weigela florida *'Albomarginata' is seen here against a* Spiraea. *The striped leaves blend well with the white flowers of the* Spiraea *in spring.*

Above: Dainty yellow primroses are charmingly set off by their own green foliage and enhanced by a fountain of yellow grass.

NATURAL EFFECT

For a natural effect in borders, try a mass planting of spring-flowering bulbs and perennials. Purple crocus and yellow aconites could be planted to flower above the marbled leaves of *Arum italicum pictum*, with the rich mauve flowers of hellebores atop leafless stems. Around these could perhaps be scattered the green-tipped white bells of snowdrops.

The strong blue of grape hyacinths with the pale yellow of primroses is another time-honoured spring combination. Or you could try a mix of hyacinths, compact tulips and narcissi. Planted closely for maximum impact, these would be as colourful as any summer bedding.

PLANTS AT THEIR BEST
EARLY SPRING

Bergenia (non-woody evergreen)
Camellia (shrub)
Crocus (bulb)
Eranthis hyemalis (bulb)
Helleborus orientalis (perennial)
Hyacinthus (bulb)
Iris reticulata (bulb)
Magnolia stellata (shrub)
Primula x *polyantha* (perennial)
Tulipa kaufmanniana (bulb)

MID-SPRING

Amelanchier (shrub/tree)
Cytisus, various (shrub)
Dicentra (perennial)
Doronicum (perennial)
Magnolia x *soulangiana* (tree)
Magnolia stellata (shrub)
Narcissus (bulb)
Prunus 'Kwanzan' (tree)
Rhododendron, various (shrub)
Ribes sanguineum (shrub)

LATE SPRING

Azalea (shrub)
Bergenia (non-woody evergreen)
Cheiranthus (wallflower)
Choisya ternata (shrub)
Clematis montana (shrubby climber)
Cytisus, various (shrub)
Dicentra (perennial)
Fritillaria (bulb)
Laburnum (tree)
Malus (tree)
Paeonia (perennial and shrub)
Phlox subulata (rock plant)
Pulsatilla vulgaris (rock plant)
Rhododendron, various (shrub)
Saxifraga, various (rock plant)
Syringa (shrub)
Tulipa, various (bulb)
Wisteria (shrubby climber)

Jobs to Do

In cold regions the weather can still be icy in early spring, but in mild climates you can make a start on many outdoor jobs, including feeding and mulching beds and borders, and spring-pruning shrubs if applicable. If sowing or planting outdoors, bear in mind that soil and air temperature are important. Few seeds will germinate if the soil temperature is below 7°C (45°F), so use a soil thermometer to check before you sow.

By mid-spring, outdoor sowing and planting can begin in earnest. You can plant container-grown shrubs, herbaceous perennials, gladioli and other summer bulbs and tubers, as well as making a start on sowing hardy annuals. Plants sown or planted in late spring often catch up with those sown a month earlier if the weather was unseasonably cold.

Late spring can be deceptive, and in cold areas late frosts can occur. Take local climate into account before planting any frost-tender plants outdoors or hardening off tender bedding plants. Watch to see when summer bedding is put out in local parks, by gardeners with local knowledge.

Prune spring-flowering shrubs, such as *Ribes sanguineum* and forsythia immediately they finish flowering. At the end of the season, you can start planting up hanging baskets and containers for summer displays.

GARDENER'S TIP

Severe late frosts can kill new shoots and buds on shrubs. Provide adequate protection if a hard frost is forecast.

Harden off Bedding Plants

It is crucial for all plants raised indoors or in a greenhouse to be hardened off. This gradually accustoms cosseted plants to withstand the harsher conditions outdoors. Place the plants in a cold frame a week or two before planting out. Close the top in the evening and on cold days, otherwise ventilate freely. If a sharp frost threatens, cover the frame with insulation material, such as bubble polythene.

Below: By late spring you can plant up your hanging baskets for a summer display like this.

PRICK OUT SEEDLINGS

1 Prick out seedlings as soon as they are large enough to handle. Fill the individual cells of a module loosely with a potting compost (soil mix) suitable for seedlings.

2 Strike the compost off level with the top of the module, but do not compress. It will settle once the seedlings have been inserted and watered.

3 Loosen the seedlings and, if possible, lift one at a time by their seed leaves. These are the first to open, and are usually smaller and a different shape from the true leaves. Do not lift them by the stems as these are fragile.

4 Using a small tool, make a hole in each cell that is large enough to take the roots of the seedlings with as little damage to them as possible. Gently firm the compost around the roots, without pressing. Water the seedlings thoroughly, then keep in shade for a few days.

PRICK OUT INTO POTS

There are a few special cases when more than a single seedling is used because they are too small to handle individually. For example, lobelias have seedlings that are tiny, and the individual plants are not very substantial when they are mature, so many gardeners choose to prick out a small group of seedlings, about five or six, together. By the time these have grown into seedlings that are large enough to plant out they look like one substantial plant.

Above: Scarlet Verbena *plants that were sown as seeds in the spring.*

Summer

THE ARRIVAL OF SUMMER ALWAYS SEEMS SUDDEN. ONE MINUTE IT IS SPRING, THE NEXT IT IS SUMMER, AND THE GARDEN IS BURSTING WITH LIFE, HEADY WITH AROMAS AND VIBRANT WITH COLOUR.

PLANTS AT THEIR BEST

Although often regarded as a continuation in gardening terms there is quite a difference between early, mid- and late summer.

Early summer carries on where spring left off, with plenty of fresh-looking foliage and bright, rich colours. Lupins, poppies, peonies and delphiniums are vital players in any display at this time of the year.

As midsummer approaches, the colours change subtly and flowers with more muted tones unfurl. Among these are *Phlox*, *Catanache* (sometimes known as Cupid's dart), pente-mons and *Gypsophila*.

By late summer colours are fading and foliage is starting to look a little tired. Autumnal tones become evident with the deep golds and russet-reds of perennials such as achilleas, heleniums and inulas.

Perennials

Summer is the height of the perennial year. The hardy geraniums (pelargoniums) are one of the mainstays of the summer border. There is a vast range to choose from.

Above: A variety of different shades of yellow are broken up by contrasting splashes of red in this summer garden.

Pelargoniums are widely grown for the visual impact of their flowers and for their coloured foliage. They can be grown in borders, or in containers.

Dahlias are useful for borders as they last for months, come in many different heights and provide lots of flowers for cutting.

Tuberous-rooted begonias, used for both bedding and container display, come in shades of pink, red, yellow and white. Seed-raised begonias that flower quickly, such as Non-stop, are also popular. They flower all summer, until cut back by frost, and are suitable for massed bedding. These are all low growing, reaching 23–30cm (9–12in) in height.

The tall – up to 1.8m (6ft) – exotic-looking cannas come into bloom early and continue until the first frost. They combine spectacular red, orange or yellow flowers with interesting foliage, mostly dark or purple bronze but some brightly variegated.

Bulbs

Summer-flowering bulbs are exceptionally good for adding highlights to a traditional herbaceous border, and can be useful for brightening up areas between shrubs that have finished flowering. It is difficult to imagine a traditional herbaceous border, for example, without groups of lilies or a clump or two of crocosmias. The crocosmia corms multiply freely, and after a year or two most plantings

Above: The pink globes of Allium christophii *contrast successfully with* Salvia sylvestris.

Above: Yellow achillea and the streaked leaves of Canna *'Striata' make an effective backdrop for* Crocosmia *'Lucifer'.*

make a bold show in late summer with arching sprays of red, orange or yellow flowers.

The round, colourful heads of alliums make stunning statements in the summer border. There are many forms including dwarf ones like the yellow *Allium moly*, *A. christophii*, with its 15cm (6in) spheres of starry, lilac flowers, and tall, majestic species such as the 1.8m (6ft) *A. giganteum* with its huge bloom. *A. sphaerocephalon* has drumstick heads of pinkish-purple flowers on thin 75cm (2½ft) tall stems. It is best grown mid-border, where other border plants can hide and support the stems. The seedheads are another delight. They can be enjoyed in the garden or used indoors in dried flower arrangements.

Shrubs

From midsummer onwards, many shrubs begin to flower. These include brightly flowering shrubs such as *Hypericum calycinum*, which, with its brilliant yellow flowers, will even flourish in shade. For a sunny spot, the bright pinks and oranges of helianthemums, or the soft-pink shades of *Cistus* are a delight. Use white-flowering shrubs such as *Cistus laurifolius* or *Philadelphus* to break up bold masses of colour and act as a backdrop to vivid shades.

Hydrangeas, with their huge mounds of blooms, prefer shady positions, where the whites will brighten up their surroundings. The delicate lacecaps are popular because of the shape of the flowers. *Hydrangea quercifolia*

Above: The glorious cascading flowers of Fuchsia *'Cotton Candy' would be a delightful addition to the summer scheme.*

Above: A white Hydrangea *thrives in a shaded border.*

combines white flowers, which become tinged pink with age, with mid-green leaves which will turn bronze in autumn. *H. aspera* 'Villosa' has mauvish-blue and pink flowers. Mophead varieties (*H. macrophylla*) bear blue flowers on acid soil, red ones on neutral soil and pink ones on alkaline soil.

Few other plants smother themselves so completely or over such a long period as fuchsias. Ranging from almost white, through pastel pink to rich purples, reds and oranges, the flower shapes and colours of fuchsias offer unlimited possibilities. Tender types have become prized bedding plants, while the often less showy hardy types can be integrated into mixed borders, where they can give years of pleasure. Some hardy fuchsias

Above: Clematis *'Purpurea Plena Elegans'* provides the interest now that its host plant, Rosa *'Cécile Brünner, climbing'*, has all but finished flowering.

make elegant plants that can stand alone as specimens in a bed or in a suitable container.

Roses are at their best in summer. Some are once-flowering and do so in the early summer, but many go on flowering throughout the whole season. Some gardeners prefer to have a separate garden or special beds for roses, while others like to mix them in with other plants.

Climbers

Interesting effects can be created using climbing roses. The rambling 'Albertine', for example, can be grown to produce a glorious fountain of salmon-pink flowers up to 6m (20ft) high.

Like climbing roses, clematis can be grown in a variety of ways, on pergolas, against walls and fences. The more vigorous types will reach into trees to provide glorious colour and height. There are many startling colours to choose from, ranging from deep rose-pink through crimson and wine red to bright purple, in small or large flower sizes. You can select from the three different groups to ensure colour throughout the summer.

PLANTS AT THEIR BEST

EARLY SUMMER

Allium
Dianthus
Geranium
Iris germanica hybrids
Paeonia
Papaver orientale
Philadelphus

MID-SUMMER

Clematis
Digitalis
Geranium
Hardy annuals
Hydrangea
Hypericum
Lavandula
Lilium
Rosa

LATE SUMMER

Dahlia
Fuchsia
Helenium
Hibiscus syriacus
Hypericum
Lavatera
Perovskia atriplicifolia
Romneya
Solidago
Summer bedding

331

Above: *Orange and blue are both powerful colours. Used together in a planting scheme, they produce an agreeable tension as is shown by the bright* Agapanthus *and orange* Crocosmia.

COLOUR COMBINATIONS

With all the colour that is around during summer, some stunning plantings are possible.

Beds and Borders

At this time of year blues can be tinged with pink, making them work well with mauves and violets. For example, *Echium* 'Blue Bedder', which comes in varying shades of blue, combines beautifully with *Penstemon* 'Sour Grapes'. To create a restful mood, try fronting spires of purplish-blue delphiniums with a mass of violet-blue *Geranium ibericum*.

Including white flowers in a planting with a lot of soft blues and pinks will soothe the whole effect; blue and

pink with occasional pure white highlights is a favourite scheme for the summer border.

While some gardeners will relish a totally hot composition, most will want to use red with some discretion at this time of the year. Even a combination of bright red and blue, achieved perhaps by planting red oriental poppies with blue anchusas, can be too strong for some. If you prefer a pink-and-pastel summer mix, do include the occasional hot red such as *Penstemon*, *Kniphofia* or *Crocosmia* to add some spice.

Above: *The stunning white bloom of the Easter or Bermuda lily* (Lilium longiflorium)

A White Border

Cool white summer plantings can be centred on white lilies, perhaps combining them with 'Iceberg' roses, hazy *Gypsophila* and white *Penstemon*. Lilies make a good focal point in the border, and will flower above a sea of

Above: The glorious white flowers of Rosa 'Madame Hardy' will enhance a traditional cottage garden.

herbaceous plants. The Madonna lily *(Lilium candidum)* is a traditional cottage garden plant that blends well with old-fashioned roses. You could fill out such a scheme with *Hebe rakaiensis* and grey-green leaved *Anaphalis triplinervis*, both white flowered. You could also include silvery-leaved plants.

Effects with Climbers

The evergreen foliage of the many types of conifers provides a superb foil for the bright blooms of summer-flowering climbers. Climbers can also be allowed to scramble through formally trained plants, creating different effects. Mixing violet-blue *Clematis* 'Ascotiensis' with the creamy white old-fashioned *Rosa* 'Albéric Barbier', for instance, produces a cool, striking result and will provide colour over a long period.

Late-flowering clematis can be encouraged to meander through heathers. The less vigorous, small-flowered viticella or texensis types of clematis, in the same colour range as the heathers, are best for this purpose (summer-flowering species would be too rampant). The flowers of *Clematis* 'Royal Velours' glow like rubies against the velvety old-gold foliage of *Erica carnea* 'Foxhollow', for instance. If you plant a clematis among winter-flowering *Erica*, however, you will have to cut it back in late autumn rather than late winter, as is generally recommended, so that the clematis does not smother the heather flowers. Clematis can also be grown up small trees to add interest to the lower section, which is without leaves.

Above: Climbers planted together prolong the colour in an area. Here Rosa *'Iceberg' is grown with* Clematis tangutica.

333

JOBS TO DO

Many of the planting and sowing jobs begun in spring can be completed during early summer – planting hanging baskets and containers, sowing hardy annuals and planting perennials, bulbs and tubers. Now is the time to sow biennials such as wallflowers and forget-me-nots and plant out any tender bedding plants.

As the display changes through the summer, it is important that the beds and borders are kept tidy and well-maintained. The flowers of each plant should be dead-headed as soon as they go over. This not only removes an eyesore, but also prevents the plant's energy from being spent on seed production. Instead, the energy is channelled back into the plant, which may then produce a second, later show of flowers.

Above: Disbud chrysanthemums if you want larger flowers later.

Some perennials benefit from being cut right back to the ground, which encourages a flush of new leaves, so they can then act as foliage plants. Lady's mantle (*Alchemilla mollis*), for example, not only looks tired and tatty if it is left, but it also seeds itself everywhere. If it is sheared back to its base after flowering, however, it will produce a set of beautiful new foliage and self-sowing will have been prevented.

Summer is the time to take semi-ripe cuttings, layer shrubs and carnations and move biennial and perennial seedlings to a nursery bed. As the season draws to a close, start planting spring bulbs and divide and replant irises.

Left: Dead-head lilacs as soon as they have finished flowering to prevent the tree's energy going into seed production.

Sow Biennials and Hardy Perennials

1 Prepare the ground, and eliminate the weeds. Competition from weeds is often the greatest enemy the seedlings face. Break the soil down into a fine, crumbly structure once it has been cleared of weeds.

3 Run water into the drill before sowing if the soil is very dry. Space the seeds thinly and evenly. This will make thinning and transplanting easier. A small dispenser tool makes the task easier.

2 Take out a drill with the corner of a hoe or rake to the depth recommended on the seed packet. The drills can be quite close together.

4 Cover the seeds by shuffling the soil back with your feet or carefully ease the soil over with the back of a rake. Remember to add a label.

GARDENER'S TIP

In dry weather do not water the drill after sowing as this will cause the soil to harden, preventing germination of the seedlings.

5 Thin the seedlings as soon as they are large enough to handle easily so that they do not become overcrowded. Gently firm the soil around the seedlings that remain in the ground.

Autumn

AUTUMN MAY WELL SIGNIFY THE END OF SUMMER, BUT IT COMPENSATES WITH A FLUSH OF GLORIOUS COLOUR. WARM YELLOWS, BURNING ORANGES AND BRONZE, AND FIERY REDS AND PURPLES ARE NEVER BETTER THAN NOW.

PLANTS AT THEIR BEST

Mellowed by the slanting autumn light, colours at this time of year become more muted, but there are still plenty of bright flowers around. Additionally, the tints and hues of foliage, berries and other fruit make this season a celebration of reds and browns which glow in the light and bring a warmth to the garden.

Above: The foliage of an Acer *tree is at its best in the autumn.*

Bulbs

Autumn-flowering bulbs are a delight, with exotic dahlias and cannas vying for attention with strident colours and bold foliage. Nerines bear their large heads of frilly, bright pink, trumpet-shaped flowers. Colchicums are found in various shades of lilac, pink and white and will grow in borders or grass in sun or partial shade. Other autumn highlights include the sternbergias, with their bright yellow, crocus-like flowers and crinums, which produce a wonderful array of large, pink, funnel-shaped flowers.

Above: The magnificent autumn flowering bulb Crinum x powellii *is also known as the Cape Lily.*

The open, cup-shaped flowers of the kaffir lily (*Schizostylis coccinea*) are available in shades of pink or red.

Perennials

Many perennial plants run on into autumn from summer but true autumn has its own distinctive flora. Michaelmas daisies (*Aster*) are one of the mainstays of the season, as are chrysanthemums, while vibrantly coloured sedums are invaluable for attracting the last of the butterflies and bees.

Yellows, oranges and bronzes are plentiful, with coneflowers *(Rudbeckia)* and sunflowers *(Helianthus)* in full flower, but there are also deep purple ironweeds *(Vernonia)*. Lilyturf *(Liriope)* has blue spikes of flowers and is useful because it is one of the few autumn-flowering plants that will grow in shade.

Above: Many shrubs have stunning berries in the autumn. Here Pyracantha *is covered with glowing orange berries.*

Above: The autumn border will look glorious with a display of Aster *x* frikartii.

Shrubs

Fuchsias, buddlejas, hibiscus and hydrangeas all continue to bloom in autumn. One of the few true autumn-flowering shrubs is *Osmanthus heterophyllus*, with fragrant white flowers. *Ceratostigma willmottianum* has piercingly blue flowers that continue well into autumn and *Eucryphia glutinosa* bears glistening white flowers with a central boss of stamens.

Foliage and Berries

The true glory of autumn, of course, belongs to foliage. Paramount for autumn beauty are the acers, trees and shrubs, which have a stunning range of leaf shades. Berries and other fruit are an added bonus; they are attractive and supply birds and other animals with a valuable food resource.

Above: The red leaves of Acer palmatum *'Sakazuki' make a fiery climax to the year.*

COLOUR COMBINATIONS

The abundance of plant material and vibrant colour in the garden during autumn can provide some stimulating effects. Autumn flower colours can be arranged to harmonize with the season's colourful berries and changing leaves.

Beds and Borders

Whilst daisy-like plants such as chrysanthemums, dendranthemas, asters and the yellow-flowered *Rudbeckia* 'Goldsturm' are the mainstay of autumn borders, there are other plants that can be utilized, too.

Daisy plants can be combined with late-flowering dazzlers such as the white-flowered *Anemone japonica* 'Honorine Jobert'. *Achillea ptarmica* 'The Pearl', also white flowered, and *Campanula lactiflora*, are also good

choices to extend the late summer border well into autumn.

Sedums take on some glowing hues now. At the front of a border, the pink-mauve flowers of the iceplant *Sedum* x *spectabile* 'Brilliant' planted with an eye-catching daisy plant like *Dendranthema* 'Raquel' would provide a long period of strong colour. Hostas could be substituted for sedums to edge a border. *Hosta* 'Honeybells' and *H.* 'Green fountain' both provide particularly glowing foliage as well as useful flowers. *Cephalaria gigantea* would make a bold display at the back of the border.

CONTRASTING SHAPES

Some interesting effects can be engineered by planting contrasting shapes and textures together. The tall, slender

Above: The autumn-flowering succulent Sedum spectabile *is a seasonal highlight.*

Above: Cortaderia selloana *'Sunningdale Silver' is at its most splendid in the autumn months.*

flower spikes of cannas, which rise above their spiralling oval leaves, often brilliantly coloured at this time of year, can be contrasted with the roundness of dahlia flowers. These range from the large open flowers of the single forms to the round, tight balls of the Pompon varieties.

Dahlias also make interesting associations with ornamental grasses. Plant them with grasses such as *Calamagrostis* x *acutifolia*, *Miscanthus sinensis* or *Cortaderia selloana* to create a graceful picture. Try placing the copper-orange spikes of *Canna* 'Wyoming' alongside *Dahlia* 'David Howard' together with the lilac-purple flowers of *Verbena bonariensis*.

Right: Autumn is renowned for the warm tones of its plants and foliage. Dahlia *'David Howard' has glowing flowers.*

PLANTS AT THEIR BEST
EARLY AUTUMN
Anemone japonica
Aster novae-angliae
Aster novi-belgii
Chrysanthemum, early-flowering garden type
Dahlia
Hibiscus syriacus
Pyracantha
Rudbeckia
Sedum spectabile
Solidago
Sternbergia lutera

MID-AUTUMN
Acer
Anemone japonica
Aster novi-belgii
Fothergilla
Liriope muscari
Schizostylis coccinea

LATE AUTUMN
Berberis
Cotoneaster
Fothergilla
Gentiana sino-ornata
Liriope muscari
Nerine bowdenii
Pernettya
Pyracantha

JOBS TO DO

Now is the time to prepare for the following year. Plant lilies and spring-flowering bulbs. Sow hardy annuals if your climate is mild enough or you can provide winter protection. Take fuchsia, pelargonium and hardwood cuttings. Divide perennials that have become over large.

Clear away dead matter and dying plants regularly to keep the autumn border looking tidy and to ensure that flowering perennials are visible.

Before winter sets in, lift, clean and store gladioli and other tender bulbs, corms and tubers. As soon as dahlias have been blackened by the first frost, lift and store them too. Protect vulnerable plants that will remain in the garden over winter.

Above: Cover tender plants with horticultural fleece or bubble polythene to protect from sharp frosts and damaging winter wind. Secure well with stakes and tie twine or string around the circumference of the plant.

If you are planning a major replanting of a border, start preparing the soil in the autumn, especially if you are planting shrubs. The ground will still be warm from the summer sun and easier to dig. This will also give the ground an opportunity to weather, with worms taking nutrients below the surface, and any remaining weeds that reappear can be cleared before planting begins again the following spring.

PLANT LILIES FOR SUMMER

1 Dig an area that will take four or five bulbs 20cm (8in) deep and mix in well-rotted manure or garden compost. Add grit and a little bonemeal.

2 Place the bulbs 15cm (6in) apart and deep enough to be covered with twice their depth of soil so that they are well anchored when fully grown.

3 Sprinkle more grit and coarse sand around the bulbs to deter slugs and reduce the risk of waterlogging. Place canes to mark the lilies' position.

PLANTING BEDDING PLANTS FOR A SPRING DISPLAY

1 Fork over the ground after clearing summer bedding plants. Apply slow-acting bonemeal after forking over and rake it in.

2 If you have raised the plants yourself, water them well about an hour before lifting them. Lift them with some soil, using a hand fork.

3 Spring bedding plants bought from garden centres or nurseries are sold in trays or strips. These are disposable, so don't be afraid to break them.

4 Space the plants out on the surface, allowing for any bulbs before planting. Arrange the bulbs, then plant from the back or one end.

LIFT AND PROTECT CHRYSANTHEMUMS

1 Lift the roots before frosts begin. Trim the tops and any long roots, to keep a compact shape. Select a tray that will take the roots in one layer.

2 Position the roots on a layer of compost (soil mix) in a tray. Cover with 2.5cm (1in) of compost and keep just moist. Store in a cool, light place.

LIFT AND STORE PELARGONIUMS

1 Lift pelargoniums that have finished flowering, before the first frost if possible. Shake the soil off the roots, and trim them to 5–8cm (2–3in) long.

2 Trim the roots and shoots. Trim off any remaining leaves.

3 Half fill a large tray with soil or sowing compost (soil mix). Position the plants and add more compost to cover the roots. Water well initially, then only when the soil becomes almost dry.

4 If you want to overwinter on a sunny windowsill, it may be more convenient to use large pots.

Above: By storing pelargoniums they will survive over the winter.

GARDENER'S TIP

A cool but frost-free garage is a sensible place to store overwintering bulbs, corms and tubers. Keep bulbs, corms and tubers where you can easily check them about once a month, to ensure they are all still sound. Any that start to rot must be removed immediately to safeguard the rest.

PLANT A POT-GROWN ROSE

1 Dig a hole large enough to contain the roots. Fork in a little bonemeal and plenty of well-rotted manure or garden compost.

2 Place the rose in the hole and use a cane laid across the top of the hole to check that the bud union is positioned about 2.5cm (1in) below the soil level.

3 Replace the soil and firm gently with your feet to ensure the rose is planted firmly with no air pockets, and so that the bush cannot be rocked by wind. Rake over and water thoroughly.

4 If the plant was unpruned when bought, cut back all the shoots to 15–20cm (6–8in) above the ground.

OVERWINTER DAHLIAS

1 Lift dahlias, using a fork, once the first frosts have blackened the foliage. Avoid damaging the roots with the prongs of the fork.

2 Cut off the stem, leaving a stump 5cm (2in) long. Stand upside-down on a supported mesh to allow moisture to drain from the hollow stems. Keep in a dry, frost-free place for a few days.

3 Remove surplus soil, trim loose bits off the roots and shorten the stem to a stump. Label each tuber and pack in a well-insulated box with peat substitute, vermiculite, wood shavings or crumpled newspaper. Store in a frost-free location.

Winter

GARDENS CAN BE FULL OF COLOUR AT THIS TIME OF YEAR. THERE IS
PLENTY TO SEE AND ENJOY, FROM STRIKING STEMS AND FOLIAGE TO
BRIGHT FLOWERS THAT WILL DISPEL THE WINTER GLOOM.

PLANTS AT THEIR BEST

Winter light shows up plants in relief.
Silvers and greys are sympathetic to
the season, and green takes on new
importance. Many evergreen shrubs,
especially those with shiny leaves, can
look particularly good in the weak
winter sunlight.

Bulbs

There are many dainty winter-flowering
bulbs and corms, including snowdrop
cultivars, winter aconites (*Eranthis
hyemalis*), early crocuses, dwarf irises,
tiny cyclamen and *Anemone blanda*.
The earliest daffodils, such as *Narcissus*
'January Gold', are slightly taller.

*Above: Winter aconites bring a touch of
colour at the end of the year.*

The Algerian iris (*Iris unguicularis*)
starts flowering in late autumn and
continues until early spring, whatever
the weather. Its mauve or purple
flowers are deliciously scented.

Perennials

Primroses (*Primula vulgaris*) often
flower sporadically at this time of
year, and sweet violets (*Viola odorata*)
will flower in warm spots. Hellebores
(*Helleborus*) are one of the mainstays
of the perennial scene in winter.

*Left: Clump-forming hellebores add
colour and architectural interest in winter.*

Above: Conifers retain their glowing colours throughout the winter.

Shrubs

Many shrubs provide plenty of interest during winter months. Winter jasmine (*Jasminum nudiflorum*) is truly a winter plant, flowering from the end of autumn through to early spring, untroubled by frost and snow. Jasmine stems taken indoors make attractive winter flower decorations.

Winter hazels (*Corylopsis*), with their lovely yellow catkins, also make excellent winter plants. Witch hazels (*Hamamelis*) produce curious flowers, resembling clusters of tiny ribbons. As well as being attractive, they have a prominent smell that fills the air. Several viburnums flower during winter. *Viburnum tinus* is evergreen and covered with flat heads of small white flowers throughout most of the winter and often right through into spring.

Coloured Stems

Some shrubs are prized for the colours of their bare stems in winter. When planted to catch the low winter sunshine, they make a wonderful display. Dogwoods (*Cornus*) are renowned for the beauty of their stems with colours ranging from red though to yellow. *C. alba* is scarlet. Vibrant *C. stolonifera* 'Flaviramea' has yellowish green bark. *Rubus* 'Golden Veil', which has bright yellow foliage in summer, sports white stems in winter.

Several of the willows (*Salix*) have beautiful winter stems, which bear distinctive catkins at the end of the season. *S. alba* produces some of the best coloured stems, but there are many other good species.

Above: Daphne burkwoodii *has an intense scent as well as delightful pink flowers.*

COLOUR COMBINATIONS

As colour is so precious at this time of year and valued in its own right, planting combinations seem to have less importance than during other seasons. Nonetheless there are some delightful associations to be enjoyed.

Brightening the Gloom

The early woodland bulbs and perennials naturally favour locations under bushes and trees where they enjoy precious sunshine before the newly-formed leafy canopy obstructs their light and they cease flowering.

Snowdrops (*Galanthus*) multiply quickly where they are growing, especially in their natural habitat in damp

Above: A welcome sight in the winter, Cyclamen coum *and snowdrops.*

woodland, and will eventually spread to carpet vast areas with white and green. In the garden, you can plant them under shrubs to create a similar, if scaled down, effect. Winter aconites (*Eranthis hyemalis*) grown this way provide welcome splashes of yellow, rather than white, in dark places.

Above: The bright red stems of Cornus *lighten a wintery scene when branches are bare.*

> ### WINTER SHRUBS
>
> (Shrubs marked * are best cut back hard each spring for their winter stem effect.)
> *Berberis temolacia**
> *Cornus alba* 'Sibirica'*
> *Cornus sanguinea* 'Winter Beauty'*
> *Cornus stolonifera* 'Flaviramea'*
> *Garrya elliptica*
> *Hamamelis mollis*
> *Mahonia* x *media* 'Charity'
> *Prunus subhirtella* 'Autumnalis'
> *Rubus thibetanus*
> *Salix alba var. vitellina* 'Britzensis'*
> *Salix irrorata*
> *Viburnum* x *bodnantense* 'Dawn'
> *Viburnum tinus*

Above: Heather can be relied on to add colour to the winter garden.

Effects with Grasses

The evergreen grass, *Stipa arundinacea*, which thrives in dry shade, can be used in a similar but altogether more stunning way, by being underplanted with a skirt of *Bergenia cordifolia*. The impact of the bergenias' purple-tinged, heart-shaped leaves beneath the arching orange-brown fronds of the grass is heightened when rose-red to dark pink, winter flowers on dark red stems come into play.

Winter Heathers

The glowing colours of winter heathers can be strikingly combined with some of the more colourful shrubs. Varieties of *Erica carnea* and *E. x darleyensis* can be mixed with the colourful stems of dogwoods (*Cornus*) and some varieties of willow (*Salix*). Selections of *Calluna vulgaris* with highly coloured foliage, such as 'Beoly Gold' (bright golden yellow) or

PLANTS AT THEIR BEST

EARLY WINTER
Hamamelis mollis
Iris unguicularis
Jasminum nudiflorum
Mahonia 'Charity'
Nerine bowdenii
Pernettya, berries
Prunus x *subhirtella* 'Autumnalis'
Pyracantha, berries
Sarcococca
Viburnum

MID-WINTER
Chimonanthus praecox
Eranthis hyemalis
Erica carnea
Erica x *darleyensis*
Galanthus nivalis
Garrya elliptica
Ilex, berries
Lonicera fragrantissima
Sarcococca

LATE WINTER
Crocus
Daphne mezereum
Eranthis hyemalis
Garrya elliptica
Helleborus
Iris unguicularis
Jasminum nudiflorum
Prunus x *subhirtella* 'Autumnalis'
Viburnum

'Robert Chapman' (gold turning orange-red) will also complement plants with interesting stems. Many heathers look good when matched with shrubs such as *Viburnum* x *bodnantense* 'Dawn' or white-stemmed birches such as *Betula utilis* var. *jacquemontii*.

Jobs To Do

Go outdoors whenever the weather allows – there is always tidying up to be done. When you are forced to stay indoors, take the opportunity to look at seed and plant catalogues and do any necessary planning. Later in the season you can start sowing indoors.

You can take hardwood cuttings from shrubs, and some plants can be propagated by taking root cuttings. Chrysanthemums that are overwintered in a greenhouse or cold frame are usually propagated from cuttings once the old stool (clump of roots) starts to produce shoots. You can also take dahlia cuttings.

Late winter is a good time to sow the majority of the frost-tender plants used for summer bedding, if you have a heated greenhouse. Because you need a lot of each kind of bedding, it is normally best to sow in seed trays rather than pots. Sow more sweet peas and pinch out the tips of autumn-sown ones to encourage bushier growth in the spring.

Throughout winter keep a regular eye on bulbs, corms and tubers in store as well as bulbs grown in pots for early flowering.

Above: Between now and early spring wash all your pots and canes with a garden disinfectant to prevent the spread of diseases.

Protect Hellebores

1 Protect winter hellebore flowers by placing a cloche over them. Close up each end if severe weather is expected.

2 Alternatively, put a few bricks on each side of the plant. Place a sheet of glass across the top of the bricks.

Take Chrysanthemum Cuttings

1 Take cuttings when your chrysanthemum stools have produced shoots about 5cm (2in) long. Choose ones coming directly from the base of the plant. Cut them off close to the base.

3 Dip the ends in a rooting hormone to improve the rate and speed of rooting. (These powders also contain fungicide to help prevent rotting.) Shake off any excess rooting hormone before planting.

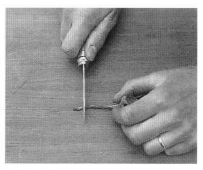

2 Pull off the lowest leaves and trim the ends of the cuttings straight across with a sharp knife.

4 Insert the cuttings around the edge of a pot containing a mixture suitable for cuttings. Then place in a propagator or cover with a plastic bag, inflated so that it does not touch the leaves. Check occasionally and remove any rotted specimens. Remove the bag when all the plants have rooted.

Left: Take chrysanthemum cuttings now for a supply next year.

Plants for Seasonal Colour

*Plants marked * require acid soil; those marked with ^ alkaline soil. Plant positions: (d) free-draining; (m) moist soil; (s) sun; (ps) partial shade; (fs) full shade.*

Latin name	Sow	Plant out	Season of interest and colour
Acer (s)	N/A	autumn/spring	autumn foliage
Achillea (s)	spring, in situ	N/A	summer, yellow/autumn, pink
Allium (s)	spring	autumn	summer, autumn
Alyssum (s, d)	spring/autumn	summer	summer, yellow or white
Anemone blanda (s, ps, d)	spring	autumn	spring, blue, pink, white
Aster x frikartii (s, ps, d)	spring/autumn	autumn/spring	early autumn, violet-purple
Aubrieta (s, d)	autumn/spring	spring/autumn	late spring, mauve
Berberis (s, ps)	N/A	autumn/spring	autumn foliage, berries
Bergenia (s, ps)	spring	summer	spring, pink
Buddleja (s)	N/A	autumn/spring	summer, mauve, pink, white
Calluna vulgaris * (s)	N/A	autumn/spring	summer, autumn, pink, white
Canna (s)	spring/autumn	early summer	summer, autumn, red, yellow
Chimonanthus praecox (s, d)	spring	autumn/spring	winter, yellow
Chionodoxa (s, d)	late spring	autumn	early spring, blue, pink
Choisya ternata (s)	N/A	autumn/spring	late spring, autumn, white
Chrysanthemum (s, m)	early spring	early summer	early autumn, many colours
Clematis summer-flowering (s, ps, d)	N/A	autumn/spring	summer, many colours
Clematis viticella (s, ps, d)	N/A	autumn/spring	summer, autumn, blue, purple
Colchicum autumnale (s)	N/A	summer	autumn, pink
Cortaderia selloana (s, d)	spring	summer	late summer, plumes
Cotinus coggygria 'Royal Purple' (s, ps, m, d)	N/A	autumn/spring	year-round, purple foliage
Crocosmia 'Lucifer' (s, ps, m)	N/A	spring	summer, red

Latin name	Sow	Plant out	Season of interest and colour
Crocus (s, most d)	N/A	autumn	late winter/early spring, many colours
Dahlia (s, d)	spring	summer	late summer/early autumn, many colours
Delphinium (s, d)	spring	autumn	summer, blue, pink, white
Dianthus (s)	spring	early summer	summer, pink, white, red
Doronicum (ps)	spring	autumn	spring, yellow
Echium vulgare 'Blue Bedder' (s, d)	summer	spring	summer, blue
Eranthis hyemalis (s)	spring	autumn	winter/early spring, yellow
Erica carnea * (s, d)	N/A	autumn	winter, purple-pink
Erica cinerea * (s, d)	N/A	autumn	summer, white, pink, purple
Forsythia (s)	N/A	autumn	spring, yellow
Fuchsia hybrids (s, ps, m)	spring	autumn	summer, pink, mauve
Galanthus nivalis (ps)	spring	autumn	winter, white
Garrya elliptica (s, d)	N/A	autumn/spring	winter, spring catkins
Geranium (s, ps)	spring	autumn	early summer, pink, mauve
Gladiolus (s, d)	spring	early summer	summer, many colours
Gloxinia (ps, m)	spring	autumn	summer, pink, lavender
Gypsophila ^ (s)	spring, in situ	N/A	summer, white, pink
Hamamelis mollis (s, ps, m)	N/A	autumn/spring	winter, yellow, orange
Hedera (s, fs)	N/A	autumn/spring	year-round foliage
Helenium (s)	spring	autumn	summer, orange, yellow
Helleborus niger (ps, m)	N/A	autumn/spring	winter, white

Plants for Seasonal Colour

Latin name	Sow	Plant out	Season of interest and colour
Hosta (fs)	N/A	autumn/spring	year-round foliage
Hyacinthus (s, d)	N/A	autumn	spring, many colours
Hydrangea (s, ps)	N/A	autumn/spring	summer/early autumn, white, blue, pink
Ilex (s)	N/A	autumn/spring	winter, berries
Iris unguicularis (s, d)	N/A	early summer	winter, white, lavender, blue
Jasminum nudiflorum (s, ps)	N/A	autumn	winter, yellow
Juniperus (s, d)	N/A	autumn/spring	year-round foliage
Kniphofia (s, ps)	spring	early summer	summer, red, orange
Lathyrus odoratus (s, m)	spring	early summer	summer, many colours
Lavandula (s)	spring	autumn	summer, lavender
Lilium * (s, ps)	N/A	autumn	summer, many colours
Liriope muscari (fs)	spring	early summer	autumn, winter, purple
Lobelia erinus (ps, m)	spring	early summer	summer, many colours
Lobularia maritima (s, d)	spring	early summer	summer, white, pink
Lonicera fragrantissima (ps, d)	spring	autumn	winter, yellow, pink
Magnolia stellata * (s, ps, m)	N/A	autumn/spring	spring, white
Mahonia (fs)	N/A	autumn/spring	winter/spring, yellow
Miscanthus (s, ps, m)	early spring	autumn	year-round foliage
Muscari armeniacum (s, m)	spring	autumn	late winter, early spring, blue
Myosotis (s, m)	spring, in situ	N/A	early summer, blue
Narcissus (s, m)	N/A	autumn	spring, white, yellow
Nerine bowdenii (s, d, m)	N/A	spring	autumn, pink
Nicotiana (s, ps, m)	spring, in situ	N/A	summer, many colours
Paeonia (s, ps)	N/A	autumn/spring	early summer, many colours
Papaver orientale (s, d)	spring	early summer	early summer, scarlet
Papaver somniferum (s, d)	spring, in situ	N/A	summer, mauve, red, white
Pelargonium (s)	late winter/ early spring	summer	summer, red, pink
Penstemon (s, ps)	spring	early summer	summer, many colours

Latin name	Sow	Plant out	Season of interest and colour
Perovskia atriplicifolia (s, d)	N/A	autumn/spring	late summer, blue
Petunia (s,d)	spring	summer	summer, pink, purple
Philadelphus (s, ps)	N/A	autumn/spring	early summer, white
Primula Polyanthus Group (s, ps, most m)	early spring	autumn	spring, many colours
Primula vulgaris (ps)	early spring	autumn	spring, purple
Pulsatilla vulgaris (s, d)	N/A	autumn/spring	late winter, yellow
Pyracantha (s, ps)	N/A	autumn/spring	autumn berries
Ranunculus ficaria (fs)	spring	autumn	spring, yellow
Rhododendron * (ps)	N/A	autumn/spring	spring, many colours
Ribes sanguineum (s, d)	N/A	autumn/spring	spring, pinkish white
Romneya coulteri (s, d)	spring	autumn	summer, white
Rosa (s, m)	N/A	autumn/spring	summer, many colours
Rudbeckia (s)	spring	autumn	summer, autumn, yellow
Salvia splendens (s, m)	spring	summer	summer, red
Schizostylis coccinea (s, m)	spring	autumn	autumn, pink, red
Sedum spectabile (s, d)	autumn	spring	early autumn, pink
Solidago (s, d)	N/A	autumn/spring	late summer/early spring, white
Spiraea 'Arguta' (s)	N/A	autumn/spring	spring, white
Stachys byzantina (s, d)	autumn/spring	autumn/spring	summer, purple
Stipa arundinacea (s, ps, d)	spring	autumn	year-round foliage
Tagetes (s)	spring	summer	summer, orange, yellow
Trillium (fs)	spring	autumn	spring, white
Tropaeolum majus (s, d)	spring	summer	summer, orange, red
Tulipa (s, d)	N/A	autumn	spring, many colours
Verbena (s, m)	autumn, spring	summer	summer, pink, purple, white
Viburnum x *bodnantense* (s, ps, m)	N/A	autumn/spring	winter, pink
Viburnum tinus (s, ps, m)	N/A	autumn/spring	winter, white
Viola Universal (s, ps, m)	summer	autumn	winter, many colours
Zinnia (s, d)	spring	summer	summer, orange, yellow

ANNUAL ATTRACTION

They may be short-lived, but annuals and biennials come in just about every shade you could want. Whether you sow them directly into the soil to fill gaps or use them as seasonal bedding schemes, they reward you with abundant colour, in many cases all summer long. Being temporary, these garden fillers allow you to experiment and ring the changes from year to year.

Beautiful Borders

When a garden is in need of an instant face-lift, annuals are the perfect answer. They provide a colourful display over a long period, yet being temporary, they allow you to experiment with different schemes each year.

What is an Annual?

The simple definition of an annual is a plant that grows from seed, then flowers, sets seed and dies all within a year. However, gardening is never that simple, and several other types of plants, including short-lived perennials and tender perennials, are often treated as annuals in the garden. Biennials are a related group which also need to be replaced, but their life cycle takes two years to complete.

Biennials and Tender Perennials

Unlike annuals, biennials are sown in one year, planted out in the autumn and flower during the following year, usually in spring or early summer. Short-lived perennials are plants, such as snapdragons and pansies, which flower best in their first year and so are normally discarded and replaced, but they can have their flowering stems removed in order to produce flowers again in the following

Above: A mixture of annuals in a large bedding scheme. Such designs can be scaled down for the small garden.

Above: *Tender perennials are often treated as annuals. Here both dahlias and verbenas belong to this group.*

summer. Tender perennials are plants, such as geraniums and dahlias, which cannot be overwintered outside in colder climates. These can be kept indoors over winter, but many people prefer to replace them, particularly when using them as bedding plants.

Hardiness
Annuals are also categorized according to their hardiness. Hardy annuals are those that can be sown outside in autumn or spring. Half-hardy annuals will not tolerate frost and are usually sown indoors for planting out when the frosts are over. Those that grow quickly enough, however, can be sown outside at the end of spring for flowering that summer. Tender annuals need to be sown in a greenhouse to ensure a long enough growing season – again, they are planted out when there is no danger of frost.

POPULAR BIENNIALS
Campanula medium
Dianthus barbatus
Digitalis purpurea
Erysimum (Cheiranthus)
Matthiola incana
Oenothera biennis
Silybum marianum
Verbascum

Above: *Honesty,* Lunaria annua, *is a versatile, self-sowing biennial.*

POPULAR TENDER PERENNIALS
Alcea rosea
Alonsoa warscewicizii
Antirrhinum majus
Argyranthemum
Chrysanthemum
Felicia amelloides
Dahlia
Impatiens
Pelargonium
Salvia splendens
Semperflorens begonias
Verbena x *hybrida*

357

VALUE FOR MONEY

The great thing about annuals is their value for money. Many are easy to raise from seed, which can be highly rewarding. Indeed, with those hardy annuals that can be sown in situ, growing them from seed is scarcely any more trouble than buying plants. Some are more difficult to germinate, but small plants can often be bought very cheaply, and in most cases they will flower for a long period, often from late spring right through to the first frosts of winter.

VARIETY

Annuals have a wide range of attributes which mean that they can be used and appreciated in a number of ways. Colour is obviously one of their main qualities. This can be from dazzling reds to very subtle pinks and blues. Some have very colourful or shapely leaves and are used as foliage plants, others have a mixture of both attractive flowers and foliage. Many have delicious scents – you only have to think of sweet peas or heliotropes.

ANNUALS IN THE GARDEN

There are many situations in the garden where annuals are useful. One of their most popular uses is as container plants. They are perfect for containers of all sorts, from hanging baskets and window boxes to a wide variety of pots, tubs and troughs. They are also frequently used as bedding plants, either in a random, informal way for a cottage-style effect, or in traditional formal bedding schemes with geometrical designs. Some annuals have a more limited flowering period and these tend to mix in with perennials very well. Some gardeners grow annuals in separate beds, often in the vegetable garden, specifically for cutting to use in flower arranging, or for exhibition purposes.

Left: Annuals are great in containers. They are colourful, long flowering and not difficult to look after.

How to Use This Chapter

This chapter will introduce you to a wide range of annuals, all of which are relatively easy to grow and will definitely enhance your garden, whether it be simply confined to a couple of hanging baskets or an area the size of a soccer pitch. As well as firing your enthusiasm, there is also plenty of practical information. *Using Annuals Effectively* gives advice on choosing plants that will suit the conditions in your garden, as well as suggestions for a variety of ways of planting annuals, depending on the style of garden you want to create. You will then find useful charts listing annuals by colour and height – invaluable information for designing bedding schemes. In this chapter you will find

Above: *Trailing petunias are perfect for hanging baskets, and come in a huge range of colours. Shades of yellow and white are used here to great effect, combined with red geraniums and busy Lizzies.*

all you need to know to create a beautiful display of colourful plants that will give you and your friends pleasure throughout the summer.

Above: *There would not be bedding without annuals. The even height and vivid colour of these geraniums makes them perfect for use in such schemes.*

Using Annuals Effectively

THE TEMPORARY NATURE OF ANNUALS MAKES THEM IDEAL PLANTS FOR EXPERIMENTING WITH INTERESTING EFFECTS. IT IS WORTH TRYING OUT UNUSUAL COMBINATIONS OF COLOUR AND FORM – IF YOU ARE NOT HAPPY WITH THE RESULTS YOU CAN CHANGE THEM NEXT YEAR.

GETTING THE CONDITIONS RIGHT

Many of the annuals grown in gardens are reasonably tolerant of a wide range of conditions, though most will perform best in a sunny, well-drained site. If your soil is very heavy, you can improve the drainage by adding plenty of horticultural grit or sand – this is especially helpful in a very wet or sunless site which might be prone to waterlogging. Shade is more difficult to counteract – light shade is fine for most annuals, but if it is very deep shade, you will be limited in your choice of plants. Foxgloves, for example, may succeed, and busy Lizzies are also worth trying – they are one of the few plants that will give a really colourful show in a shady spot, yet they are also happy in sun.

Above: Some annuals self-sow freely once they have flowered. Here, they have sown themselves a little too closely together, but if thinned out they should flower again with no further attention.

Above: These sweet Williams are a mixture of colours that harmonize together very well. Care would be needed when adding other plants to the scheme, so as not to spoil the effect.

GETTING THE SCHEME RIGHT

Annuals are versatile plants. You may choose to use them simply as flowering plants mixed in with perennials in the border – this can be a good way to create a cottage-garden effect, particularly if you allow the plants to self-sow randomly. They can also be used as temporary fillers in a more planned mixed border.

Many gardeners, on the other hand, prefer to create bedding schemes made up entirely of annuals, and this is an ideal way to create a formal design. Whichever way you want to use annuals, their ephemeral nature means that you can try out a different scheme each year. Since annuals offer such a wide range of bold, bright colours, as well as more delicate, subtle ones, there is plenty of scope for imaginative self-expression.

GETTING THE PLANTS RIGHT

If you want to make things easy for yourself, particularly if you are new to gardening, you will probably do well to choose from the many plants that are widely available in garden centres, or those that you see flourishing in other people's gardens. The reason for their popularity is usually their reliability – often these are the plants that will flower for a long period, suffering few problems. However, you may wish to be more adventurous. Seed catalogues will offer a far wider range

Above: This delightful spring border, combining deep blue forget-me-nots and pink daisies with delicate tulips, shows a careful use of colour while still creating an attractively informal effect.

of plants, so if you grow from seed you will be able to create more interesting and unusual effects. Some of the less common plants may have shorter flowering periods, but you can allow for this when planning your scheme. If you do not want to raise seeds, try mail-order plant suppliers – many of these will produce a wider range than you can find at most garden centres.

BEDDING SCHEMES

Many annuals, particularly the smaller varieties, will grow very uniformly in terms of height, size and colour. These are ideal for bedding schemes where blocks or patterns are required.

Above: *This design has been created entirely from foliage plants, showing that different leaf colours can produce an effect as striking as flowers.*

The possibilities for creativity here are endless – it is a good idea to visit public parks and gardens for inspiration, particularly if you want to make a traditional, formal scheme. However, there is no need to restrict yourself to traditional patterns. Geometrical shapes can also be used in new and striking ways, or you may want to create a softer effect, perhaps with swirling lines or colours subtly merging into one another. If your design contains intricate details, make sure you choose only small, neat plants that will suit the scheme.

COLOUR AND TEXTURE

Bedding plants can be used almost like a paintbox – indeed, you might even find inspiration for your design by visiting an art gallery for colour ideas, as well as the more obvious approach of wandering around garden centres looking at different plants and placing them together to see how they combine. Do not overlook the value of foliage plants – many bedding plants are grown purely for their foliage, and these are often silver-leaved, with interesting furry textures. There are also some with deep red or purple leaves, or variegated plants such as coleus, with many colour variations.

Above: *Large triangular blocks of colour, here using geraniums and busy Lizzies in shades of pink and purple, create a vivid impact in this border.*

GARDENER'S TIP

Remember that the smaller and neater the plants you use, the more detailed and intricate your design can be.

Infilling with Colour

Blocks of colours can be used to fill in shapes within an outline, which can be 'drawn' either with a single variety of small annual – foliage plants are often a good choice – or with a line of permanent small hedging plants such as box. The latter is the classic method for creating a traditional parterre. Though this will be a permanent feature, you will still be able to vary the annuals that are planted within the shapes.

Varying the Height

Plants of different heights can be used to great effect in bedding schemes. You need to be careful with detailed patterns – if taller plants are hiding smaller ones the effect can be spoiled. However, by grading the heights so that taller plants

Above: A neatly clipped box parterre with a filling of summer plants. When these are finished they will be replaced by colourful winter pansies.

are towards the back of a border, or in the centre of an island bed, you can create a design that still looks very neat and regular while gaining extra interest from the added vertical dimension.

Creating the Design

It is often difficult to imagine how a scheme will look when it is planted out, and it can be helpful to draw it on paper first, using crayons or coloured pencils. If you make your drawing to scale, you can also use it to work out how many plants you are likely to need – this is particularly useful if you are covering a large area.

363

MIXING IT

Many of the annuals work well in a mixed border with perennials, in an informal cottage-garden style. This is particularly good for more subtle and unobtrusive flowers, such as the soft blue or white love-in-a-mist, or toad-flax in various delicate colours. These also have short flowering seasons, making them less suitable for bedding schemes, but in an informal border they can come and go, and can be allowed to self-sow. It is less easy to fit in some of the more strongly-coloured annuals, such as busy Lizzies, so choose your plants carefully.

Above: The temporary gaps between these young shrubs are being planted with nasturtiums, which will soon spread out and fill the space.

TEMPORARY FILLERS

Annuals are perfect candidates for filling gaps in a border. If for example you have just planted a number of shrubs, then it will be several years before they have filled their allotted space and during that time the gaps can be filled by annuals. In the perennial border, early season plants finish flowering and their remains, often unattractive, can be hidden by planting annuals in front of them. Winter annuals can be used to fill beds that will be planted up permanently in the following spring. Filling temporary gaps with annuals not only improves the appearance of the garden, avoiding boring expanses of bare soil, but the plants can also act as a useful ground cover, especially if planted relatively close together. This will reduce the occurrence of weeds, as well as preventing erosion of the empty soil by the weather.

Above: The pale pink shades of Cleome *blend in well with the perennials in this mixed border.*

GOING UP IN THE WORLD

There are a handful of annuals which are climbing plants, the best-known being sweet peas and nasturtiums. Some tender perennial climbers are also used as annuals, such as *Cobaea scandens* – this could also be grown in a tub and overwintered indoors. Climbers can be used to scramble up through other plants, perhaps providing colourful blooms after the host plant's flowers have finished. They can be grown up sticks in the centre of a bedding scheme, trained up trellising or allowed to spread out to make colourful ground cover.

Above: *Climbing annuals, such as this* Ipomoea lobata, *can be used to fill vertical space in a border. They help to relieve boring flat spaces.*

Above: *No cottage garden would be complete without the delicious scent of sweet peas.*

POPULAR ANNUAL CLIMBERS

Asarina erubescens
Cobaea scandens
Convolvulus tricolor
Eccremocarpus scaber
Ipomoea
Lablab purpureus
(syn. *Dolichos lablab*)
Lathyrus odoratus
Lathyrus sativus
Mikania scandens
Rhodochiton atrosanguineum
Thunbergia alata
Tropaeolum majus
Tropaeolum peregrinum

Planning Annuals for Colour

WITH SO MANY PLANTS TO CHOOSE FROM, PLANNING A SCHEME FOR A GARDEN CAN SEEM A DAUNTING PROSPECT. HOWEVER, WITH ANNUALS YOU CAN TRY SOMETHING DIFFERENT EACH YEAR, AND YOU WILL SOON FIND OUT WHAT WORKS WELL IN TERMS OF STYLE AND COLOURING.

RED ANNUALS
Adonis aestivalis
Alcea rosea 'Scarlet'
Cosmos bipinnatus 'Pied Piper Red'
Dianthus chinensis 'Fire Carpet'
Impatiens Tempo Burgundy
Lathyrus odoratus 'Winston Churchill'
Linum grandiflorum
Lobelia erinus 'Rosamund'
Papaver rhoeas
Pelargonium (many red varieties)
Petunia 'Mirage Velvet'
Salvia splendens
Semperflorens begonias
Tagetes patula 'Scarlet Sophie'
Verbena 'Blaze'

ORANGE ANNUALS
Alonsoa warscewiczii
Antirrhinum majus (various varieties)
Calceolaria (various varieties)
Calendula officinalis (various varieties)
Emilia javanica
Erysimum (*Cheiranthus*) 'Fire King'
Eschscholzia californica
Helichrysum bracteatum (various varieties)
Impatiens 'Mega Orange Star'
Mimulus (various varieties)
Nemesia 'Orange Prince'
Rudbeckia hirta (various varieties)
Tagetes erecta (various varieties)
Tithonia rotundifolia 'Torch'
Tropaeolum majus (various varieties)
Zinnia (various varieties)

BLUE ANNUALS
Ageratum houstonianum
Borago officinalis
Brachyscome iberidifolia
Campanula medium
Centaurea cyanus
Cynoglossum amabile
Echium 'Blue Bedder'

Echium vulgare
Felicia bergeriana
Gilia
Godetia bottae 'Lady in Blue'
Legousia pentagonica
Limonium sinuatum 'Azure'
Limonium sinuatum 'Blue Bonnet'
Linanthus liniflorus
Lobelia erinus
Myosotis
Nemophila menziesii
Nigella damascena
Nolana paradoxa 'Blue Bird'
Petunia
Primula (blue varieties)
Salvia farinacea 'Victoria'
Viola x *wittrockiana*

VIOLET AND PURPLE ANNUALS
Antirrhinum 'Purple King'
Callistephus chinensis (various varieties)
Centaurea cyanus 'Black Ball'
Cleome spinosa 'Violet Queen'
Eschscholzia californica 'Purple-Violet'
Eustoma grandiflora
Heliotropium
Hesperis matronalis
Impatiens (purple varieties)
Lathyrus odoratus (various varieties)
Limonium sinuatum 'Midnight' or 'Purple Monarch'
Lunaria annua
Malva sylvestris subsp. *mauritanica*
Orychiophragmus violaceus
Papaver somniferum (purple varieties)
Petunia (purple varieties)

PINK ANNUALS
Alcea rosea 'Rose'
Antirrhinum majus (numerous varieties)

Centaurea cyanus (pink forms)
Dianthus (numerous varieties)
Diascia (numerous varieties)
Godetia grandiflora 'Satin Pink'
Helichrysum bracteatum 'Rose'
Impatiens Impact Rose
Lathyrus odoratus
   (numerous varieties)
Lavatera trimestris 'Mont Rose'
Nicotiana 'Domino Salmon-Pink'
Nigella damascena
   'Miss Jekyll Pink'
Papaver somniferum
Pelargonium (numerous varieties)
Petunia (numerous varieties)
Semperflorens begonias

WHITE ANNUALS
Anoda cristata 'Silver Cup'
Clarkia pulchella 'Snowflake'
Cleome spinosa 'Helen Campbell'
Cosmos bipinnatus 'Purity'
Digitalis purpurea f. albiflora
Gypsophila elegans 'Covent Garden'
Helianthus annuus 'Italian White'
Hibiscus trionum
Impatiens Tempo White
Lathyrus odoratus (various varieties)
Lavatera trimestris 'Mont Blanc'
Limonium sinuatum 'Iceberg'
Lunaria annua var. albiflora
Malope trifida 'Alba'
Malope trifida 'White Queen'
Nemesia 'Mello White'
Nemophila maculata
Nicotiana sylvestris
Nigella damascena 'Miss Jekyll Alba'
Osteospermum 'Glistening White'
Papaver somniferum (various varieties)
Pelargonium (various varieties)

YELLOW ANNUALS
Alcea rosea 'Yellow'
Anoda cristata 'Buttercup'
Antirrhinum majus (yellow varieties)
Argemone mexicana
Argyranthemum frutescens
   'Jamaica Primrose'
Calendula officinalis 'Kablouna'
Chrysanthemum segetum
Cladanthus arabicus
Coreopsis 'Sunray'
Glaucium flavum
Helianthus annuus

Limnanthes douglasii
Limonium sinuatum
   'Forever Moonlight'
Limonium sinuatum 'Goldcoast'
Lonas annua
Mentzelia lindleyi
Mimulus (various varieties)
Sanvitalia procumbens
Tagetes erecta (yellow varieties)
Tagetes patula (yellow varieties)
Tripleurospermum inodora
   'Gold Pompoms'
Tripleurospermum inodora
   'Santana Lemon'
Tropaeolum majus (yellow varieties)
Tropaeolum peregrinum
Viola x wittrockiana (yellow varieties)

MIXED-COLOURED ANNUALS
Antirrhinum majus
Linaria maroccana
Dianthus barbatus
Dianthus chinensis
Lathyrus odoratus
Nemesia
Primula
Salpiglossis
Schizanthus
Tagetes
Viola x wittrockiana

ANNUALS FOR FOLIAGE
Brassica oleracea
Canna
Coleus blumei
Euphorbia marginata
Galactites tomentosa
Helichrysum petiolare
Ocimum basilicum 'Purple Ruffles'
Onopordum acanthium
Ricinus communis
Senecio cinerea
Silybum marianum
Tropaeolum majus 'Alaska'

ANNUAL GRASSES
Agrostis nebulosa
Briza maxima
Chloris barbata
Hordeum jubatum
Lagurus ovatus
Panicum miliaceum
Tricholaena rosea
Zea mays

Choosing Annuals

THIS QUICK REFERENCE SECTION CAN BE USED TO HELP SELECT THE MOST SUITABLE ANNUALS FOR A VARIETY OF DIFFERENT PURPOSES AND CONDITIONS. IT INCLUDES ANNUALS AND BIENNIALS AS WELL AS TENDER AND SHORT-LIVED PERENNIALS THAT ARE USED AS ANNUALS.

Plant Name	Height	Flower Colour
Ageratum HH/A or B b (t) C	up to 30cm (12in)	blue, pink and white
Alonsoa HH/A b t hb w C	up to 45cm (18in)	scarlet and orange
Amaranthus HH/A b mb C S	up to 1.5m (5ft)	red-purple
Antirrhinum H or HH/SP b t mb C	up to 45cm (18in)	wide range (not blue)
Arctotis H or H/A TP b C	up to 60cm (2ft)	most colours except blue
Argemone HH/A b mb C F	up to 1m (3ft)	white and yellow
Argyranthemum TP b mb t hb w C	up to 60cm (2ft)	pink and yellow
Atriplex H/A b mb F	up to 1.2m (4ft)	foliage red
Begonia Semperflorens TP ps/s b t hb w C	up to 15cm (6in)	white, pink, orange, red and yellow
Bidens ferulifolia HH/SP b t hb w C	up to 90cm (3ft)	yellow
Borago officinalis HH/A b C F He	90cm (3ft)	blue and white
Brachyscome iberidifolia H/A b t hb w C	23cm (9in)	blue, pink and white
Calceolaria HH/A b t hb w C	up to 30cm (12in)	yellow and orange
Calendula officinalis H/A b C He	45cm (18in)	orange, yellow and cream
Callistephus chinensis HH/A b t C Sc	up to 60cm (2ft)	all colours
Canna TP b mb C F	up to 1.5m (5ft)	orange and red, purple foliage (some)
Centaurea cyanus H/A b C	60cm (2ft)	blue, pink and white
Cerinthe major H/A b t C	30cm (12in)	purple flowers, grey foliage
Cheiranthus cheiri H/B b (t) mb C Sc	45cm (18in)	orange, yellow and red

Calceolaria

Lathyrus odoratus

Chrysanthemum TP b t w C Sc Cu	1.2m (4ft)	all except true blue
Clarkia HH/A b t hb w C	up to 50cm (20in)	pink, red and mauve
Cleome HH/A b mb C S	up to 1.2m (4ft)	pink, white and purple
Collinsia H/A b tolerates ps C	up to 30cm (12in)	bicoloured in pink and purple
Consolida HH/A b (t) C	up to 45cm (18in)	blue, white, pink and purple
Convolvulus tricolor HH/A b hb C	up to 30cm (12in)	tricoloured mainly blue with white and yellow
Coreopsis tinctoria H/A b (t) C	up to 1.2m (4ft)	yellow, red, purple and brown forms
Cosmos HH *or* H/A b mb C	90cm (3ft)	red, pink and white
Dahlia TP b C Cu	1.2m (4ft)	all colours except true blue
Dianthus chinensis H/A b (t) mb e C	up to 23cm (9in)	pink, red and white
Echium H/A *or* B b t w C	up to 60cm (2ft)	blue, purple and pink
Eschscholzia HH/A b mb C	up to 15cm (6in)	orange, cream and yellow
Eustoma grandiflorus T/A *or* B b C	up to 45cm (18in)	blue, purple, pink and white
Felicia HH/A b t hb w C	up to 60cm (2ft)	blue and white
Gomphrena globosa T/A b C	up to 60cm (2ft)	red, pink, purple and white
Helianthus H/A b C S	up to 2.5m (8ft)	yellow
Helichrysum HH/A *or* TP b t hb w C F	up to 60cm (2ft)	white, pink and yellow
Heliotropium HH/A b (t w) C Sc	45cm (18in)	violet
Hesperis matronalis H/B b mb C Sc	1.2m (4ft)	mauve and white
Hordeum jubatum H/A grass b C S	up to 45cm (18in)	
Iberis H/A b e t C	up to 30cm (12in)	white and pink
Impatiens TP b t hb w tolerates ps C	up to 30cm (12in)	red, orange, purple, pink and white
Ipomoea T/A b C	up to 5m (15ft) climber	blue, pink, purple and red
Isatis tinctoria H/B b C He	up to 1.2m (4ft)	yellow
Lathyrus odoratus H/A b C Sc Cu	up to 1.8m (6ft) climber	red, pink, mauve and white
Lavatera trimestris H/A b C	up to 1.2m (4ft)	pink and white
Limnanthes douglasii H/A b e C Be	15cm (6in)	bicoloured yellow and white

Dahlia

Hesperis matronalis

Linum grandiflorum H/A b mb C	up to 75cm (30in)	red
Lobelia erinus HH/A b e t hb w C	up to 15cm (6in) some trailing	blue, purple and white
Lobularia maritima H/A b e t hb w C	15cm (6in)	white and pink
Lunaria annua H/B b tolerates sh Sp C F	up to 1m (3ft)	purple and white, also variegated foliage forms
Matthiola HH or H/A b t C Sc	up to 45cm (18in)	pink, mauve and white
Melianthus TP b mb F C S	up to 3m (10ft)	red, foliage silver
Moluccella laevis HH/A b C	up to 1m (3ft)	green
Myosotis H/A b t hb w mb tolerates ps C	up to 30cm (12in)	blue
Nemesia HH/A b t hb w C	up to 30cm (12in)	white, blue, yellow and purple
Nicandra physalodes H/A b C F	up to 1m (3ft)	blue
Nicotiana HH/A b t hb w C Sc (some)	up to 2.1m (7ft)	white and pink
Nigella H/A b mb C	60cm (2ft)	blue and white
Oenothera H/B b mb C Sc	90cm (3ft)	yellow, orange and pink (in evening)
Omphalodes linifolia H/A b mb C	up to 25cm (10in)	white
Papaver H/A b mb C	up to 90cm (3ft)	red, mauve, pink and white
Pelargonium TP b t w C F Sc (some)	up to 75cm (30in) some trailing	red, pink and white, some scented foliage
Petunia HH/SP b t hb w C Sc (some)	25cm (10in)	all colours
Phacelia H/A b C	up to 50cm (20in)	blue, lavender and white
Phlox drummondii HH/A b (t) C	up to 45cm (18in)	purple, pale blue, pink and white
Portulaca HH/A b C	up to 20cm (8in)	most colours
Ricinus HH/A b F	up to 3m (10ft)	red, foliage red and bronze
Rudbeckia HH/A b mb C	up to 1m (3ft)	yellow, gold, orange-red and brown
Salpiglossis HH/A b t C	up to 60cm (2ft)	most colours
Salvia farinacea HH/SP b mb hb t w C	up to 38cm (15in)	scarlet, blue, pink and purple

Lunaria annua

Impatiens

Salvia splendens HH/SP b mb hb t w C	up to 38cm (15in)	scarlet, blue and pink
Salvia viridis HH/A b mb hb t w C	up to 38cm (15in)	scarlet, blue and purple
Sanvitalia H/A b t hb w C	up to 20cm (8in) creeping	yellow
Senecio cineraria (S. maritima) TS b t hb w F	up to 60cm (2ft)	flowers yellow, foliage silver
Silybum marianum H/B mb F	up to 75cm (30in)	flowers purple, white-veined leaves
Tagetes HH/A b t hb w C	up to 30cm (12in)	yellow and orange
Tithonia HH/A b mb C	up to 1.2m (4ft)	orange
Tropaeolum majus H/A b (t) C	up to 90cm (3ft) climber	orange, red and yellow
Verbascum H/B b mb S C F	up to 2m (7ft)	yellow
Verbena x hybrida TP b hb mb t w C	up to 30cm (12in)	red, purple, pink and white
Viola x wittrockiana H/SP b hb mb t w tolerates ps C	25cm (10in)	all colours

KEY TO SYMBOLS

Unless otherwise stated the plants all prefer a sunny position

H = Hardy
HH = Half-hardy
T = Tender
TS = Tender Shrub
A = Annual
B = Biennial
SP = Short-lived Perennial
TP = Tender Perennial
b = beds
e = edging
hb = hanging baskets
mb = mixed borders
t = tubs

(t) = mainly used in beds but some could be used in tubs, pots or similar containers
w = window boxes
ps = partial shade
sh = shade
Be = Grown to attract Bees
C = Grown for Colour
Cu = Grown for Cutting
F = Grown for Foliage
He = Grown as Herb
S = Grown for Shape
Sc = Grown for Scent
Sp = Grown for Seed Pods

Verbena

Tagetes

PERENNIALS

Planted on their own in the
herbaceous border, or among
structural shrubs in a mixed bed,
perennials form part of the permanent
planting. They provide flower and
foliage interest from spring through to
the end of autumn, when they die
down for the winter. There are types
to suit every garden condition, style
and colour scheme, and a carefully
planned planting will ensure interest
and colour throughout the year.

Everlasting Perennials

PERENNIALS ARE REGAINING THEIR POPULARITY AT THE FOREFRONT OF GARDENING. WHILE SHRUBS PROVIDE THE BASIC STRUCTURE OF A BORDER AND ANNUALS TEMPORARY COLOUR, PERENNIALS FORM THE PERMANENT PLANTINGS THAT CREATE THE MAIN INTEREST.

WHAT IS A PERENNIAL?

In theory, perennials are plants that live more than one or two years. However, in gardening terms there are certain perennials that fit this definition but are not generally included in this category: woody plants, such as trees and shrubs, for example. Within this group some sub-shrubs, including *Dianthus* and *Perovskia*, are usually

Above: Perennials are suitable for any garden style, such as this lush planting.

included as perennials. Alpines, most of which are perennials, are also often considered as a separate category. Bulbs are usually excluded as a group but individuals such as lilies are included. Many perennials are herbaceous plants in that they die back each year below ground and reappear in spring, but there are also those, some irises for example, that wholly or in part remain evergreen throughout the winter.

WHY CHOOSE PERENNIALS?

Perennials form the backbone of a garden, adding a wealth of colour, shape and texture. They have the advantage over annuals in that they reappear every year, basically recreating the same border, so that you do not have to worry about the overall picture each year, just the detail. Their versatility is astonishing, as there are plants for every type of garden situation as well as for every style and type of border design. No matter whether you live in the countryside, by the sea or in the middle of town, you will find that there are ample perennials to suit all your needs.

How to Choose Perennials

As when choosing any other garden plants, it is important to consider the physical environment in which you live: the type of soil, whether it is moist or dry, whether it is in sun or shade or exposed to winds. Generally this will limit your choice of plants to some degree but there will still be plenty to choose from. The design is a much more personal matter: deciding which plants will create the look you want. It is important at this stage to consider the colour, shape and texture of not only the flowers but also the foliage and overall planting to obtain the most pleasing effect.

Above: The contrasting shapes of perennials give the gardener plenty of scope for designing interesting and dynamic borders.

Above: This classic mixed border of spring-flowering perennials contains a wonderful mixture of fresh, bright colours.

375

SELECTING HEALTHY PLANTS

From the maintenance point of view it is important to select only plants that are healthy and strong. Some perennials are very tough, in terms of resisting both the weather and disease. These are not necessarily unattractive plants, many having come down to us through cottage gardens, and are always worth considering for a trouble-free garden. Many of the modern cultivars are more brightly coloured and have larger flowers but do not have the same resistance, so select your plants or seeds with care. It is always useful to look at other gardens in your area: plants that are obviously thriving in your neighbours' gardens are also likely to do well for you.

Above: *This border has a distinctive layered effect, with winter aconites in front of* Helleborus foetidus.

THE IMPORTANCE OF FORM

The next aspect to consider is the look of the plant. There are innumerable permutations of colour, shape, texture and size, of both the flowers and the foliage, and all these aspects must be taken into consideration when combining plants together to form an attractive border. For example, however much you may like it, a tall red-flowered plant is no substitute where a short red one is required; you will either need to choose another plant, or change the design. It is always best to think about the design, and the function of the plants in the border, before you buy them. The texture and shape of the plant and its foliage are just as important as flower colour and size.

Above: *There are many perennials, such as these primroses, that are robust and will thrive in most garden conditions.*

Above: The tall spikes of stately Lythrum salicaria *provide a mass of mauve flowers in the summer. Plant them where they will be noticed.*

A Plant for All Seasons

Another important thing to remember about perennials is their flowering periods. Many only have a relatively short time in flower. This must be co-ordinated with other plants. You will be disappointed if you have two pink plants that you hope will look stunning together, if one flowers in May and the other in September. Likewise, if you choose carefully the border can be full of colour throughout the growing season and often during the winter as well. Many plants also remain attractive when not in flower.

How to Use this Chapter

In this chapter you will find a comprehensive guide to using perennials in a variety of ways. *Perennials in the Garden* gives advice on designing gardens in different styles, taking account of the conditions in your garden, and suggests ways of using perennials to create the effect or garden style that you want. *Perennials for Different Conditions* will help you choose suitable plants for every part of your garden, whether wet or dry, sunny or shady. *Seasonal Splendour* shows you how to maintain interest in your garden throughout the year using shrubs that flower at different times of the year and colourful evergreen foliage. Finally, you will find useful charts listing perennials by colour, size and season of interest, to help you find the plants you need when creating your beds and borders.

Above: Snapdragons are quite short and should be placed near the front of a border for maximum effect.

Perennials in the Garden

THERE ARE COUNTLESS USES FOR PERENNIALS IN THE GARDEN. THEY CAN HELP TO CREATE A WIDE VARIETY OF STYLES, FROM THE FORMAL TO THE ROMANTIC. THEY ARE EQUALLY EFFECTIVE IN THE SMALL GARDEN OR IN THE WIDER SPACES OF A LARGE PLOT.

CONSIDERING YOUR SITE

As with most plants, it is best to grow perennials in sites where they will thrive rather than forcing them into situations where they will languish and probably die. This is not quite as serious as it may sound as most gardens provide areas that will grow a wide variety of plants. However, there are some things to think about. There is no point in growing sun-loving plants in the shade or shade-loving plants in the sun (some shade-loving plants will grow in the sun if the soil is moist enough). Some plants need a moist soil and will soon fade away in dry conditions, and vice versa.

So when considering the style of garden you want, do think about the conditions you can provide and how this will influence your choice. For example, very few silver foliage plants will grow in the shade. The best way to garden successfully is to work with nature and not against it. It may be possible to change the conditions – chop down a tree to let in more light or create a damp area in part of the garden, for example – but this will mean additional work.

Above: Using your own style and colour preferences will provide you with a garden that is uniquely yours and will be a source of inspiration for others.

CHOOSING A STYLE

The style of the garden is largely a matter of personal taste, as perennials will lend themselves to most designs. However, there may be a few restrictions. The site has already been mentioned. It is also important to consider the use of the garden as a whole. For example, if children are regularly playing in the garden, it may be difficult to maintain a formal border – an informal planting will be much more suitable. Similarly, a natural wildflower planting can look very out of place in a formal setting. However, in both these

Above: You will make a bold statement with a Mediterranean-style planting. There are plenty of plants to choose from and it can be very colourful.

cases, it may be possible to succeed with such a border if it is isolated, perhaps in its own area of the garden.

The gardener's personality is also important. It is inadvisable to consider having a neat formal border if you are a naturally untidy person who will soon let the border deteriorate. Similarly if your lifestyle is frenetic, with little time to spare, avoid complicated borders that are very time-consuming and perhaps choose something formal where maintenance may be minimal. Frequently style is dictated by needs. If you want to attract wildlife to your garden, then an informal style with plants that bear seeds or nectar will be important, as birds, bees and other beneficial insects rely on them for food.

Above: Aquilegia *and* Meconopsis cambrica *are more suited to an informal or cottage style garden where little maintenance is required. They will tolerate sun or light shade.*

379

HERBACEOUS BORDERS

These are the traditional ways of growing perennial plants. They consist of borders containing nothing other than herbaceous plants. They are usually planted in drifts, generally with the taller specimens at the back and shorter ones at the front. The colours are carefully planned so as to present a harmonious whole. The traditional colour scheme is hot, strong colours in the centre with cooler, softer ones at the ends. Some attractive herbaceous borders can be made by restricting the flowers to one colour, such as red, or perhaps two, such as white and gold or yellow and blue.

Perennials mostly look their best when they are set off against a green background, either shrubs or, better still, a yew hedge. Traditional herbaceous borders were long and often consisted of two parallel beds with a broad path between them. However, they can be of any shape you like to fit in either with your own designs or with the shape of your garden. Herbaceous borders can be quite labour-intensive but if you combine mulching with a "little and often" approach to maintenance, they are surprisingly easy to look after and are very rewarding. A wide range of plants, running to many thousands, are suitable.

Above: *A herbaceous border on a grand scale, with two parallel beds separated by a wide path. With a careful choice of plants it can be kept attractive from spring to autumn.*

Above: A mixed border of perennials and shrubs in early summer, planned to have plenty of colour later in the season.

Above: Island beds can be very effective in a larger garden. Create a path around them with grass, gravel or chipped bark.

MIXED BORDERS

Nowadays very few gardeners have herbaceous borders in the strictest sense. Most mix in a few other types of plants, such as roses and perhaps a few annuals. There is very little point in being a purist and sticking to one type of plant when the whole object is to create an attractive border. It makes sense to use whatever is available. A few shrubs will add a permanent structure to the border. The foliage of the shrubs can be used to set off the flowers of the plants in front of them. They can also provide a little shade for those plants that need it. In gardening terms there is very little difference between a mixed border and a herbaceous one. The shapes and design can be the same and apart from using other plants, aesthetically the two borders are likely to look very similar in style.

ISLAND BEDS

These are exactly the same as herbaceous and mixed beds except that they can be seen from all sides rather than from one or two. The main problem is that there is no background for the plants, so it makes sense to put taller plants in the middle, enabling the others to be seen against them. Shrubs or trees often make a good centre feature as they prevent the eye running straight over the bed to what lies beyond.

> PERENNIALS FOR HERBACEOUS, MIXED AND ISLAND BEDS
>
> *Achillea*
> *Aster*
> *Campanula*
> *Delphinium*
> *Geranium*
> *Heliopsis*
> *Nepeta*
> *Paeonia*
> *Rudbeckia*
> *Solidago*

COTTAGE STYLE

Traditional cottage gardens can be very attractive but they can also be a lot of work. Essentially they are borders with a profusion of old-fashioned flowers growing in them. Originally they had little structure with everything just planted where there were spaces, creating a joyous mixture of colour, shapes and sizes. Nowadays it is often more organized, with tall plants at the back and shorter ones at the front, and the colours planted a little more harmoniously. However well-organized, it should still represent a riot of colour. Self-sowing annuals are usually included with the perennials.

COTTAGE GARDEN PERENNIALS
Alcea rosea
Aquilegia vulgaris
Aster
Astrantia major
Campanula persicifolia
Dianthus 'Mrs Sinkins'
Doronicum
Geum rivale
Lathyrus latifolius
Lupinus Russell hybrids
Primula vulgaris
Salvia officinalis

INFORMAL STYLE

Many gardeners prefer an informal style, especially if there are children who play in the garden. Here the perennials are used along with shrubs

Above: *A cottage garden, with a mixture of various types of flowers and plants spilling out in profusion over the path, gives an informal impression.*

and perhaps bulbs to create a colourful, comfortable background for family life. Small borders with tough plants that will stand a little neglect or the occasional football are what is required. Foliage plants are a good choice, as they have a long season and need little maintenance, along with colourful long-flowerers such as geraniums.

FORMAL STYLE

Creating a formal garden involves a layout with clean lines, often straight or with regular curves, such as circles. The planting is also regular, frequently using plants with clear lines and shapes, such as cordylines or yuccas, with their fountains of strap-shaped leaves. Edges may be tightly clipped box, lavender, or small, neat flowers. Repetition and symmetry are important. Small gardens are often ideal, especially if they are mostly paved.

WILDFLOWER GARDENS

An increasing number of gardeners are growing wildflowers to compensate for their loss in the countryside.

Below: A formal garden with repeated rhythms moving away from the house. The predominance of white and pink flowers helps to unify the garden.

This sounds simple, but can be as difficult as other types of garden. Wildflowers are best grown in a meadow or overgrown lawn, which should be mown regularly to avoid getting coarse grasses that will overpower the flowers. To start with, grow the flowers in pots and plant them into the meadow. These will establish more easily than if sown into the grass. Only grow wild plants that are appropriate to your area and soil.

PERENNIALS FOR
A FORMAL GARDEN

Cordyline australis
Euphorbia characias
Iris
Miscanthus sinensis
Phormium tenax
Santolina pinnata subsp. *neapolitana*
Yucca gloriosa

383

Perennials for Different Conditions

ALL GARDENS HAVE A VARIETY OF DIFFERENT CONDITIONS IN WHICH
TO GROW PLANTS. THERE ARE USUALLY AREAS OF SUN AND OTHERS
OF SHADE. MANY GARDENS HAVE PONDS AND WITH THEM PATCHES OF
RELATIVELY MOIST GROUND.

SUNNY AREAS

Most, but not all gardens have sun for
at least part of the day. The majority
of herbaceous plants will tolerate full
sun. However, there are a number that
will not and some that can only be
grown in sun under special circum-
stances. Some plants that prefer shade,
such as hostas, will grow in the sun if
the soil is kept moist, but once it dries
out they start to wilt. Others will
grow in the sun but they should be
protected from the really hot midday
sun, violas being a good example.
Some plants, especially those from

*Above: Silver foliage plants need to grow
in a sunny position. In the shade they will
languish and eventually die. Here silver
Stachys byzantina is mixed with a sun-
loving Nepeta.*

Mediterranean climates, really thrive
in hot, sunny conditions and are ideal
for hot dry areas. These are particularly useful in areas that are close to
house walls and receive little rain, or
in gardens with light, dry soil. Most
plants that need sunny conditions will
not grow well in the shade.

*Left: Grasses need a sunny position –
very few of them will grow successfully
in shade. When planted together they can
make an interesting semi-formal planting.*

SHADY AREAS

When planting in shady areas, the choice is slightly more limited than for sun, particularly with flowers, but so long as the soil is moist there are still a large number of suitable plants. Most of the flowering woodland plants flower in the spring, before the leaves appear on the trees – lily-of-the-valley and pulmonaria are good examples. However, there are still plenty of foliage and some flowering plants that will create a good display in the summer and into the autumn. If the area is dry, particularly under a large tree that takes a lot of moisture and nutrients from the soil, the choice is much more restricted. Some bulbous plants, such as anemones and cyclamen, are able to survive because they become dormant before the dryness of summer really sets in. Those plants that will tolerate dry shade, such as *Euphorbia amygdaloides* var. *robbiae* should be planted in drifts so that you will get maximum benefit from them.

Creating Shade

If your garden is always sunny it is worth creating some shade just to enable you to grow a greater variety of plants. This can be achieved by planting trees or even large shrubs. Remove some of the lower branches so that light but not midday sun reaches the ground. A trellis screen covered with climbers, or perhaps a

Above: Geranium macrorrhizum *is one of the best shade plants, seen profusely flowering here in spite of being in quite dense shade. It will happily spread and form excellent ground cover.*

pergola or arch, will also provide some shade as well as creating an attractive feature. Keen gardeners often create shade beds by suspending netting on a framework above the bed. This is not very elegant but does allow you to extend your range of plants and also gives you time to establish a tree.

FLOWERING PERENNIALS FOR SHADE

Anemone nemorosa
Brunnera macrophylla
Convallaria majalis
Eranthis hyemalis
Euphorbia amygdaloides var. *robbiae*
Helleborus viridis
Lamium galeobdolon
Lathyrus vernus
Liriope muscari
Polygonatum
Sanguinaria canadensis
Smilacina
Trillium

WATERSIDE AREAS

There are a large number of perennials that will grow in water or in the mud surrounding it. These tend to be specialist plants that will only grow in these conditions. Waterside planting can add another dimension to the garden. Because they have a plentiful supply of water, the plants' foliage tends to stay fresh for most of the year, often creating an oasis in an otherwise dry garden. The colours are predominantly yellow and blue, but most other colours can be found, allowing an attractive planting scheme to be developed. The main problem with water plants is that many of them can be invasive. These will need to be reduced every so often, or planted in bottomless pots in the ground, to allow the more delicate plants to survive.

PERENNIAL WATERSIDE PLANTS
Aruncus dioicus
Astilbe x *arendsii*
Caltha palustris
Cardamine pratensis
Gunnera manicata
Iris ensata
Lobelia cardinalis
Lythrum salicaria
Onoclea sensibilis
Persicaria bistorta
Primula japonica
Rodgersia pinnata

MOIST AREAS

Many people with ponds also have a damp area next to them in which to grow the wide range of plants that like a moist but not waterlogged situation. Other gardeners deliberately create such an area as they want to grow moisture-loving plants but cannot have a pond for safety reasons. Such areas, often called bog gardens,

Above: Primulas and many irises are ideal plants for a streamside position.

Above: The arum lily can be planted either in shallow water or in marshy margins. It can also be used in a bog garden.

can be a very attractive feature. Many of the plants are colourful and some, such as gunnera, can grow very large, creating eye-catching features.

DRY AREAS

Areas with light, free-draining soil can become very dry in summer, particularly when they also receive a lot of sun. Mediterranean-type plants love these conditions. However, many gardens with light soil will still become very wet in the winter, because of higher rainfall than occurs in the Mediterranean climate, which can be a problem for these plants. There are still many plants that can tolerate these conditions, but it is a good idea to increase the moisture-retentiveness by adding plenty of organic material to the soil, and also mulching. This will enable you to grow a wider range of plants.

Mediterranean Beds

In recent times Mediterranean-style beds have become very popular. A lot of gravel is added to the borders, so that they drain very quickly, preventing the plants becoming waterlogged in winter. This type of bed is ideal for very dry climates. A wide range of plants can be grown, and the beds can look very attractive and require little maintenance.

PLANTS FOR A DRY GARDEN
Allium hollandicum
Cistus purpurea
Cordyline australis
Euphorbia characias subsp. *wulfenii*
Lavandula angustifolia
Ophiopogon planiscapus 'Nigrescens'
Papaver somniferum
Rosmarinus
Salvia nemorosa 'Superba'
Sedum
Stachys byzantina
Verbascum

Above: A small, sunny courtyard can be an ideal site for Mediterranean garden plants that tolerate dry conditions.

387

Choosing Perennials with Special Qualities

WITH SUCH A LARGE RANGE OF PERENNIALS AVAILABLE TO THE GARDENER IT IS NOT SURPRISING THAT MANY HAVE INTERESTING FEATURES THAT CAN BE USED IN A VARIETY OF DIFFERENT WAYS, EITHER INDIVIDUALLY OR MIXED WITH OTHER PLANTS.

FRAGRANT PERENNIALS

Many perennials have a smell of one kind or another. Some are delightfully sweet, such as dianthus, others are rank and foetid; *Dracunculus vulgaris,* for example. As always there is an in-between group, represented by such plants as *Phuopsis stylosa,* the smell of which some people find attractive and others repulsive. One tends to think

Above: Phlox has an intoxicating fragrance from mid- to late summer. It is ideal for the back of a border.

Above: The scent of roses varies dramatically from one variety to another.

of fragrance in terms of flowers, but many plants have fragrant foliage and this can be an important element in the garden. However, it is the flowers that most people love the best, particularly those that fill the whole area around them with fragrance. Lily-of-the-valley *(Convallaria majalis)* is one such plant, and it will rapidly spread to form large drifts, producing an intoxicating scent.

Aromatic Foliage

Most aromatic foliage needs to be crushed or at least brushed before it issues its scent. One of the best scents is that of monarda, which releases a wonderful fragrance at the slightest touch. If possible plant them near a path where they can be touched or brushed against.

Scent for Different Times

Fortunately, not all flowers are scented at the same time. Surprisingly, a large number of winter-flowering plants – *Iris unguicularis*, for example – are highly scented, probably because they need to attract pollinating insects and there are not many around in winter. Spring is also good, but it is the height of summer when the warm weather brings out the greatest number of perfumes. Plants also vary in their scents during the course of the day, many reserving their smell for the evening to attract the night-flying moths. *Cestrum parqui* is a curiosity as it has a savoury smell during the day, probably to attract flies, and a sweet scent in the evening to attract moths.

Using Scents

While a scented garden provides a great deal of pleasure and sensuous stimulation, mixing too many scents together is self-defeating, as you end up smelling none of them. It is better to spread the scents out so that you come

Above: Nepeta *has the advantage of scented leaves and attractive flowers.*

on them one at a time. Areas where you sit and relax are good places for scented flowers. Beds near the house where fragrance can waft through open windows can also be delightful.

SCENTED PERENNIALS

FLOWERS
Alyssum maritinum
Cestrum parqui
Convallaria majalis
Cosmos atrosanguineus
Dianthus
Erysimum cheiri
Filipendula ulmaria
Iris
Mirabilis jalapa
Phlox
Viola odorata

FOLIAGE
Agastache foeniculum
Anthemis punctata subsp. *cupaniana*
Melittis melissophyllum
Monarda
Morina longifolia
Nepeta
Salvia

CLIMBING PERENNIALS

There are a small number of climbing perennials that add variety to the range of plants when you are planning your border. However, with the exception of golden hop, *Humulus lupulus* 'Aureus', they are generally not as vigorous as many of their shrubby counterparts. They are relatively short growing but this can make them ideal for inclusion in the herbaceous or mixed borders. Climbing perennials are treated in exactly the same way as ordinary perennials. Some are self-clinging or twining and will even attach themselves to their supports, but others will need to be tied in.

Supporting Climbers

Some climbers, such as a selection of the violas and geraniums, are scrambling plants rather than true climbing

Above: The golden hop is a perfect plant for growing over an arch or pergola.

Above: This viola and thrift are growing through a rose providing an extended period of colour and interest.

plants and are extremely useful for growing through the base of low bushes. Others, and here many of the geraniums such as 'Ann Folkard' or 'Salome' are perfect, will happily scramble across other plants, often providing colour when their host plant has finished flowering. If you choose carefully you can extend the flowering period considerably.

The true climbers can also be draped over other plants, but they are best supported in some other way. The majority, being relatively low growing, can be used in the border supported by wigwams of twiggy sticks to create attractive mounds of colour. The golden hop, being vigorous, may be used in a more conventional climbing way. It can be trained to grow over pergolas or arches, or up poles.

Herbaceous Clematis

Most clematis are shrubby but there are just a few that are herbaceous in character and die back each autumn. These tend not to be tall climbers but are well worth considering both for foliage colour (*Clematis recta* 'Purpurea') and for their flowers (*C. durandii*). Again, twiggy sticks form the best kind of support.

PERENNIAL CLIMBERS

Clematis erecta
Eccremocarpus scaber
Humulus lupulus 'Aureus'
Lathyrus
Solanum dulcamara 'Variegatum'
Tropaeolum speciosum
Vinca major

GROUND COVER

There are generally two main reasons for using ground-cover plants: either to suppress weeds, or to provide a low-maintenance covering for an area where not many types of plants will thrive, such as a shady area or a bank. In the latter case the ground cover may also help prevent soil erosion. Either way, perennials are perfect. Virtually any perennial, if planted close enough together, will form ground cover, the basic requirement for weed suppression being that the foliage prevents light reaching the soil. Some make better cover than others as their foliage is dense or large, creating shade. Hostas are a prime example.

Suppressing Weeds

If the plants are covering the ground effectively, any weed seeds that germinate will quickly die from lack of light. However, ground cover will not suppress perennial weeds if their roots are already in the soil. For this reason it is

Above: Persicaria affinis *makes a dense carpet of foliage that is the perfect weed-suppressing ground cover.*

vital to remove all perennial weeds before planting the ground cover. Otherwise, they can be difficult to eradicate without digging up the whole bed.

PERENNIALS FOR GROUND COVER

Acaena
Anthemis punctata cupaniana
Bergenia
Epimedium
Geranium macrorrhizum
Hosta
Pulmonaria
Stachys byzantina
Vinca minor

FOLIAGE PERENNIALS

Among the perennials are some truly delightful foliage plants. Some are used purely as foliage plants, either not producing flowers or having all the flowers removed as these spoil the effect. Others are ordinary flowering plants but they also have very good foliage. This attribute is rather useful when the plant is flowering as well as before and after flowering. *Alchemilla mollis* is a good example.

Above: Silver foliage has a softening effect in a border. Two popular species are Stachys *and* Artemisia.

The Qualities of Foliage

Foliage is attractive for several different reasons. Although the majority of perennials have green foliage there is also a wide range of other colours, including variegation where more than one colour is present. Then there are the size and shape, which can vary from thin strap-like leaves to huge rounded ones. The texture is also important. Shiny leaves, for example, are useful

Above: These rodgersias have a wonderful ribbed texture that contrasts well with the smoothness of the water. The fans of leaves also complement the foliage of the iris.

FOLIAGE AND ARCHITECTURAL PERENNIALS
FOLIAGE
Canna
Cordyline
Cynara
Grasses
Gunnera manicata
Hosta
Rheum
Rodgersia
Stachys byzantina
ARCHITECTURAL
Acanthus spinosus
Angelica archangelica
Cortaderia selloana
Cynara cardunculus
Gunnera manicata
Phormium tenax
Rheum
Stipa gigantea

for example, has large eye-catching leaves, while cordyline has narrow leaves arranged in such a beautiful way that they cannot but attract attention. These plants will act as focal points in the garden, and this should be remembered when planning the design. They may be used at the end of a straight path or at a bend in a curved one. The feature may be away in the distance at the end of a lawn or on the boundary of the garden. Often this attraction accentuates the length of a path or of a garden, making it look bigger than it is. Architectural plants can also be effective in a border, perhaps in the middle or at regular intervals to set up a rhythm, which is particularly useful in a formal setting.

for illuminating dark areas. Light and shade play an important part in the use of foliage. Foliage plants can simply be used as a foil for other plants, or they can be decorative in their own right, either among flowering plants or in a purely foliage border. Mixing foliage with contrasting characteristics always creates interesting designs. It can also be used as a break between two plants with flower colours that do not quite go together visually, so that they do not jar on the eye.

ARCHITECTURAL PLANTS

There are some plants with a striking, statuesque shape that immediately draws the eye, foliage generally being the most important element. *Gunnera manicata*,

Above: Gunnera manicata *has some of the largest leaves of any garden perennial. A clump of these certainly creates an imposing sight.*

393

Seasonal Splendour

MANY PERENNIALS FLOWER FOR RELATIVELY SHORT PERIODS, AND THOUGH THIS CAN SOMETIMES SEEM A DRAWBACK, IT DOES GUARANTEE A CONSTANTLY CHANGING PICTURE. BY CAREFULLY PLANNING YOUR PLANTING, YOU CAN ENSURE INTEREST THROUGHOUT THE YEAR.

SPRING

This is the season of birth and renewal. It is the time when barren earth suddenly springs into life in a myriad of colours, each with its own kind of freshness. The predominant colours are yellow and blue, but all the other colours are also present. It is not only the flowers that are exciting and new; it is also the foliage, which appears in a seemingly limitless number of shades of green.

Planting for Spring

A good way to plan your spring planting is to choose those colours that represent the freshness and vitality of the season, such as yellow primroses, blue anemones and red pulmonarias. The silver-spotted foliage of the pulmonarias will continue to look attractive for a long time, but most of the spring-flowering perennials add little to the scene once they have finished flowering.

Above: *Spring is a wonderful time of year with many old favourites, such as primulas, aquilegias and forget-me-nots, coming into flower.*

SPRING PERENNIALS

Aubrieta deltoidea
Bergenia cordifolia
Caltha palustris
Doronicum 'Miss Mason'
Euphorbia polychroma
Helleborus orientalis
Primula vulgaris
Pulmonaria angustifolia
Sanguinaria canadensis
Smilacina racemosa
Trollius europaeus
Viola odorata

Above: An important perennial in any spring garden is Euphorbia polychroma, *which forms a perfect dome of gold up to 75cm (30in) high.*

Indeed many, such as the anemones, die back below ground and are not visible. Plant these types of flowers towards the back of the border or between other plants where they will show up in spring when the shoots are only just beginning to appear, but will be hidden when the later plants are fully grown.

No special maintenance is required for spring perennials except to remove any dead foliage as it appears. Try to weed and mulch the borders before too much growth has been made to avoid damaging the plants.

Woodland Plants

Many spring plants are of woodland origin, and appear, flower, seed and die back before the trees come into leaf. This allows them to make full use of the available light and moisture. Anemones and celandines are of this type. In the garden, they can be planted under deciduous shrubs and trees, where later-flowering plants would not thrive because of the shade created by the foliage. Some perennials that keep their foliage, such as primroses, hellebores and pulmonarias, can also be used in such places.

Above: The soft greyish pink of this dicentra is unusual in spring.

EARLY SUMMER

At this time, the spring-like quality of freshness is still in evidence in the garden, and yet the multitude of colours and abundance of lush vegetation give a decidedly summery feel. As yet the sun is usually not too strong and so the colours have a brightness and intensity that they lose as summer progresses. Spring is colourful, but this colour is mainly seen against bare earth. By early summer the foliage has nearly all developed and the flowers are viewed against a wide range of foliage colours and shapes, which enhances them considerably.

Above: *Early summer would not be complete without the towering spires of blue produced by delphiniums.*

Planting for Early Summer

The plants for early summer seem to be quite distinct from those later in the summer. In a late season many are left over from spring and the two periods can merge, with dicentras lasting into summer and *Geranium pratense* starting in spring. Although it is a good idea to try to co-ordinate the colours in the border, do not place all the early-flowering plants together or there will be gaps later in the year when they die; try to spread them among the later-flowering plants.

Long-lasting Plantings

Some plants have modern hybrids that flower for longer than the older varieties. For example, old-fashioned pinks tend to flower only once, in early summer, whereas many of the modern pinks, although not so attractive to many people and often less fragrant, do flower throughout the whole summer and well into autumn. Some plants that start to flower in early summer, such as the Mexican daisy, *Erigeron karvinskianus*, or *Erodium manescaui* continue to flower profusely throughout the whole summer and often until the first frosts appear. Some plants that do not flower for very long can be used as foliage plants for the later part of the summer. Either cut them back to the ground and let them regenerate, as you can with alchemilla, or remove the flowering heads, for example with lupins. Some

plants, such as *Alchemilla mollis* and delphiniums, may well flower again later in the year if cut back.

Early Summer Maintenance

In the initial part of early summer, while the plants are still putting on lots of growth, be certain to stake

Above: Alchemilla mollis *often flower twice if cut back in mid-season.*

Above: There are many perennial wallflowers, which are valuable for their cheerful colours in the early summer.

them. If this is done now, the plants will hide the staking under the new foliage. Deadhead as plants go over. If the borders have been properly mulched there should be no need to water, but if there is a prolonged dry spell it may become necessary.

EARLY-SUMMER PERENNIALS
Alchemilla mollis
Baptisia australis
Campanula persicifolia
Centaurea montana
Delphinium
Dianthus 'Mrs Sinkins'
Geranium pratense
Hemerocallis
Lupinus Russell hybrids
Papaver orientale

High Summer

The borders in high summer can be drenched in sunshine. Some of the brighter colours, such as the reds, still stand out but many of the others have lost the freshness of early summer and are subdued into a haze. It can be one of the best times in the garden, but so often things begin to flag and steps should be taken to overcome this.

Summer Colours

To create a border that retains its colour at this time of year, it is best to use hot reds or oranges, such as some of the kniphofias and heleniums. White also holds up well in this light, especially if seen against green. Most of the soft pastel colours are bleached even paler by the bright light, but with hazy, romantic borders the effect can be enhanced – perfect for lazy summer days.

Flagging Foliage

Much of the foliage has been around since spring and it is beginning to look tired and ragged. Try to offset this by cutting back plants that have finished flowering earlier in the year, so that they produce fresh leaves to brighten up the borders. Regular deadheading will also help to keep the borders looking neat. Mulching should have helped to keep the moisture in the soil, but in a hot summer reserves may be used up and it may be necessary to water copiously until the ground is again fully saturated and the plants are revived.

Above: Helenium *'Indian Summer'* brings an orange glow with its sun-loving flowers.

Above: Lilies are always popular for their attractive blooms and range of colours.

Beside the Water

By midsummer the water in the ponds has warmed up and the water plants are in full growth. This is one of the fresher-looking parts of the garden, both in the water and along its margins. Water lilies and irises are at their best and the colours are still vibrant. In dry gardens, where this time of year may be a problem, it is worth creating a water feature to provide an oasis of fresh greenery and colourful flowers.

The Importance of Planning

In the spring and early summer enthusiasm for gardening is high, and along with this the tendency to buy and plant out new plants. However, one's eye is often caught by plants that are in flower rather than ones yet to flower. This can easily upset the balance of plants in the garden with a preponderance of plants for spring and early summer and far less for high summer. Try to be forward-looking and plan for this period too.

FLOWERS FOR HIGH SUMMER
Acanthus
Astilbe
Campanula
Dianthus
Eryngium
Geranium
Helenium
Hemerocallis
Kniphofia
Lilium
Phlox
Veronica

Above: Different yellows with soft pink astilbes make a lovely summer border.

399

AUTUMN

As autumn sets in, nature begins to wind down, but with good planning this can be one of the most colourful times of the year in the garden. By now, many plants are usually looking decidedly the worse for wear, but with judicious cutting back it should be possible to remove the more unsightly plants and dead flowers so that the autumn colours have a chance to shine through. A lot of the end-of-season look that many gardens have during this time of year can be avoided simply by cutting out spent material.

Autumn Colours

This season is a time of warm and hot colours with many yellow daisies, such as helianthus and rudbeckias, as well as fiery autumn foliage. However, there are still plenty of other colours. The Michaelmas daisies, in particular,

Above: Michaelmas daisies are among the stars of the autumn garden. They come in a wide variety of colours.

produce a wide range of colours including blues, pinks and whites. Vernonias also have some wonderfully rich purples as well as whites.

Moving Plants

One of the problems with perennial gardening is to manage to accommodate enough plants in a border to maintain a continuous supply of colour from flowers and foliage. By mid-autumn many of the plants have finished, leaving large gaps in the arrangements. This is not so much a problem at other times of the year as there are always plants in leaf, although they may not yet be in flower. One solution is to move some plants. This works well with shallow-rooted plants, of which Michaelmas

Above: Rich gold is one of the prime colours of the autumn scene and long-flowering rudbeckias provide it.

AUTUMN-FLOWERING PERENNIALS

Anemone x hybrida
Aster
Boltonia
Chelone
Chrysanthemum
Helianthus
Kirengeshoma
Liriope
Nerine
Ophiopogon
Rudbeckia
Schizostylis
Sedum
Solidago
Tricyrtis

Above: A number of sedums flower in the autumn and these are not only valuable for their colour but also for the way that they attract butterflies and bees.

daisies are the prime candidates. Surprisingly these can be moved in full flower without any detrimental effect. Grow them in a spare bit of ground or the back of the border. Soak them well as they come into flower. Dig up the clump with a good rootball of soil still attached, replant it in a gap in the border and then water again. This is real instant gardening.

Wildlife

Autumn is a wonderful time for butterflies, moths and bees in the garden. Fortunately there are plenty of plants, such as the sedums and the Michaelmas daisies, that provide food for these visitors. It is worth making certain that you grow several attractant plants, as the sight of these creatures adds another dimension to the garden. If you want to provide winter food and shelter for birds and insects then you should leave

some areas of herbaceous material such as seed heads for them to feed on during the winter, although this may mean that the garden looks less neat and tidy than it would otherwise.

Above: The dainty flowers of Schizostylis *appear in the autumn. They come in a range of reds and pinks.*

401

WINTER

This is the most difficult time of year in the garden. And yet in some ways it can be the most interesting as it certainly is a challenge. The weather can vary dramatically from region to region and in some areas there may be total snow cover throughout the darkest months, in which case the main interest in the garden will be trees and shrubs. On the other hand there are mild areas that can support a surprisingly large range of material. In the middle are those that have a mildish winter with a few cold snaps here and there. Where the ground can be seen, as long as it is not frozen or waterlogged, there are always a number of plants to be grown.

Above: Iris reticulata *gives a warming splash of colour in late winter.*

Winter Flowers

There are only a handful of perennials that flower in the winter but combined with other plants, such as bulbs and shrubs, they can make up a good display. Some of the most popular winter plants are the hellebores. There are a number of species and an ever-increasing number of cultivars in a wide range of colours. The foliage of many species is very attractive and the plants are worth growing for this alone. Another worthwhile winter perennial is the winter iris, *I. unguicularis*. This flowers over a long period, throughout most of the dullest months. It has wonderful soft blue or mauve flowers that have a delightful scent. It has one other advantage in that it can be grown in the poorest of soils. Indeed an ideal spot is in a dry, rubble-filled soil next to a wall.

Surprise Appearances

If you are not in too much of a hurry to cut everything to the ground in autumn, it is surprising how many plants can continue to flower if the weather is mild, right into the middle of winter and beyond. Penstemons are good examples of this long- and late-flowering ability. Similarly in a mild winter many of the spring flowers will flower early. Sweet violets, *Viola odorata,* are usually flowering in winter, as are a number of primroses and ground-covering pulmonarias.

Where to Plant

Because winter flowers are generally not very interesting for the rest of the gardening year, they can be planted towards the back of the border or under deciduous shrubs where they will clearly show up in the winter but be covered by other plants when they are not looking at their best. If you have a large garden and can afford the space you might create a special winter garden, which you only visit at this time of the year.

ALL-YEAR-ROUND PLANTS

Some perennials have all-year-round qualities that make them especially useful if you have limited space. Although pulmonarias have their

Above: The appearance of winter aconites is a welcome sign as it shows that winter will soon be over.

flowers in late winter and spring, they can be used as a foliage plant for the rest of the year. If all the foliage is cut back after flowering, new leaves will quickly regrow and will retain their freshness. Bergenias have spikes of pink, red or white flowers in spring, but, again, retain their attractive leaves for the rest of the year.

Above: The unusual, delicate pale green flowers of these hellebores brighten up the garden in the winter.

WINTER-FLOWERING PERENNIALS
Eranthis hyemalis
Euphorbia rigida
Galanthus
Helleborus niger
Helleborus orientalis
Helleborus purpurascens
Iris ungicularis
Primula vulgaris
Pulmonaria rubra
Viola odorata

Perennials for Colour

OF ALL THE QUALITIES OF PERENNIALS, COLOUR IS PROBABLY THE MOST IMPORTANT. IT IS THE FIRST THING MOST PEOPLE NOTICE ABOUT A PLANT AND IT GENERALLY MAKES THE MOST IMPACT.

RED PERENNIALS

Alcea rosea (various)
Astilbe 'Fanal'
Astrantia major 'Ruby Wedding'
Canna (various)
Centranthus ruber
Cosmos atrosanguineus
Dahlia (various)
Dianthus 'Brympton Red'
Geum 'Mrs Bradshaw'
Hemerocallis 'Stafford'
Lobelia 'Cherry ripe'
Lupinus 'Inverewe Red'
Lychnis chalcedonica
Monarda didyma 'Cambridge Scarlet'
Paeonia (various)
Papaver orientale (various)
Penstemon 'Cherry Ripe'
Persicaria amplexicaulis
Potentilla 'Gibson's Scarlet'
Zinnia (various)

ORANGE PERENNIALS

Canna 'Orange Perfection'
Crocosmia (various)
Dahlia (various)
Gazania (various)
Geum 'Borisii'
Helenium (various)
Kniphofia (various)
Potentilla 'William Rollison'

YELLOW PERENNIALS

Achillea
Anthemis tinctoria
Asphodeline lutea

Helenium
Helianthus
Hemerocallis
Lysimachia punctata
Oenothera
Primula veris
Primula vulgaris
Sedum (various)
Trollius
Verbascum

BLUE AND VIOLET PERENNIALS

Agapanthus
Ajuga reptans
Aquilegia flabellata
Baptisia australis
Campanula
Delphinium (various)
Echinops ritro
Eryngium
Gentiana
Iris (various)
Limonium platyphyllum
Nepeta
Perovskia atriplicifolia
Scabiosa
Tradescantia Andersoniana Group (various)
Veronica

PURPLE PERENNIALS

Aster (various)
Echinacea purpurea
Erigeron 'Dunkelste Aller'
Erysimum 'Bowles Mauve'
Geranium (various)
Lythrum

Osteospermum jucundum
Penstemon 'Burgundy'
Phlox 'Le Mahdi'
Primula denticulata
Senecio pulcher
Tradescantia Andersoniana Group (various)
Verbena bonariensis

PINK PERENNIALS

Anemone x *hybrida*
Aster (various)
Astilbe (various)
Bergenia cordifolia
Dianthus (various)
Diascia
Dicentra
Erodium manescaui
Geranium (various)
Helleborus (various)
Lamium roseum
Linaria purpurea 'Canon Went'
Malva moschata
Monarda didyma 'Croftway Pink'
Papaver orientale 'Cedric Morris'
Penstemon 'Hidcote Pink'
Persicaria (various)
Phlox (various)
Phuopsis stylosa
Primula (various)
Sedum (various)
Sidalcea

WHITE PERENNIALS

Achillea ptarmica 'The Pearl'
Anemone x *hybrida* 'Honorine Jobert'
Anthemis punctata subsp. *cupaniana*
Campanula lactiflora alba
Convallaria majalis
Crambe cordifolia
Dicentra spectabilis 'Alba'
Geranium (various)
Gypsophila
Helleborus (various)
Penstemon (various)
Phlox (various)
Polygonatum hybridum

Silene uniflora
Trillium grandiflorum
Zantedeschia aethiopica

CREAM PERENNIALS

Anemone lipsiensis
Aruncus dioicus
Kniphofia 'Little Maid'
Rodgersia (various)
Sisyrinchium striatum
Smilacina racemosa
Trollius 'Alabaster'

MIXED

Aquilegia
Chrysanthemum
Dianthus
Gazania
Hemerocallis
Lupinus
Penstemon
Phlox
Primula
Zinnia

FOLIAGE

Alchemilla mollis
Bergenia
Canna
Hosta
Pulmonaria
Sempervivum

Best Perennials for Your Garden

USE THIS QUICK REFERENCE CHART TO SELECT THE PLANTS MOST SUITABLE FOR YOUR DESIGN AND GARDEN CONDITIONS. UNLESS OTHERWISE STATED, ALL PLANTS SHOULD BE SOWN OR PLANTED OUT IN THE SPRING (OR AUTUMN IN MILDER AREAS).

Plant Name	Height/Spread	Colour/Period of Interest	Method of Propagation
Acanthus	150cm (5ft)	white and purple/summer	seed
Achillea	120cm (4ft)	yellow, white, pink/summer	division
Actaea	180cm (6ft)	white/summer and autumn	seed or division
Agapanthus	90cm (3ft)	blue, white/summer	division
Alchemilla	38cm (15in)	yellowish green/summer	seed
Allium B	90cm (3ft)	all colours/summer	seed or division
Alstroemeria	90cm (3ft)	all colours/summer	division
Anemone	90cm (3ft)	white, blue, pink, yellow/spring	autumn division
Anthemis	75cm (30in)	white, yellow/summer	cuttings or division
Aquilegia	60cm (2ft)	all colours/spring, early summer	seed
Artemisia	120cm (4ft)	yellow, brown/silver foliage/summer	cuttings or division
Aruncus	2m (7ft)	cream/summer	division
Aster	2m (7ft)	all colours/summer and autumn	division
Astilbe	120cm (4ft)	white, pink, red/summer	division
Astrantia ps	60cm (2ft)	greenish, pink, red/late spring, summer	division
Bergenia s or ps	45cm (18in)	pink/evergreen foliage/spring	division
Caltha ms	45cm (18in)	yellow/summer	seed or division
Campanula	120cm (4ft)	blue, white/summer	seed or division
Canna	150cm (5ft)	Red, pink, yellow/summer and autumn	division
Cardiocrinum fs B	3m (10ft)	white/summer	seed or division
Catananche	45cm (18in)	blue/summer	seed
Centaurea	120cm (4ft)	purple, red, pink, yellow/summer	seed or division
Centranthus	75cm (30in)	reddish pink, white/summer	seed
Cephalaria	2m (7ft)	yellow/summer	seed
Chelone	90cm (3ft)	pink/autumn	division
Chrysanthemum	180cm (6ft)	various colours/autumn	cuttings or division
Clematis	180cm (6ft)	blue, white/summer	cuttings

Above: Crocosmia *'Lucifer'*

Above: Geranium sanguineum *'Album'*

Convallaria S	20cm (10in)	white/late spring	division
Coreopsis	75cm (30in)	yellow/summer into autumn	division
Cortaderia G	2.5m (8ft)	various colours/all year round	division
Cosmos S	45cm (18in)	mahogany/summer	cuttings or division
Crambe S	180cm (6ft)	white/early summer	division
Crinum B	120cm (4ft)	pink/late summer	seed or division
Crocosmia B	120cm (4ft)	orange, red, yellow/late summer	division
Cynara	2.5m (8ft)	purple/silver foliage/late summer	division
Dahlia T	120cm (4ft)	various colours/summer into autumn	division or cuttings
Delphinium	2m (7ft)	blue, pink, white/summer	cuttings, division or seed
Dianthus S	Up to 38cm (15in)	pink, white/summer	cuttings
Diascia	38cm (15in)	pink/summer into autumn	cuttings
Dicentra	75cm (30in)	pink, white/late spring into early summer	division
Dictamnus	90cm (3ft)	purple, white/summer	seed
Dierama	150cm (5ft)	pink/summer	seed or division
Digitalis	180cm (6ft)	purple, yellow, brown/summer	seed
Doronicum	90cm (3ft)	yellow/spring	division
Echinacea	150cm (5ft)	summer	division
Echinops	180cm (6ft)	blue, white/summer	seed
Epimedium ps	45cm (18in)	yellow, white, pink/late spring	division
Eremurus	2m (7ft)	pink, yellow/summer	seed or division
Erigeron	60cm (2ft)	purple, blue, pink, white/summer	division
Eryngium	2m (7ft)	blue, green/good foliage/summer	seed or division
Eupatorium	2m (7ft)	pink, white/summer and autumn	division
Euphorbia	150cm (5ft)	yellowish-green/spring into summer	seed or division
Filipendula S	120cm (4ft)	pink, white/summer	division
Foeniculum	2m (7ft)	yellow/good, fragrant foliage/summer	seed
Francoa	75cm (30in)	pink/summer	seed
Fritillaria B	90cm (3ft)	various colours/spring	seed or division
Gaura	90cm (3ft)	white/summer	seed
Gentiana	90cm (3ft)	blue, white, yellow/summer and autumn	seed or division
Geranium	90cm (3ft)	purple, pink, blue, white/spring into autumn	seed, cuttings or division
Geum	45cm (18in)	red, yellow, pink/spring into summer	division
Gladiolus B	120cm (4ft)	in various colours/summer	division
Gunnera	2.5m (8ft)	green/large foliage/summer	division
Gypsophila	120cm (4ft)	white, pink/summer	seed or cuttings
Helenium	150cm (5ft)	yellow, orange, brown/summer	division

Above: Anemome ranunculoides

Above: Gypsophila paniculata

Helianthus	2.5m (8ft)	yellow/summer into autumn	division
Heliopsis	150cm (5ft)	yellow/summer into autumn	division
Helleborus	60cm (2ft)	various colours/winter into spring	seed or division
Hemerocallis	120cm (4ft)	yellow, orange, red, pink/summer	division
Heuchera	90cm (3ft)	white, pink/good foliage/summer	division
Hosta	60cm (2ft)	blue, white/good foliage/summer	division
Humulus C	6m (20ft)	green/good foliage/summer	division
Inula	2.5m (8ft)	yellow/summer	seed or division
Iris	150cm (5ft)	various colours/summer, winter	division
Kirengeshoma ps	90cm (3ft)	yellow/autumn	seed or division
Knautia	75cm (30in)	crimson, pink/summer	division, cuttings or seed
Kniphofia	180cm (6ft)	red, orange, yellow/summer into autumn	division
Lamium	60cm (2ft)	pink, purple, white/good foliage/summer	cuttings or division
Lathyrus C	120cm (4ft)	various colours/spring into summer	seed or division
Ligularia	180cm (6ft)	yellow/summer into autumn	seed or division
Lilium some S	180cm (6ft)	various colours/summer	seed or division
Limonium	90cm (3ft)	blue/summer	seed or division
Linaria	180cm (6ft)	yellow, purple, pink/summer	seed
Linum	45cm (18in)	blue/summer	seed
Liriope	38cm (15in)	purple/autumn	division
Lobelia	150cm (5ft)	various colours/summer into autumn	cuttings, division or seed
Lupinus S	150cm (5ft)	various colours/early summer	seed or cuttings
Lychnis	75cm (30in)	red, cerise, pink, orange/summer	seed
Lysimachia	120cm (4ft)	yellow, white, red/summer	seed or division
Lythrum	120cm (4ft)	purple/summer	cuttings or division
Macleaya	2m (7ft)	pink, white/summer	root cuttings or division
Meconopsis	150cm (5ft)	blue, yellow, white, red/summer	seed or division
Miscanthus G	2.5m (8ft)	various/all year round	division
Monarda SF	150cm (5ft)	red, pink, purple, white/summer	division
Nepeta SF	150cm (5ft)	mauve, blue, white, and yellow/summer	cuttings or division
Nerine B	45cm (18in)	pink/autumn	division
Oenothera	150cm (5ft)	yellow, orange/summer into autumn	seed
Origanum SF H	45cm (18in)	purple/summer	seed or division
Osteospermum	Up to 38cm (15in)	purple, white/summer	cuttings
Paeonia	75cm (30in)	red, pink, white, yellow/ spring into summer	seed or division
Papaver	75cm (30in)	various colours/summer	seed or division
Pennisetum G	90cm (3ft)	various colours/all year round	seed or division

Above: Rheum   **Above:** Astrantia major

Penstemon	90cm (3ft)	various colours/summer	cuttings
Perovskia	120cm (4ft)	blue/summer	cuttings
Persicaria	120cm (4ft)	pink, white/summer	division
Phlox	120cm (4ft)	various colours/summer	cuttings or division
Phormium	180cm (6ft)	red, green/good foliage/summer	division
Physostegia	90cm (3ft)	pink, white/summer	seed or division
Polemonium	90cm (3ft)	blue, white, pink, yellow/summer	seed or division
Polygonatum ps	90cm (3ft)	white/spring into summer	division
Potentilla	60cm (2ft)	red, yellow/summer	division
Primula	60cm (2ft)	in various colours/winter/summer	seed or division
Pulmonaria ps	30cm (12in)	blue, red, white/some good foliage/ late winter into spring	division
Rodgersia	120cm (4ft)	pink, cream/good foliage/summer	division
Rudbeckia (cone)	2m (7ft)	yellow/summer into autumn	division
Salvia	150cm (5ft)	in various colours/summer into autumn	cuttings or division
Scabiosa	75cm (30in)	lilac, pink, yellow/summer	seed or division
Schizostylis B	60cm (2ft)	pink, crimson/autumn	division
Sedum	60cm (2ft)	pink, red, yellow/summer	cuttings
Sidalcea	120cm (4ft)	pink, white/summer	division
Silene	60cm (2ft)	pink, white/spring into summer	seed or division
Sisyrinchium	60cm (2ft)	yellow, blue, white, purple/summer	seed or division
Stachys	60cm (2ft)	purple, pink, yellow/silver foliage/summer	some division
Stipa G	2m (7ft)	various colours/all year round	division
Thalictrum	180cm (6ft)	various colours/summer	seed
Tradescantia	60cm (2ft)	blue, purple, white/summer	division
Trillium ps	45cm (18in)	various colours/spring	seed or division
Trollius ms	75cm (30in)	yellow, orange/spring into summer	seed or division
Veratrum	180cm (6ft)	green, red/summer	division
Verbascum	180cm (6ft)	yellow, pink, white/summer	seed
Verbena	180cm (6ft)	purple, blue/summer	seed or division
Veronica	120cm (4ft)	blue, pink, white/summer	division
Viola	30cm (12in)	various colours/summer	cuttings
Yucca	2m (7ft)	cream/summer into autumn	division
Zantedeschia ms	90cm (3ft)	white/summer	division

KEY TO ABBREVIATIONS

s = sun	fs = full shade	H = herb	SF = scented foliage
ms = moist soil	B = bulbous	G = grasses	T = tuberous
ps = partial shade	C = climber	S = scented	

Above: Lathyrus latifolius

Above: Aquilegia

SCENT IN THE GARDEN

In addition to plenty of visual impact, a garden should be full of delicate scent, sensual perfume and intriguing aroma, by night and day. Not only do delightful smells lift the spirit and help us relax, but they also attract beneficial insects. Scented plants can be found for every style and for every time of the year, even in the depths of winter. The handy checklist at the end of this chapter will ensure your garden is never short on fragrance.

Delicate Aromas

SCENT IS OFTEN THE MOST MEMORABLE ELEMENT OF A GARDEN, EVEN MORE POTENT IN ITS IMPACT THAN FLOWER COLOUR OR THE HARMONY OF SHAPES AND TEXTURES. THE FAINTEST WHIFF OF FRAGRANCE CAN UNLOCK THE DOOR TO A HOST OF MEMORIES.

In the plant kingdom scent functions mainly to attract pollinators, but for the gardener it is the most elusive of all the senses and the hardest to define. Scents cannot be recorded and transmitted like sounds or images, nor is it always easy to put into words how we experience them. Moreover, our sense of smell is notoriously under-developed compared with that of the cats, dogs and other domestic animals we share our lives with.

There is even a variation of sensitivity within the human species itself. Some people seem to have a highly developed sense of smell while others have the misfortune to lose the faculty altogether. While women are said to have the keener sense of smell, according to Dr Alex Comfort, men are more responsive to it, so there is no battle of the sexes here.

Our reactions to scent tend to be individual, and it is not always easy to pinpoint a particular aroma. Although we might be able to distinguish between two or three different scents, if more are added the nose becomes anaesthetized, making distinctions difficult. Scent can, however, be used to produce

Above: *The evening primrose* (Oenothera biennis) *releases its fragrance at night.*

Above: Hypericum *'Hidcote' is a useful plant for ground cover and has leaves that are aromatic when crushed.*

a sense of calm and wellbeing, or, conversely, to stimulate and invigorate, ensuring that your garden is a place of regeneration as well as tranquillity.

Types of Scent

Difficult to describe though they are, scents in the garden can be divided into several broad groups.

The commonest examples are usually defined as aromatic. They are generally sweetly spicy and always appealing: we seem never to tire of them. They are found in the almond-like fragrance of heliotropes and the clove essence of carnations and pinks. Violet scents are sharper and more transitory. As well as violets (*Viola*), mignonettes (*Reseda*) and *Iris reticulata* belong to this group.

Roses are usually fruity and spicy, pleasing both up close and at a distance. Some tulips also have this type of scent. Interestingly, many roses seem to belong to a further group, with citrus or lemon overtones. These fragrances are almost universally perceived as pleasant and exhilarating.

Citrus smells are light and refreshing, while herbal ones, such as thyme and lavender, tend to have a calming effect. Some herbal scents are more astringent, however, with notes of eucalyptus that not everyone finds pleasing, although many experience them as invigorating.

A musk-like odour can often be detected in honey-scented plants, and such fragrances seem warm and enduring. They are most commonly encountered among the orchids.

Some flower scents combine more than one note and seem to be "layered". We usually think of these as exotic, as they can be so rich and heady as to be almost cloying.

Above: Perovskia *smells of eucalyptus.*

Above: *Creeping thymes (*Thymus*) can be planted to be trodden gently underfoot.*

Benefits of Scented Plants

Apart from the pleasure they give to gardeners, scented plants are of inestimable value to the garden's ecology, given their appeal to pollinating insects. A diverse insect population is the best way of keeping down garden pests – whose attacks on plants also make them vulnerable to disease – since their predators are more likely to be present.

Brightly coloured plants are usually designed to attract birds, which have no sense of smell, so such flowers are often scentless. Many of the most fragrant plants have simple, cup-shaped flowers, for easy access to the pollen.

Night-scented plants have evolved to attract moths and other nocturnal insects. These plants include night-scented stock (*Matthiola longipetala* subsp. *bicornis*), tobacco plants (*Nicotiana*) and the exquisitely fragrant South American sub-shrub, willow-leaved jessamine (*Cestrum parqui*).

How to Recognize Scented Plants

Latin botanical names often provide good clues as to whether a plant is scented or not. Any genus name followed by the descriptive word *fragrantissima*, *odora* or *suaveolens* is bound to be fragrant. Sometimes the type of scent is indicated: *citriodora* means lemon-scented, and *moschata* is musky. But beware: *pungens* implies a strong (or pungent) scent that is not necessarily appealing.

Scent is not always betrayed by the name, however: *Magnolia grandiflora* refers only to the size of the flowers, not to their bewitching fragrance.

Above: *The characteristic scent of* Eucalyptus *is carried by its volatile oils.*

Parts of the Plant

Speak of scent in the garden and most people immediately think of flowers. While it is true that in most cases it is the flowers that provide the most intoxicating of garden fragrances, other parts of plants can be aromatic, even though they must sometimes be crushed, rubbed or bruised to release their attraction. This is the case with most herbs, but there are other well-known garden plants that have "secret" scents. *Hypericum* 'Hidcote' is widely grown for its yellow flowers and robust qualities, but its aromatic leaves give it a distinction of quite a different kind. *Perovskia*, a sub-shrub valued for its hardiness and late summer lavender-coloured flowers, has white-bloomed stems that smell of eucalyptus oil. Such scents are not always appealing, however: the crushed leaves of skimmias have a somewhat bitter note.

Anyone who has wandered through an apple orchard in autumn will recall the evocative, slightly alcoholic cider smell that arises from bruised windfalls. On a warm day you will see wasps buzzing drunkenly around, intoxicated by the fermenting juices.

Gum trees (*Eucalyptus*) have resinous bark, as do most conifers, so the many genera are not listed separately here. *Chimonanthus* has fragrant leaves, wood, flowers and seeds and is a delight in the winter garden.

Above: *'Constance Spry', one of the most richly scented of all roses, is superb when trained against a wall.*

PLANTS WITH AROMATIC
WOOD, BARK OR LEAVES
Aloysia triphylla
Cercidiphyllum (fallen leaves)
Cistus
Eucalyptus
Helichrysum italicum
Hypericum 'Hidcote'
Laurus nobilis
Liquidambar styraciflua
Myrtus communis
Perovskia
Populus balsamifera
Rosmarinus officinalis
Ruta graveolens
Santolina
Skimmia
Thymus

415

COMBINING PLANTS

Devising a planting scheme that includes a large proportion of strongly scented plants can be even more difficult than planning a colour scheme, for which you can at least get some ideas by playing around with colour swatches. Trying to balance and harmonize the whole range of natural aromas and notes in a collection of plants is a more abstract process, since you cannot reproduce garden scents in the comfort of your sitting room.

On the whole, within a single bed scents are best in pairs or at a maximum of three. More confuse the nose and can seem to anaesthetize it, meaning that none of the scents makes its full impact. Rich, heavy smells are best combined with lighter, fresher

Above: Bergamot (Monarda) *is an aromatic that can be used in potpourri.*

scents: hence the value of underplanting roses with lavender. Alternatives would be old-fashioned, clove-infused carnations (*Dianthus*) – especially if you have alkaline soil – or sweet violets (*Viola*). Some scents are best appreciated on their own, and that applies especially to the powerfully scented *Magnolia grandiflora*, with its lemon-scented, waxy-textured flowers. It is often best to combine such plants with non-scented ones. For example, you could introduce a sweetly scented mock orange (*Philadelphus*) into a white garden if you are relying on 'Iceberg' as the main rose, since this has only a light fragrance. For scent later in the year add some lilies, such as *Lilium regale*, or plant the creamy white *Paeonia* 'White Wings'.

Above: Conifers such as Thuja plicata, *with resinous bark, are highly scented.*

SITING PLANTS

Finding the right position in the garden for your scented plants can increase their impact considerably.

Where you site the plants will largely depend on how they distribute their scent. The mock orange, for example, a large shrub that wafts its scent far and wide, is ideal for the back of a large border, especially since it is rather dull when out of flower. But large plants whose flowers you want to bury your head in, such as *Rosa* 'Constance Spry', need to be sited for easy access, and they are ideally trained over a pergola spanning a walkway or against a house wall, close to where you sit in the evening. House walls are also ideal for other scented climbers, such as the vigorous jasmine (*Jasminum polyanthum*) and the deliciously fragrant star jasmine (*Trachelospermum jasminoides*).

A sheltered garden will seem to trap scent, making a veritable bower of fragrance. In a more open, windy site, locate the most sheltered areas (such as in the lee of a wall or a group of shrubs) and place your fragrant plants there, otherwise you will scarcely notice the scent because it will be borne away on the breeze.

Plants that need to be touched to release their fragrance, such as the herbs lavender (*Lavandula*) and rosemary (*Rosmarinus*), should be placed where you can rub their leaves as you pass. Some prostrate plants are tough enough to stand the occasional (light) footfall and can be planted in the

Above: *The leaves of* Skimmia japonica *have a curious, rather bitter aroma that is released when they are crushed.*

Above: Pelargonium triste *is an unusual member of this genus: its flowers emit a freesia-like scent at night.*

SEASONAL FACTORS

Aromatic plants, such as the conifers and woody herbs that originated in Mediterranean countries, give off most scent during hot weather, so you will be particularly aware of them in high summer. Other plants, however, seem to smell sweeter during mild, damp weather or after a shower of rain, when the moisture in the atmosphere holds the scent in some way. You will particularly notice the scent of the late-flowering climbing rose 'New Dawn' on a cool, damp morning in early autumn. Winter-flowering plants tend to be at their most fragrant on mild, sunny days, when their pollinators stir from their dormancy.

cracks in paving to make a scented carpet. The creeping thymes (*Thymus*) are ideal for this purpose, but you could try the slightly less robust camomile (*Chamaemelum nobile*), *Rosmarinus prostratus* or pennyroyal (*Mentha pulegium*), which are also ideal plants for the top of a retaining wall or the edge of a raised bed.

Many scented plants can be grown in containers and placed on a patio where you sit out in summer. Some are suitable for window boxes or hanging baskets that can be suspended from a pergola over a patio or near a barbecue area. A position near an open window will allow you to enjoy the fragrance from indoors.

Above: Like most members of the pea family, laburnums produce sweetly scented flowers.

NIGHT AND DAY

Unlike other attributes, such as colour, texture and shape, scent is not a constant. Flowers give off their scent when their pollinators are active. Often this is during the hottest part of the day, and there are few more evocative sights and sounds than those of bees, moving from flower to flower on a hot summer day, collecting pollen. Those that are most fragrant when dew is in the air will smell most strongly early in the day and at dusk.

Above: The epiphytic orchid Oncidium *'Sharry Baby' has striking flowers that smell of chocolate.*

A few precious plants are scented at night because they are pollinated by night-flying insects. They are particularly appreciated by those who have daytime jobs and who look forward to the delights of a fragrant evening garden at the end of a stressful day.

HOW TO USE THIS CHAPTER

This quick and easy guide to planning a scented garden begins with a section that covers all the main plant groups, giving recommendations for the best scented plants in each group. *Scent for All Seasons* explains how those plants can be used to give all-year-round fragrance. Finally, *Scent for Every Style* suggests ways in which gardens can be designed to include many favourite aromas.

NIGHT-SCENTED PLANTS

Brugmansia suaveolens
Cestrum parqui
Hemerocallis citrina
Matthiola longipetala subsp. *bicornis*
Mirabilis jalapa
Nicotiana alata
Oenothera biennis
Pelargonium triste
Reseda odorata

Scented Plants in the Garden

EVERY GROUP OF GARDEN PLANTS INCLUDES DELICIOUSLY SCENTED SPECIES, FROM QUICK-TO-GROW ANNUALS TO EXOTIC FLOWERING TREES. THE FOLLOWING SELECTION INCLUDES IDEAS TO HELP YOU FILL A GARDEN WITH FRAGRANCE, WHATEVER ITS SIZE AND STYLE.

BULBS AND CORMS

Valued primarily for their vivid bursts of colour, many of the flowers that grow from bulbs and corms also supply a rich fragrance that more than doubles their appeal. Try to mass them, where possible, to make the most of their brief but intoxicating moments of glory.

Bulbs and corms are among the most versatile plants in the garden, and most are easy to grow. Early bulbs, usually dwarf, are harbingers of spring, studding the bare earth with jewel-like colours, often at the coldest time of the year. Bulbs are also excellent in containers, and this is much

Above: Muscari armeniacum *is a diminutive plant with a delicate scent – good for planting* en masse *in the garden.*

the best way to appreciate the scent of low-growing species that you cannot get down low enough to sniff in the garden. Crocuses, dwarf narcissi, irises, tulips and grape hyacinths can all be grown in shallow pans of gritty compost (soil mix).

Some early bulbs are traditionally grown for enjoyment indoors, notably hyacinths (*Hyacinthus*) and *Narcissus papyraceus*. Remember that these are by no means hot-house plants. They are adapted to a hard life, so keep them outdoors in a cool, light but sheltered spot (perhaps against a house wall) and bring them indoors only when the flower buds start to show colour. After flowering they can be planted outside.

Freesias and *Hymenocallis*, which are not hardy in cold climates, can be grown in pots in an alpine house. Florists' cyclamen (usually unnamed varieties of *Cyclamen persicum*) are sold as winter-flowering houseplants. As they are always sold in flower you can be sure to choose the most fragrant. They enjoy a cool but light position. Store them dry in summer and water and feed in autumn to bring them back into growth.

Summer bulbs include the glorious lilies, though many garden forms are not scented. Look for the species *Lilium regale* and the later-flowering *L. speciosum*. The sumptuously fragrant

BULBS WITH FRAGRANT FLOWERS
Amaryllis belladonna
Crinum
Crocus
Cyclamen persicum
Freesia
Galanthus
Galtonia candicans
Gladiolus tristis
Hyacinthus
Hymenocallis
Iris reticulata
Lilium (some)
Muscari
Narcissus
Tulipa clusiana
Tulipa sylvestris

Easter lily (*L. longiflorum*) is unfortunately not hardy, so must be grown under glass in cold districts. It is easily raised from seed. The bulb season ends with the dramatic South Africans: *Amaryllis belladonna* and *Crinum*, both with trumpet-like flowers.

Above: Lilium regale *is a strongly scented species lily for the summer border.*

Above: *Hyacinths have possibly the most distinctive scent of any bulbous plant.*

421

ANNUALS AND BIENNIALS

Annuals are generally used in the garden for instant impact, for the brilliance of the flowers and the ready way in which they are produced. Many have little or no scent, and most gardeners will want to grow them for their visual beauty alone, but there are also a number of wonderfully fragrant varieties which no scented garden should be without.

In addition to a description of the flowers, seed packets carry full instructions on germination and aftercare. If you do not have time to raise plants from seed, buy young plants from a garden centre in spring. However, you will have less choice.

Annuals are almost without exception flowers of high summer, needing warmth and light to perform at their

Above: New cultivars are introduced regularly, so consult the latest catalogues to keep abreast of these.

best. Biennials, however, usually flower earlier, in late spring. It is also possible to make a late summer sowing of hardy annuals for over-wintering. These will be the earliest to flower in the following season.

Above: Annual nasturtiums have a light, peppery scent, and both the flowers and young leaves are edible. They are one of the easiest annuals to grow, and will self-seed year after year.

Above: Sweet peas (Lathyrus odoratus), which can be sown in autumn or spring, are an essential component of any scented garden. There are countless varieties, in many delicate colours.

422

Choosing Varieties for Scent

As a rule, scented annuals are less showy than those grown for splendid flowers, so it is a good idea to mix scented varieties with other strains. Night-scented stock (*Matthiola longipetala* subsp. *bicornis*) is a case in point: it is a spindly plant with modest little flowers of a bleached mauve. Scatter the seed among other plants, such as the showier gillyflower (*M. incana*), for the best of both worlds. Sweet peas (*Lathyrus odoratus*) are typical cottage garden plants. Despite the common name, not all cultivars are equally fragrant, so it is worth experimenting to find a variety that particularly pleases you, and many of the old-fashioned plants are among the most fragrant, if not the most

Above: Sweet-scented Heliotropium 'Marine' *is actually a perennial, but it is usually treated as an annual in cold districts.*

colourful. Nasturtiums (*Tropaeolum*) have a fresh, peppery scent, reminiscent of the related watercress. Both flowers and leaves are edible, even if the taste is an acquired one.

ANNUALS AND BIENNIALS WITH SCENTED FLOWERS

Amberboa moschata
Erysimum cheiri
Exacum affine
Iberis
Lathyrus odoratus
Limnanthes douglasii
Lobularia maritima
Matthiola
Oenothera biennis
Reseda odorata
Tropaeolum

423

Shrubs and Perennials

These plants are the mainstay of the garden, flowering year after year and gradually increasing in size and importance. Nowadays, they are frequently used together to make low-maintenance mixed borders that provide interest over a long period.

Aromatic Shrubs

Leaving aside the shrubby herbs, there are a number of shrubs with aromatic foliage, and those that are also evergreen will supply scent all year round.

Many conifers are dwarf and compact or so slow-growing that they can be treated as shrubs for a good few years. They are traditionally combined with heathers, but also work surprisingly well with grasses planted in island beds. But if conifers are not

Above: Dianthus *'Cobham Beauty'* has a light, pleasing scent. Small fragrant pinks make ideal edging plants near a path.

to your taste, try skimmias or Mexican orange blossom (*Choisya ternata*), although you will have to bruise the leaves to enjoy their aroma. The young leaves of the sweet briar (*Rosa eglanteria*) smell distinctly of apples after a shower of rain.

Above: Buddleja alternifolia *has honey-scented flowers in midsummer.*

*Above: The common myrtle (*Myrtus communis) *has an unmistakable aroma.*

Flowering Shrubs

As far as scent is concerned, there is almost a surfeit of shrubs. Mahonias have yellow flowers with a fragrance like lilies-of-the-valley, and some of the berberises, both deciduous and evergreen forms, are similar. *Viburnum* is also a genus richly endowed with flowering species. One of the best is the hybrid *V.* x *burkwoodii*, an elegant plant with heads of sweetly fragrant white flowers in spring.

The scent of lilacs (*Syringa*) seems to embody late spring, but some of the species have flowers with a fetid smell. The hybrids of *S. vulgaris* have the typical lilac scent.

Buddleias are indispensable for their honey-scented, mauve, white or purple flowers. The butterfly bush, *Buddleja davidii*, is almost too well known in some gardens, where it self-seeds with abandon. *B. alternifolia* has a more elegant form, particularly when it is trained as a standard.

> **SCENTED SHRUBS**
>
> *Berberis sargentiana*
> *Buddleja*
> *Camellia sasanqua*
> *Cestrum parqui*
> *Choisya ternata*
> *Citrus*
> *Cytisus battandieri*
> *Daphne*
> *Deutzia*
> *Elaeagnus* x *ebbingei*
> *Erica arborea*
> *Hamamelis mollis*
> *Mahonia* x *media*
> *Myrtus communis*
> *Osmanthus decorus*
> *Philadelphus*
> *Skimmia japonica*
> *Syringa vulgaris*
> *Viburnum*

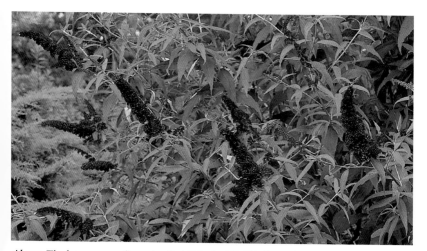

Above: *The late summer-flowering* Buddleja davidii *'Black Knight' is dramatically coloured and richly scented.*

425

Fragrant Roses

If ever a group of plants was prized for its scent, it is the roses. Not all roses are scented, but it is a myth that only old varieties have fragrance. Some, such as 'Nevada', have a light scent, which seems to hang on the air some distance from the plant. Others bear their scent on their stamens, and this is usually a rich, heady fragrance that you have to drink in by burying your nose in the flower.

Above: Besides its unique colouring, Rosa *'Escapade' has a delicious fragrance.*

Scented Perennials

This large and diverse group of plants contains some of the most exquisitely scented species.

The herbaceous clematis are less well known than the climbers, but they make excellent additions to the border, flowering in early summer. *Clematis recta* needs staking but pro-

duces a mass of starry, creamy-white flowers, held on stems up to 1.2m (4ft) tall. Herbaceous peonies also need staking, but few gardeners would

SCENTED ROSES
'Apricot Nectar'
'Blue Moon'
'Buff Beauty'
'Céleste'
'Constance Spry'
'Escapade'
'Fantin-Latour'
'Fragrant Cloud'
'Lady Hillingdon'
'Margaret Merril'
'Mme Hardy'
'Mme Isaac Pereire'
'Reine Victoria'
R. rugosa
'Sheila's Perfume'
'Whisky Mac'

Above: Cytisus battandieri *deserves its common name of pineapple broom. The flowers both look and smell like pineapples.*

think that a problem when confronted by their sumptuous flowers, many blessed with a rich, spicy fragrance unmatched in this group of plants. The pink 'Sarah Bernhardt' is an old but reliable cultivar, and 'Kelway's Supreme' has huge, bowl-shaped, satin-textured flowers, but all the cultivars are ravishing, and specialist nursery catalogues are usually temptingly illustrated. The single-flowered forms are more likely to be scented than those with double flowers.

The daylilies (*Hemerocallis*) now form a huge group. New cultivars have a longer flowering season, and some are night-flowering. Many are sweetly scented, but check the catalogues of the specialist breeders. Lily-of-the-valley (*Convallaria majalis*) is almost too familiar, but it has an unmistakable scent and is ideal for growing in a shady spot. It can be forced for winter flowering indoors if you pot up the "pips" in autumn and bring them into an unheated greenhouse or conservatory (sunroom). A little more warmth in midwinter will produce earlier flowers than appear outside. Give the plants a rest after flowering and return them to a position outdoors.

Carnations and pinks (*Dianthus*) make ideal edging plants, which are attractive when out of flower with their sheaves of steel-blue leaves. The clove-scented cultivars are particularly

SCENTED PERENNIALS
Clematis recta
Convallaria majalis
Cosmos atrosanguineus
Dianthus
Helleborus lividus
Hemerocallis
Hosta plantaginea
Iris unguicularis
Phlox
Primula
Smilacina racemosa
Verbena bonariensis

sought-after. Not all the newer forms are scented, although they have the advantage of a longer season.

One of the most intriguing of all plants is *Cosmos atrosanguineus*, whose blood-red flowers smell of melted chocolate. If you are a chocoholic, this is the plant for you.

Above: The delicate scent of primula flowers is best appreciated when they are grown in sizeable drifts in a mixed border.

TREES WITH SCENT

A tree adds dignity and style to a garden, and several species are scented. Choose carefully, however, because not only will a tree often outlive the gardener, but many trees will also eventually outgrow their allotted space.

Flowering Trees

A scented tree in full flower will be one of the glories of the garden. In a mild climate, where frosts are unlikely, an airy acacia, such as *Acacia dealbata* or *A. baileyana*, will charm with its bobbly, duckling-yellow mimosa flowers in early spring. In a cold area, grow it against a warm wall or in a conservatory (sunroom). Acacias are among the few trees that positively thrive in a

TREES WITH SCENTED FLOWERS
Acacia dealbata
Aesculus hippocastanum
Laburnum x watereri 'Vossii'
Magnolia delavayi
Magnolia kobus
Magnolia x loebneri
Malus floribunda
Malus hupehensis
Prunus 'Amonagawa'
Prunus x yedoensis
Styrax japonica
Tilia x euchlora
Tilia petiolaris

container. Hardier and rather grander are the magnolias, with sumptuous, chalice-like flowers, usually of a creamy ivory white, although pinks and purples also occur. In cold areas choose a position out of the morning sun, since the flowers can be blackened by a

Above: *The pure white flowers of* Magnolia x loebneri *'Merrill' are delicately scented.*

Above: Acacia dealbata *produces masses of flowers from late winter to early spring – it makes a magnificent specimen in a sheltered garden.*

sudden rise in temperature after a clear, frosty night. Ornamental cherries (*Prunus*), usually prized for the wealth of their blossom, also include some scented cultivars among their number. The same is true of the crab apples (*Malus*). The musty scent of hawthorn blossoms (*Crataegus*), so evocative in the wild, is possibly best kept out of small gardens and its use restricted to boundary planting.

The evergreen Chinese privet would be an unusual choice. Normally used for hedging (in which case the flowers are generally sacrificed by the tight clipping necessary for a neat surface), this makes a surprisingly elegant specimen or back-of-the-border plant. A warning note must be struck, however: not everyone finds the scent of the creamy summer flowers appealing.

Limes (*Tilia*) are too large for most gardens, but anyone who has one growing nearby (such as in a village square or as a pavement planting) will know the heady scent the flowers, though inconspicuous, release on warm evenings in early summer.

Bark, Stems and Leaves

Most conifers are scented, usually because of their sticky, resinous stems. You will especially notice this in a hot summer, when pines (*Pinus*) in particular give off a characteristic scent, but you will also be aware of it if you cut stems from your conifers for winter decoration indoors – do not be put off by the synthetic 'pine fragrance' used in household cleaning products. Eucalyptus scent is also familiar from cough medicines and other remedies.

The scent of the balsam poplar (*Populus balsamifera*) is unmistakable when the leaves unfurl in spring. At the other end of the growing season, one of the most appealing of all scented trees is *Cercidiphyllum*, whose leaves smell of burnt toffee when they fall to the ground in autumn.

TREES WITH AROMATIC BARK,
WOOD OR LEAVES

Cercidiphyllum
Eucalyptus
Laurus nobilis
Liquidambar styraciflua
Populus balsamifera
Populus x *candicans*

AROMATIC HERBS

Most herbs are not so much scented as aromatic, a quality that is often not immediately apparent but is released only when the leaves or stems are bruised or crushed. The many forms of mint (*Mentha*) are a good example. Most of the plants that are defined as herbs have scents that are refreshing and invigorating, but they are not always appealing. Sometimes a plant's aromatic qualities are a defence mechanism to deter browsing animals. In addition, herbs have been so widely used in medicines that they have acquired connotations beyond gardening. Nevertheless, in any scented garden, herbs will play a major role.

Most of the fragrant herbs have culinary uses, so they are doubly valuable in the garden. Fragrant sage

HERBS WITH SCENTED LEAVES
Aloysia triphylla
Artemisia arborescens
Laurus nobilis
Lavandula
Mentha
Monarda didyma
Ocimum basilicum
Origanum vulgare
Rosmarinus officinalis
Salvia officinalis
Santolina
Thymus

(*Salvia*), rosemary (*Rosmarinus officinalis*) and thyme (*Thymus*) are as well known to cooks as they are to gardeners, but a scented garden will also have room for an aromatic evergreen bay (*Laurus nobilis*) and annual basil (*Ocimum basilicum*). Ornamental herbs, such as the attractive, ever-popular lavender (*Lavandula*) is also grown for its deliciously scented flowers, and cotton lavender (*Santolina chamaecyparissus*) for its aromatic foliage.

Because most of the culinary herbs are native to countries around the Mediterranean, they need to be grown in well-drained soil in full sun. They are particularly well suited to growing in containers, which tend to be well drained and, if space in the garden is limited, can be moved to sunny positions as the plants come into flower. Bear in mind, however, that many of the cultivated forms with golden or variegated foliage will do better in light or dappled shade.

Above: *Lemon balm (*Melissa officinalis*) is very easy to grow and smells strongly of citrus when crushed.*

Take care when handling some of these plants, especially common rue (*Ruta graveolens*). People with sensitive skin may be allergic to the foliage, which can cause rashes.

Harvesting and Preserving

Many herbs can be used fresh in cooked dishes, added to salads or used to make refreshing tisanes. Such herbs should be grown close to the house to make harvesting easy. Many herbs can also be dried or frozen for use out of season, and drying can sometimes enhance the flavour.

Harvest in fine, sunny weather, picking the leaves and shoots early in the day, when the plants are at their freshest. If you intend to dry the plants, wait until the dew has evaporated before picking. Dry the leaves and stems on a metal rack in a warm, dry, well-ventilated place or in a very

Above: All forms of lavender have that characteristic scent, but the Mediterranean Lavandula stoechas *stands out.*

low oven. If necessary, the leaves can then be removed from the stems by rubbing. Once dried, herbs should be stored in airtight containers.

Above: 'Tricolor' is an ornamental variegated form of the culinary herb sage (Salvia officinalis)*.*

431

CLIMBING PLANTS

Most climbers are naturally big, rampant plants, and this is really part of their charm, since they will cast their scent far and wide.

Trained over pergolas, they can be used to create a delightful shaded place to sit and relax on a warm summer's day, or they can be planted to ramble through trees, which is logical when you consider that this is how they grow in the wild. They can also be grown over shrubs in the border to lengthen the period of interest, flowering either before or after the host plants (or simultaneously for a briefer but glorious display). Many can also be trained against house walls: a good way of growing plants that are not reliably hardy, since they will benefit from the reflected heat and extra shelter that the wall provides.

Above: Lonerica *has an intoxicating fragrance in the evening.*

Types of Climber

Climbing plants are usually categorized according to the way they cling (if they cling at all) to their support.

Twining climbers have stems that grow in a spiral, in the wild wrapping themselves around the stems of a host plant. The honeysuckles (*Lonicera*) are the most familiar example, but the group also includes the hop (*Humulus lupulus*) and wisteria. These plants are good for growing into trees or over trellis panels, either free-standing or attached to a wall.

Leaf stalk climbers, such as clematis, have specially adapted stalks that twist and grip the thin stems of a host plant. Some types of trellis are too coarse for these, so choose either a light trellis, pig wire or a framework of wires against a wall. They are also excellent rambling through shrubs.

Self-clinging climbers have special pads that adhere to the host, so no system of support is necessary. These are ideal for covering a wall.

Thorny plants, such as roses (*Rosa*), produce long, flexible stems that attach themselves to the bark of host plants by means of their sharp thorns. These usually need a little help in the garden. To train them into a tree, support the stems initially on long canes until the rose has a good grip. Against a wall, use a trellis or system of wires, and train the growing stems as near the horizontal as possible.

Above: '*Blairii No. 2*', *a sweetly scented Bourbon rose, is repeat-flowering and can make a spectacular climber.*

Above: *Free-flowering and prolific, this particular* Clematis montana *will scent the air far and wide in late spring.*

A Scented Bower

For many, the scent of honeysuckle defines summer, and it can be enjoyed over a long period, since there are early- and late-flowering forms. Equally familiar is the common jasmine (*Jasminum officinale*). The sweet-scented *Jasminum polyanthum* bears large clusters of white flowers but is not hardy, so it must be grown in a conservatory (sunroom) in cold areas. Even more richly scented is the star jasmine (*Trachelospermum jasminoides*), an evergreen with curious white flowers from summer to autumn, that benefits from the protection of a warm wall.

Another plant that benefits from the support of a warm wall is wisteria, surely the most dramatic of all flowering climbers. In this case, the plant is fully hardy, but it needs a good roasting in summer to ensure that it flowers well the following year. Wisteria is also spectacular when it is grown more informally, through a large deciduous tree.

It is a pity that the large-flowered clematis are mostly unscented. For fragrance you need to look to the smaller flowered species. *Clematis montana* is a rampant plant, but not all cultivars are scented. Curiously, a montana can lose its scent from one year to the next for no apparent reason. The deliciously scented *Clematis flammula* and *C. rehderiana* are particularly valued for their late season – from late summer to autumn.

SCENTED CLIMBERS
Akebia quinata
Clematis (some)
Jasminum
Lonicera (some)
Rosa
Trachelospermum jasminoides
Wisteria

GROUND-COVER PLANTS

There are a few useful, stalwart plants that can provide scent as well as fulfilling the overriding need to cover large areas of otherwise bare ground or to create weed-suppressing mats of herbage.

Violets make excellent ground cover, especially in a woodland garden, where they revel in the cool, slightly damp conditions. Another valuable woodlander is lily-of-the-valley (*Convallaria majalis*), provided you can get it established. It is also attractive in a shady rock garden. In a more open site (but still with some shelter), primulas could be charming, but remember that not all species are fragrant.

For covering large tracts of rough ground, *Crambe cordifolia* can be magnificent, although it must be admitted that not everyone finds the scent of the clouds of white summer flowers

SCENTED GROUND-COVER PLANTS
Cistus
Convallaria majalis
Crambe cordifolia
Dianthus
Geranium macrorrhizum
Melissa
Mentha
Petasites
Thymus
Verbena

appealing. Another perennial, *Geranium macrorrhizum*, has velvety-textured leaves that emit a resinous fragrance when bruised. They have the added distinction of turning red in autumn.

Many climbers can be used as ground cover, particularly over a bank. Peg down the stems to encourage rooting. Besides strengthening the plant, this will keep down weeds.

Above: Applemint, like all the mints, makes good aromatic ground cover – perhaps too good, as it can be invasive.

Above: Houttuynia cordata *is a fine plant for ground cover or as a bog plant; the leaves smell of oranges when crushed.*

434

WATER PLANTS

Many water lilies are scented, but in a large pool it can be difficult to get close enough to appreciate this. You are more likely to catch the fragrance of plants at the water's edge.

The sweet rush (*Acorus calamus*) has deliciously scented, handsome, sword-like leaves and can be grown either in wet soil or in shallow water as a marginal plant. The straight species is of scant ornamental value, and only the variegated form, 'Variegatus', is widely grown.

An intriguing bog plant, which can also be grown in borders provided the soil does not dry out, is *Houttuynia cordata*, which has attractive arrow-shaped leaves that look as though cast in bronze. Crush a leaf between your fingers, however, and you will find it

*Above: Many water lilies (*Nymphaea*) are described as fragrant. But how are you supposed to get close enough to tell?*

smells distinctly of Seville (Temple) oranges. The cultivar 'Flore Pleno' has appealing double white flowers; 'Chameleon' has attractive leaves that are marbled with yellow and red. All forms make excellent ground cover.

All species of mint (*Mentha*) prefer reliably moist soil, but water mint (*M. aquatica*) actually likes to have its feet in water. A rather coarse plant, it can be invasive if given its head.

SCENTED BOG AND WATER PLANTS

Acorus calamus 'Variegatus'
Houttuynia cordata
Mentha aquatica
Nymphaea
Primula

Scent for All Seasons

IF YOU CHOOSE CAREFULLY FROM THE MANY SCENTED PLANTS
AVAILABLE, YOU WILL BE ABLE TO ENJOY FRAGRANCE IN THE GARDEN
THROUGHOUT THE YEAR. THE FOLLOWING PAGES DESCRIBE AND
ILLUSTRATE A SELECTION OF PLANTS FOR EACH SEASON.

THE FRAGRANT GARDEN

A surprisingly large number of plants
produce scent all year round. Conifers
are always fragrant, though obviously
you will be more aware of this during
hot, dry weather in summer when the
resin oozes from the branches. It is
well worth passing your hands over

*Above: Aromatic bay (*Laurus nobilis*) is
one of the most desirable of all evergreens.*

the leaves in the dead of winter to
remind yourself of their invigorating
scent. All the woody evergreen herbs,
such as bay (*Laurus nobilis*) and rosemary (*Rosmarinus*), retain their scent
all year round, as do other evergreens,
such as skimmias and choisyas.

Indoors, scented-leaf pelargoniums
and citrus can be relied on to provide
scent for all seasons.

Planning for Scent

Achieving year-round scent in your
garden will be a matter of trial and
error. Plant catalogues and encyclope-
dias are often vague when it comes to
flowering times – necessarily so, since
this can vary with the weather from
year to year and will also depend on
the local conditions.

For scent in winter, look to those
shrubs that flower intermittently during mild periods, such as *Viburnum* x
bodnantense, which has intensely fragrant, deep pink flowers from late
autumn to spring. Spring flowers
begin with dwarf bulbs, then come the
magnolias and shrubs, many divinely
scented. Summer is the peak of the

gardening year, when you can hardly count the different scents: this is the season of peonies, roses and all the many deliciously perfumed annuals.

Autumn is a quiet time in the garden, when everything in it is dying back – a season for taking stock of your successes and failures. This is a good time for planting to plug all those gaps in the succession of scent that you noticed throughout the year. But as you do so, you will also catch the scents of ripening fruits and seeds. And the deliciously sweet-scented ice plant (*Sedum spectabile*), beloved of bees, often flowers well into autumn.

Above: Fragrant in all their parts, the various members of the Citrus *genus provide year-round scent but need winter protection in cold areas.*

Above: A scented-leaf pelargonium will provide fragrance when you touch the plant, perhaps most noticeably in warm, dry weather.

SPRING

Many gardeners' favourite season, spring is the time when everything is fresh and full of promise. Most spring scents are appropriately fresh, light and airy.

Bulbs and Corms

Many spring bulbs produce scented flowers. Among the many daffodils and narcissi, those with short cups tend to have the sweetest fragrance, especially the Tazetta hybrids, such as 'Geranium' and 'Cragford'. *Iris reticulata* is delicious but unfortunately not reliably perennial. Dwarf bulbs that will multiply year after year include *Crocus tommasinianus* or forms of *C. chrysanthus*. Some of the more robust hybrids are

Above: Viburnum carlesii *'Diana' has one of the richest fragrances of any of the spring-flowering shrubs.*

strong enough to compete with grass and can be planted to create scented drifts in a lawn. Prolific to the extent of becoming weeds are the sweetly scented grape hyacinths (*Muscari*).

Queen of all the spring bulbs, at least so far as scent goes, is the hyacinth (*Hyacinthus*). In appearance flowers are stiff and uncompromising: they are best grown in formal beds *en masse* if you have the space; otherwise they are ideal in containers.

Few tulips are scented – they have been bred for flamboyance of flower – but you could try the dainty lady tulip, *Tulipa clusiana*. To add scent to a dramatic bed of hybrid tulips, combine them with biennial wallflowers (*Cheiranthus*), which have perhaps the spiciest, most evocative perfume of any of the spring flowers. Look for dwarf varieties in shades that will complement the tulips.

Shrubs and Perennials

If you have acid soil, try some of the azaleas (*Rhododendron*). Not all cultivars are scented, but those that are often have a rich, lily-like fragrance entirely in keeping with their exotic-looking flowers.

Spring is the season of viburnums, such as *V.* x *burkwoodii* and *V. carlesii*, both richly perfumed and tolerant of any soil. There is rich scent to be found among the skimmias, which have a powerful lily-of-the-valley fragrance.

438

Skimmias are extremely versatile and make an elegant choice for containers and tubs near the front door with their squat, compact habit.

If you have light, acid soil, the tree heath (*Erica arborea*) will be a joy in this season with its honey-scented flowers. More tolerant of a range of soil types are the berberises and the handsome *Osmanthus decorus*.

Among perennials, do not overlook lily-of-the-valley (*Convallaria majalis*), a modest plant that is charming where allowed to push itself up through cracks in paving. It is one of the few scented plants that thrives in shade.

Climbers and Trees

There are not many climbers that flower in spring, and those that do tend to have no scent. However, two clematis are worth having for their scent. The evergreen *C. armandii* is handsome, with vanilla-scented flowers

Above: *The herbaceous* Clematis recta *is scented, unlike the large-flowered climbing hybrids.*

around mid-spring. More rampant is *C. montana*. Cultivars vary, but 'Elizabeth' (pale pink) and 'Alexander' (white) are sweetly scented.

Ornamental cherries and magnolias are generally chosen for their looks rather than their scent, but many will reliably perfume the air as well. Among magnolias, *M. denudata* is ravishing, with large flowers that open before the leaves unfurl. *M. salicifolia* has orange-blossom-scented flowers.

For later in the season, consider some of the crab apples (*Malus*), with their delicate blossoms, and lilacs (*Syringa*), which take the shrub season into summer with what is perhaps the most wonderfully potent scent in the entire garden.

SCENTED PLANTS FOR SPRING

Clematis armandii
Convallaria majalis
Crocus
Erica arborea
Erysimum cheiri
Hyacinthus
Magnolia (some)
Muscari armeniacum
Narcissus (some)
Primula (some)
Rhododendron (some)
Syringa
Viburnum

SUMMER

This is the peak of the gardening year, when the well-planned garden will be filled with an apparently unending succession of flowers. At this time of year, there is an abundance of choice to ensure that delicious scents greet you whenever you step outside on a sunny morning.

Shrubs and Perennials

The summer season is heralded by the peonies, stately plants with gorgeous flowers that are usually of an intoxicating spiciness matched by no other group of plants. Old-fashioned forms of clove-scented carnations and pinks (*Dianthus*) also have a part to play, provided you can supply the conditions that suit them – well-drained, alkaline soil in full sun. Some do best in a rock garden.

Summer is the season of roses, and no garden worthy of the name should be without them. All rose scents are appealing, but while some are light and fresh, others have deeper base notes that make them richer and more complex. One of the best is the climber 'New Dawn', which has a very pronounced, but not cloying, fruity scent that is at its best towards the end of the season as the nights become cooler and damper.

A group of roses known as hybrid musks includes the delightful 'Buff Beauty', with deliciously fragrant flowers of soft apricot-orange that

Above: Roses vary surprisingly in the strength and character of their fragrance – always try them before buying, if possible.

Above: If you have acid soil, plant the heather Erica vagans *'Summertime', which prefers such conditions.*

fades to a creamy white in sun. The rambling rose 'Albertine' is virtually unsurpassed for scent, although the myrrh-like notes of 'Constance Spry' run it close. Among modern roses, the aptly named 'Fragrant Cloud' has a rich scent that hangs on the air. 'Margaret Merril' is also incomparable for a white garden. The bleached mauve of 'Blue Moon' does not appeal to all tastes, but the scent is full and lemony.

Mock oranges (*Philadelphus*) are richly, even cloyingly scented. The flowers are exclusively white. 'Virginal' is a good double, but eventually makes a large shrub up to 3m (10ft) in both directions. The cultivar 'Belle Etoile' has single flowers with appealing purple blotches at the centre.

Above: Genista lydia, *which flowers in early summer, is a fine scented plant for a Mediterranean-style garden.*

P. coronarius 'Aureus' has the added distinction of yellow-green leaves, but needs a sheltered position out of full sun to avoid scorching.

SCENTED PLANTS
FOR SUMMER
Buddleja
Cestrum parqui
Clematis recta
Clematis rehderiana
Hesperis matronalis
Lilium regale
Lonicera (some)
Matthiola longipetala subsp. *bicornis*
Nicotiana
Philadelphus
Syringa
Wisteria

Trees

Scented summer-flowering trees are rare but delicious. In the past, limes (*Tilia*) were a popular choice for avenues leading up to stately homes, and now they are mature we can enjoy their fragrance. The pale yellow flowers, though they look insignificant, have an unforgettable scent.

In a small garden, the Mount Etna broom (*Genista aetnensis*) is a good choice. It is a light, airy tree that casts little shade but pours forth its fragrant yellow flowers at the height of summer. It needs a well-drained spot in full sun. Sophoras are equally desirable, but not all the species are hardy, and even those that are need long, hot summers to flower reliably.

Annuals and Biennials

Mignonette (*Reseda odorata*) is a charmingly old-fashioned flower with a sweet scent, ideal for a cottage garden. Stocks (*Matthiola*) are also fragrant, and there are many strains of varying colours. The spires of gillyflowers (*M. incana*) are in white and shades of pink, mauve, violet and purple. Sweet alyssum (*Lobularia maritima*), in white or purple, is low-growing and makes an excellent edging plant. Where happy, it will seed itself obligingly in paving cracks. Look out for new strains of another cottage garden favourite, sweet William (*Dianthus barbatus*), which will flower the same year as it is sown and make an invaluable addition to the border.

Above: *Buddleja davidii 'Peace' is a white form of this highly fragrant species.*

Night-scented Flowers

For flowers that are fragrant in the evening look to the aptly named night-scented stock (*Matthiola longipetala* subsp. *bicornis*) or to tobacco plants (*Nicotiana*). These hang their heads in the most pensive way during the heat of the day but revive as the temperature falls to release a potent, incense-like fragrance. *Hesperis matronalis* has the charming common names of dame's violet or sweet rocket. The flowers, which are mauve, purple or white, are carried in phlox-like heads.

Cestrum parqui, a sub-shrub of borderline hardiness, possesses panicles of curious, star-like, lime green flowers. You realize the point of the plant as night falls, when the flowers release a unique, bubble-gum fragrance to attract the night-flying moths that

Above: Paeonia *'Alice Harding', like nearly all the hybrid peonies, has spicily scented flowers.*

pollinate them. Position the plant in a warm corner of the garden where you relax in the evening.

Herbs

Most of the aromatic herbs are at their best in summer, when their essential oils are freely produced. On a really hot day, the curry plant (*Helichrysum italicum*) will give off its characteristic spicy odour without you having to bruise its leaves. The sweetly scented flowers of lavender (*Lavandula*) and thyme (*Thymus*) are a must, both for their unforgettable fragrance and their attraction for bees and other insects. Lavender can also be harvested and dried for scenting linen.

443

AUTUMN

Scents tend to be in short supply at this time of year, when most plants are busy setting seed and ripening their fruits. Many of the autumn-flowering plants have no scent at all, though it is worth keeping an eye on new dahlia hybrids: scented forms are being developed using a species that has not hitherto made its way into the garden.

Cheating Nature

Until such time as scented dahlias are widely available, we have to rely on a few tricks. For scent in the autumn garden, you can make a few late sowings of fragrant annuals to be planted out from midsummer. Tobacco plants (*Nicotiana*) will carry on flowering until the first frosts and will reward you with their deliciously scented flowers well into autumn. Pruning *Buddleja davidii* in late spring will delay its flowering season, and as long as the summer is not too hot, flowers should still be coming at this time of year.

Many roses have an autumn display that matches the summer one. 'Buff Beauty' is, if anything, even better in autumn, since the flowers hold their distinctive soft orange colour for longer before they fade to white.

In a good year, you can expect the evergreen *Magnolia grandiflora* to push out a few more flowers in autumn. In a cold area train this against a warm wall or look for the cultivar 'Victoria', which is apparently

Above: Autumn foliage is often spectacular.

Above: Most crab apples not only bear fragrant spring flowers but also have aromatic fruits.

*Above: The medlar (*Mespilus germanica*) has edible fruits that develop a honeyed sweetness when softened by frost.*

impervious to the cold. There is no need to cheat nature in the case of *Elaeagnus* x *ebbingei*, as it actually flowers at this time of year. All its cultivars are evergreen and some are attractively variegated. The flowers are inconspicuous but exude a sweet, powerful scent even on chilly days.

Fruits and Foliage

Apples and pears are well known, but the queen of fruits so far as scent is concerned must be the quince (*Cydonia oblonga*). Pick a few and place them in a bowl in a warm room, where they will soon release their distinctive sweet and spicy aroma. They are not edible raw, but make a sublime addition to apple pies and crumbles. Quince jelly is a precious treat. The fruits of the little-grown medlar

(*Mespilus germanica*) develop their fragrance as they begin to rot after the first frost; indeed, this is the point at which they become edible.

The leaves of walnuts (*Juglans*) and *Cercidiphyllum japonicum* are also unusually fragrant after they have fallen from the tree, bringing a special pleasure to an autumn stroll through any woodland or arboretum where they are planted.

> ### SCENTED PLANTS FOR AUTUMN
> *Acidanthera bicolor*
> *Amaryllis belladonna*
> *Camellia sasanqua*
> *Cercidiphyllum japonicum*
> *Chaenomeles*
> *Cydonia oblonga*
> *Elaeagnus* x *ebbingei*
> *Juglans*
> *Magnolia grandiflora*
> *Mespilus germanica*

WINTER

Far from being a dead time of year, winter is a season when the garden can be full of scent. Indeed, the fragrance of a winter garden seems to have an added poignancy when so much is lifeless and barren.

Winter Shrubs

One of the best shrubs is the witch hazel (*Hamamelis mollis*) which has spidery, ochre yellow flowers that are sweetly scented. It will do best in a sheltered spot and prefers acid to neutral soil. It is slow-growing, so it will be some years before you will feel happy about cutting branches for indoors. Another desirable plant is the

Above: The winter flowers of Sarcococca *have an almost overpowering scent and are quite happy to grow in shade.*

winter-sweet, *Chimonanthus praecox*, although this, too, is slow-growing. Rather faster are the excellent sarcococcas, low-growing evergreens with glossy, pointed leaves. They make excellent ground cover, even under trees. The scent of the inconspicuous white flowers is almost overpowering, and even a couple of branches brought into the warm indoors will scent the whole house.

Viburnum x *bodnantense* is excellent and reliable, flowering on and off throughout winter. Of even greater distinction is *Daphne bholua*, which benefits from a sheltered spot. Plant it near the front door so that you can appreciate its incomparable scent.

A number of shrubs are of small value when in leaf but earn their keep through the fragrance of their winter

Above: Viburnum x bodnantense *'Dawn' is one of the most sweetly-scented of all winter-flowering shrubs.*

Above: Daphne bholua *is a wonderful shrub for planting near the front door, where visitors will appreciate its scent.*

flowers. One such is the shrubby honeysuckle, *Lonicera fragrantissima*, a good plant for a wild garden.

On a warm wall, you could try *Acacia dealbata*, which produces fluffy yellow flowers towards the end of winter. In mild areas this makes an excellent specimen tree. Another plant that benefits from wall protection is *Abeliophyllum distichum*, with fragrant, white, forsythia-like flowers.

> SCENTED PLANTS FOR WINTER
> *Abeliophyllum distichum*
> *Acacia dealbata*
> *Chimonanthus praecox*
> *Daphne bholua*
> *Hamamelis mollis*
> *Iris unguicularis*
> *Lonicera fragrantissima*
> *Mahonia* x *media*
> *Sarcococca*
> *Viburnum* x *bodnantense*

A Special Iris

The Algerian iris (*Iris unguicularis*) is unique. It produces its large flowers in the depths of winter. To appreciate them to the full, pull them from the plant while they are still in bud and watch them unfurl in a warm sitting-room, where they will release a delicious fragrance. The plant itself is tough and hardy, but, betraying its geographical origins, it needs a hot position (preferably at the base of a warm wall) in well-drained soil of low fertility. Once established, it should be left alone, and the flowering display will improve year on year, as long as the rhizome gets a good baking in the previous summer.

Above: The yellow flowers of Mahonia x media *bring the fragrance of lily-of-the-valley to the winter garden.*

Scent for Every Style

TELEVISION MAKEOVER PROGRAMMES AND STYLE MAGAZINES HAVE MADE DESIGNERS OF ALL OF US, AND NOW NEARLY ALL GARDENERS CONSIDER DESIGN AN ESSENTIAL ASPECT IF THE GARDEN IS TO BE MORE THAN JUST A COLLECTION OF PLANTS.

DEFINING STYLE

In gardening the word style is a convenient way of categorizing or of sorting plants into groups and arrangements that seem homogeneous, meaningful and aesthetically pleasing. When we design a garden or a section of a garden, we will choose plants that will help us create the effects we want to achieve, opting, for example, for those with a regular shape, such as many conifers or skimmias, or those that can be clipped and topiarized, such as box or privet, to create a formal garden. A cottage garden style implies a more relaxed approach to both planting and weed control, involving plants that are easy to cultivate and do not need endless trimming and pruning to look their best. If, in addition to achieving a particular visual style, we want to incorporate scented plants,

Above: *Aromatic herb gardens can be defined by formal, clipped hedges.*

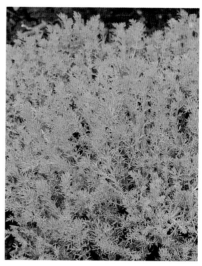

Above: *Terracotta containers are perfect for growing informal groupings of aromatic herbs.*

Above: *Camomile can be used to create a fragrant lawn that needs no mowing and releases scent as you walk over it.*

our plans might need to be modified to varying degrees to accommodate this extra dimension.

SELECTING A STYLE

The overall guideline that you should select a style for your garden that reflects your own personality and lifestyle is a truism, but it is nevertheless worth observing: there is no point opting for a garden that relies on summer bedding for scent, colour and definition if you do not have time to raise, plant out and then lift the spent plants at the end of the season. Given this caveat, however, there is a wide range of styles that can be adapted to include the many scented plants described in the previous section.

When scent is as important a factor in your garden design as colour or ease of maintenance, your plant selection should reflect this. It is well known that some roses, for example, are more fragrant than others, and this is true of several other plant groups. There are many more cultivars and strains available today than in the past, but even given this vast choice, there may be occasions when your wish to include a fragrant plant may have to override other design considerations, such as colour or form. Nevertheless, the gardener who longs for scent will find plants of almost every conceivable shape, colour and habit of growth to fit in with the most demanding of schemes.

449

COTTAGE GARDEN

The idealized picture of a cottage garden, with bees buzzing lazily above lavender and other sweetly scented flowers, is an appealing one, even if it exists more in the popular imagination than in reality. Contrary to what you might expect, planting a scented cottage garden requires the careful selection of fragrant cultivars and the exclusion of other, strongly growing but less aromatic varieties.

Choosing Plants

Typically, the cottage garden consists of simple plants that are easy to grow. The beds and borders should be overflowing with a profusion of plants.

Borders can be edged with box or lavender, both fragrant in different ways, which may be formally clipped or allowed to grow more freely. Roses

Above: Skimmia japonica *is a useful evergreen shrub with sweetly scented flowers in early spring.*

are essential, but choose from the many scented varieties. Old roses are traditional, but many flower only once, and there is no reason to exclude modern roses that have a longer season.

For climbers, think about the climbing roses ('Zéphirine Drouhin' is an old favourite, with magenta flowers over a long period), jasmine or honeysuckles. If these can be persuaded to frame the front door or sitting room window, so much the better. If you have a garden gate, it is a charming idea to train climbing plants over an archway spanning the path at the entrance to the garden.

Perennials include scented pinks (*Dianthus*); some have appealing names, such as 'Gran's Favourite', 'Sops in Wine' and 'Fair Folly'. Peonies, such as hybrids of *Paeonia officinalis* (often sold unnamed), are cottage garden

Above: Scented roses in profusion are an essential part of cottage garden style.

Above: A cottage garden is a pleasing jumble of colourful and fragrant plants, at its best in high summer.

classics. All the perennial herbs belong in such a garden; traditionally they were used to provide potpourri and were often spread on the floor to cover damp smells, to say nothing of their value in the kitchen and as medicines. The Madonna lily (*Lilium candidum*), with white, scented flowers, is also a typical cottage garden plant. For annuals, try dame's violet (*Hesperis matronalis*), old-fashioned tobacco plants (*Nicotiana*) and sweet peas (*Lathyrus odoratus*), which can also be incorporated in a vegetable plot to provide cut flowers for the house.

Above: Fragrant cottage garden pinks (Dianthus) have been grown for centuries.

SCENTED COTTAGE GARDEN PLANTS

Convallaria majalis
Dianthus
Geranium macrorrhizum
Hesperis matronalis
Lathyrus odoratus
Lilium
Lobularia maritima
Matthiola
Nicotiana
Paeonia officinalis
Philadelphus
Reseda odorata
Rosa

451

MEDITERRANEAN GARDEN

In recent years, as climate change has made summers in much of the northern hemisphere drier and hotter, the Mediterranean-style garden has become increasingly popular. This popularity has been fuelled by an increased use of aromatic herbs in the kitchen and by the fact that many of these herbs are not only attractive but also easy to maintain.

The Best Conditions

The Mediterranean style implies a warm, sunny site and soil that is both free-draining and low in fertility. Lushness is the antithesis of this style. Basking in heat and starved of nutrients, Mediterranean plants develop a gaunt appearance that is an essential part of their appeal.

A sun-baked slope is ideal. Most Mediterranean plants do not mind wind, and some are coastal. White concrete terraces will help to reflect heat and light, as will a top-dressing of gravel, which will also improve drainage – vital for all these plants.

Choosing Plants

Height and structure should really be provided by pines, which exude their resinous sap as the temperature climbs in summer. There are plenty of dwarf varieties for the small garden. That also goes for junipers (*Juniperus*), though these are a little less "giving" of their fragrance. Another traditional conifer of the Mediterranean is the cypress (*Cupressus sempervirens*). Elegant, pencil-thin forms are the most desirable. For a cold climate, be

Above: Using gravel allows you to grow a wide range of scented sun-loving plants.

Above: Citrus trees in pots are an essential feature of the Mediterranean garden.

Above: The distinctive scent of lavender is associated with the Mediterranean style.

sure to look out for the hardy forms that have been developed in recent years. Another excellent tree for this style of garden is the Mount Etna broom (*Genista aetnensis*) which produces a shower of yellow, scented pea blossom in summer but is so light and airy that it casts little shade.

Bulk out the borders with the excellent cistuses, grown mainly for their crinkled, papery summer flowers but of value here for their sticky, resinous stems and leaves. All the woody herbs suit this style of gardening.

Many favourite culinary herbs are indispensable additions to this type of garden and can be used to provide colour as well as scent. Lavender and rosemary are obvious candidates. Remember box (*Buxus sempervirens*), an excellent edging plant that can be clipped to shape or not, as the fancy

takes you. Box borders have been discovered in excavations of Roman villas, so there is classical precedence for its use. It has a quite distinctive scent that is released during hot weather or after a shower and that most gardeners learn to love.

SCENTED PLANTS FOR A MEDITERRANEAN GARDEN

Artemisia
Buxus sempervirens
Cistus
Citrus
Cupressus sempervirens
Genista aetnensis
Helichrysum italicum
Juniperus
Laurus nobilis
Lavandula stoechas
Olea europea
Phlomis fruticosa
Pinus
Rosmarinus
Salvia officinalis

FORMAL GARDEN

The formal style is more a matter of design than the other garden types discussed in this book. The gardener who is attracted to formalism is more interested in the structure and shape of the garden – what might be referred to as the manipulation of an exterior space – than such incidentals as flowers. Nevertheless, scent need not be excluded from such a scheme.

Choosing Plants

While formality can be achieved through non-plant material, through the lie of paths, walls and formal pools, it would be almost a contradiction in terms to banish plants from the

Above: Use scented bedding plants as a backdrop to formal features.

garden entirely. Plants that lend themselves to clipping obviously answer well the requirements of formalism. Unfortunately, extensive pruning – a gardening discipline in its own right – is often carried out at the expense of flowers. This is where plants with scented leaves come into their own. Box (*Buxus sempervirens*) is ideal for edging a planting area, in containers or clipped to shape.

Less versatile, but with an equally distinctive smell, are the curry plant (*Helichrysum italicum*) and lavender (*Lavandula*). A few tastefully positioned conifers, especially those that grow into a perfect shape without the intervention of the gardener, could complete a planting that would be low-key and subtle but would have the benefit of fragrance.

A specimen tree (possibly in a container) would make an excellent focal point. Bay (*Laurus nobilis*), with aromatic evergreen leaves, can be clipped to shape, though in some areas it needs some protection from cold, drying winds in winter (horticultural fleece would be adequate on a frosty night). An acacia (*Acacia dealbata*), citrus or olive (*Olea europea*), all with fragrant flowers, could also look extremely stylish, although none is reliably hardy.

If you cannot imagine life without flowers, consider the sculptural perfection of lilies. These can be grown in

Above: In a formal garden, a raised bed is ideal for bringing scent close to the gardener.

SCENTED PLANTS FOR A
FORMAL GARDEN

Buxus sempervirens
Citrus
Conifers
Laurus nobilis
Lavandula
Ligustrum lucidum
Myrtus communis
Rosmarinus
Santolina

pots and distributed around the garden in a formal arrangement. Earlier in the year, hyacinths planted in containers would have a comparable distinction, and their stiff, upright habit is entirely apposite in these surroundings. Annuals recommended for bedding are excellent when they are grown in formal blocks. Look for single colour strains of stocks (*Matthiola*), tobacco plants (*Nicotiana*) – 'Lime Green' is a sophisticated choice – and sweet alyssum (*Lobularia maritima*).

Above: This formal garden has been filled with a range of plants to appeal to the senses, including roses and lavender.

455

MODERN GARDEN

The essence of the modern style is determined by a desire for simplicity. A contemporary garden is based on pure form and texture, creating an environment that is both stimulating and calming. The planting must be carefully considered and should include some well-chosen scented plants.

Choosing Plants

No plant is actually modern in the generally accepted sense of the term, but trends in gardening come and go. Plants fall in and out of favour, partly as a result of television programmes and partly as new cultivars are promoted. The beautifully scented *Lilium* 'Star Gazer' is an example of a bulb that is currently in vogue. Its deep, rose-red flowers, edged with white, is perfect for adding a splash of colour to a muted, contemporary scene. Other scented lilies that are suitable for a modern setting are *Lilium regale* with its large, trumpet-shaped white flowers and *Lilium candidum*, the Madonna lily.

Hostas can be grand and architectural, but they are usually grown for their leaves rather than their flowers. The exceptions are *H. plantaginea* and a hybrid derived from it, 'Honeybells'. Both of these have shining green

Above: *This sleek, black slate bench, with lilies planted close by, provides the perfect resting place to sit and enjoy the fragrances of the garden.*

*Above: Cotton lavender (*Santolina*) grows in a pleasing dome shape that lends itself to contemporary plantings.*

leaves and sweetly scented white flowers in the summer, and unlike most hostas, they are best in full sun. Both are excellent in containers.

One of the most architectural of all herbaceous perennials is *Angelica archangelica* (sometimes a biennial), which carries its large, dome-shaped heads of greenish-yellow summer flowers on stems up to 2m (6ft) tall. It is aromatic in all its parts.

A High-tech Garden

The modern garden uses a range of materials. Galvanized, beaten metal containers are part of the style, as is recycled glass, often moulded into "pebbles" in place of gravel (which is less acceptable these days, since it is not a renewable resource). Even old CDs can be recycled for use as a paving material. The traditional colours of stone and terracotta are less in keeping with the high-tech style.

Genetic modification will no doubt be used to introduce scent into previously unscented flowers, such as gladioli and chrysanthemums, but in the meantime, the modern gardener looks to such plants as *Yucca filamentosa*, a perennial with spiky, sword-like leaves and panicles of scented white flowers in late summer, *Mahonia* x *media*, a group of gaunt shrubs with richly fragrant, yellow flowers in winter above pointed, holly-like leaves, or the stiffly formal hyacinths (*Hyacinthus*), which flower in spring. All have the characteristic high-tech look that is appropriate to a garden designed in a contemporary style.

Above: A bank of highly scented hyacinths add colour and form.

Plants for Scent

MOST OF THE PLANTS LISTED BELOW ARE MORE FULLY DESCRIBED
ELSEWHERE IN THIS CHAPTER, BUT THIS CHECKLIST IS PROVIDED AS A
QUICK REFERENCE TO HELP YOU CHOOSE A RANGE OF SCENTED
PLANTS FOR ALL SEASONS WHEN PLANNING YOUR GARDEN.

Plant name	Part of plant scented	Season	Day/night
Acacia t HH–FRH	flowers	winter–spring	day
Akebia quinata c FH	flowers	spring	day
Aloysia triphylla h FRH	leaves	spring–summer–autumn	day
Artemisia arborescens h FH	leaves	spring–summer–autumn	day
Berberis sargentiana h FH	flowers	spring	day
Buddleja s FH	flowers	summer–autumn	day
Camellia sasanqua s FH	flowers	autumn–winter	day
Cercidiphyllum t FH	fallen leaves	autumn	day
Cestrum parqui s FRH	flowers	summer–autumn	night
Choisya ternata s FH	flowers/leaves	spring	day
Cistus s FH	stems	summer	day
Citrus s/t FRH	flowers/leaves	all year	day
Clematis armandii c FH	flowers	spring	day
Clematis flammula c FH	flowers	summer–autumn	day
Clematis montana c FH	flowers	spring	day
Clematis recta p FH	flowers	spring–summer	day
Clematis rehderiana c FH	flowers	summer–autumn	day
Convallaria majalis p FH	flowers	spring	day
Cosmos atrosanguineus p FRH	flowers	summer	day
Crambe cordifolia p FH	flowers	summer	day
Crocus b FH	flowers	spring	day

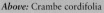

Above: Crambe cordifolia   ***Above:*** Paeonia *'Bowl of Beauty'*

Cytisus battandieri s FRH	flowers	summer	day
Daphne s FH–FRH	flowers	winter/spring	day
Deutzia s FH	flowers	spring–summer	day
Dianthus p/a FH	flowers	spring–summer	day
Elaeagnus x *ebbingei* s FH	flowers	autumn	day
Erica s FH–FRH	flowers	all seasons	day
Erysimum cheiri p FH	flowers	spring	day
Eucalyptus t FH	stems	all year	day
Genista aetnensis s/t FH	flowers	summer	day
Genista lydia s FH	flowers	summer	day
Hamamelis mollis s FH	flowers	winter	day
Hebe cupressoides s FH	stems	all year	day
Helichrysum italicum h FH	leaves	all year	day
Heliotropium arborescens a FH	flowers	summer	day
Hemerocallis p FH	flowers	summer	day/night
Hesperis matronalis bi FH	flowers	spring–summer	night
Hosta 'Honeybells' p FH	flowers	summer	day
Hosta plantaginea p FH	flowers	summer	day
Hyacinthus orientalis b FH	flowers	winter–spring	day
Hypericum 'Hidcote' s FH	leaves	spring–summer	day
Iris p/b FH	flowers/bulb	winter/spring/ summer	day
Jasminum c FH–FRH	flowers	winter/summer	day
Laurus nobilis s/h FRH	leaves	all year	day
Lavandula h FH–HH	flowers/leaves	spring/summer– autumn	day
Lilium b FH–HH	flowers	summer	day/night
Liquidambar styraciflua t FH	leaves	spring–summer	day
Lobularia maritima a FH	flowers	summer–autumn	day
Lonicera c/s FH	flowers	summer/winter	day
Magnolia s/t FH	flowers	spring	day
Mahonia s FH	flowers	winter–spring	day
Matthiola a FH	flowers	summer	day/night

Above: Dianthus 'Louise's Choice'

Above: Lonicera japonica 'Halliana'

Melissa h FH	leaves	spring–summer–autumn	day
Mentha h FH	leaves	spring–summer–autumn	day
Muscari b FH	flowers	spring	day
Myrtus s FRH	flowers	summer	day
Narcissus b FH–HH	flowers	spring	day
Nicotiana a FRH–HH	flowers	summer–autumn	night
Nymphaea wp FH–FRH	flowers	summer	day
Osmanthus s FH	flowers	spring	day
Paeonia s/p FH	flowers	spring–summer	day
Pelargonium p FRH (scented-leaf)	leaves	all year	day
Perovskia s FH	stems	spring–summer–autumn	day
Petasites p FH	flowers	winter–spring	day
Petunia a HH	flowers	summer	day
Philadelphus s FH	flowers	summer	day/evening
Phlomis s FH–FRH	flowers	summer	day
Phlox p/al FH–HH	flowers	summer	day
Populus balsamifera t FH	leaves	spring	day
Primula p/al FH–FT	flowers	spring/summer	day
Reseda odorata a FH	flowers	spring–summer–autumn	day
Rhododendron s FH–FT	flowers	spring–summer	day
Rosa s/c FH	flowers	summer–autumn	day
Rosmarinus h FH–HH	leaves	all year	day
Ruta graveolens h FH	leaves	all year	day
Salix triandra s FH	flowers	winter–spring	day
Santolina s FH	leaves	all year	day
Sarcococca s FH	flowers	winter	day

Above: Pelargonium *'Little Gem'*

Above: Santolina chamaecyparissus

Skimmia s FH	flowers/leaves	winter–spring	day
Smilacina racemosa p FH	flowers	spring	day
Spartium junceum s FH	flowers	summer	day
Syringa s FH	flowers	spring	day
Thymus h FH	leaves	spring–summer	day
Trachelospermum c FRH jasminoides	flowers	summer	evening
Tulipa b FH	flowers	spring	day
Verbena p/a FH–FT	flowers	summer	day
Viburnum carlesii s FH	flowers	spring	day
Viburnum s FH x bodnantense	flowers	winter	day
Viola p/a FH	flowers	summer/winter	day
Wisteria c FH	flowers	summer	day

KEY TO ABBREVIATIONS

a = annual   c = climber   t = tree
al = alpine   h = herb   wp = water plant
b = bulb   p = perennial
bi = biennial   s = shrub

FT = frost tender = may be damaged by temperatures below 5°C (41°F)
HH = half hardy = can withstand temperatures down to 0°C (32°F)
FRH = frost hardy = can withstand temperatures down to –5°C (23°F)
FH = fully hardy = can withstand temperatures down to –15°C (5°F)

In the United States, throughout the Sun Belt states, from Florida, across the Gulf Coast, south Texas, southern deserts to Southern California and coastal regions, annuals are planted in the autumn, bloom in the winter and spring, and die at the beginning of summer.

Above: Rosa 'Ispahan'

Above: Ruta graveolens 'Variegata'

HANGING BASKETS

Whatever the time of year, there is
nothing more welcoming than a
prettily planted basket hanging on a
wall or near the door. Even if you
have no garden at all, you will almost
certainly have somewhere for a basket
or two. This chapter contains all the
information you need, from choosing
the right basket and the best plants
to tips on regular maintenance
for keeping the arrangement
in tip-top condition.

Miniature Gardens

HANGING BASKETS ADD AN EXTRA DIMENSION TO GARDENING –
POSITIONED JUST ABOVE EYE LEVEL, THEY INVITE YOU TO LIFT YOUR
GAZE SKYWARDS. WHETHER YOU PLANT FOR SUBTLETY OR GO FOR A
RIOT OF COLOUR, THEY MAKE FOR INSTANT APPEAL.

ENJOYING HANGING BASKETS

Hanging baskets are a form of gardening that is available to everyone, even those who have no garden. Fixed to house walls, they are an extension to the home, bringing pleasure every time you walk through the door. They are democratic: delightfully framing the doorway of an elegant town house, they are equally at home at the entrance to a country cottage. They can be fixed near a kitchen window – if you want to grow herbs, for instance. They can also be suspended on either side of a patio door and enjoyed from inside when it is too wet or cold to venture outdoors. They are also the ideal way for a city-dweller to experience something of the thrill of growing things.

DECIDING WHAT YOU WANT

A wealth of plants can be grown in baskets, not just the traditional lobelias, pelargoniums and fuchsias, splendid though these are. While they are generally associated with summer, you can plant baskets for spring, autumn or even winter interest, because many plants flower at these cooler times of year, even if the choice may not be as great.

Hanging baskets are also extremely versatile as they can be enjoyed in many ways. Most people think of them as vehicles for vibrant summer flowers, but they can be used not just for flower plantings, but also for plants with variegated or coloured leaves, herbs, and even fruit and vegetables. In a conservatory (sunroom), use them for trailing rainforest plants, such as cacti, ferns and orchids.

Above: *Extend a border vertically by using the same colours in an eye-level arrangement of plants.*

MAKING AN IMPACT

As with many other types of container, hanging baskets offer boundless opportunities to experiment. You can try out all kinds of colour combinations and be as subtle as you like or as ritzy as you dare. You can use an arbitrary mix of flowers that will certainly be cheerful if not elegant or you can adopt a more sophisticated approach and plan the effect from the outset. Hot vibrant colours, such as red, orange and yellow, will always make an impact, while soft blues, pinks, cream and white are more soothing. Purples are ambivalent, adding drama to an already brilliant planting but sounding deeper notes in a gentler pastel scheme.

Above: *This charming planting uses polyanthus, pansies and dwarf narcissi to brighten a gloomy corner in spring.*

Below: *This subtle arrangement makes effective use of the silky-textured, silver-leaved* Helichrysum petiolare.

DECIDING ON STYLE

Some of the best hanging baskets are to be found in municipal schemes and adorning the streets of towns, where they are often paid for by the shop-keeper. The baskets are usually planted for summer interest and often contain bright, eye-catching colours. You can, of course, copy these at home, but there is no reason you cannot add a personal touch. An informal mixture of plants suits a cottage garden, for instance, whereas an elegant, white-painted, stuccoed house needs a more tightly controlled look, perhaps involving no more than two colours. If you favour a very minimalist style, try a few hanging rat's-tail cacti with perhaps a spiky aloe for height. For a funky look, try using one of the more compact grasses, such as *Festuca glauca*.

INTEREST THROUGH THE YEAR

Hanging baskets are traditionally associated with summer, but they can also be enjoyed at other times of year. Spring baskets, possibly involving some dwarf bulbs, such as daffodils, irises or crocuses, with a few early bedding plants, are always a delight, but it is also possible to enjoy baskets in autumn with a combination of tender perennials – which seem to go on flowering for ever – with the addition of some late-sown annuals. Winter baskets offer less scope, but it is still possible to have some choice of colour. Choose robust, winter-flowering heathers and hardy pansies, and even dainty ivies, whether colourful variegated varieties or plain green, can be surprisingly interesting and attractive.

SUN OR SHADE

Once you have decided where your baskets are to go, the amount of sun or shade the position offers will influence your choice

Above: This glorious display uses pale pink nemesias to offset the rich purples of the verbenas and pansies.

Left: Coelogyne velutina *is a robust orchid with trailing flower stems, which, together with the upright leaves, create an unusual effect.*

reason. However, a large basket would be first choice for growing fruit and vegetables, which normally need a good root run to develop properly. Smaller baskets create a daintier effect but perhaps offer less scope for exciting colour combinations.

of plants. Many of the summer flowers are sun worshippers, but remember that in a very sheltered spot against a warm wall, the heat on a hot summer's day will be intense. Reserve such a favoured spot for real exotics, such as South African osteospermums. Many plants will thrive in shade. Lobelias are shade tolerant, and begonias and busy Lizzies actually prefer it. Fuchsias usually do best if kept out of direct sun.

SIZE MATTERS

The size of the basket is an important consideration. Although large baskets are the most spectacular and can house the greatest number of plants, they will take up a lot of space when the plants are mature and will be heavy, particularly when wet. That can be an issue if you need to move the basket for any

HOW TO USE THIS CHAPTER

You will find all the information you need for creating successful baskets on the following pages. *Getting Started* deals with such practical matters as choosing a suitable basket, selecting an appropriate potting mix, buying plants, planting the basket and maintaining it. Watering, feeding and dealing with pests and diseases are also covered. The subsequent sections are full of ideas, with *Baskets for All Seasons* illustrating a range of baskets planted for seasonal appeal, whether your taste is for subtle or brilliant or for dramatic foliage effect. Herb, fruit and vegetable baskets are also given due attention. In *Satisfying the Senses* you will find ideas for plants to smell and touch as well as stimulating the eye. Finally, there is a useful summary of seasonal tasks, followed by a list of recommended plants with information on plant type and size, season of interest, flower colour and cultivation tips.

467

Getting Started

ONCE YOU HAVE DECIDED WHAT YOU WANT YOUR HANGING
BASKETS TO PROVIDE, YOU CAN BEGIN TO EXPLORE THE MANY TYPES
THAT ARE AVAILABLE AND DECIDE WHICH BEST SUITS YOUR NEEDS AND
THE STYLE OF PLANTING YOU HAVE IN MIND.

TYPES OF HANGING BASKETS

Hanging baskets come in all shapes and sizes, and when you come to shop for one you will be amazed at the range available. The traditional basket is half a sphere and is usually made of plastic-coated wire, with three chains to hang from. Wrought iron is also sometimes used, especially for hay baskets, which are meant to be fixed directly against a wall. More ornate antique baskets (and, increasingly, reproductions of these) can be found, but decorative as these are, they are usually less sturdy, so are less suitable for a very heavy planting. Decide whether it is the basket itself or the plants that you grow in it that will be the focus of interest.

Some baskets really are baskets and are made of wicker or bamboo or some other twiggy material. Many are beautiful to look at and are perhaps best with a simple planting. It is not always possible, or indeed desirable, to plant through the sides of such containers. Unless they have been treated with some kind of preservative, they

Above: Plastic-coated wire baskets.

Above: Wrought iron and galvanized wire baskets.

468

will be vulnerable to changes in the weather and may dry out and split in hot sun. They may need to be replaced after a few seasons, while a metal basket is virtually indestructible and will last for many more years than those made of wicker or bamboo.

The ideal basket is strong but lightweight. It will be heavy enough once it is full of moist soil and all the plants have reached their optimum size so you do not want to start off with a heavy basket that is going to add substantially to the overall weight.

Some baskets are sold already lined with plastic, but remember to pierce this before use to allow for drainage.

Above: Small hanging baskets often look most effective when a single flower colour is used.

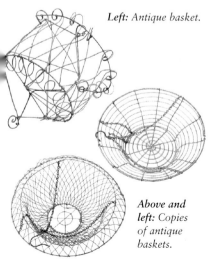

Left: Antique basket.

Above and left: Copies of antique baskets.

Brackets and Other Fixings

All hanging baskets have to be mounted, and usually some form of wall bracket is required. To determine the size of the bracket, you need to calculate how wide the basket will be once it is planted up and mature, then divide this figure by two. This is the minimum distance it will need to hang from the wall so that the plants can be displayed properly. Look for sturdy brackets that will not buckle under the weight of the basket and that are made from rust-proof material. Hanging baskets can also be suspended from hooks attached to the cross-beam of an archway or pergola or screwed to the ceiling of a conservatory (sunroom).

469

Above: This antique wicker bird cage is such a thing of beauty that it needs only the simplest planting.

Other Types of Container

Apart from the traditional hemispherical shape, other types of container are available. Your choice will often be determined by the type of plant you wish to grow.

Orchid baskets are shallow, usually square and made of wooden slats. They are designed to allow plant roots to grow through and grip the sides. Orchid potting mix is coarse enough not to slip through the openings. The baskets are usually designed for indoor use and are not robust enough to stand up to the weather. Similar baskets are available for other tropical plants that need air around their roots, such as some ferns and cacti.

Ideas for Improvising

If you like to experiment, keep a sharp eye out for objects that were intended for quite different purposes but that can be used as hanging baskets. Antique bird cages are very beautiful and make a witty statement hanging from the branches of a tree. For a cottage kitchen look, use an old metal colander. These are particularly effective and appropriate for culinary herbs or other edible crops. Look out for them in flea markets and junk shops. Car sales and second-hand stores are also a valuable source of unusual but usable hanging containers.

Above: Slatted baskets are ideal for orchids and other tree-dwelling plants.

470

Left: Recycled cardboard is increasingly popular as a liner. Most have pre-cut holes that can be punched out.

Some products, often based on recycled sisal, look remarkably natural. Coir lining is sometimes sold in rolls or ready cut to fit certain sizes of basket. Convenient pressed cardboard liners are pre-formed to fit various sizes of basket.

Remember that once the planting is mature, the liner will be all but invisible, so a material that at first glance looks a little unsympathetic will soon be hidden from view. This is especially the case with summer baskets.

Different Linings

What you line your basket with is a matter of choice. The traditional material is moss, but, like peat, this is not a renewable resource, and many feel that alternatives are preferable.

Above: This unusual edible hanging basket partners dwarf beans with decorative curled parsley. Sage or summer savory would look just as attractive as the parsley.

Choosing a Compost

There are a number of different composts (soil mixes) on the market, some all-purpose, others tailored for specific needs. Loamless mixtures, which are light, are usually best.

Loam-based compost

is based on soil. It is high in nutrients but also heavy. It can easily be lightened by adding perlite or vermiculite.

Lime-free (ericaceous) compost

is specially formulated for those plants that will not grow in limy conditions, such as many of the heathers and azaleas.

All-purpose compost is cheap and light to handle, but many are based on peat, which is not a renewable resource, and most gardeners now prefer to look around for more ecologically acceptable peat-free alternatives.

Peat-free compost

is also an all-purpose compost, but, for ecological reasons, is usually based on a renewable resource such as coir or bark.

Hanging basket compost

is lightweight and often contains some water-retaining crystals and slow-release fertilizers, but it may be peat-based.

Above: If the compost does not already contain water-retaining gel, you can mix some in before planting, pre-soaking if necessary so that it expands with water.

Above: Pelleted fertilizers, which are very easy to use and can feed for a whole season, are a low-maintenance option.

Orchids and cacti need specially formulated, free-draining, proprietary composts. Ordinary composts retain too much moisture and are not suitable for these plants.

WATERING AND FEEDING

You can cut down on watering by adding water-retaining gel. Make sure the compost does not already contain any – an excessive amount will cause problems when it swells up. Most new composts contain some plant food, but this is usually exhausted after 6 weeks. To keep the plants flowering well, you should give a high-potash plant food. Tomato fertilizers are suitable, but you can also buy special hanging basket formulas. Pelleted

fertilizers are easy to handle and feed the plant as they break down in the compost. One application will last for a whole season, but check, as individual products vary.

Liquid feeds are sold either as powders to be dissolved in water, as liquids to be diluted or as ready-mixed products. They are usually watered into the compost as a root drench at intervals, depending on the product. Some can be sprayed directly on to the foliage as a foliar feed, and these are especially good for giving your plants an instant boost if they have suffered a set-back, such as an unexpected cold spell or pest attack – but a certain amount of the product is inevitably lost.

Above: Using the right compost and feeding regularly will ensure that the plants in your hanging baskets flower for longer.

473

Getting Started

THINKING AHEAD

Hanging baskets have to be planned far in advance. Although it is possible to buy plants in flower for instant impact, this is an expensive option and the flowers are likely to be short-lived if they have been forced out of season. As a general rule, you need to plant up your baskets 6–10 weeks before the main season of interest. Spring-flowering bulbs, for instance, are sold in autumn and winter and should be planted at that time.

BUYING PLANTS

The best advice when buying plants is to go to a reputable garden centre or nursery. Bedding plants are sold in strips, but larger plants such as ivies, pelargoniums and fuchsias are usually potted individually. "Plugs", basically young plantlets with well-developed root systems, are often sold via mail order by seed merchants; busy Lizzies, fuchsias, pelargoniums and begonias are often marketed this way.

If possible check the plant before purchase to make sure that it is not harbouring any pests or diseases. Bedding plants should have fresh, bright green foliage, with no hint of yellowing, and should be compact, not straggly. Potted plants should have a good root system. If possible, slide the plant from the pot. The roots should fill the pot nicely without being tightly coiled. Select plants that have plenty of healthy buds that are not yet open.

Bulbs are sold when dormant (usually in autumn and winter). Buy them from a reputable garden centre or nursery and look for firm, plump bulbs that show no signs of withering or fungal disease.

Left: Pansies can be relied on to provide a colourful display over a long period. They are available in a wide variety of shades, either singly coloured or in bold combinations such as this bright yellow and maroon pairing.

PLANTING

The aim when planting a hanging basket is to use as many plants as you can. The normal rules of carefully spacing plants to allow them to reach their full potential do not apply.

1 If you are using moss or an equivalent to improve water retention, place a circle of plastic, pierced to allow drainage, at the base of the basket.

2 Line the basket with the chosen liner, making holes in the liner with scissors or a sharp knife, if necessary.

3 Fill the basket about one-third of the way up with the appropriate compost (soil mix), tamping it down lightly with your fingers to remove any air pockets.

4 Push trailing plants through the side of the container, resting the rootballs on the surface of the compost.

5 Add more compost and plant the top of the basket. Angle the plants at the edge slightly so that they will trail outwards and cover the rim of the basket.

HANGING THE BASKET

You need good do-it-yourself skills to fix the brackets to the wall. Hanging baskets are heavy for their size when they are moist and full of mature plants and they can also be blown about in strong winds, so proper fixing is essential for safety. Use rawl plugs and long screws to hold them securely in position.

ROUTINE CARE

Hanging baskets need a certain amount of regular care and attention if they are going to give the display you want. Don't forget that you are asking the plants to outperform their garden counterparts, and, crammed into the basket, they are competing for water, light and nutrients.

Watering

Even if you added water-retaining gels to the compost (soil mix), you will find that the compost in summer baskets quickly dries out. You will need to water the basket every day, and twice a day during the long hot days of summer. Morning or evening is the best time, because leaves can scorch if they

Above: An automatic drip feed system can save time and effort and will be useful if you go away.

get wet in the full heat of the sun. You may find that the compost is dry even after a rainy spell as dense leaf coverage makes it difficult for water to reach the compost.

Water with a can, making sure the tip of the spout reaches the compost. If you can lift only a small can, one canful may not be enough.

Watering winter and spring baskets is a matter of judgement. The plants are unlikely to be growing strongly and will need watering only when the compost is dry. Over-wet compost in cold weather can lead to root rot.

Feeding

To keep the plants growing strongly and flowering well you will need to feed them. Unless you added a slow-release fertilizer to the compost, apply a high-potash liquid feed every two to three weeks.

Above: Use a watering can with a spout so that you wet the compost thoroughly.

Above: Pinching out fuchsias and pelargoniums regularly will give a fuller plant with a better shape and more flowers.

Pinching Out

This involves removing the growing tips of young plants to make them bush out and thus produce more flowering stems. Use just your thumb and forefinger to remove the tips. If this is done regularly the plant will have a better, more even shape.

Deadheading

Removing faded flowers not only keeps the baskets looking good, but encourages the plants to produce further flowers rather than expending their energies on seed production. As the flowers begin to go over, either pinch back the stems or trim them off with secateurs (pruners) or scissors. If you want to propagate the plant from seed, to provide plants for the following year, allow a few flowers to go to seed at the end of the season when they can be collected and stored.

Pruning

Few hanging basket plants will need pruning, but you may find that woody-stemmed plants, such as fuchsias, will benefit from a trim if they start to become a bit leggy and overgrown. Trim them back as necessary, cutting just above a leaf joint. Ensure that you use sharp secateurs so that you achieve a clean cut.

Above: Deadheading flowers as they fade will encourage a succession of blooms.

477

USING PESTICIDES

Plants in hanging baskets are usually grown for one season before they are discarded, which means that they rarely succumb to diseases. They are, however, susceptible to attack by pests. Although keeping your plants healthy by feeding and watering them regularly will increase their resistance, you may find it necessary to use chemicals to keep pests under control.

There are two main types of pesticide. Contact pesticides are sprayed directly on to the pests and are usually instantly effective. Use specific formulations to avoid harming beneficial insects, such as ladybirds (ladybugs), hoverflies and bees. Systemic pesticides are watered into the compost and are absorbed by the plant so that insects that feed on the plant are killed. The effect is not immediate, but this is a good way of dealing with sap-sucking pests, such as aphids.

Aphids

These are one of the most common plant pests. These sap-sucking insects feed on the tender growing tips of plants and can transmit diseases. Green- and blackfly are most often seen, clustering on young shoots and the undersides of leaves. Pirimicarb is the best chemical spray as it is aphid-specific, and insecticidal soap is an effective organic alternative.

Mealy Bugs

Often affecting plants under glass, these look like spots of white mould. Biological or chemical controls are usually effective.

Caterpillars

The occasional caterpillar can simply be picked off the plant and disposed of, but a major infestation can strip a plant before your eyes. Contact insecticides are usually effective in these cases.

Red Spider Mite

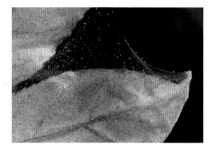

The mites are prevalent in warm, dry conditions in the garden. The spider mite is barely visible to the naked eye, but infestation is indicated by fine webs and mottling of the plant's leaves. Keep plants misted, and remove the worst affected leaves. The mites are often resistant to pesticides, but some may be effective.

Vine Weevils

These white grubs are a real problem. The first sign of an infestation is the sudden collapse of the plant, which has died as a result of the weevil larvae eating its roots. Systemic insecticides or natural predators can be used as a preventative, but once a plant has been attacked it is usually too late to save it. Never re-use the soil from an affected plant. The picture shows an adult weevil.

Snails

These will often travel up walls and hide behind baskets during the day, coming out at night to feed. Chemical controls are not recommended, since birds will be harmed by eating the poisoned snails, but you can easily catch them by shining a light on the basket at night.

Whitefly

These tiny white flies, often a problem under glass in dry conditions, flutter up in clouds when disturbed from their feeding places on the undersides of leaves.

Baskets for All Seasons

ALTHOUGH THEY ARE USUALLY ASSOCIATED WITH SUMMER, HANGING BASKETS CAN BE DESIGNED TO PROVIDE INTEREST THROUGHOUT THE YEAR. IF YOU PLAN CAREFULLY, YOU CAN HAVE FRESH, BRIGHT FOLIAGE AND COLOURFUL FLOWERS SEASON AFTER SEASON.

SPRING BASKETS

This is the season of dwarf bulbs, many of which can be grown with ease in baskets. However, they tend to be stiffly upright. Few flowering plants at this time of year are natural trailers, so to soften the edges of the basket, you will have to rely on the old stalwarts, ivy (*Hedera*) and periwinkle (*Vinca*).

Early dwarf bulbs include the indispensable snowdrops (*Galanthus*) and two irises, *Iris danfordiae* (yellow) and *Iris reticulata* (mostly in shades of blue and purple). Most bulbs need

PLANTS AT THEIR BEST IN SPRING
Crocus
Galanthus
Myosotis
Narcissus (dwarf cultivars)
Primula
Vinca minor
Viola

good drainage, so remember to choose a light, free-draining compost (soil mix). When they have finished flowering, plant the bulbs out in the garden.

Your hanging baskets can be a last-minute inspiration, if you neglected to plan ahead. Simply dig up clumps from the garden and plant them up.

Planting Partners

Polyanthus (*Primula*), grown from seed sown the previous year, are delightful, low-growing plants with flowers in a range of jewel-like colours. Some have attractive markings in more than one colour. Use them on their own or to contrast with or complement dwarf narcissi, such as 'Tête-à-Tête', 'Jenny' or 'Jumblie'.

Left: A classic spring combination, forget-me-nots, miniature narcissi and pansies always look delightful together.

Above: Dwarf tulips, grape hyacinths and cheeky-faced violas make for a vibrant colour combination.

Easy-to-grow grape hyacinths *(Muscari armenaicum)* are more subtle, with deep purple-blue flowers like miniature bunches of grapes. They go well with the brighter blue of forget-me-nots *(Myosotis)*. Crocuses are also a good bet, especially sturdier cultivars such as 'Snow Bunting' (white) and 'Dutch Yellow' (yellow).

Extending the Display

Most bulbs have brief seasons compared to other plants you might be using at this time of year. To extend the period of interest of the basket, plan for a succession of bulbs – for instance, early crocuses, followed by mid-season daffodils, then late dwarf tulips – and pot them up in containers, one type in each. As the buds of the

earliest bulbs start to show colour, plunge the pot into the centre of the basket. When the flowers have faded, replace the pot with the one holding the later bulbs, and so on.

Planning Ahead

Plant iris bulbs in autumn to winter when they become available in shops and garden centres. Snowdrops are best planted up as growing plants.

Above: Planting bulbs in pots means you can replace them after flowering.

481

SUMMER BASKETS

No matter how much time and attention you lavish on your hanging baskets at other times of the year, summer is their peak season, as it is for the garden at large. At no other time of year will you have such a wide choice of plant material, offering you a wealth of colour, form and scent. This is the time when all your plans will pay off.

If it is properly cared for, a summer basket will provide pleasure for up to three months of the year, and possibly even longer. At the height of summer, the basket itself and the lining material should be invisible, covered by a mass of flowers.

Different Styles

Plant baskets the way you would plant any other area in your garden. If the cottage garden style appeals to you, use simple plants in a range of colours. Many cottage favourites, such as pinks (*Dianthus*) and nasturtiums, are ideal basket material if you stick to shorter cultivars. For a sophisticated look, team pastels with grey-leaved *Helichrysum petiolare*.

An Airborne Rose Garden

If you have a passion for roses, extend that towards some of the many miniatures and patio roses, which are ideal for containers of all kinds. Many of the so-called ground-cover roses

Above: Fuchsias, petunias and lobelias are the epitome of summer plantings.

the place of more familiar fuchsias and pelargoniums. These plants are often sold unnamed in many florists, sometimes out of season. In a mild spell in spring, autumn or even winter, you could use one as a temporary planting. If you want the basket to be permanent, protect the roots from frost in winter – they are more vulnerable than plants in the ground. Remember that, if you are intending to use a rose, you will have to watch out for the attendant problems. You may need to spray occasionally against troublesome blackspot and aphids. However, most modern varieties are robust despite their dainty appearance, and you should not experience any big problems.

have long, flexible stems, which will trail over the edge of a hanging basket in a most appealing way, but watch out for thorns if you site it near a doorway or walkway.

The miniature roses are dainty, twiggy plants that are ideal as the centrepiece of a basket and can take

PLANTS AT THEIR BEST IN SUMMER

Begonia
Bidens
Dorotheanthus
Fuchsia
Impatiens
Lobelia
Pelargonium
Petunias

Fuchsias and Pelargoniums

These woody-based plants are the mainstay of many a summer hanging basket, and rightly so. Few plants can rival their ease of cultivation and length of flowering season. They both usefully have a number of different forms. Upright cultivars are perfect as the central plant of a large basket, while trailing forms are excellent cascading down the sides.

Tender Perennials

This group of plants is growing in popularity and nurseries and garden centres offer new species and cultivars every year. In addition to the marvellous osteospermums, there are bidens, felicia and argyranthemum, all of which produce their vivid flowers over a long period.

Annuals

Hardy and half-hardy annuals are the mainstay of the summer garden, and most are easily grown from seed. Alternatively, they can be obtained as plugs or plantlets, ready to be planted out in early summer.

Above: Yellow-leaved lysimachia is an excellent trailing plant and a good substitute for ivy in a predominantly yellow basket.

Above: Pelargonium 'Eclipse' produces masses of pink flowers in large open heads.

Perhaps most familiar of all summer annuals are lobelias, trailing forms of which have been specially bred for containers. Colours include different shades of blue, as well as purple, with white and red. Equally noteworthy are the petunias, which can be found in a wide colour range, including white, yellow, cream, red and blue, with some bicolours. Double forms and those with ruffled petal edges are particularly appealing. Look out especially for the trailing types.

Foliage

At the height of summer a hanging basket can be virtually a ball of flowers, but don't underestimate the value of pure green to tone down a scheme. Ivies and periwinkles can be

484

relied on to give a long-lasting performance, to which can be added the tender helichrysums, with felted leaves of grey or soft lime green, or the pick-a-back plant (*Tolmiea menziesii*), with its fresh green, toothed leaves.

Summer Problems

While summer is the time for sitting back and enjoying the fruits of your labours in the garden at large, you cannot just relax and let your hanging baskets get on with it. They need care and attention. Tender leaves can easily scorch with too much sun, and flowers will rapidly fade. This is the ideal time – from the plant's point

> **GARDENER'S TIP**
>
> If the basket dries out, stand it on a bucket and give it a good soaking. Allow it to sit in the bucket until the compost (soil mix) is saturated. Adding a few drops of dishwashing detergent to the water will help water absorption.

of view – for setting seed. At this time you need to increase your watering, giving the basket a thorough soaking once or twice a day. If the weather is very hot, you might even need to move the basket to a more shady position. If you have baskets at the front and back of the house, swap them around every

Above: *Yellow-flowered bidens is a tender perennial that is often treated as an annual. It produces dainty flowers on trailing stems all summer long.*

few days, and turn them. Keep up the deadheading, or the flower display will be shortened. On the plus side, succulent plants, such as Livingstone daisies (*Dorotheanthus*), will positively revel in the heat and flower their hearts out, as will pelargoniums. Plants with aromatic leaves will release their oils now.

If you want your baskets to give pleasure throughout the season, look for plants that are in flower over a long period. Most floriferous of all are probably the pelargoniums, with flowers in shades of white, pink, salmon and red. The ivy-leaved

Above: *These osteospermums and diascias in subtle pastel colours are slightly tender but will carry on flowering until the first frosts appear.*

varieties are trailing, so are ideal for the sides of a basket, with perhaps a more upright cultivar at the centre. Fuchsias also have a long period of interest, often surviving into late autumn, and there are trailing as well as more upright cultivars.

Make sure you include some foliage plants, such as ivies and helichrysum, which will provide a solid background throughout the season.

All plants will flower for longer if regularly deadheaded. This diverts the plant's energy away from seed production and encourages it to produce further flowers.

Left: *Nasturtiums are among the easiest annuals to grow. 'Alaska' has the added attraction of variegated leaves.*

Things to Watch Out For

In a very hot spell baskets can easily dry out and delicate plants will scorch. Remember that their roots are well above ground level and hence can easily bake, because there is little moist soil to keep them cool. The problem is made worse if the basket is next to a wall that reflects the heat. A wall that has been in the sun for most of the afternoon will continue to radiate heat well into the evening when the sun is no longer on it. If necessary, take the basket to a position where it will be shaded when the sun is at its scorching strongest.

> **GARDENER'S TIP**
>
> Pelargoniums and many tender perennials can be over-wintered in a cool, light, frost-free place, such as an unheated bedroom or a porch (sunroom).

Flowering plants run to seed faster in hot weather, so keep up your deadheading regime. But remember that plants with succulent leaves, such as Livingstone daisies, will thrive in baking conditions. Most of the grey-leaved plants, especially those with fine hairs covering the leaves, will also flourish in hot weather.

Above: This riotous mix of fuchsias, lobelia, petunias, scarlet pelargoniums, nemesias and verbena has been planned for maximum impact.

Autumn Baskets

A surprising number of plants are at their best in autumn. Shortening days bring cooler temperatures, and although there may not be as many flowers, they will last longer in the gentle autumn sun. Many annuals, particularly if sown late, will carry on until the first frosts, but others to enjoy later in the year include fruiting plants, such as bright red capsicums.

Annual capsicums, with their cheerful red, yellow or orange ball-like fruits, are appealing, as are the cultivars of *Gaulthesia mucronata*, the colourful fruits of which are beginning to ripen at this time of year to give additional interest to the basket.

Many members of the daisy family reach their peak at this time of year, and some dahlias and chrysanthemums make ideal basket plants. A dwarf chrysanthemum could be the central plant, surrounded by small ivies or possibly a late sowing of lobelias or helichrysum. This is also the season when the tuberous begonias are glorious, giving a show of colourful blooms. Look out especially for trailing cultivars such as 'Cascade Orange'.

Above: *Autumn is the season of the tuberous begonias, here partnered by pink diascias,* Helichrysum petiolare *and a fuchsia.*

488

and diascias, will also continue to flower. A late feed will give all such plants a boost, but they will not survive the first autumn frosts. This is the time to look to the true plants of autumn, such as chrysanthemums, which produce satisfying mounds of colour, and sedums. Winter-flowering heathers will even provide colour into the darker days of winter.

Above: The perennial bidens can be relied on to produce its starry yellow flowers well into autumn.

Maintaining Interest

Autumn is an unpredictable season at the best of times. If the summer was cool and the autumn continues mild, many annuals will carry on flowering, provided they are deadheaded regularly. Many of the tender perennials, such as osteospermums, felicias

GARDENER'S TIP

After flowering, dry off the tubers of begonias and store them over winter in a cool, dry, frost-free place for planting out again the following year. When new buds appear, you could propagate them by cutting the tubers in sections and planting them like cuttings.

Above: With its perfectly formed flowers and arching habit, 'Dark Eyes' is an ideal fuchsia for a hanging basket.

PLANTS AT THEIR BEST IN AUTUMN

Calluna vulgaris
Capsicum annuum
Chrysanthemum
Fuchsia
Gaultheria mucronata
Impatiens
Sedum
Solenostemon

489

Winter Baskets

It is possible to have colour and fragrance even in winter, but your choices are obviously more restricted then, since this is the time of year when most plants are resting. Winter-flowering pansies, invaluable though they are, will actually flower only during mild spells. For colour in the very depths of winter, you should look to the heathers (some of which have foliage that takes on attractive tints as the temperature dips) and dwarf berrying shrubs, such as gaultherias. The latter need lime-free (ericaceous) compost (soil mix), but winter heathers will tolerate lime.

> PLANTS AT THEIR BEST
> IN WINTER
> *Buxus*
> *Erica carnea*
> *Galanthus*
> *Hedera*
> *Skimmia japonica*
> *Viola* (winter-flowering)

This is also the time that the ivies come into their own. They exhibit a quite astonishing range of leaf shape (some being attractively crinkled at the edges) and variegation. Some are tinged pink or bronze in cold weather. A basket planted with ivies alone can be more attractive than you might think. You could even try tiny dwarf conifers or a hebe for leaf contrast. Small varieties of skimmia are also a possibility. Choose either a berrying female or the compact male form, 'Rubella', which has red-edged leaves and pink flower buds, which develop in autumn and last throughout winter, finally opening in spring. Plant them out in your garden the following year or pass them on to friends.

Left: Variegated ivies are an obvious choice for a winter basket, here livened up by yellow and bronze winter-flowering pansies.

Above: A hanging basket planted solely with one or two cultivars of small-leaved ivies will be a real eye-catcher once the plants are mature.

Danger Zones

Not only is the weather at its harshest in winter, but there is usually precious little light or sun. Although many plants tolerate wet and even a light covering of snow, evergreens in particular hate cold, drying winds, which will seriously damage their foliage if they do not kill the plant outright. Make sure your baskets are not hanging in a wind funnel. At this time of year, it also makes sense to hang your baskets only in the most sheltered spots. If particularly severe weather is threatened, move your baskets under cover. Even the shelter of a porch or a covered car port should be sufficient to protect the plants and keep them in good health.

Above: A miniature clipped Buxus *will provide sculptured interest and colour.*

Above: Erica *comes in a range of colours that will brighten up a winter basket.*

491

HANGING BASKETS INDOORS

If you are fortunate enough to have a conservatory, greenhouse or sunroom, you could grow plants that thrive in hanging baskets and can be kept in such situations all year round. In this way hanging baskets can be more than just a seasonal pleasure.

Plants for Indoor Baskets

The first choice for baskets indoors should be those plants that are actually airborne in the wild. These are the plants known as epiphytes, which cling to trees without actually deriving any nutrients from them. Many orchids come into this category, and there are plenty of modern hybrids that have been specially developed to tolerate the conditions found in the typical centrally heated home. Those

Above: With its trailing stems, this rainforest cactus makes an obvious choice for a hanging basket.

with trailing flower stems are especially well suited to baskets. Rainforest epiphytic cacti that can be grown in baskets include the familiar Christmas cactus (*Schlumbergera*) and cultivars of *Epiphyllum*. A few ferns are also natural tree-dwellers.

Trailing houseplants, such as wandering Jew (*Tradescantia*) and the popular spider plant (*Chlorophytum comosum*), are also worth including.

Above: The orchid Coelogyne flaccida *is well adapted to being above ground level and tolerates indoor conditions.*

PLANTS FOR INDOOR HANGING BASKETS

Chlorophytum comosum
'Vittatum'
Nephrolepis exaltata
'Bostoniensis'
Orchids (epiphytic species)
Platycerium bifurcatum
Schlumbergera
Tradescantia fluminensis
'Albovittata'

Caring for Baskets Indoors

Rainforest plants are generally adapted to growing in low light levels and need to be shaded from hot sun. Conversely, most are best if they are given maximum light in winter, so be prepared to move your plants around or alter the shading of any window they are near. They will not tolerate freezing temperatures, so move them well away from the glass when the winter is at its coldest.

It is worth spending more to buy the special composts (soil mixes) that cacti and orchids require. These are usually very free-draining, since the plants are accustomed to free passage of air among the roots, and orchid compost usually contains bark.

Unless your baskets are suspended over a solid floor with a drain,

*Above: Graceful, arching ferns, such as the Boston fern (*Nephrolepis exaltata *'Bostoniensis'), are ideal for baskets.*

watering can be a problem. The best solution is to mist them, twice a day or more when in active growth, and just occasionally in winter to keep the foliage plump and fresh looking. For the same reason, feed with a foliar feed rather than a root drench.

In summer you can move your hanging baskets to a cool, sheltered place outdoors. Gradual controlled exposure to outdoor conditions firms the growth and makes the plants more disease-resistant.

*Above: When it is slightly pot-bound, the spider plant (*Chlorophytum comosum*) will produce plantlets on trailing stems.*

GARDENER'S TIP

If you need to give your baskets a thorough watering, hang them in the shower, making sure the setting is at cold. Allow them to drain thoroughly before attempting to move them back to their permanent position.

493

Satisfying the Senses

PLANTS APPEAL TO OUR SENSES IN MORE THAN ONE WAY. WHILE WE ALL REJOICE IN THE COLOURS AND BEAUTY OF THEIR FLOWERS, WE SHOULD NEVER OVERLOOK THEIR MORE SUBTLE APPEAL TO OUR SENSES OF TOUCH, TASTE AND SMELL.

USING COLOUR

Colours make an immediate impact. Strong yellows, oranges and reds are known to increase the heartbeat slightly and are always considered exciting. Blues and pinks are more calming, and most restful and soothing to the eye of all is plain green.

Think of the position of the basket when you are choosing colours. Strong vibrant reds and yellows work best in

Above: This riotous mix of sweet peas uses a range of colours together, harmonized by the abundance of fresh green leaves and stems.

> ### GARDENER'S TIP
>
> When you choose a colour scheme remember that pale colours, such as pastel shades of blue, pink and yellow, tend to recede and appear further away, while strong oranges, reds and purples always seem to be nearer to the viewer and will dominate a display.

hot sun, but creams, pinks and lavenders tend to bleach out and look white. Conversely, pale colours will glow in half-light or shade, while deep reds and purples will look almost black.

Combining Colours

Use combinations of different colours as a painter would. Complementary colours (red and green; blue and orange; purple and yellow) tend to fizz when they are placed next to each other, making some exciting effects. If you add some grey to such a combination, in the form of foliage plants, it can soften the impact. If you decide to base a planting scheme on complementaries, however, it is best to avoid adding white, which tends to flare out, preventing the eye from finding a resting place.

494

Different tones of the same colour always look pleasing together. Creams and apricots blend happily with oranges and reds, for instance, as do lavenders and mauves with purples. Clear red and blue seldom make good bedfellows, but a rich purple can be enlivened with the right shade of red. You will soon learn what works.

If you are using a combination of pinks, try not to mix those that tend towards blue with those that have some orange in them. Try the bluish pinks with warm mauve and purples, and the orange-pinks with red and yellow. Potential clashes can always be softened by the use of plain green or grey foliage.

Above: The vivid colours of nasturtiums and French marigolds combine to create an eyecatching arrangement.

Below: The begonias and diascias used here could have clashed were it not for the presence of the ever-dependable Helichrysum petiolare.

495

Dramatic Effects

Bearing in mind the effects the different colours have on the senses, the most dramatic plantings involve rich, deep, saturated colours, such as purple, orange, yellow and red. A typical planting might involve a richly coloured petunia or fuchsia – several cultivars have red or purple flowers – surrounded by dark blue, trailing lobelias with a few orange and red nasturtiums tucked in for added vibrancy. Purple on its own, or as the principal colour, would certainly be dramatic, but if you are mixing purples beware:

red-purples and blue-purples make unhappy bedfellows. Play for safety and include plants with grey foliage or some ivies, which will bring a welcome calming note to the scheme.

> STRIKINGLY COLOURED
> PLANTS
> *Antirrhinum*
> *Fuchsia*
> *Lobelia*
> *Nasturtium*
> *Pelargonium*
> *Petunia*
> *Verbena*
> *Viola*

Above: Pink flowers are always enhanced by silver-grey foliage, and these warm pink pelargoniums and diascias make a beautifully subtle planting with Helichrysum petiolare.

Above: The combination of a virginal white pelargonium with purple daisies and verbenas is undeniably romantic.

Above: As well as the familiar strident colours, busy Lizzies come in some lovely soft shades.

Soothing Schemes

For subtlety, choose pastels. Creams, pinks, blues and lavenders always work well together, though the results can be insipid unless you include a few deeper shades of those colours. In theory, white should be the most calming of all, and silver and white baskets are undeniably romantic, but again you have to be careful where you place them. In full sun, the flowers tend to bleach, and a subtle scheme might end up looking washed out. On the whole, white flowers are best used to highlight other pale colours.

A simple planting might surround a pale fuchsia (there is no clear white, but some of the pink varieties are very pale) or pelargonium with white lobelias and cream, lavender or white petunias. The ever-reliable grey-leaved *Helichrysum petiolare* could give the planting substance. You can warm up a cool scheme by using pinks with a touch of orange in them – a colour usually called salmon. Diascias are among the most desirable, many having flowers of a smoky apricot.

PLANTS WITH PALE
FLOWERS

Diascia
Fuchsia
Lobelia
Nemesia
Osteospermum
Pelargonium
Petunia
Viola

Using Foliage

Although planting schemes are usually planned around the flowers, you could plant a basket for the appeal of foliage, either on its own, for a subtle look, or combined with flowering plants. A dramatic combination would be black lilyturf (*Ophiopogon nigrescens*) mixed with silver-leaved *Helichrysum petiolare*. Blue fescue (*Festuca glauca*) would be a more understated alternative. For richer, bolder effects, annual coleus (*Solenostemon*) would give as vivid a display as any combination of flowers and over a much longer period. Coleus seedlings vary and can never be accurately predicted, but colours include red, brown and gold. Foliage begonias (*Begonia rex*) have purple or

---

PLANTS WITH SILVER OR GREY FOLIAGE

Artemisia
Dianthus
Festuca glauca
Helianthemum 'The Bride'
Helichrysum petiolare
Nepeta
Santolina
Senecio
Stachys byzantina

---

silver leaves with a pronounced metallic sheen.

Be careful where you place baskets planted for foliage effect, however. Most need some sun to enhance the colour, but the leaves can scorch in too hot a position – somewhere sheltered from the midday sun is usually best.

The ever-popular spider plant (*Chlorophytum comosum* 'Vittatum') is generally grown as a houseplant, but there is no reason not to allow it an excursion outdoors in the frost-free months. It is an ideal basket plant, with green-and-white striped, arching leaves, and new plants attractively hanging from the tips of long runners.

Left: A sumptuous combination of purple heuchera, orange and brown pansies, mimulus and golden lysimachia. The purple foliage sets off the pansies.

Above: The green foliage of Helichrysum petiolare *'Aureum' makes a striking partner to blue anagallis and pansies.*

Combining Foliage with Flowers

For the best of both worlds, try blending foliage plants with flowering ones. Alaska Series nasturtiums solve the problem in one, because the leaves, which are beautifully marbled with splashes of pink and cream, are almost as appealing as the orange, yellow and red flowers. Otherwise, try matching leaf colour with flower colour. An ivy with cream variegated foliage will echo any cream flowers you may have chosen, for instance. The yellow-leaved *Lysimachia nummularia* 'Aurea' works splendidly as a foil to red and orange flowers and is a dramatic complement to purple verbenas,

but take care when combining it with other shades of yellow – you should experiment with different shades to find out what works best. Purple- and bronze-leaved plants are also striking when used in conjunction with red or yellow flowers. For a more sophisticated effect, try combining them with cream or white flowers.

If you like variegated plants it is probably best to stick to one variety only in each basket, combined with plain-leaved plants as a foil. If you include too much variegation there is a danger of creating a visually confusing look, whereas with a single, well-chosen variety you can ensure maximum effect.

PLANTS WITH COLOURED
FOLIAGE
Begonia rex
Chlorophytum comosum
'Vittatum'
Festuca glauca
Fuchsia 'Autumnale'
Gynura
Hedera (variegated forms)
Helichrysum
Lysimachia nummularia 'Aurea'
Ophiopogon nigrescens
Solenostemon (annual)
Tradescantia fluminensis
'Albovittata'
Tropaeolum Alaska Series

Satisfying the Senses

Introducing Scent

The scent of plants is as important a part of their appeal as is the colour of their flowers, and you may wish to plant a few baskets with this as the principal theme. A minority of plants have a distinctly unpleasant smell, but many have a potent fragrance that promotes a sense of well-being.

Some flowers have a scent that is emitted only at certain times of the day – when their natural pollinators are active. Night-scented plants, such as *Nicotiana*, for instance, are usually pollinated by nocturnal moths. Scents can also vary in intensity at different times of day according to the moisture content of the atmosphere. Roses are often at their sweetest when the dew hangs in the air.

Types of Scent

Scent is the most elusive of the senses and not everybody reacts in the same way to particular fragrances. For some, they awake precious memories stored up from childhood, while others are completely indifferent to them. One gardener might find that a particular scent has strong and positive associations while another might be completely unmoved by it.

Citrus smells are light and refreshing, while herbal scents such as thyme and lavender tend to be calming and relaxing. Some herbal scents are more astringent and often have notes of eucalyptus that not everyone finds pleasing, although many people experience them as invigorating. Musky scents can be very provocative, though these essences are rare in the plant world. Some flower scents combine more than one note and often seem to be "layered". Such scents, which we usually think of as exotic, are so rich and heady as to be almost cloying, though undeniably intoxicating. The commonest scents in the garden are usually defined as aromatic. They are usually sweetly spicy and always appealing, and we seem never to tire of them. They are often found in the distinctly

Above: Baskets filled with fragrant ground-cover roses make a summer focal point at the end of the pergola.

almond-like fragrance of heliotropes and the warm clove scent of old-fashioned carnations and pinks. Violet scents are sharper and more fatiguing but also more transitory. Mignonettes (*Reseda*) and *Iris reticulata* as well as violets have scents in this group.

Rose scents are usually fruity and spicy, pleasing both up close and at a distance. They are best in a sunny spot where the warmth brings out their fragrance. Some varieties of tulips as well as roses have these lovely scents. Interestingly, many of the roses have scents that seem to belong to a further group, the citrus or lemon group. These scents are almost universally perceived as pleasant and exhilarating rather than calming. Distinctive honey-scented tones are occasionally

Above: Few pansies are scented, but orange forms are sometimes fragrant, recalling their link to sweet violets.

detected in plants and their fragrance is warm and enduring. They are most commonly found among the orchids.

Above: White Lobularia maritima *has a delicate, pleasing scent that gives this simple scheme an added appeal.*

Positioning Scented Plants

Bearing in mind the power of scent, you need to think carefully where you place hanging baskets containing scented plants. While it is a joy to fling open a window and breathe in a heady mix of roses and jasmine, you may find such smells too cloying if they are near a bedroom window that is open on hot, sultry nights. Nevertheless, a basket of predominantly night-scented plants can be a pleasing addition to a pergola over a paved area where you dine *al fresco* on balmy summer evenings.

Plants with aromatic leaves, such as most of the herbs, especially woody-stemmed ones like artemisia, lavender and rosemary, are richest in their essential oils at the height of summer, and these tend to be released only when they are crushed. Site these in full sun somewhere where you regularly pass by, perhaps near a doorway or suspended from a garden arch, so that you can reach up and rub a few leaves between your finger and thumb to release their fragrance. Hanging them near a barbecue area will allow you to

Above: *Include some late-flowering narcissi with* Anemone blanda *and ivy for a fragrant spring display. Make sure you hang the basket where you can appreciate the scent.*

Above: Dwarf lavender has scented grey leaves as well as strongly fragrant flowers. It prefers a sunny site.

Above: Blue petunias, here planted against a sunny wall, often have a rich scent not found in the other colours.

have material close at hand to garnish grilled steaks, lamb or fish or simply to fling on the flames to release their evocative aroma.

Heavy scents, of the kind found in such plants as jasmine and stephanotis, are rich and penetrating and are delicious when caught on the passing breeze. Within the confines of a greenhouse or conservatory, or in the house itself, they can be overpowering. For fragrance indoors, you could consider growing some of the *Dendrobium* or *Coelogyne* orchid hybrids or *Cyclamen persicum* hybrids, but note that not all of these are scented. Look for plants in flower and sniff out their potential before you make a purchase.

SCENTED PLANTS

Convallaria majalis
Crocus (some)
Cyclamen persicum
Dianthus
Iris (some)
Lathyrus odoratus
Lavandula
Lobularia maritima
Muscari armeniacum
Narcissus (some)
Nicotiana
Petunia (some)
Pelargonium (scented-leaved)
Phlox
Reseda odorata
Rosmarinus
Narcissus (some)
Primula (some)
Tulipa (some)
Verbena

Benefits of Scented Plants

Scented plants have the inestimable value of attracting beneficial insects, such as hoverflies and ladybirds (ladybugs), into the garden. A healthy ladybird population will help keep aphids at bay, since they feed on these pests. The poached egg plant (*Limnanthes douglasii*), with its saucer-shaped, yellow and white flowers, will be alive with bees throughout summer. Butterflies are an ornament to the garden in their own right.

Many plants are believed to have healing qualities, and they have been used in traditional medicines for centuries. A cup of mint tea helps settle the stomach after a meal, while an infusion of lemon balm can be very soothing. Feverfew is said to alleviate

Above: Lavandula stoechas *ssp.* pedunculata *is a form of lavender from Provence that is particularly attractive to bees.*

headaches and migraines, but no herb other than the familiar culinary ones should be taken in any form for its health benefits without consulting a medical practitioner.

Citronella oil is widely used as a component of insect repellents. Growing citrus-scented plants, such as lemon balm (*Melissa officinalis*), in a basket near a favourite evening sitting place may help to deter mosquitoes and other unwelcome nighttime insects provided you rub its leaves periodically to release the lemon scent.

Left: The silver-leaved thyme is a strong feature of this basket and will be alive with bees when it is in flower.

Combining Scented Plants

Placing two or three scented plants together can be detrimental to the effect of each and can confuse the nose. You will achieve the most pleasing results by restricting yourself to one scented plant in each basket, particularly if the scent is a heavy one. However, the aromatic herbs and scented-leaved plants, such as pelargoniums, which are fragrant only when bruised, can work well together, because you have some control over when the scent is actually released. In a mixed basket, a succession of scents is possible. The leaves of some nasturtiums (*Tropaeolum*), for instance, have a fresh, peppery scent when young, and this could be enjoyed before later, scented flowers – pansies or petunias,

***Above:** An elegant planting with an added dimension: the scent of the purple lobularias will attract a host of insects.*

for example – appear. Alternatively, use these plants with herbs or pelargoniums that owe their scent to aromatic oils, which are at their richest when the weather is hottest – from mid- to late summer. Misting the plants will help to release their fragrance.

PLANTS THAT ATTRACT BEES
AND BUTTERFLIES

Aster (dwarf forms)
Aubrieta deltoides
Lavandula species
Limnanthes douglasii
Lobularia maritima
Sedum 'Vera Jameson'
Thymus species
Viola tricolor

***Left:** In addition to the beauty of its abundant mauve flowers,* Pelargonium *'Little Gem' has the advantage of soft-textured, lobed leaves, which exude a warm, rose-lemon fragrance.*

PLANTS TO TOUCH

Good gardeners love to handle their plants, some of which seem to grow just to be touched, especially those with furry or silky leaves and those with aromatic leaves that release their fragrance when bruised. This characteristic is, perhaps, the subtlest of pleasures that plants can give us, and appreciation of it is one to be encouraged. Some people believe that plants that are caressed regularly grow more vigorously and are more disease-resistant, although it is obviously difficult to demonstrate this scientifically. Touching may imitate the contact that plants would receive in the wild from passing animal life.

Above: *The leaves of the triphylla-type fuchsia 'Thalia' – at the centre of the basket and yet to bear its orange flowers – are velvety and eminently strokeable.*

506

> ### PLANTS WITH TEXTURAL LEAVES
> *Fuchsia* (triphylla types)
> *Gynura*
> *Helichrysum*
> *Pelargonium* (scented-leaved)
> *Rosmarinus*
> *Stachys byzantina*

Leaf Texture

Waxy and furry coatings to leaves developed as a response to climate, to protect the plants from hot sun by helping the leaf to retain moisture. Such textures are at their most pronounced, therefore, when the sun is at its hottest, so a basket featuring these is best sited in a sunny position that will encourage the plants to build up their protective coatings.

Plants with smooth, waxy leaves include, most obviously, succulent plants such as *Schlumbergera*. The nearest hardy equivalents are the sedums, with their fleshy, almost glassy leaves, which can assume a grape-like bloom as the temperature rises. Furry-textured leaves have an irresistible appeal to children, who love to stroke the charmingly and aptly named lambs' ears (*Stachys byzantina*), which is usually used to edge a flower

Right: The silver-grey foliage of Convolvulus cneorum *is a delightful foil to the white flowers.*

border but also makes an excellent basket plant, particularly in one of its non-flowering forms such as 'Silver Carpet'. *Helichrysum petiolare* also has soft, velvety leaves, though they are firmer-textured and, being smaller, not quite so easy to stroke. An attractive alternative is *Convolvulus cneorum*, with its silky-textured, silver-grey leaves that are no less appealing than the glistening white, funnel-shaped flowers. This is actually a Mediterranean shrub, but its lax habit makes it perfect for a basket.

Leaves that are soft, thin and silky usually need some shelter from hot sun, and most will do best in shade. Triphylla-type fuchsias are outstanding here, with large, usually bronze-flushed leaves with a metallic sheen. *Gynura aurantiaca* 'Purple Passion' has purple hairy leaves that shine almost blue, making a strong appeal to our tactile sense. Popular as a houseplant, there is no reason this should not find its way into a hanging basket outdoors provided there are no great temperature fluctuations and it is sheltered from any strong winds. Another useful trailing foliage plant is wandering Jew (*Tradescantia*). Their leaves have a glittering crystallized appearance, almost as though they have been lightly sprinkled with sugar.

Above: The yellow leaves of Helichrysum petiolare *'Limelight' bring their distinctive texture to a colourful summer basket.*

Satisfying the Senses

EDIBLE PLEASURES

In an age when commercial crops are routinely sprayed against pests and diseases and fed with chemicals to increase crop size and extend shelf life, many gardeners are attracted to the idea of growing their own fruit and vegetables at home. You do not have to have a large area of flat ground, as you might imagine, and growing edible crops in hanging baskets is actually a very practical option if you have only limited space. This way you can be sure that they are always ready to hand to be picked. Moreover, home-grown crops are always tastier and fresher than their shop-bought equivalents.

Make sure that your edible baskets are positioned near to the kitchen so that you do not have too far to walk in wet weather. Remember, though, that all vegetables need an open, sunny site to grow properly, so if the area near your kitchen door is shady, you may need to hang your basket elsewhere for the best crops.

What to Grow

Look out for quick-maturing, dwarf, trailing forms that have been specially developed to meet the needs of gardeners with limited space. All edible crops are greedy plants so will need a lot of feeding to give you the results you want. Lettuces and other salad leaves are an ideal crop for growing in hanging baskets. 'Little Gem' is a reliable dwarf variety. The cut-and-come-again varieties, such as 'Frisby', are particularly useful, because you can simply snip off the leaves you need for a salad and the plant will carry on producing more, so you do not have to remove a whole plant at a time. Some are decorative in their own right, with red or crinkly-edged leaves.

Cherry tomatoes are also an excellent choice and, of course, look

Above: The pretty flowers of the trailing tomato plants, here combined with nasturtiums (also edible), give a hint of tasty crops to come.

Left: This sumptuous basket combines perennial herbs with fragrant flowers.

is truly beautiful to look at as well as a valued food source. Beware of overplanting the basket, however. If the vegetables have to compete for the water and nutrients, they may not produce the tasty crops you want.

Maintaining the Basket

The demands of the majority of vegetables are much greater than those of flowering plants, which should be considered when deciding what to grow. They need a free-draining compost (soil mix), so choose a lightweight type that will not compact with the frequent watering. Because free-draining composts tend to be low in nutrients, and vegetables demand greater amounts of fertilizer, feed the baskets with a soluble variety. Tomato fertilizers are quite high in potassium, to promote good fruiting, but tend to encourage other leafy vegetables, such as lettuces, to bolt. For these, look for a high-nitrogen feed. If the idea of using chemicals to enhance an edible crop does not appeal, there are also organic equivalents, usually based on seaweed extract. Apply all fertilizers at the manufacturer's recommended rate. Overfeeding (and overwatering) can impair the flavour of the crop.

extremely attractive as the cherry-like fruits ripen in late summer. 'Tumbler' is the cultivar generally recommended.

Beans have the advantage of pretty flowers before the beans form. Be sure to harvest the beans regularly while they are still small and sweet. Older beans will be tough and stringy. Sadly, root crops, such as carrots, parsnips and potatoes, are definitely not suitable for such a limited space. They need a deeper root run than it is possible to achieve in a hanging basket.

You could try adding some flowers to the planting, to create a basket that

GARDENER'S TIP

Seed merchants bring out new varieties every year, so check their catalogues for the latest additions. For success with edible crops, use baskets no less than 35cm/14in in diameter.

Growing Herbs

If you do not have a herb garden – or even if you do – you might like to grow some herbs in a basket that you can hang near the back door or kitchen window so that they are always within reach. Held aloft as they are, hanging baskets offer what most herbs need above all – good drainage. Unlike many other plants, herbs thrive in relatively poor soil, so feed less often than you would a flowering basket. However, you will need a very free-draining compost (soil mix), so be sure to add perlite or vermiculite so that there is no danger of waterlogging.

Some herbs are perennials, which means that the basket can be a year-round feature. You can also include herbs in mixed baskets – sage and parsley make particularly attractive additions to flower baskets. It would be a practical idea to grow basil with tomatoes, because the two flavours complement each other so nicely, and you would have the ingredients of a tasty salad growing together.

Nearly all the herbs that are suitable for hanging baskets are sun-lovers. Indeed, sun is often needed to enhance their aromatic properties. Most have tough leaves – sage, lavender

Below: With its crops of parsley, sage and tarragon, this basket is every cook's dream. It will produce fresh leaves over a long period of time if trimmed regularly.

Above: Chives have pretty flowers, but if you want to reserve your plants solely for culinary use it is best to nip them off before they are fully formed.

they are unlikely to run to seed, but if flowers should begin to form, nip them out with finger and thumb or scissors.

You might, however, allow herbs such as lavender, rosemary and thyme to flower. Not only are the flowers pretty in themselves, but they will provide a valuable nectar source for bees and other pollinating insects.

> HERBS FOR A
> HANGING BASKET
> Basil (annual)
> Chives
> Lavender
> Parsley (annual)
> Rosemary (prostrate varieties)
> Sage

and rosemary – but those with more delicate leaves, such as basil and tarragon, may need some shelter from the midday sun during the hotter months. The exception is mint, which is not only shade-tolerant but demands reliably moist soil if it is to prosper. Make sure that you keep mint baskets well watered.

Maintaining a Supply

Herbs actually benefit from being harvested regularly. Not only does this keep the plants neat and compact, but it prevents them from flowering and setting seed and makes them put out fresh young leaves, always the most tender and tasty. Basil and parsley are annual herbs, which tend to become coarse if allowed to bolt and lose their characteristic flavour. If you pick from them regularly to provide garnishes,

Above: Herbs can please the eye as much as the taste buds. This striking scheme combines mint, parsley, lavender and thymes with alpine pinks.

511

Growing Strawberries

Believe it or not, you can even grow strawberries in hanging baskets, and at least you can be sure you'll experience no problems with mice, the scourge of many a fruit garden. Pick and choose among the varieties. Alpine strawberries are the best, being naturally small and neat-growing, but you could also experiment with some of the larger fruited varieties. All strawberries have the additional attraction of white flowers in spring.

You can either raise plants from seed or buy plantlets, probably the better option if you are short of time. Look for compact cultivars. You will have most success with those that are recommended for container growing.

It is also worth checking when the cropping season is. Some fruit in early summer, others in midsummer, while a third group provides late crops. A few varieties produce relatively small crops but over a long period, and these may be the best choice for a busy town-dweller. Make sure that any variety you choose is self-fertile, unless there are other strawberry plants grown nearby.

Below: Two types of strawberry are used here, the large-fruited 'Maxim' and smaller alpine plants. A crimson pelargonium adds a dash more colour.

Above: This half basket uses attractive alpine strawberries almost as much for the appeal of their foliage as for their fruits. Red petunias and a variegated helichrysum sit above them.

Strawberries are susceptible to mildew, a common fungal infection encouraged by high humidity and fluctuating temperatures – the kind of conditions that often prevail in late summer and autumn. Spray at the first sign of disease, but make sure that any product you use will not taint the fruit or damage wildlife.

Even if you can't grow a large enough crop to make preserves, you can still have alpine strawberries to add to your breakfast cereal or cornflakes in the summer or to make tiny pots of compote for enjoying with scones (biscuits) and cream. Alpine strawberries are also traditionally eaten in France dropped in a glass of champagne – a custom certainly well worth importing.

RECOMMENDED
STRAWBERRIES

'Calypso' (perpetual-fruiting)
'Mignonette' (alpine)
'Temptation' (perpetual-fruiting)

Planting Combinations

You need not restrict yourself to one strawberry cultivar, but two or three is probably the maximum you will manage in one basket. Allow an alpine strawberry to trail at the edges of the basket and place a larger fruited type in the centre.

Strawberries are such attractive fruits that they can be used in conjunction with flowers for a display that is as much for the eye as the taste buds. Small pelargoniums, petunias or nasturtiums are possibilities, and if you stick to shades of red you can be sure to have a vivid display. There are also a few white strawberry cultivars, which would look charming mixed with a few cream petunias.

GARDENER'S TIP

Most strawberries ripen best in an open, sunny site. Alpine strawberries, however, will ripen perfectly well in light shade, so if the only position available is shaded, restrict yourself to these varieties. As the fruits begin to ripen, protect strawberry baskets with a piece of netting, otherwise the birds may help themselves to the entire crop.

Edible Flowers

Some flowers are edible and make colourful additions to salads and drinks. A bowl of chilled punch at a summer party will be considerably enhanced by the presence of a few viola or borage flowers floating on the surface, and they can also be used to garnish desserts, either fresh from the plant or given a coating of egg white and sugar. Flowers for culinary use are best picked when they have just opened, but before they are fully open and beginning to fade.

The pink flowerheads of chives make a delicious addition to salads, but the flowering stems are tough and best not used.

Borage flowers can also be frozen in ice cubes to add to drinks, allowing you to revisit in a modest way the pleasures of summer once the plants that produced the flowers are spent. Place individual flowers in each compartment of an ice tray and fill with water. Once frozen, release the cubes

Below: Leaving aside the blue felicia, this chirpy planting provides parsley leaves as well as marigold flowers, both of which can be used in the kitchen.

from the trays and bag them up separately for storing in the freezer.

Nasturtium flowers can be used as a last-minute garnish to salads and have a fresh, peppery taste. Pansy flowers have a less distinctive flavour, but they have a lovely velvety texture.

Rose or marigold petals can be used to flavour butters or to scent oils and vinegars, adding to the appeal of your salad dressings. Soften butter (preferably unsalted) first and gently mash the flowers into it. The idea is to release some of the oils into the butter while preserving the integrity of the flowers. Flavoured butters are best used fresh, before the flowers discolour, otherwise the butter turns rancid.

Oils and vinegars act as preservatives, so have a longer shelf life than butter. Choose a lightly flavoured oil, such as sunflower. Wine or cider vinegar should be gently warmed before adding the flowers. Steep for two weeks on a sunny windowsill, shaking occasionally, then strain the liquid.

The petals of pot marigolds (*Calendula*) can be used to colour rice in place of saffron but will not impart any flavour. To dry marigold petals, lay the individual flowers on sheets of

Above: Not only can nasturtium leaves and flowers be used in salads and cooked dishes, but the seeds can also be pickled.

absorbent kitchen paper and allow them to dry naturally in a well-ventilated area. Once dry, pull the petals from the centre of the flower (which can then be discarded) and store them in an airtight screwtop jar.

To keep your plants producing new flowers, remove faded ones promptly.

Combining Plants

Using edible flowers in conjunction with other edible plants means that your useful baskets can be as attractive to look at as baskets planted for appearance alone. Try marigolds with nasturtiums, for instance, with a few added parsley plants for bulk. This type of planting also gives you more scope for variations in colour, flower and leaf shape and scent.

EDIBLE FLOWERS

Borago officinalis
Calendula
Rosa
Tropaeolum
Viola

515

Seasonal Tasks

GOOD TIME-MANAGEMENT WILL HELP YOU SUCCEED WITH HANGING
BASKETS. THE FOLLOWING CALENDAR PROVIDES A TIMETABLE THAT
WILL ENABLE YOU TO KEEP PACE WITH TASKS AS THEY NEED TO BE
DONE, AND TO MAINTAIN HEALTHY BASKETS ALL YEAR ROUND.

SPRING

Early spring
- plant up evergreens, such as herbs and ivies, for a permanent display
- tidy up permanent plantings and remove any dead leaves
- sow seed of vegetables under protection
- coax overwintered fuchsias, pelargoniums and chrysanthemums back into growth with bottom heat if necessary
- take cuttings of overwintered fuchsias and chrysanthemums as they come into growth

Mid-spring
- plant herbs and ivies for a permanent display
- sow seed of flowering annuals, such as nasturtiums and marigolds
- sow seed of annual herbs, such as basil and parsley
- bring dormant begonia tubers back into life
- prune woody plants such as roses
- lightly trim evergreen herbs

Late spring
- start feeding permanent plantings as they come back into growth
- buy bedding plants suitable for baskets from garden centres
- plant up baskets for summer interest
- pot up spent bulbs for use the following year or plant out in the garden

Above: *A cheery display for a spring basket.*   **Above:** *A glorious summer combination.*

SUMMER

Early summer
- make late sowings of annuals for autumn baskets
- start feeding summer baskets with a high-potash fertilizer
- order bulbs from bulb suppliers for planting in autumn

Midsummer
- begin harvesting cut-and-come-again crops
- begin harvesting dwarf beans
- begin harvesting strawberries
- begin harvesting annual herbs
- sow seed of winter pansies and keep the seedlings cool
- deadhead flowering plants to keep up the display

Late summer
- take cuttings of herbs and other woody plants for overwintering
- take cuttings of tender perennials for overwintering
- continue harvesting strawberries

AUTUMN

- sow seed of hardy annuals for early flowers the following season
- sow seed of biennials, such as *Myosotis,* for an early spring display in 18 months
- gradually dry off fuchsias and pelargoniums for overwintering
- dry off begonia tubers and store dry over winter
- plant up baskets of dwarf bulbs

WINTER

- order seed of annuals and vegetables from seed catalogues
- order strawberry plants from commercial suppliers
- protect permanent plantings from heavy frosts
- continue to care for baskets indoors, watering to keep them just moist

Above: *Fuchsias provide colour in autumn.*

Above: *An evergreen basket for winter.*

517

Best Hanging Basket Plants

THIS QUICK REFERENCE CHART CAN BE USED TO SELECT THE MOST
SUITABLE PLANTS FOR YOUR HANGING BASKETS IN TERMS OF THEIR
REQUIREMENTS AND SEASON OF INTEREST. NOTE PARTICULARLY THE
PLANTS' PREFERENCES FOR SUN OR SHADE.

Plant name	Height	Flower colour	Season of interest
Allium schoenoprasum FS	25cm/10in	herb	spring/summer
Anagallis Tr FS	10cm/4in	blue, red, pink	spring/summer
Antirrhinum hh FS	30cm/12in	pink, red, purple, yellow, bronze, orange, white	summer
Argyranthemum fh FS	30cm/12in	white, pink	summer/autumn
Asarina Tr FS	5cm/2in	purple	summer
Aster FS	25cm/10in	white, pink, violet, purple, red	summer/autumn
Begonia t Tr PS (tuberous and semperflorens)	20–60cm/ 8–24in	white, yellow, orange, red	summer/autumn
Bellis perennis FS	15cm/6in	white, pink, red	spring
Bidens fh Tr FS	25cm/10in	yellow	summer
Buxus FS/S	15cm/6in	foliage	all year
Calendula officinalis FS	25cm/10in	cream, yellow, orange	summer
Calluna FS	15cm/6in	white, pink, purple, crimson	summer/autumn
Chamaemelum FS	10cm/4in	foliage	all year

Plant name	Height	Flower colour	Season of interest
Chlorophytum comosum t Tr PS	25cm/10in	foliage	all year
Convallaria majalis Sh	20cm/8in	white	spring
Crocus FS	10cm/4in	white, yellow, purple, lilac	late winter/spring
Diascia FS Tr	30cm/12in	pink, lilac, apricot	summer
Dwarf beans FS	30cm/12in	vegetable	summer
Erica FS	30cm/12in	white, pink, purple	winter/spring
Eschscholzia FS	30cm/12in	cream, pink, orange, white, red, yellow	summer
Felicia t FS Tr	25cm/10in	blue	summer
Fuchsia hh PS Tr (some)	25cm/10in	pink, red, purple	summer/autumn
Galanthus officinalis PS	15cm/6in	white	late winter
Glechoma hederacea 'Variegata' FS/PS Tr	15cm/6in	foliage	all year
Gynura aurantiaca t PS Tr	30cm/12in	foliage	all year
Gypsophila FS Tr	30cm/12in	white	summer
Hedera (small-leaved) FS/Sh Tr	15cm/6in	foliage	all year
Helichrysum petiolare hh FS Tr	15cm/6in	foliage	all year
Impatiens t PS/Sh Tr (some)	15cm/6in	white, pink, red	summer/autumn
Lathyrus odoratus FS Tr	25cm/10in	white, pink, red, violet	summer
Lavandula FS	45cm/18in	blue, purple	all year

Plant name	Height	Flower colour	Season of interest
Lobelia hh S/PS/Sh Tr (some)	10cm/4in	white, blue, purple, red	summer
Lobularia maritima FS	10cm/4in	white, purple	summer
Lysimachia nummularia 'Aurea' PS Tr	5cm/2in	foliage	all year
Mentha Sh	45cm/18in	herb	spring/summer/autumn
Mimulus PS Tr (some)	15cm/6in	yellow, orange, red, pink	summer
Muscari armeniacum FS	12cm/5in	purple, white	spring
Myosotis FS	30cm/12in	blue	spring
Narcissus FS	15–30cm/ 6–12in	white, cream, yellow	spring
Nemesia hh FS	20cm/8in	cream, orange, pink, blue, purple, yellow	summer
Ocimum basilicum hh FS	25cm/10in	herb	summer
Orchids t Sh Tr (some)	30cm/12in	all colours	any time of year
Pelargonium t FS/PS Tr (some)	30cm/12in	white, pink, red	summer
Petunia hh FS Tr	20cm/8in	white, purple, blue, red	summer
Primula PS	15cm/6in	white, pink, yellow, red, orange, purple	spring
Rosa (miniature and ground-cover) FS	25cm/10in	white, pink, yellow, red, orange	summer/autumn
Rosmarinus officinalis FS Tr (some)	30cm/12in	herb	all year

Plant name	Height	Flower colour	Season of interest
Salpiglossis hh FS	45cm/18in	yellow, orange, red, purple, blue	summer
Salvia officinalis FS	30cm/12in	herb	all year
Schlumbergera t PS Tr	20cm/8in	red, pink, white	winter
Solenostemon hh PS	30cm/12in	foliage	spring/summer/autumn
Strawberries FS Tr	12cm/5in	fruit	summer
Tanacetum parthenium FS	45cm/18in	white	summer
Thymus vulgaris FS	12cm/5in	herb	all year
Tomatoes hh FS Tr (some)	15cm/6in	fruiting vegetable	summer
Tradescantia t PS	20cm/8in	foliage	all year
Tropaeolum FS Tr (some)	20cm/8in	yellow, orange, red	summer
Verbena hh FS Tr	25cm/10in	red, pink, blue, mauve, white	summer
Vinca PS/Sh Tr	15cm/6in	white, blue, purple	foliage all year
Viola FS/PS	20cm/8in	white, violet, yellow, orange, maroon, black	spring/summer/ autumn/winter

KEY TO ABBREVIATIONS

t = tender (needs minimum 5°C/41°F)

hh = half hardy
(survives lows of 0°C/32°F)

fh = frost hardy
(survives lows of -5°C/23°F)

Unmarked plants are fully hardy
(down to -15°C/5°F)

FS = full sun

PS = partial shade
(i.e. best protected from hot sun)

Sh = shade

Tr = trailing

WINDOW
BOXES

Chosen to complement the style of a
house, window boxes can add the
perfect external finishing touch and
offer considerable scope for year-
round planting schemes. On a kitchen
windowsill they can be filled with
herbs or even planted as mini-
vegetable gardens. This chapter gives
you all the information you need to
create beautiful displays, from
choosing the best boxes and plants to
caring for them and keeping them
looking good all year round.

Dressing up Windows

AN EMPTY WINDOWSILL IS A MISSED OPPORTUNITY, AND FOR ANYONE WHO LOVES PLANTS A WINDOW BOX CRAMMED WITH COLOUR WILL BE PURE DELIGHT. THE CHALLENGE IS KNOWING JUST HOW TO TRANSFORM THAT EMPTY SPACE INTO SOMETHING MAGICAL.

THE PLEASURE OF WINDOW BOXES

For many apartment dwellers, window boxes provide their only view of garden plants and flowers, and are like a breath of fresh air. For garden owners they can be important as exterior decoration, adding colour and design to the façades of their homes and forming a link with their gardens.

Above: A window box planted with soft pale pink petunias and deeper-hued verbenas provides a link between house and garden.

Left: This window box, bursting with petunias, Brachyscome *daisies and* Convolvulus, *brightens the window from outside and within the house.*

There are so many wonderful plants to use and so many ways to use them, that creating the right window box for your home can be tricky. But once you know the basic principles involved in planting containers and window boxes, you can display your creative skills.

DECIDING WHAT YOU WANT

Before you buy containers and plants, you need to decide exactly what you want a window box to do for you and your home. You can make it blend with the decorative style, or create a contrast. Alternatively, you might want to continue the theme of your garden, extending the planting right up to your windows.

You may choose a country style of planting, or opt for a classic, modern or Mediterranean look. Perhaps a mass of colour appeals to you or just one or two accents, or you might prefer a subtle blend of foliage, scent for open windows or doorways, or the window box to be of culinary use.

MAKING AN IMPACT

How you use colour will affect the success of your window box. You can throw together a mix and end up with a cheerful bunch of flowers, or you can colour co-ordinate for a more sophisticated approach, and to complement the external decoration of your home. Hot colours are loud and exciting, cool or pastel colours calm and relaxing.

The height and shape of the plants you choose also contribute to the overall effect. Clipped topiary and the erect, compact outlines of dwarf conifers suggest classic design, while wispy stems create a romantic image. Large leaves make bold statements, whereas fronds soften an arrangement. Flowering or colourfully leafed trailing plants are invaluable for window boxes for their ability to drop curtains of colour from the sill. This adds depth to a planting and softens the outline. Trailing lobelias and

Above: A bold black wooden window box is softened by the delicate cascades of foliage and flower.

Helichrysum petiolare are especially valuable; they team well with many plants and can completely camouflage a dull container or soften a plain wall.

CREATIVE CONTAINERS

For maximum impact the window box or container itself should fit comfortably with the style of the house and garden and complement the planting it contains. Material, shape and colour all contribute to the final effect. If you cannot find exactly what you need, you can often improvise by decorating or customizing a box or even adapting some other type of container. Pots, bowls, cans, even old boots can be employed.

Left: This stylish box planted with Heuchera, Senecio, *lavender and* Brachyscome *daisies would be more suitable for an elegant town house than a country cottage.*

525

Decorative Styles

You can of course plant your window box in any way you wish, but a few identifiable styles are worth considering. Country style reflects a relaxed attitude to planting, with mixed colours and loose outlines. A classic style is altogether more restrained and formal, with tighter control over colour. A modern style involves the use of plants with interesting structure and foliage in unorthodox arrangements. A hot and exotic style uses sun-loving plants, many of which come in vibrant colours, combined with soft grey foliage and often includes spiky cacti and other succulents.

Right: Osteospermum daisies keep their petals furled in cloudy weather so require a sunny position. Here O. 'Buttermilk' combines delightfully with yellow violas and white Bacopa.

Left: A hot and exotic style planting of succulents in a terracotta window box will enjoy a sunny position.

Interest Through the Year

The traditional approach to planting window boxes is a splash of fresh colour for the spring, usually supplied with bulbs and a few early bedding plants, followed by an exuberant show of summer bedding plants. But you can do much better than that.

Colourful plants are available at all times of the year and containers can be planted to make the best of each season. They can be replanted as one season gives way to the next, either in the same style or differently.

Alternatively, you can plant a window box to provide interest for the whole year. Use evergreen plants with colourful and interesting foliage for the permanent structure, and seasonal plants to add a succession of colour.

PLANNING AHEAD

To ensure good results at all times with your window boxes, you need to plan ahead. Although you can buy plants when you are planting up your containers, you will not always find exactly what you want in the right colour when you want it. To avoid problems you can sow your own seed and grow the plants on until they are the right size for your container. Find a spare corner in the garden to act as a nursery for growing plants, as well as those that are resting at the end of their season of interest. You can even plant up containers ahead of time, so that they can be put on to a windowsill only when they are looking their best.

Above: Mesembryanthemum *need a hot sunny position.*

SUN AND SHADE

When planning your containers, consider how much light your windowsills receive and try to plant accordingly. Sun-loving plants will look sick and lose colour if they are kept in perpetual shade, and those preferring dark, moist conditions may die in hot sun.

HOW TO USE THIS CHAPTER

You will find all the information you need to create delightful window boxes on the following pages. The beginning of the chapter describes the types of containers and compost you can use as well as providing planting information. *Seasonal Splendour* explains how you can achieve interest during the entire year. Read *Knowing Your Style* to help you decide on a planting approach, and then *Satisfying the Senses* to find out how to plant for colour, scent and how to grow edible produce in containers. To help you with your window box planning there is a calendar of *Seasonal Tasks*. Finally, a quick-reference list gives useful information on cultivation requirements and season of interest for a selection of recommended plants.

Above: Ferns are ideal for a dark, damp and shady spot.

527

Getting Started

TO GET THE BEST FROM YOUR WINDOW BOXES YOU WILL NEED TO SELECT THE RIGHT CONTAINERS TO SUIT THE STYLE OF YOUR HOUSE. IT IS ALSO IMPORTANT THAT YOU KNOW HOW TO PLANT THEM UP CORRECTLY TO GIVE THE PLANTS A GOOD START.

TYPES OF WINDOW BOX

You can buy a wide range of attractive window boxes to blend in with your setting or planting design. There is something to suit every taste and budget, from modern lightweight materials and simple rustic boxes through stylish terracotta to the grandest stone trough. They are available plain or decorated and in many colours. Some containers have a built-in reservoir, which is useful if you are unable to water daily during a hot, dry summer. These are usually made of plastic or fibreglass.

Window boxes with a removable liner enable the contents to be lifted out at the end of a season.

Plastic

These boxes are often plain, but are lightweight and practical, needing less watering than boxes made of porous materials. However, they are often less attractive.

Above: A simple galvanized tin window box is a perfect foil for the showy contents.

Wood

There are styles of wooden container to suit every taste. Protect with wood preservative to ensure they age attractively.

Terracotta

Available in a range of sizes and styles, terracotta looks good and improves with age. However, it is heavy and susceptible to frost damage.

Plastic

Wood

Terracotta

528

Lightweight fibre

These boxes are a practical alternative to plastic, although they will not last as long. They are useful for lining baskets or rustic twig containers.

Bark

These are lightweight containers that have a rustic appeal, ideal for a country-garden setting.

Galvanized tin

Once only a utilitarian material, tin now makes a fashionable and smart window box that will make an eyecatching display when planted.

Fibreglass

Lightweight and durable, fibreglass planters are often moulded and finished to give the appearance of metal or terracotta.

MAKING THE RIGHT CHOICE

When choosing a window box, decide first whether you want it to blend in with the setting of either the house or the garden. Choose with care: a rustic planter will be in keeping with a cottage but may look out of place in front of an elegant town house. Bear proportion in mind, too, and look for a window box that fits comfortably on

Above: A trug planted with pot marigolds and herbs has informal appeal. Culinary herbs can be grown near to the kitchen window for convenience.

the sill or bracket without crowding the space or looking lost in front of a very large window.

If you cannot find exactly the style or colour you want, you could make your own or adapt another container to make a window box. Alternatively, you could decorate a shop-bought one.

Lightweight fibre

Bark

Galvanized tin

Fibreglass

Improvising with Unusual Containers

Many containers not normally associated with planting can be adapted for use as window boxes, to give striking visual effects. These can include small metal buckets or watering cans, unusual pots, copper kettles and old wooden boxes.

Large cans, perhaps painted in dramatic colours, can look good lined up on a windowsill. Baskets can also be used as window boxes, provided they are generously lined with moss or plastic before planting up. The only considerations are that the container is not so tall as to obscure the view from the window and that it fits on to the sill. It must also be possible to fix it safely on the windowsill without danger of it falling off or being blown

Above: A small oval old metal bucket has been converted into an attractive container for lily-of-the-valley.

over by the wind. It will also be necessary to add drainage holes. These can be simply made using a drill with the appropriate bit for the material of the container.

Above: Vivid red geraniums dominate this rustic, home-made window box, which is an ideal choice to complement an unpainted window frame.

CUSTOMIZING WINDOW BOXES AND OTHER CONTAINERS

If a container is not exactly what you want, you can paint or decorate it to suit your requirements.

Wooden, terracotta and plastic containers can be painted to tone in with your house or to complement a planting theme for maximum impact. You can even change the paint colour seasonally to suit different plantings. The paint can be applied as flat colour, in bold designs or with special effects such as marbling or crackle glaze.

As most window boxes are flat-fronted, they are easy to decorate with different materials, such as sea shells, using self-hardening clay or a glue gun. For a mosaic effect, pieces of coloured china, broken tile or

Above: These brightly painted pots look stunning in a sunny spot, filled with vibrant geraniums and herbs.

mirror can be applied to create a pattern, using water-resistant tile adhesive and grout. Sketch out your design on paper before you start, to avoid mistakes.

Above: Mussel shells on a small terracotta window box prettily complement this colour-themed planting of lavender and violas.

COMPOSTS

There are several types of compost (soil mix) available for using in containers, and it is worth thinking about which is best suited to the plants you want to grow. The most commonly used is "multi-purpose", and this is indeed suitable for many purposes. It is usually peat-based, but peat-free versions are available, which are preferable because of the environmental damage caused by peat removal. Both versions have similar properties: they are light and can be difficult to moisten if they are allowed to dry out completely, and their nutrient content will be rapidly used up, so the plants will need regular feeding. Special container composts are available which are largely similar, but often have water-retentive granules added. (Make sure you don't add more water-retentive granules, if this is the case.)

For long-term plantings, or for growing fruit or vegetables in window boxes, a loam-based compost is preferable. It is heavier than multi-purpose, but contains more trace elements and will not run out of nutrients so quickly. Plants will still need feeding, however, and permanent plantings will also benefit from yearly top-dressing – removing the top layer of soil, taking care not to damage the roots, and replacing it with fresh.

Ericaceous compost is the best choice if you are growing lime-hating plants, such as many of the summer-flowering heathers (most of the winter ones are fine in standard compost). Herbs will also tolerate standard compost, but will grow best in a loam-based type with sharp grit added to make it really free-draining.

Below: Window boxes are high-maintenance, but can be spectacular.

MULCHES

A layer of protective material placed over the compost or soil helps to retain moisture, conserve warmth, suppress weeds and prevent soil splash on foliage and flowers. It should also provide an attractive backdrop for plants before they have filled out and completely covered the surface.

Composted bark

Coarse bark is an effective mulch, as weeds that have germinated are easily removed. As it rots down, it also conditions the soil. It works best when spread in a layer at least 7.5cm (3in) thick, and is therefore not ideal for small containers.

Stones

Smooth stones can be used as decorative mulch for large plants grown in containers. You can save stones dug out of the garden or buy them from garden centres. Try to find colours that will complement your buildings.

Gravel

This makes a decorative mulch for container plants and provides the correct environment for plants such as alpines. It is available in a variety of sizes and colours, which can be matched to the scale and colours of the plants used.

WATER-RETAINING GEL

You can reduce the frequency of watering needed by adding water-retaining gels to the compost. Sachets of gel are available from garden centres. You mix it with the compost at the recommended rate, though some types may need soaking in water first. Ensure you don't add it to special container composts that already contain a water-retaining gel, as large amounts can froth up out of the compost.

Above: Water-retentive gel holds many times its weight of water and is useful for containers.

PLANTING UP WINDOW BOXES

Most solid window boxes are easy to plant, but need some initial preparation to ensure best results.

1 It is essential to provide all types of window boxes with some form of drainage material in the base. In small window boxes this can be broken pieces of pot – known as crocks – or gravel, which is available in various sizes from garden centres.

2 When planting up large window boxes, it is more economical to recycle polystyrene plant trays as drainage material. Lumps of polystyrene are excellent for this purpose, and, as they retain warmth, they are an additional benefit to the plants.

3 Partly fill the container with compost (soil mix) and arrange the plants. Adjust the level of the compost to ensure the tops of all the rootballs are at the same height, about 2.5cm (1in) below the rim of the container. Fill up around the plants with compost, adding slow-release plant food granules at the same time, and gently press it down. Water thoroughly.

> GARDENER'S TIP
>
> Some plants that have been grown in small pots for a length of time can become "pot-bound". When replanting gently tease out the roots around the bottom and edges to encourage the roots to grow down into the container.

Above: A variegated periwinkle, Vinca minor 'Aureovariegata', blue-leaved hostas and summer-flowering busy Lizzies (Impatiens) will brighten a gloomy corner for many months. The periwinkle will bear blue flowers in the spring.

Planting Wicker Baskets

If you use an open container such as a wooden container with a slatted bottom or a basket, you may need to line it to prevent the compost falling out.

Above: A wicker basket will be able to retain moisture if it is lined with moss.

Plastic Boxes

When buying plastic window boxes, check that the drainage holes are open. Some manufacturers mark the holes,

Above: With plastic window boxes the drainage holes sometimes need to be drilled before you can begin planting.

but leave it to the customer to punch or drill them out as required. Make sure there are enough holes, and that they are large enough to prevent any danger of waterlogging.

Plant Supports

Most window boxes are planted with fairly low-growing plants, so as not to cut out too much light from the window, but sometimes height may be required, and this can be achieved by training climbers up canes or a small trellis. Ivies work well for a year-round box, or for a riot of colour in summer, try dwarf sweet peas, which will provide a gorgeous scent as well as colour, nasturtiums or morning glories.

Above: Climbing plants may simply be allowed to trail, but you can grow them up plastic or wooden trellising.

Seasonal Splendour

WINDOW BOXES CAN LOOK MAGNIFICENT DURING EVERY SEASON OF THE YEAR, WHETHER YOU DECIDE TO CREATE A DIFFERENT SCHEME EVERY FEW MONTHS WITH FLORAL COMBINATIONS, OR A DISPLAY THAT LASTS FOR THE WHOLE YEAR.

SPRING WINDOW BOXES

After the gloomy winter months, spring boxes need to be bright and cheerful. Bulbs are plentiful, and their crisp, exquisite colours, with plenty of white and yellow, work extremely well with fresh green foliage. Many species have dwarf varieties, which are ideal for small containers or window boxes.

GARDENER'S TIP

To save bulbs for next year allow the leaves to die right back and then dig up and store in a cool, dry place.

Left: Different varieties and shades of yellow and white daffodils and pansies herald the arrival of spring.

Hyacinths, available in an enormous number of delicate and intense shades, provide a heady scent. Spring bedding in jewel colours, such as pansies, auriculas and polyanthus, provide more joy. As the season progresses the strong colours seem to give way to softer ones, with blues and pinks leading into summer.

Evergreen plants such as ivies and periwinkle *(Vinca minor)* make valuable contributions to early spring boxes when foliage can be sparse.

Above: Potted daffodils, pansies and tulips provide a cheerful display.

Planting Partners

Early bulbs look good massed together in pots, but you can fill the gaps around less tightly packed ones with vividly coloured bedding plants. Double-flowered daisies make excellent backdrops for yellow daffodils and the variously coloured tulips.

Blue and yellow is a common spring combination, starting with early blue-flowered bulbs accompanying daffodils, and later yellow tulips with blue and yellow hyacinths, blue pansies and forget-me-nots. Blue also makes a striking combination with red; try red tulips with forget-me-nots.

Maintaining Interest

Plant up a spring window box so that its interest increases from winter to summer. Follow late crocuses, daffodils, narcissi and pansies with hyacinths, tulips, forget-me-nots, bluebells and wallflowers.

> **PLANTS AT THEIR BEST IN SPRING**
>
> *Bellis perennis*
> *Crocus*
> *Erisymum cheiri*
> *Hyacinthoides*
> *Hyacinthus*
> *Muscari armeniacum*
> *Myosotis*
> *Narcissus*
> *Primula*
> *Primula auricula* hybrids
> *Primula* Polyanthus Group
> *Tulipa*
> *Viola*

If you did not plant up your spring boxes in the autumn, you can create an instant spring arrangement by using pots of plants already in flower. Simply arrange them in a window box and fill around the pots with bark to hide them. As soon as a plant is past its best, replace it with something new. Old pots of bulbs will flower again next year.

Above: *An old strawberry box carrier makes an attractive and unusual spring window box for a group of beautifully marked auricula primulas, planted in old-style terracotta pots.*

SUMMER WINDOW BOXES

Window boxes need flowering and foliage plants that are going to look good throughout the summer months. Use plenty of bushy, but not very tall bedding plants, such as pansies and petunias, dwarf snapdragons, flowering tobaccos *(Nicotiana)* and compact pot marigolds. Many border perennials are also useful for creating a variety of different heights.

Over the years, plant breeders have produced myriad varieties of summer bedding in every colour imaginable, so it is unlikely you will be unable to find the exact colour you want to fit into any scheme. There is such an abundance of colour that care needs to be taken to avoid ending up with a garish mix.

Above: White tobacco flowers and pale pink geraniums make a lovely summer display, with variegated ground ivy trailing attractively over the sides of the box.

Below: Scented petunias, delicate white marguerites and star-flowered Isotoma *make a stunning layered arrangement.*

Planting Partners

With so many varieties of summer bedding you can create just the right colour scheme to suit you. Compact and trailing fuchsias are stunning and you can use them to conjure up pretty combinations in whites, pinks and purples. Try them with sweet alyssum, violas, *Impatiens*, tobaccos and lobelias. Blue *Felicia amelloides* will combine well with *Osteospermum*, petunias and verbenas.

Use brightly flowered *Impatiens* with colourful trailing plants, including ivies, lobelias and *Tradescantia*, and with attractive foliage plants such as long-lasting begonias and coleus. They can also be teamed with architectural hostas, bergenias and ferns for a shady windowsill.

Above: White osteospermums make a good background, accentuating bolder colour choices.

Lobelias combine well with many summer bedding plants, such as dwarf snapdragons, nemesias and *Tagetes*, as well as with foliage plants like begonias and *Chlorophytum*.

The silvery *Helichrysum petiolare* sets off summer's bright colours, especially blues, mauves and pinks.

Above: Alaska nasturtiums, with cream-splattered leaves, are planted with yellow snapdragons, Gazania and Brachyscome daisies to make an extended summer display.

Maintaining Interest

To extend the season, plant a window box so that there is a succession of interest, with new flowers replacing plants that are past their best. For example, a container of pink geraniums *(Pelargonium)* such as 'Tomcat', *Lavandula pinnata*, salvias and alyssums, with blue *Brachyscome* daisies and

Convolvulus sabatius will only improve as the season progresses. By the end of summer, the pinks, reds and purples of the geraniums, salvias and lavenders will be at their most prolific. Many plants will continue flowering well into autumn, if they are properly maintained with regular watering, feeding and deadheading.

If you are using individual pots in a window box, now is the time to include annuals or exotic bulbs such as *Tigridia* as they come into flower. Perhaps intersperse the arrangement with some foliage plants or trailing ivies.

Left: *The bold blooms of* Pelargonium, *ranging from pinks to reds, will provide a long-lasting summer display.*

Below: *All the plants in this pink arrangement are still in their pots. As soon as one is past its best, a new pink plant can easily replace it.*

To ensure window boxes look their best, remember to deadhead regularly. Once a plant begins to set seed flowering will reduce. With some prolific plants deadheading may be necessary on an almost daily basis.

Watering is another important task that must not be overlooked. During summer, containers dry out very quickly and require watering daily. If this is neglected, the plants will soon suffer stress, lose their leaves and become vulnerable to disease. If the weather is very hot, you may even need to water twice a day, in the morning and in the evening. If you do water in the morning, avoid wetting the leaves, otherwise the sun can scorch them, causing them to turn brown and die off, and spoiling the display.

Above: The plants in this shallow planter require little depth for their roots, but they will need watering and feeding often.

PLANTS AT THEIR BEST IN SUMMER

Ageratum
Antirrhinum
Argyranthemum
Calendula
Dianthus
Fuchsia
Gazania
Impatiens
Lobelia
Lobularia maritima
Nasturtium
Nemesia
Nicotiana
Osteospermum
Petunia
Salvia
Tagetes
Verbena
Viola

AUTUMN WINDOW BOXES

As summer fades into autumn, the low sun casts its spell on the autumnal hues as bright summer colours mellow into russets, golds and purples. Golden rudbeckias bloom well into autumn. Chrysanthemums are prolific, with masses of rust, maroon, orange, gold and red flowers that last for weeks; the dwarf varieties are ideal choices for window boxes. Michaelmas daisies and autumn heathers come into their own with pink to purple flowers; the heathers often have interesting foliage shades, too. Depending on the variety, all these bushy plants will supply flowers throughout the season. In addition, blue gentians and bulbs, such as *Colchicum* and the pink *Amaryllis belladonna*, will provide some unexpectedly bright highlights with their wide range of colours.

Above: Dwarf chrysanthemums provide colour over a long period.

Planting Partners

Red-tinged foliage works especially well in autumn light. Choose red or rust coleus, and bronze or purple heuchera to complement the season's flowers. If you have space for it, a container-grown Japanese maple will appear to burn with glorious colour outside your window.

Above: A bark window box provides a sympathetically rustic container for autumn-flowering heathers.

Maintaining Interest

Many of the long-flowering summer plants will continue well into autumn, providing plenty of colour. Asters and kaffir lilies *(Schizostylis)* bridge the gap from summer into autumn. As these start to fade, introduce ice plants *(Sedum spectabile)*, heathers and autumn-flowering bulbs such as nerines and sternbergias for the middle of the season. Chrysanthemums will continue to show until the cold of winter finally arrives. Autumn crocuses can flower right through the season.

Michaelmas daisies and chrysanthemums are prone to grey mould *(Botrytis)* and powdery mildew, which can disfigure the plant. Remove and destroy affected areas but if the problem persists spray with a fungicide.

Berries are attractive to birds, which rely on them for an autumn feast. While you may resent their gluttony, view it as a spectacle to enjoy from inside your window. The more berry plants you have, the longer brightly coloured fruits will last for both you and the birds to appreciate. For larger containers, low, spreading cotoneasters can be a real boon with their fiery-red berries.

PLANTS AT THEIR BEST IN AUTUMN

Amaryllis belladonna
Aster novae-angliae
Aster novi-belgii
Calluna vulgaris
Colchicum
Cyclamen
Fuchsia
Impatiens
Nerine
Rudbeckia
Schizostylis
Sedum

Above: *Autumn-flowering crocuses* (Colchicum) *provide a beautiful and delicate colour that is best appreciated at close quarters.*

WINTER WINDOW BOXES

To dispel midwinter gloom you need robust plants with plenty of colour and interesting foliage in your window boxes. Evergreen plants come into their own at this time of year, providing permanence of structure and colour that lasts, no matter what the weather does. There are many shades of green, with blue, silver-grey and golden hues as well as creamy and yellow variegations; colours that become almost magical in the crisp winter light.

Above: Pot-grown dwarf conifers, variegated ivies and red polyanthus provide instant winter cheer.

Planting Partners

Box (*Buxus*) can be trimmed into interesting shapes to form miniature topiary, which can be combined with dwarf conifers (including cultivars of *Chamaecyparis* and *Thuja*).

Some berried plants can be included in winter boxes. Although it is fast growing, wintergreen *(Gaulheria procumbens)*

Above: The copper leaves of Cordyline *work well with the softer texture of a dwarf conifer and miniature hebe for interest in the winter.*

544

can be contained for a couple of years, before it needs to be replanted in the garden. It has big red aromatic berries and its glossy leaves are red when young, and would combine well with *Juniperus squamata* 'Blue Carpet'. In mild areas, the green, orange and scarlet berries of winter cherry *(Solanum pseudocapsicum)* make a contribution.

Another seasonal partnership is a combination of white variegated ivy, cheerful *Euonymus fortunei* 'Emerald 'n' Gold' and a silver-leaved senecio such as 'Sunshine'.

Foliage plants such as bergenia, heuchera and ivies, especially variegated ones, make important contributions to winter containers. Combine them with multi-coloured winter-flowering pansies, pink cyclamen and, for late winter, white snowdrops to bring precious cheer to window boxes.

Maintaining Interest

Winter-flowering pansies often bloom stoically through the cold of winter. Varieties of *Cyclamen persicum* also bloom throughout winter, while *C. coum* continues into spring. Others that flower at the end of the season are multi-coloured polyanthus, yellow winter aconites, snowdrops, iris, and *Erica carnea*, in shades of pink and white.

If you are using individual pots in your window boxes, they can be planted up with winter-flowering pansies, which are available in a bright array of bold colours, polyanthus or *Cyclamen coum* in shades of red, pink or white. You can also plant hellebores – *Helleborus niger* (the Christmas rose) and *H. orientalis* produce their delicate white, pink or purple flowers in winter or early spring. When they have finished flowering, you could remove the pots and plant them out in the garden.

Danger Zones

Cold, wind and rain are the combined perils of winter. Any terracotta containers you have must be frost-proof if you live in a frost zone, otherwise they will absorb moisture, which will freeze during frost and result in cracking. Self-watering containers should be drained before winter to prevent frost damage. If strong wind is expected you may need to protect taller plants.

PLANTS AT THEIR BEST IN WINTER

Bergenia
Buxus sempervirens
Cyclamen
Dwarf conifers
Erica carnea
Euonymus fortunei
Galanthus
Hedera
Heuchera
Primula Polyanthus
Viola

Above: *Winter pansies are wonderfully resilient and will often bloom bravely throughout the winter as long as they are regularly deadheaded to promote new buds. They make a dramatic and cheerful display, especially in an old wooden trug, as here.*

YEAR-ROUND WINDOW BOXES

In the same way that a garden has certain plants that provide structure throughout the year, evergreens can provide the backbone of a year-round window box. Evergreen plants come in many shapes, sizes and shades and should be carefully selected to supply height and depth to the planting. Before you start planting, plan the positions of the plants so that the colours and shapes look well balanced. Plant the structure plants first, then add the colour plants. Extra colour can be introduced each season by including smaller flowering plants.

Topiary shrubs and dwarf conifers are important structural plants for the year-round display, and can be supplemented with evergreen trailers to add depth and soften outlines. Choose

Above: Choosing foliage plants with differently shaped leaves creates a structured planting scheme for year-round interest.

variegated varieties of evergreen plants such as ivies (*Hedera*) and periwinkle (*Vinca minor*) to add further interest.

Above: Evergreen Skimmia reevesiana *'Rubella' and* Arundinaria pygmaea *provide height while trailing* Cotoneaster conspicuus *and variegated periwinkle soften the edges of this year-round window box. Heathers supply winter colour.*

Planting Partners

Evergreen plants have a surprising range of foliage colours and textures, and many colourful combinations are possible. *Cordyline* has dramatic, spear-shaped leaves and many varieties are red or purple. Planted with golden dwarf conifers or tufts of golden grass, the effect can be stunning. Adding more colour, such as a blue-green hosta with broad leaves or a bright green, tiny-leaved hebe, would only heighten the interest. Grasses always add grace and movement to a planting, no matter what their colour.

Tiny topiary plants, clipped in several different shapes, would make an intriguing group for a container. Be creative with your shapes for an eye-catching display. Box (*Buxus*) is the most suitable plant for this treatment.

A collection of pretty alpines arranged in a small trough would make a charming permanent planting. Try compact species and cultivars of armeria, aubrieta, campanula, dianthus, phlox, sempervivum and saxifrage together with tiny hebes.

A mulch of gravel for such plants is both attractive and practical as it prevents soil splashing on to the leaves of the plants. A trough like this should last a number of years before it needs replanting.

Above: A selection of easy-to-grow alpine plants have been grouped together in this basket-weave stone planter to create a miniature garden.

Maintaining Interest

You can ring the changes in a permanently planted box by including some seasonal highlights in the planting. Bulbs can be part of the permanent planting, emerging when their flowering time is due. There are bulbs for almost every season – snowdrops, spring and autumn crocuses, narcissus and daffodils, hyacinths, tulips, crocosmia, lilies, nerines, cyclamen and many more. If you include some perennials for spring and summer interest, you will hardly need to disturb the planting.

Below: Hyacinths add a welcome burst of colour and a glorious scent to the early spring window box.

Above: Winter-flowering pansies progress through to spring to add brilliance to Narcissus *as they bloom.*

Adding Bedding Plants for Variety

A permanent planting of foliage can start to look a bit lifeless after a couple of seasons. It can be given seasonal highlights by adding a succession of bright bedding plants, replacing plants as they fade.

By rotating winter- and summer-flowering pansies you can sustain the appearance of the window box through the year. But by planting any of the spring and summer bedding plants you will change the overall effect. Choose plants with long flowering periods.

Such a window box might include creeping Jenny *(Lysimachia nummularia), Arabis caucasia,* rock cress *(Aubrieta deltoidea)* and bellflowers *(Campanula)* as constant residents. These provide beautiful edging and trailers and may need to be divided or cut back every couple of years.

Above: Lysimachia nummularia, *heather and* Lobelia *would combine well.*

The scheme could include deep maroon heathers in winter followed by hyacinths and crocuses for spring. Trailing lobelia and *Pelargonium* (geranium) could supply both summer and autumn colour.

EVERGREEN PLANTS FOR
WINDOW BOXES

Buxus
Cordyline
Chamaecyparis pisifera
Cotoneaster conspicuus
Dwarf conifers
Euonymus fortunei
Grasses
Hebe
Hedera helix
Vinca minor

Right: Topiaried Buxus *in a window box makes a stylish year-round statement. In spring, the dainty, white flowers of* Bacopa *enhance the effect.*

Knowing Your Style

BEFORE YOU SET ABOUT PLANTING A WINDOW BOX YOU NEED TO
MAKE A DECISION ABOUT VISUAL STYLE IN YOUR CHOICE OF CON-
TAINER AND PLANTS AND HOW BEST TO ACHIEVE AN EFFECT THAT
WILL SUIT YOUR TYPE OF HOME.

COUNTRY STYLE

Cottage gardens are an exuberant mix of differently coloured flowers planted unrestrictedly or self-sown. You can re-create a scaled-down version of this relaxed style in a window box by allowing charming, cottage-garden-style plants to tumble from the container in an almost chaotic display. Country-style window boxes are appropriate for small houses and cottages, where informality is the order of the day.

When choosing plants, select soft colours and shapes that mix harmoniously, but without appearing to be at

Below: Dainty scented geranium and trailing variegated ground ivy, verbena and petunias are combined to create the archetypal country-style window box.

all contrived. Very solid, bold or acidic colours suggest flowers from exotic parts of the world and would not work in a cottage setting.

Containers

To reinforce the country theme, use containers that look country-made or rustic. Appropriate materials are basketweave, bark, logs or rough wood. Simple terracotta would also look the part, as long as it is plain and without classical decoration. Discarded containers such as old metal baths, which have a rural look, may also be suitable.

Above: The sunny flowers of Nemesia, *pot marigolds and nasturtiums mingle chaotically with the cool, soft green* Helichrysum petiolare *and blue-green nasturtium leaves.*

Colour Combinations

Whilst colours can be bright and mixed in a country garden, some combinations produce a more successful effect than others.

Frothy pinks and mauves with hazy purples and soft blues combine well together, especially when mixed with a hint of white. Pastel yellow with white is also effective. For louder associations, orange and green is a good combination.

Maintaining Interest

Many traditional plants have short flowering periods, so it is wise to plant boxes with this in mind. You can aim for continued interest, or consider replanting during the summer season with a different selection.

COUNTRY-STYLE PLANTS

Aster
Calendula
Dianthus
Iberis
Nasturtium
Nemesia
Osteospermum
Pelargonium
Verbena
Viola

Dianthus, violas and candytuft are delightful traditional plants, which together make a pretty, pink-themed display during late spring and early summer. The candytuft will peak first, and when they have all finished flowering they can be replaced with summer favourites such as nemesia, pot marigolds and nasturtiums in fiery oranges and yellows.

Above: *Violas and* Dianthus *put on a pretty show for early summer; the candytuft has already peaked. They will soon all be replaced with later summer flowers.*

Knowing Your Style

CLASSIC STYLE

Window boxes planted in a classic style are contrived and often formal in their arrangement. Colours are tasteful and carefully co-ordinated, and the structure of the planting is planned. These smart, tidy containers would complement elegant period houses and modern ones built and decorated in a fairly classical style.

The plants' bearing also needs to be quite formal. Loose, frilly plants with gaudy flowers and untidy habits will not do. Dwarf conifers, tiny compact foliage plants like hebes and topiarized box are all good candidates. Ivy can be trained into interesting shapes. Elegant flowers with stiff stems and dignified blooms such as lilies all add to the effect.

Containers

The right style of window box will reinforce the rather formal effect: terracotta window boxes with classical motifs, smartly painted wooden containers with clean lines, and classical stone containers are all suitable. Plastic containers can be painted in an appropriate colour to disguise their material and tone in with the décor and planting scheme.

Above: *The plants selected for this classic-style container have been arranged carefully to create a symmetrical and pleasing effect in tones and forms.*

Colour Combinations

Classic style says sophistication. Many arrangements are centred on permanent evergreen foliage plantings, where splashes of strong, bright seasonal colour are important. For arrangements that depend more on seasonal plants, colour combinations must be carefully considered. Blue is a cool colour and mixed with pinks creates a calm atmosphere. Yellow and blue are a classic colour combination. Blues set against silver or grey foliage create an interesting effect that is distinct yet soft. White is associated with purity, peace and tranquillity, and white flowers add sophistication to a scheme, especially if mixed with green and silver foliage. Cream introduces a sense of luxury.

Maintaining Interest

There are plenty of bulbs to add elegant shapes and colours to formal boxes throughout the year. These can be used in arrangements on their own or combined with more permanent structural plantings. Crocuses, snowdrops, early irises, hyacinths and tulips will see the window box from winter through spring, while nerines and colchicums are useful for autumn. Alliums provide a range of fascinating summer flowers, and some short-growing lilies are also useful such as *Lilium* 'Côte d'Azur' and *L. mackliniae*. Many will require an acid compost (soil mix), for example the beautiful

Below: The stunning orange blooms of stately lilies add a touch of elegance to a formal window display.

Lilium formosanum var. *pricei* which is white, strongly flushed with purple and grows to 10–30cm (4–12in) high.

Small bulbs can be left in the container all year round, to re-emerge when their season is due; larger ones such as narcissi and tulips benefit from being lifted and stored elsewhere through their dormant season.

For summer, fuchsias provide a spectacular, long-lasting display and any of the neat, compact bedding plants can be used as formal edging.

CLASSIC-STYLE PLANTS

Allium
Buxus
Colchicum
Crocus
Dwarf conifers
Fuchsia
Galanthus nivalis
Hedera helix
Iris reticulata
Lilium formosanum var. *pricei*
Nerine bowdenii

Left: Dwarf sunflowers (Helianthus annuus) *grow very well in small pots. Start them from seed sown in spring.*

inside the roll within the container and drape the strands over the branches to create a gothic arrangement.

Some of the intriguing-looking plants may be frost tender, in which case the container will have to be moved to a conservatory or frost-free greenhouse for winter in certain areas.

Containers

Choose containers that will work with the plants, complementing their unusual appearance. Weathered terracotta is ideal for succulents, perhaps because it is suggestive of the parched environment they originate from. A mulch of small pebbles completes the effect.

MODERN STYLE

Window boxes in a modern style are planted unconventionally, and are eye-catching and interesting, or fun. The plants are chosen for their architectural or dramatic appearance, with unusual shapes, foliage or colour. Succulents, which come in a vast array of shapes and textures, are appropriate for this image. Grasses have fine, graceful leaves and fronds with the added advantage that they move and shimmer in a breeze. Flowers are less of a key feature and, if included, need to be striking in appearance or employed in an unusual way.

Simplicity is often the essence of modern planting. For example, twisted willow branches pushed into a deep container offer an attractive support for ivy. Simply insert a roll of chicken wire into the container to hold the branches upright. Place a pot of ivy

Above: A well-matched combination of container and contents will give you the best effect.

Left: A contemporary planting of architectural grasses, miniature hebe and fragrant, yellow-flowered santolina in a metal container would suit a modern setting.

Year-round Interest

Plants with architectural interest are often best grown in isolation, so the full impact of their outline can be appreciated. There are occasions, though, when combinations can work; the rounded leaves of sedums, for example, make a contrast with the spikes of cordyline and agaves, as well as the toothed edges of the latter. You can also use variegated or coloured leaves to increase the foliage interest.

Underplantings for architectural plants can be either long term or seasonal. Bold foliage could be softened by the addition of some daisy flowers such as *Argyranthemum frutescens*, and *Pelargonium* or *Impatiens*, which

would also add summer interest. The felted leaves of trailing *Helichrysum petiolare* would have a similar softening effect that lasts all year.

Planting Partners

Small trees grown as standards with rounded heads always look dramatic. These can be planted in a container at ground level near a window so that the foliage is at eye level. Small camellias, bays or even *Elaeagnus pungens* 'Maculata' look good when sympathetically underplanted. Try jaunty *Narcissus* 'Tête à Tête' for spring, and colourful fuchsias or *Impatiens* for the summer. Pansies would work for winter or summer, while periwinkle cascading over the side of the box would look smart all year round with the bonus of blue flowers during summer.

A row of the same plants is another way of making a strong statement. Dwarf conifers or tiny topiary, shaped into pyramids or globes from box, bay or holly, will carry a lot of impact.

MODERN-STYLE PLANTS

Aloe
Cordyline
Crassula
Echeveria
Hakonechloa
Sansevieria

555

against whitewashed or coloured walls where the hot summer sun will shine on them.

Cacti and succulents can also be used in window containers to create a hot, dry planting effect. They dislike wet conditions, so extra care must be taken at preparation to provide good drainage, and some will need protection from cold in temperate areas.

HOT AND EXOTIC STYLE

Arid area plants with hot flower colours and small, tough, drought-resistant leaves, which are often also silvery or spiny, suit the hot and exotic style. Many of them originate from the Mediterranean area where they have adapted to the intense heat. They will really look the part if you place them

HOT AND EXOTIC STYLE PLANTS

Crassula
Dorotheanus
Gazania
Kalanchoe
Lampranthus
Lavandula
Pelargonium (geranium)
Portulaca
Rosmarinus, prostrate
Thymus

Containers

Terracotta is the obvious choice for this style of planting. It is ubiquitous in the Mediterranean region and often painted with bold designs in bright, vibrant colours.

Above: These brightly coloured, hand-marbled terracotta pots make exciting exotic-style containers which set off simple foliage plants.

Colour Combinations

The tough silvery-greys or dull greens of many Mediterranean plants blend naturally with flowers in shades of purple, purplish-blue and pink. Lavender, thyme, rosemary and sage are typical warm-climate foliage plants with beautiful summer flowers in these warm shades. Some sages have purple or variegated foliage.

Hotter red and orange flowers combine more readily with green foliage. Red geraniums *(Pelargonium)*, orange marigolds *(Calendula)*, and bright yellow *Portulaca* will bloom freely in sunny spots, as will *Potentilla eriocarpa*, producing yellow flowers throughout the summer.

The flowers of cacti and succulents are usually startlingly vivid in colour, emerging from tough, leathery plants, which in the case of cacti are covered with spines. When combining these plants, group those requiring similar conditions together and protect them from cold if necessary.

Maintaining Interest

Many of the plants you can use have attractive long-term foliage, which is useful for a permanent display. The flowers may be brief, however, and to maintain flower colour you will have to supplement it. Alliums are useful for additional summer colour, and you can use ornamental garlics to continue the hot-climate look. For hotter colours, *Dorotheanus* will flower all summer long in shades of crimson, red, orange-gold, yellow and white.

Above *Arrange cacti sparsely to emulate a hot, dry landscape. A top dressing of gravel adds to the sense of aridity.*

557

Satisfying the Senses

WINDOW BOXES APPEAL TO OUR SENSES IN MORE THAN ONE WAY.
THEY SHOULD ALWAYS BE VISUAL FEASTS, BUT CAN ALSO BE USED TO
SATISFY OUR SENSE OF TOUCH, TASTE AND SMELL BY INCLUDING
TEXTURED, SCENTED AND EVEN EDIBLE PLANTS.

USING COLOUR

How you use colour in a window box
will depend on what you want to
achieve. You can create a carefully
co-ordinated planting or make a brash
statement. You can plant in a single
colour or use several together to create
a witty image.

Your use of colour will influence
the mood of the planting. Hot colours
introduce excitement into a planting.
Intense blues will cool things down.
White imparts a sense of purity and
tranquillity. Pastels introduce a
romantic tone.

When planning your window boxes
remember that light affects colours.
Strong, hot colours, especially red,
work better in strong light, as does
variegated foliage. Pastels become
bleached out in strong
light and respond better
to shade.

*Above: Make a bold
statement with flame-
coloured flowers in an
area with plenty of light.*

*Left: A well-filled con-
tainer of large white
geraniums* (Pelargonium)*,
verbenas, marguerites*
(Argyranthemum) *and
white-flowered* Bacopa*,
with silver-leaved* Senecio*,
is a joy to the eye as well
as deliciously fragrant.*

GARDENER'S TIP
Try to position blue flowers
where they can be seen at dusk,
when their colours become far
more intense and are a treat not
to be missed.

Colour Combinations

Not all colours mix well and it is
usually best to place plant colours that
harmonize next to each other. White
and blue seem to work with almost
any other colour, and pastels are easy
to arrange together. The ones to be
careful of are brilliant oranges with
strong magenta.

Above: White-flowering tobaccos
(Nicotiana), *pink* Impatiens *and tumbling,
white, variegated geranium* (Pelargonium)
*and lobelia have been planted to create a
visually satisfying linear effect.*

*Above: Shocking pink petunias and verbenas dominate this container, which also
features softer pink marguerites to delight the eye. The silver-leaved* Stachys byzantina *are
a perfect colour foil as well as being delightful to touch.*

Satisfying the Senses

USING FOLIAGE FOR VISUAL IMPACT
With its variety of shapes and colours, foliage is an essential element of garden design, whether in the garden flower beds or in a window box. Foliage comes in a vast number of colours and shades, including white, cream, gold, silver, red and purple. It is possible to create window boxes using only foliage plants, either with contrasting colours or within a narrow range. For example, you could use only foliage with yellow or golden tinges, but with plenty of variation in shape, and perhaps set off by a plant with darker green leaves. Also leaf colours change through the year. Variegated hosta leaves can deepen in colour as the year progresses.

> COLOURFUL FOLIAGE
>
> *Begonia rex*
> (red, black or silver variegations)
> *Coleus blumei*
> (multi-coloured leaves)
> *Hedera helix* (variegated)
> *Helichrysum petiolare* (silver)
> *Ophiopogon* (black)
> *Pelargonium* (variegated)
> *Senecio* (silver)

Blending Foliage with Flowers

More commonly, though, foliage is regarded as a part of a planting that features flowers, and the type of foliage can be chosen specifically for its ability to work well with certain flower colours. Dark green works well with strong hot colours. Soft greens and silver suit cool blues and pinks.

Above: *The intense purple of this heliotrope is teamed with a purple-leaved dahlia with dark red flowers and purple- and red-flowered trailing verbenas.*

560

Maintaining Colour

To sustain a colourful display over a whole season, use evergreen foliage plants for the basis of the planting. You can team them with plants that have a long flowering season, or keep a colour scheme going by replacing fading plants with different ones in the similar colours.

For spring, a succession of bulbs with polyanthus and pansies provide good value. For summer, annuals and bedding plants provide the bulk of bright colour; ageratum, sweet alyssum, antirrhinums, flowering begonias, marigolds, and *Impatiens* are all excellent. Geraniums (*Pelargonium*) also give some spectacular displays. The many varieties of compact and trailing

Above: The blue-green leaves of the nasturtium contrast dramatically with the bronze leaves of Fuchsia fulgens 'Thalia'.

fuchsias produce their elegant flowers over a long period, and combine well with petunias and lobelias, also reliable performers. Remember to deadhead flowers regularly to maintain a constant supply of fresh buds.

Above: Fuchsia has a long flowering period and is used here to striking effect with vibrant crimson and purple petunias.

561

Satisfying the Senses

SCENT

Fragrant flowers or aromatic herbs in a window box will scent the air as it wafts in through an open window. Choose the type of fragrance to complement the use of the room. A bedroom window box will allow you to wake up to sweet-smelling flowers on summer mornings, but take care as anything too heady can be overpowering and even interrupt sleep. For a kitchen window the aroma of fresh herbs would be more suitable.

> **GARDENER'S TIP**
> During the summer, pick and dry the leaves of scented geraniums for use in pot-pourri or in muslin bags to scent linen.

Plants with fragrant foliage release their scents more readily when they are bruised. Site these where they will be brushed against. Scented geraniums *(Pelargonium)* have an incredible diversity of scents: lemon, spice and peppermint. They need to be overwintered in a greenhouse in frost areas.

Above: *A selection of scented geraniums* (Pelargonium fragrans) *will release their delicious fragrance when you brush against their leaves.*

Additional Benefits

Many plants have healing qualities and, while they should not be used to treat a health condition without first checking with your medical practitioner, some have provided successful country remedies for centuries. Lavender soothes headaches and rosemary is a general pick-me-up. Camomile is used in herbal teas and feverfew is said to alleviate migraines. If you have a problem that can be relieved by a simple remedy, why not grow the herb on a windowsill for a ready supply?

Some herbs can be used to repel insects. Pennyroyal rubbed around an area will deter ants, and black basil keeps flies at bay. Conversely, some sweet-smelling flowers are irresistible to butterflies, especially ice plants, which flower in autumn.

Above: *The leaves of lemon verbena, a deciduous shrub, have a powerful scent. Here they are combined with scented geranium* (Pelargonium).

SCENTED PLANTS

AROMATIC
Calendula
Mentha x gracilis 'Variegata'
Nasturtium
Origanum onites
Origanum vulgare
Pelargonium, scented
Thymus

SWEET
Lavandula
Pelargonium, scented
Petunia
Verbena

Left: *The scented flowers of many herbs, including marjoram and thyme, are irresistible to butterflies.*

TASTE

Nothing tastes as good as freshly picked vegetables, fruit or herbs, and window boxes can be used for growing many of these as well as edible flowers. Containers are perfect for anyone who likes the taste of home-grown food but does not have a garden to grow it in.

Decide on your priorities and how practical it will be to grow the crops you are interested in. A sunny position is best for vegetables, fruit and herbs; choose a sill sheltered from wind for vegetables. You will be limited to vegetables with fibrous or shallow roots, but it makes sense to grow items that cost a lot in the shops or taste many times better when they are freshly picked. Or perhaps you are interested

in growing something that is difficult to buy. If you want to include flowers in your cooking, it will be virtually impossible to buy them from a shop. A fresh source close at hand will be a real advantage.

If you place your edible window box at a kitchen window, it will be convenient to harvest your crops as and when you need them. And you will be able to inspect them daily, which will allow you to take action against any pests or diseases that may attack.

If you sow seed directly into a container on a sill, you may need to give protection to tender seedlings.

Below: An old fruit box filled with herbs is both pretty and useful. It has been colour-washed to tone with the herbs.

Maintaining a Supply of Edible Plants

Once you have decided which food, herbs or flowers you want to grow, you can start sowing seed or buying small plants. Make sure you buy and sow the seeds in good time. With salad crops, such as lettuces, radishes and spring onions, you can sow every few weeks to ensure a regular supply. Vegetables can also be started in pots so that as you harvest one plant another strongly growing one will be ready to replace it in the window box. If you want to grow herbs, make sure you have plenty of those you use often so that you do not run out.

Above: Fresh herbs cram a terracotta window box. Regular cutting of the plants will encourage plenty of new growth.

Make your food or herb window box attractive; there is no reason why the container should not be prettily planted, and, to make it perfect, it can include some fragrant flowers.

Below: You may be surprised to find how many different vegetables can be grown in a small space.

Herb Window Box

Fresh herbs make a huge difference to the taste of food, so it is always useful to have plenty growing close to hand, and a kitchen windowsill is especially convenient. You can grow virtually any herb in a container, but some do grow rather bushy and they will need to be cut frequently to keep them compact. Concentrate on growing those herbs that you tend to use most of in your cooking. There is no reason, however, why you should not also grow some others simply for the pleasure of their fragrance and appearance.

GARDENER'S TIP

Herbs are at their most flavoursome and aromatic before they flower, so as soon as the plants are well established you can start picking them for use in the kitchen.

Some herbs are available in attractively coloured varieties. Sage, mint and thyme all have variegated versions, and sage can also be purple.

Herbs can also be grown in individual pots placed on the windowsill. This is especially useful for mint, which has very invasive roots, and for any that need to be overwintered indoors.

Sun and Shade

The amount of sun your windowsill receives during the day will determine what type of herbs you can grow there successfully. The Mediterranean herbs especially are sun loving. Rosemary, sage, marjoram and thyme will thrive on a hot sill. Soft leafy herbs often prefer a cooler, shady situation to look and taste their best. Mint requires moist roots, and a pot could share a shady sill with sorrel, chives, lemon balm and parsley.

Left: This window box is packed with fresh culinary herbs. It contains chervil, coriander, fennel, garlic, purple sage, French tarragon, savory and basil. All these edible herbs can be successfully grown on a warm, sunny windowsill.

Vegetable and Salad Window Boxes

Most types of vegetable can be grown in a window box, but shallow-rooted, compact and quick-maturing types are most suitable, given the limited space. Many crops also look decorative. A window box is beneficial to tender plants as the house walls provide some warmth and shelter.

Compact but heavy-fruiting tomato plants have been specially bred for growing in containers and you can try these in a window box in full sun. Team them up with other salad vegetables and/or herbs such as compact lettuce, chives and parsley. Tomatoes are thirsty plants and need to be kept moist. Feed them with a proprietary tomato food.

If you have a very sheltered and sunny windowsill, consider growing (bell) peppers, chillies and small-

VEGETABLES FOR WINDOW BOXES
Carrot
Beetroot (Beets)
Dwarf French beans
Garlic
Lettuce
(Bell) Pepper
Radish
Shallot
Spring onion (scallion)
Tomato

fruited aubergines (eggplants). You can also grow dwarf beans, beetroots (beets) and stump-rooted carrots.

As space in the window box is rather cramped, it is a good idea to sow vegetable seeds elsewhere and transplant seedlings as they are ready, except for those vegetables that are best sown in situ.

Below: This salad window box contains compact tomatoes, lettuces, radishes, chives and parsley.

567

Fruit Window Boxes

Some apples, lemons and peaches can be successfully grown in deep containers. Standard gooseberries and redcurrants also grow well in containers and look highly decorative when they are fruiting. These can be sited close to a window where they will be enjoyed. For most window boxes, however, strawberries are the only realistic choice. They grow happily in containers and make good ornamental plants with their interesting leaves and colourful fruit.

Ordinary strawberries need plenty of sun to ripen, but the much smaller alpine strawberries can produce delicious fruit in light shade. These alpine types also make good edge planting in window boxes.

There are some very heavy cropping types, and you can buy varieties to fruit at different times to extend the season. Some even produce a second crop in the autumn. Generous and regular watering when the fruits are ripening will increase a plant's yield. To ensure a good crop next year, cut the leaves of large strawberries right back after fruiting.

Above: *A window box combination of strawberries, ivy and herbs planted in an agricultural metal basket.*

Above: *Strawberries can be successfully grown in window boxes in full sun. They look decorative as well as having a finer taste than shop-bought ones.*

Edible Flowers

In addition to herbs, some garden flowers are edible and make unusual but pretty additions to salads and drinks or can be used to garnish other dishes. Edible flowers can also be frozen with ice cubes.

In the kitchen, flowers can be used to colour butter and to scent oil, vinegar and sugar. With the addition of egg white and sugar they are transformed into crystallized flowers, which can grace cakes, cookies, mousses and sweet or savoury roulades.

To keep the plants producing flowers for as long as possible, deadhead regularly. Once a plant has set seed, it will produce fewer and fewer flowers. Wash them before use.

Use nasturtium flowers in salads; they not only look spectacular but also add a lovely peppery flavour. Chive

EDIBLE FLOWERS
Calendula
Chive
Courgette (zucchini)
Daisy
Lavandula
Lemon verbena
Nasturtium
Pansy
Rose
Sweet violet

and thyme flowers also make attractive additions to salads. Rose petals and violets make delightful crystallized cake decorations, and lavender can be used in desserts or with chicken cooked on a barbecue.

Below: Nasturtium, pansies, chives and marigolds (Calendula) *fill this window box, making a decorative display of edible flowers. They can be used in sweet and savoury dishes.*

Seasonal Tasks

KNOWING WHAT TO DO WHEN IS PART OF THE SECRET OF SUCCESSFUL
WINDOW BOX DISPLAYS. THIS QUICK GUIDE SUMMARIZES THE IMPOR-
TANT TASKS ACCORDING TO SEASON. THE JOBS HAVE BEEN LISTED IN
THE ORDER THEY GENERALLY WOULD NEED TO BE DONE.

SPRING

Early Spring
- plant herbs in containers for permanent display
- plant strawberries in containers for summer display
- plant edible flower plants in containers for summer display
- sow seed for vegetables under protection

Mid-spring
- plant herbs in containers for permanent display
- plant edible flower plants in containers for summer display
- plant ferns for spring and summer display
- sow seed for vegetables under protection
- sow seed for sunflowers

Auricula

Late Spring
- sow seed of biennial bedding (polyanthus, wallflowers etc)
  in seed beds or trays for display next spring
- start overwintered dahlia tubers into growth and plant out in
  containers when all danger of frost is past
- sow nasturtium seeds, about 4 to 6 weeks before you plant
  your window box
- feed ferns
- lift tulips after flowering and hang to dry in a cool, airy place
- plant containers for summer display
- plant succulents for summer display
- plant overwintered geraniums (*Pelargonium*) in containers for
  summer display
- plant herbs in containers for permanent display
- plant vegetables in containers for summer display
- sow seed for vegetables outdoors

Tulip

SUMMER

Early Summer
- sow seed of biennial bedding (polyanthus, wallflowers etc) in seed beds
  or trays for next spring
- sow seed of forget-me-nots outdoors
- sow seed of daisies outdoors
- plant containers for summer display
- plant succulents for summer display
- plant overwintered geraniums (*Pelargonium*) in
  containers for summer display
- plant chrysanthemums and marguerites in containers for summer display.
  Place in a bright, sheltered position
- plant sunflower seedlings for late-summer display

Geranium

- pinch out shoots of chrysanthemums, marguerites and *Osteospermum* to encourage bushy plants
- deadhead bedding plants regularly to ensure new buds develop

Midsummer
- feed greedy plants like geraniums an occasional foliar feed
- cut back lavender heads after flowering
- deadhead bedding plants regularly to ensure new buds develop

Late Summer
- pot up geraniums (*Pelargonium*) and overwinter indoors. Reduce height of each plant by at least half and it will soon send out new shoots
- trim flower stems of perennial plants like *Dianthus* and overwinter in situ
- pot up *Scaevola* and *Convolvulus* and overwinter on an indoor windowsill or in a frost-free greenhouse. Cut plants right back
- pot up *Gazania* and *Osteospermum* and overwinter fairly dry in a frost-free place ready for planting out in the garden in spring
- plant bulbs for spring display
- plant biennial bedding plants in containers for spring display (raised from seed sown during previous year)
- plant bulbs for autumn display

Gazania

AUTUMN

Early Autumn
- plant bulbs for spring display
- plant biennial bedding plants in containers for spring display (raised from seed sown during previous year)
- plant heathers for autumn display
- buy polyanthus and winter-flowering pansies and plant in containers for winter display
- buy wallflowers and forget-me-nots and plant in containers for spring display
- buy daisies (*Bellis perennis*) and plant in containers for spring display

Crocus

Mid-autumn
- plant bulbs for spring display

Late Autumn
- lift tender fuchsias and overwinter on an indoor windowsill or in a heated greenhouse. Cut back by half.
- pot up *Campanula* and overwinter in a frost-free greenhouse. Cut back
- dig up dahlia tubers after first frosts, cut stems back to 15cm (6in), dry off then overwinter in slightly damp peat in a frost-free shed
- cut back all fern foliage when it begins to die back. Add a fresh layer of bark to protect plants
- move tender succulents indoors for the winter
- plant winter heathers for winter display
- plant tulip bulbs for spring display

Petunia

WINTER

- protect vulnerable shoots from frost as necessary
- move frost-vulnerable terracotta containers indoors
- protect taller plants from strong winds
- select seeds from seed catalogues and order for next spring

Ivy

Best Window Box Plants

THIS QUICK REFERENCE CHART CAN BE USED TO SELECT THE MOST SUITABLE PLANTS FOR YOUR WINDOW BOXES IN TERMS OF THEIR REQUIREMENTS AND SEASON OF INTEREST.

PLANT	COMPOST (SOIL MIX)	WHEN IN FLOWER
Ageratum (FS)	standard, moist	midsummer to first frost
Allium sativum (H) (FS)	standard	year-round foliage
Allium schoenoprasum (H) (PS)	standard	summer*
Aloe (t) (FS)	standard	year-round foliage
Aloysa triphylla (fh) (FS)	standard, dryish	late summer*
Anagallis (t) (FS)	standard, moist	summer
Antirrhinum (hh) (FS)	standard, moist	summer into autumn
Arabis caucasica (FS)	standard	late spring
Argyranthemum (hh) (FS)	standard	late spring to early autumn
Argyranthemum frutescens (hh) (FS)	standard	summer
Armeria (FS)	standard	late spring, summer
Arundinaria pygmaea (FS)	standard, moist	year-round foliage
Aster novae-angliae (PS)	standard, moist	late summer to early autumn
Aster novi-belgii (PS)	standard, moist	late summer to mid-autumn
Aubrieta (FS)	neutral, alkaline	spring
Bacopa (syn. *Sutera*) (t) (FS)	standard	summer to autumn
Begonia rex (t) (PS)	neutral, slightly acid	year-round foliage
Bellis perennis (PS)	standard	winter and spring*
Bergenia (PS)	standard	spring/year-round foliage
Bidens (t) (FS)	standard	midsummer to autumn
Borago officinalis (H) (PS)	standard	summer*
Brachyscome (hh) (FS)	standard	summer
Buxus (some fh) (PS)	standard	year-round foliage
Calendula (PS)	standard	summer to early winter*
Calluna vulgaris (FS)	acid/ericaceous	midsummer to late autumn
Camellia (some t) (PS)	acid/ericaceous	winter or spring
Campanula carpatica (PS)	standard, moist	summer
Campanula isophylla (PS)	standard, moist	summer
Chamaecyparis, dwarf cultivars (S)	neutral, slightly acid	year-round foliage

Argyranthemum

Calendula

Calluna

572

PLANT	COMPOST (SOIL MIX)	WHEN IN FLOWER
Chlorophytum (t) (PS)	standard	year-round foliage
Chrysanthemum (some hh) (FS)	standard	autumn
Colchicum autumnale (FS)	standard	autumn
Coleus blumei (t) (PS)	standard	year-round foliage
Convallaria majalis (FS)	standard, moist	late spring
Convolvulus sabatius (fh) (FS)	gritty	summer to early autumn
Cordyline (t to hh) (PS)	standard	year-round foliage
Cotoneaster conspicuus (FS)	standard	berries autumn into winter
Crassula (t to hh) (FS)	gritty	year-round foliage
Crocosmia (some fh) (PS)	standard, moist	mid- to late summer
Crocus (FS)	gritty	spring
Crocus nudiflorus (fs) (FH)	standard	autumn
Cyclamen (PS)	standard	autumn, winter or early spring
Dianthus (FS)	neutral, alkaline	early summer to autumn
Echeveria (t) (FS)	standard	year-round foliage
Eranthis hyemalis (DS)	standard	late winter to early spring
Erica carnea (FS)	acid, slightly alkaline	winter to mid-spring
Erisymum cheiri (FS)	alkaline, neutral	spring
Euonymus fortunei (PS)	standard	year-round foliage
Felicia amelloides (t) (FS)	standard	summer to autumn
Ferns (S)	standard	spring to autumn foliage
Foeniculum vulgare (H) (FS)	standard, moist	spring to autumn foliage
Fuchsia (hardy to t) (PS)	standard, moist	summer to autumn
Galanthus nivalis (PS)	standard	late winter
Gazania (t to hh) (FS)	gritty	summer
Gaultheria procumbens (PS)	standard, moist	summer/fruit autumn to spring
Grasses (PS)	standard, moist	year-round foliage
Hakonechloa (PS)	standard, moist	year-round foliage
Hebe, dwarf cultivars (PS)	standard	summer, year-round foliage
Hedera helix (PS)	preferably alkaline	year-round foliage
Helianthus annuus (FS)	neutral, alkaline	summer
Helichrysum petiolare (hh) (FS)	neutral, alkaline	year-round foliage
Heliotropium (hh) (FS)	standard, moist	summer
Heuchera micrantha (FS, PS)	standard	year-round foliage
Hosta (PS)	standard, moist	year-round foliage

Convallaria

Fuchsia

Hedera

Hosta

PLANT	COMPOST (SOIL MIX)	WHEN IN FLOWER
Hyacinthoides (DS)	standard, moist	spring
Hyacinthus (PS)	standard	spring
Iberis (FS)	moist, neutral, alkaline	summer
Impatiens New Guinea Group (S)	standard, moist	summer to autumn
Kalanchoe (t) (PS)	standard	late winter, spring or summer
Lampranthus (t) (FS)	standard	summer to early autumn
Lavandula (some hh) (FS)	standard	summer*
Lilium (FS) (fh, hh)	acid, neutral	summer
Lobelia erinus (t) (PS)	standard, moist	summer to autumn
Lobularia maritima (FS)	standard	summer, early autumn
Lysimachia nummularia (PS)	standard, moist	summer
Melissa officinalis (H) (PS)	standard	summer*
Mentha (H) (PS)	standard, moist	summer*
Muscari armeniacum (FS)	standard, moist	spring
Myosotis (PS)	standard, moist	spring to early summer
Narcissus (DS)	standard, moist when growing	spring
Nemesia (fh to hh) (FS)	moist slightly acid	summer
Nepeta mussinii (PS)	standard	summer
Nerine (some hh) (FS)	standard, moist when growing	autumn
Nicotiana (t) (PS)	standard, moist	summer, autumn
Ocimum basilicum (t) (H) (FS)	standard	summer foliage
Ophiopogon 'Nigrescens' (PS)	slightly acid	year-round foliage
Origanum majorana (H) (fh) (FS)	preferably alkaline	summer*
Origanum onites (H) (fh) (FS)	preferably alkaline	late summer*
Origanum vulgare (H) (FS)	preferably alkaline	midsummer, early autumn*
Osteospermum (t to hh) (FS)	standard	late spring to autumn
Pelargonium (t) (FS)	neutral, alkaline	spring to summer
Petroselinum crispum (H) (PS)	standard, moist	summer
Petunia (hh) (FS)	standard	late spring to late autumn
Phlox (FS, PS)	standard	summer
Portulaca (t to hh) (FS)	standard, dryish	summer
Primula Auricula (PS)	standard, moist	spring
Primula Polyanthus Group (PS)	standard, moist	late winter to mid-spring
Primula vulgaris (PS)	standard, moist	early to late spring

Lobelia

Narcissus

Osteospermum

PLANT	COMPOST (SOIL MIX)	WHEN IN FLOWER
Rosmarinus officinalis (H) (fh) (FS)	standard	mid-spring, early summer
Salvia officinalis (H)	standard	early and midsummer*
Salvia splendens (t) (PS)	standard, moist	summer to autumn
Sansevieria (t) (FS)	neutral, slightly alkaline	year-round foliage
Saxifraga (some fh or hh) (some FS, some PS)	neutral, alkaline; some gritty, some moist	spring, summer
Scaevola (t) (DS)	standard, moist	summer
Schizostylis (FS)	standard, moist	late summer, early winter
Sedum (some fh or t) (FS)	neutral, slightly alkaline	summer, early autumn
Sempervivum (FS)	gritty	year-round foliage
Senecio cineraria (fh) (FS)	standard	year-round foliage
Skimmia reevesiana (S)	moist	autumn and winter buds
Solanum pseudocapsicum (t) (FS)	neutral, slightly alkaline	winter berries
Solenopsis (syn. *Isotoma*) (t) (FS)	standard	spring to late autumn
Sternbergia (fh) (FS)	standard	autumn, winter
Tagetes (hh) (FS)	standard	late spring to early autumn
Thuja, dwarf cultivars (FS)	standard, moist	year-round foliage
Thymus vulgaris (H) (FS)	neutral, alkaline	spring, early summer*
Tradescantia (t) (PS)	standard, moist	year-round foliage
Tropaeolum majus (FS)	standard or gritty	summer to autumn*
Tulipa (FS)	standard	mid- to late spring
Verbena x *hybrida* (t) (FS)	loam-based with sand	summer, autumn
Vinca minor (FS)	standard, moist	mid-spring to mid-autumn
Viola x *wittrockiana* cultivars (PS)	standard	spring to summer or autumn to winter

Vinca minor

Viola

KEY

(t) = tender: need minimum 5°C (41F°); they need to be overwintered indoors or in a cool or temperate greenhouse

(hh) = are half hardy and can withstand temperatures down to 0°C (32°F)

(fh) = are frost hardy down to −5°C (23°F)

Unmarked plants are fully hardy

* = edible flowers

(H) = herbs, grown mainly for their leaves

(FS) = full sun

(PS) = partial shade

(DS) = dappled shade

(S) = shade

INDOOR
PLANTS

There is a vast choice of houseplants
available, ranging from easily cared-
for favourites to demanding and
unusual exotics, but any selection
must depend on how hot or cool you
like to keep your rooms and how dry
or humid the atmosphere. This
chapter contains all you need to know
about basic care and dealing with
common problems, to help you grow a
stunning collection of plants to
beautify your home.

Living with Houseplants

HOUSEPLANTS CAN INSTANTLY CHANGE THE ATMOSPHERE OF ANY ROOM IN YOUR HOME, BRINGING THE BEAUTY OF LIVING NATURE INTO YOUR EVERYDAY SURROUNDINGS. MOST REQUIRE VERY LITTLE EFFORT TO KEEP THEM PERFORMING WELL AND LOOKING GOOD FOR MANY YEARS.

Left: Given the right conditions plants will flourish in your home.

GROWING HOUSEPLANTS

Generally, most plants are easy to look after if they are provided with the right conditions, especially light, moisture and nutrition. If well tended they will look attractive, often varying their appearance with seasonal flowers or colourful bracts. Those plants that require exacting conditions not normally found in a home will be high maintenance, and could become a chore to look after, so you

Above: Pot plants in flower will add colour and warmth to a room.

may prefer to choose from the wide selection of plants that are easy to care for and require minimum attention.

Most indoor collections found in garden centres and florists consist of a combination of easy-care, long-lasting foliage plants and seasonal plants. Flowering pot plants are often regarded as short-term colour, more like long-lasting cut flowers, but with careful pruning, deadheading and feeding, some can be treated as perennials and will flower again the following year.

HUMIDITY

The amount of heat and light in your home is major consideration. The dry heat caused by central heating can be damaging. Tropical plants especially require moisture in the atmosphere. Fortunately, the majority of houseplants can survive in low levels of humidity, particularly in summer when windows are open. In winter, when heating is turned up, commercial room humidifiers will moisten the air, but a more economic solution would be to select plants that do not need very humid conditions.

Above: *Change the colour scheme of a room by introducing a bold group of plants.*

ACHIEVING DIFFERENT EFFECTS

Plants can entirely change the atmosphere of a room, or introduce a new mood or even colour scheme from season to season. Fragrant spring bulbs, pots of herbs, autumnal toned chrysanthemums or a bowl of brightly coloured cyclamen will all add to the mood of their particular time of year.

Some plants are better suited to certain types of interiors than others, and should be compatible in size and shape as well as colour. Small plants that complement fabrics and wallpapers work well with a traditional, cottagey décor. Stark modern interiors can take big, bold "architectural" plants. Be prepared to invest in one or two really good specimens if necessary because they have far more impact than half a dozen cheaper plants.

SHOPPING FOR HOUSEPLANTS

Plants are living, perishable things, and supplies often fluctuate widely according to season and what the commercial growers decide to market.

Whenever possible, buy where the plants are well cared for in surroundings conducive to good growth: warmth, freedom from icy blasts, high humidity (though this is not important for cacti and succulents), and a high level of diffused light or artificial lighting designed for plant growth. Wilting, diseased or dying plants should not be on display.

Look beneath the pot – some roots will have grown through if capillary matting has been used for watering, but masses of long roots indicate that the plant needs to be repotted. Always check the plant for signs of pests and diseases. Turn over one or two of the leaves – pests may be lurking out of sight.

With flowering plants, timing is everything. You may get several weeks of pleasure if you buy a plant just coming into flower rather than one that is already at its peak.

GARDENER'S TIP

Houseplants tend to grow slowly and are sold in a range of sizes. If a room requires a large plant, select one at the right height or slighter smaller than required. Otherwise, you could wait a long time for a small specimen to reach the necessary size.

Left: Mauve flowers look very effective against a light grey or pale blue wall.

Below: Plants benefit from being placed in strong but indirect light. It is a good idea to move them occasionally if light is low.

COLOUR

Houseplants come in every possible colour. Even foliage comes in many shades of green, in variegated forms, and with silver or bronze tints. Plants can be used to add colour or to complement different decorative schemes.

Heavy, dark green foliage, distinctive in itself, would dominate a softly toned wallpaper or delicate paint effect. Conversely, pale fern fronds or a pastel-and-white flowering plant would enhance a soft colour scheme. While most plants would complement pale plain-coloured walls,

placing foliage or flowering plants in front of a patterned wallpaper or furnishings, especially a floral design, could be problematic. If you have patterned paper or fabric, take a piece with you when you buy plants to help you select a complementary green.

SUN AND GOOD LIGHT

In a typical house it is usually difficult to give houseplants enough light for really healthy and even growth, yet ironically a position on a windowsill in full sun will probably injure or kill most of them. Sun through unshaded glass is much more intense than sun in the open – it acts like a magnifying glass and will often scorch vulnerable foliage. Although most plants will benefit from gentler early and late sun, when the intensity is not too great,

---

SUN-LOVING PLANTS

Ananas
Coleus
Pelargonium
Roses, miniature
Yucca elephantipes

PLANTS FOR SHADE

Asplenium nidus
Dracaena
Fatsia
Hedera helix
Philodendron

---

you need really tough sun-lovers to tolerate the hot midday sun intensified through glass.

Most cacti and succulents are ideal for a windowsill position. *Echinocactus, Ferocactus, Opuntia, Parodia* and *Rebutia* are all readily available.

Succulents such as *Lithops* and *Kalanchoe* are also excellent for hot windowsills. There is more variation in shape and growth habit among succulents than cacti, but if you want yet more variety there are other true sun-lovers you can try.

Some plants that benefit from softer winter sun may be harmed by the harsher summer sun that will scorch tender leaves.

SHADE

Plants that tolerate lower light levels are especially useful. They can be positioned by shady windows and within any room, perhaps on a table or sideboard, and still survive for a reasonable time. You can use any plant in these conditions, but after a while most will become sickly and deteriorate. You will then have to move them into better light or buy a new plant.

FOLIAGE

Purely foliage plants are anything but dull. Leaves come in a vast range of greens, many are variegated, some are more colourful than many flowers, and all last much longer. Many also have contrasting textures and shapes.

FOLIAGE PLANTS

Aglaonema hybrids
Asparagus densiflorus 'Sprengeri'
Begonia, foliage
Dracaena marginata
Fatsia japonica
Ficus benjamina 'Starlight'
Hedera helix, variegated
Monstera deliciosa
Philodendron scandens
Sansevieria trifasciata 'Laurentii'
Syngonium podophyllum
Yucca elephantipes

Plants grown for their leaves will form the backbone of most arrangements and groupings. They can also form a backdrop for flowers.

SHAPE

Interesting shape will compensate for any lack of colour in a leaf. Plants such as philodendrons and *Ficus benjamina* create as much interest as those with bright flowers or brilliant foliage, and they do it in a restrained way that creates the right mood for a room.

Above: *A selection of plants showing interesting foliage and texture.*

TEXTURE

Leaf texture adds variety. There are rough, hairy and puckered leaves, all of which can add extra interest and contrast to a group. Some demand to be touched, providing tactile as well as visual stimulation.

RELIABLE FLOWERING
PLANTS

Aechmea fasciata
Begonia, elatior type
Chrysanthemum
Clivia miniata
Exacum affine
Hydrangea
Jasminum polyanthum
Kalanchoe
Pelargonium, Regal
Primula obconica
Saintpaulia
Stephanotis floribunda
Tillandsia cynea
Vriesea

FLOWERING PLANTS

Houseplants with flowers are usually a little more difficult than foliage plants to keep long-term. However, they add brilliance and colour that even the boldest foliage plants find difficult to match, and some have the extra bonus of fragrance.

A few flowering plants are available throughout the year (chrysanthemums, kalanchoes and African violets are examples), but most flower in a particular season. This is no bad thing because it prevents your displays becoming predictable or boring. Some are annuals, or treated as annuals, and have to be discarded when flowering is over. These short-term flowering pot plants are especially useful for creating instant displays of stunning colour anywhere in the home. They also make it possible to continue a colour scheme throughout the year using different plants.

SCENT

Houseplants allow you to enjoy natural fragrances the year round. Sometimes a single, strongly scented plant is sufficient for an entire room. You will need several in succession, but this gives you the chance to enjoy different kinds of perfume over the seasons.

Above: Flowering houseplants may need more care, but they give so much pleasure with their colourful blooms and bright green foliage.

Above: A miniature rose provides both colour and fragrance.

For late winter and early spring there are numerous varieties of scented hyacinths and narcissi. During autumn, plant up individual pots with hyacinths every fortnight to give you fragrance in late winter.

In summer, many shrubs and plants provide scent. Aromatic pelargoniums (geraniums) start flowering in late spring and will continue into autumn, if placed on a sunny windowsill. You will need several together to make an impact, and grow them where you will brush their leaves as you pass.

Some lilies provide a concentrated perfume from late afternoon into the evening. Plant specially prepared bulbs at intervals during winter to provide scented blooms from summer into autumn.

How This Chapter Works

In this chapter you will find practical advice on choosing plants that will best suit you and your home. *Getting Started* describes the basic tools and equipment you will need for keeping houseplants, with information on the many kinds of containers available. *Caring for Houseplants* covers all the techniques needed for looking after them, including repotting and methods of propagation to increase your stock. *Troubleshooting* discusses common pests and diseases, together with other problems that can affect your plants, and suggests effective ways of dealing with them. Finally, a comprehensive *A–Z of Houseplants* describes a wide selection of recommended plants, giving details of the preferred conditions and care requirements in each case.

SCENTED PLANTS
Hoya bella
Gardenia jasminoides
Hyacinthus
Jasminum officinale
Lilium (oriental hybrids)
Narcissus
Stephanotis floribunda

Getting Started

ONCE YOU HAVE DECIDED WHICH PLANTS YOU WANT TO GROW, YOU
NEED TO STOCK UP ON BASIC TOOLS AND EQUIPMENT, INCLUDING THE
CORRECT SOIL FOR POTTING, AND TO CHOOSE THE APPROPRIATE
CONTAINERS TO DISPLAY YOUR PLANTS TO BEST ADVANTAGE.

TOOLS AND EQUIPMENT

You can look after your houseplants
without any special tools. However,
the right tools do make the jobs easier,
and usually more pleasant. The tools
described here won't cost much. Take
particular care over the choice of a
watering-can and a mister – both
should be in daily use, so don't skimp
on these.

Canes (stakes) – usually made from
bamboo, used for supporting plants.

Dibber – a tool used for making a hole
in potting soil.

Fertilizer – food for plants, which
comes in various forms.

Knife – useful for taking cuttings and
other indoor gardening tasks.

Leaf shines – products for putting a
shine on glossy leaves.

Leaf-wipes – tissue-type leaf shine.

Mister – a sprayer producing a fine
mist.

Insecticide – for pest control.

Insecticidal plant pins – insecticide-
impregnated strips to push into potting soil.

Raffia – a natural tying material.

Rooting hormone – stimulates root
formation on cuttings.

Scissors – useful for cutting ties and
deadheading.

Water indicator – indicates moisture
level in soil.

Watering-can, indoor – one with a
long, narrow spout for precision
watering.

Wire – plastic-coated to protect stems.

Mister · Various pots · Watering-can · Leaf-wipes · Water indicator · Raffia · Insecticide · Leaf shines · Plastic coated wire · Fertilizers · Insecticidal plant pin · Rooting hormone · Knife · Scissors · Dibber · Canes (stakes)

POTTING SOIL

Plants depend on an appropriate potting soil to provide vital nutrients essential for growth, and act as a reservoir for moisture.

Loam-based potting soil – heavy, but it may be the best choice for some plants. Tall or large plants that are top-heavy may benefit from the extra weight in the pot. Some plants,

Loam-based mix

including most succulents, benefit from the good drainage and reserve of nutrients provided by loam-based mix.

Peat-based (peat moss) mixtures – light and easy to handle, but usually require supplementary feeding after a month or so. They can dry out and become difficult to re-

Peat-based (peat-moss) mix

wet, and they are more easily overwatered. They can vary greatly in quality. Some gardeners are reluctant to use peat-based products on the grounds of depleting wetland areas. Alternative products are available, including mixes based on coir (waste from coconuts).

Orchid mixtures – are unlike any others that you will use. They are free-draining and contain no loam (soil). Bark is a common ingredient.

Orchid mixture

Cactus potting mix – very free-draining, and will contain plenty of grit or other material to ensure that the roots don't become waterlogged.

Ericaceous potting mix – for acid-loving, or lime-hating, plants such as azaleas.

Cactus mix

Lime or other alkaline materials are not used in the mixture, and the pH is more acidic than in normal soils.

Water-absorbing granules – sometimes used as an additive to potting soil. They swell when wet and hold many times their own weight of water. They can be useful if you are often away for a few days and find it difficult to water regularly.

Fine gravel – helps with drainage if mixed with the soil when potting up a plant, and can be used as an attractive mulch on the

Fine gravel

surface of the soil to prevent your plant drying out as quickly.

Choosing Pots and Containers

Pots and containers can form part of the room décor. The right container will enhance an attractive plant and can compensate for a mediocre one. Part of the fun of growing houseplants is displaying them with imagination. Many everyday items can be used.

The bigger the plant, the smaller the pot or container should be in relationship to it. Small, bushy plants look best in pots that are either roughly their size or slightly smaller. A tall plant, 25–60 cm (10–24 in) in height, looks best in a pot about a quarter of its height. The pot must also be sufficiently heavy to provide a solid base when the soil dries out, otherwise the plant might topple over.

Half pots, which stand about half the height of ordinary pots but have the same diameter, suit cacti which do not have a large root system, as well as azaleas.

Below: Many types of container are suitable for houseplants.

Galvanized Metal Containers and Cache-pots

These have a waterproof base and no drainage holes. They are useful for flowering plants that are on display for a short time only and for fast-growing plants that require frequent repotting.

You do need to be careful about watering. Make sure that the plant pot is easily lifted out for watering or place on a bed of crocks or stones.

Glass

These containers allow for imaginative presentation. You can surround the plant pot with visually attractive material such as coloured stones, marbles, sand or a thick layer of moss or pine cones.

Planters and Self-watering Containers

Large containers are ideal for displaying a group of plants. Some planters are self-watering with a reservoir at the

Glazed ceramic

Terracotta

Planters

bottom, which means you can leave several days between watering. Plants generally thrive in these.

BASKETS

Many plants look especially attractive in wicker, moss-covered or wire baskets. If you use a basket not specifically intended for plants, line it with a protective sheet of flexible plastic, otherwise water will seep through and spoil the surface underneath. The plastic should not be visible once the basket has been planted.

Ordinary hanging baskets are unsuitable for using indoors because of the problems with drips. Choose one with a drip tray or water reservoir.

TERRACOTTA

Large terracotta containers are good for specimen plants. The weight gives stability to plants with thin trunks and wide, arching branches.

The orange tone of terracotta can be softened by weathering it outside over winter. Or it can be artificially aged by applying a weak solution of a pale-coloured, water-based paint.

Match the drip tray to the pot and make sure that it is internally glazed, otherwise water will seep through and spoil the surface it is resting on. For a plant that requires humidity, choose a drip tray large enough to take stones or water-retaining granules as well as the plant pot.

GLAZED CERAMIC

Solid coloured ceramic containers are more versatile than patterns and can be useful for linking a plant's foliage with a room's colour scheme.

Many glazed containers do not have drainage holes; to overcome this, quarter-fill a large one with pebbles, cover with a thin layer of charcoal and top with potting soil.

Wire baskets

Wicker basket

Galvanized metal pail

587

Caring for Houseplants

IF YOU WANT LUSH, HEALTHY HOUSEPLANTS YOU MUST CARE FOR
THEM ROUTINELY AND APPLY REMEDIAL TREATMENT AS SOON AS A
PROBLEM OCCURS. TO INCREASE AND REJUVENATE YOUR STOCK,
SOME PROPAGATION TECHNIQUES WILL BE USEFUL.

WATERING

Some plants require water daily, others, once or twice a week. In winter, some may not need water for weeks. Cacti and succulents resting during winter, for example, should not be kept constantly moist.

Feel the surface of the soil and water when it has dried out but before the plant is affected by lack of water. Don't allow the pot to stand in surplus water as this will waterlog the soil. Most plants benefit from being stood in water for 30 minutes before being returned to their original position.

Above: *Choose a watering-can with a long, narrow spout so that you can control the flow easily. You want the water around the roots, not over the leaves (or on your table or windowsill).*

HUMIDITY

Raising the humidity level will benefit most plants, except sun-lovers. Covering the soil surface with moss, stones or shells will reduce water evaporation. Placing plants on wet pebbles immediately raises the level of humidity around a plant; make sure the roots are not in contact with the water.

Misting plants daily will give a better texture to the leaves and help keep them free of dust, as well as improving humidity for a short time. Use tepid water and ideally mist your plant in the morning so the leaves dry before nightfall.

FEEDING

Slow-release fertilizers feed a plant for months, while controlled-release types release the fertilizer only when the soil is warm enough for most plants' active growth. Granules can be mixed before potting; pellets or sticks can be pushed into the soil around an established plant. Liquid feeds feed the soil for a set period, so when the plant is resting, you can stop feeding it. The amount required depends how vigorously a plant is growing.

VACATION CARE

There are plenty of ways to take care of your plants if you are going away on holiday.

Move your plants into a few large groups in a cool position out of direct sunlight. Stand them on a tray of

Above: Group plants together in a tray or large container and water thoroughly before you go away, leaving a little water in the bottom of the outer container.

gravel, watered to just below the level of the pot bases. This will not moisten the potting soil, but the humid air will help to keep the plants in condition.

Supply the most vulnerable plants with some kind of watering system. There are various proprietary devices on sale, but many of these are suitable if you have a few plants only. Porous reservoirs and ceramic mushrooms are both simple, effective systems, but you need one for each pot.

Wicks, which are inserted into pots placed above a reservoir of water, are suitable for a handful of plants.

Drip feeds, sold for greenhouse and garden use, are good, but expensive.

CAPILLARY MATTING

You can use capillary matting, sold for greenhouse benches, in the sink or the bath. The system works best with plastic pots that have nothing placed over the drainage holes. Water the plants thoroughly first.

For the sink, cut a length of matting to fit the draining area and reach the bottom of the sink. Fill the sink with water, or leave the plug out but let a tap drip on to the mat to keep it moist. If you do the latter, have a trial run to make sure that it keeps the mat moist without wasting water. (If filling with water, stand the plants on the draining area only, not in the water.) Do the same for the bath, but if you leave water in it, place the mat and plants on a plank of wood on bricks.

Above: Capillary wicks will draw water from a reservoir. Make sure the wicks are soaked and put one end deeply into the potting soil. The other end must reach the reservoir base.

GROOMING

Regular grooming of your plants will keep them looking good. Apart from picking off dead flowers whenever you notice them, grooming is a weekly task. Most jobs need doing less frequently than this, but by making a routine of tidying up your plants you will detect pests, diseases and nutritional problems that much earlier.

DEADHEADING

Removing flowers as they fade keeps the plant looking neat, and in many cases encourages the production of more flowers. It also discourages diseases; many fungal infections start on dead flowers. Remove the stalks as well as the flower spikes, using a pulling and twisting motion. Cut whole flower heads or spikes back to just above a pair of leaves.

FOLIAGE

Remove dying and fallen leaves. These will spoil the appearance of a plant and can harbour disease. Most can be pulled off with a gentle tug, but tough ones may have to be cut off.

Dust settles on foliage, and can prevent the plant from breathing properly, and block light. If the leaves are delicate or hairy dust them using a soft paintbrush.

Large, glossy leaves can be wiped clean using a soft damp cloth or sponge or proprietary leaf-wipes. Plants with small glossy leaves may have too many to make the use of leaf-wipes a sensible option. Stand these outside in a shower of light rain in the summer or spray them with water. In winter, plants can simply have their leaves swished gently in a bowl of tepid water.

1 Plants with large, glossy leaves can be wiped clean. Commercially produced leaf-wipes are convenient to use, but check that they don't carry a warning against using them on certain plants.

2 Cacti, succulents and plants with hairy leaves such as *Saintpaulia* are much more difficult to clean. These should be brushed carefully with a soft paintbrush kept for the purpose to remove dust.

PRUNING

The shape of many houseplants can be improved by pinching out the growing tips to prevent them from becoming tall and leggy. Removing the tips of the shoots makes the plant bushier. *Hedera*; *Hypoestes*; *Pilea* and *Tradescantia* are among the many plants that benefit from this treatment. Start when the plants are young, and repeat it whenever the growth looks too thin and long. This is especially useful for trailers: a dense cascade will look better than weedy-looking shoots twice the length. If any all-green shoots devel-

Right: Train new growth of climbing plants before it becomes difficult to bend. Twist stems carefully into position to avoid breaking tender shoots.

Above: If you want a bushy rather than a tall or sprawling plant, pinch out the growing tips a few times while it is still young. This will stimulate the growth of sideshoots and produce a bushier effect.

op on a variegated plant, prune to the point of origin.

Climbers and trailers need regular attention. Tie in any new shoots to the support, and cut off any long ones.

Pruning can also be a good opportunity for propagating your houseplants, as longer shoots can be treated as cuttings to pot up for new plants.

> ### GARDENER'S TIP
> Pests and diseases can spread more easily and rapidly from plant to plant when they are in close proximity, and you may be less likely to notice early symptoms on leaves hidden by other plants. Make grooming a regular routine to minimize the danger.

REPOTTING PLANTS

Sooner or later most plants need repotting, and it can give an ailing plant a new lease of life. Not all plants respond well to frequent repotting, and some prefer to be in small pots.

Repotting a plant should only be done when the plant needs it. Young plants require it much more frequently than older ones. Once a large specimen is in a big pot it may be better to keep it growing by repotting into another pot of the same size, by top-dressing, or simply by additional feeding when required.

WHEN TO REPOT

The sight of roots growing through the base does not indicate that repotting is necessary. Check by inverting the pot and knocking the rim on a hard surface while supporting the plant and soil with your hand. It is normal for some roots to run around the inside, but if there is also a solid mass of roots it is time to pot on.

Above: A plant with tightly packed roots needs to be potted on.

HOW TO REPOT

1 Prepare a pot that is one or two sizes larger than the original. Cover the drainage hole of a clay pot with pieces of broken pot. Don't cover the holes in a plastic pot that you intend using with a capillary watering mat.

2 Place a small amount of potting soil in the new pot. Knock the pre-watered plant out of its pot and position it so that it is at the right height.

3 Trickle potting soil around the sides. Gently firm the soil with your fingers. Leave a gap of about 1–2.5 cm (½– 1 in) between the top of the soil and the rim of the pot. Water thoroughly. Place in the shade for about a week and mist the leaves daily.

SIMPLE PROPAGATION

In the late spring and summer it is possible to multiply some of your plants by means of simple propagation. It is usually best to do this in spring or early summer. Always take several cuttings from the plant in case some fail.

STEM CUTTINGS

Many plants will respond to this method. Choose a piece of stem 7.5–13 cm (3–5 in) long and cut just below a leaf. Make the cut straight, not at an angle, using a razor blade or sharp knife. Remove most of the leaves from the lower half of the cutting. Stand the cutting in a glass of water in a light position, making sure no leaves are in contact with the water. Pot up the cutting when the new roots are 2.5–4 cm (1–1½ in) long. Change the water as necessary.

The Swiss cheese plant and many philodendrons can become straggly with age. They can be divided into several plants by taking stem cuttings with noticeable root nodules at their bases. Place them in water in good light as before.

PLANTLETS

The tiny plantlets produced by some plants, including spider plants, mother of thousands and piggyback plants, can be inserted directly into soil or can be rooted in water as for stem cuttings. Wait until a good root system has developed before potting up.

LEAF CUTTINGS

Take leaf cuttings of African violets, begonias and succulents.

1 Cut a mature leaf, with about 5 cm (2 in) of stalk attached, from the base of a plant. Make a straight cut.

2 Fill a pot with a rooting medium and make a hole using a pencil at a 45-degree angle. Insert the cutting with the back of the leaf towards the outside of the pot and the base just above the soil. Firm gently, then water.

3 Place short canes close to the leaf and place an airtight plastic bag over the pot. Secure with a rubber band. Place in a light position, out of direct sunlight.

Troubleshooting

REGULAR INSPECTION OF YOUR PLANTS WILL ALERT YOU TO ANY
SERIOUS PROBLEMS, DISEASE OR INFESTATIONS IN TIME TO TAKE THE
NECESSARY REMEDIAL ACTION.

PHYSICAL PROBLEMS

Upper Leaves Turn Yellow: affects lime-hating plants, and is caused by watering with hard water containing too much calcium. Use boiled or filtered water only.

Brown Spots or Patches on Leaves: may be due to insect infestation, too much direct sunlight or splashing water on leaves.

Leaves Curling at the Edges and Dropping: can be caused by too cool an atmosphere, overwatering or a cold draught.

Brown Tips and Edges to Leaves: usually too little humidity and too much direct sun. Can be due to either overwatering or overfeeding.

Wilting Leaves: underwatering, or if soil is waterlogged, then overwatering. In this case the roots will have rotted.

Dull Leaves: Lifeless leaves may require a wipe with a damp cloth. May also indicate too much light or the presence of red spider mites.

Sudden Leaf Fall: may occur after repotting or when a plant has been relocated. Can be the result of a sharp rise or fall in temperature, an icy draught or underwatering.

No Flowers: usually caused by insufficient light. If the flower buds develop but drop before opening, this is probably due to dry air or underwatering. Flowers that develop but fade quickly may be getting too much heat, too little light and not enough water.

Variegated Leaves Turning Green: due to lack of light, which generally results in pale, small leaves and a leggy growing habit.

Rotting Leaves and Stems: probably due to a disease and often caused by overwatering, poor drainage and insufficient ventilation.

Left: If the potting soil has become very dry, with a hard surface, loosen the surface with a fork to help a dried-out root-ball absorb water.

PESTS AND DISEASES

Mealy Bug: small insects covered with white fluff that form colonies in leaves and in leaf axils. The leaves eventually turn yellow, wilt and drop off. Wipe off the bugs with alcohol-impregnated swabs, or spray with malathion.

Vine Weevil: a creamy-coloured grub that lives in the soil and eats roots. The adult dark brown beetle chews leaves. If caught early, leaves and soil need spraying with pesticide.

Whitefly: tiny, moth-like flies that deposit a sticky honeydew on the undersides of leaves, encouraging black mould to develop.

Above: Whitefly damage houseplants and look unsightly. They can be killed with a pesticide spray.

Red Spider Mites: almost too small to see, these pests suck sap, causing black spots and yellowed leaves. Infestation is indicated by the presence of fine webs and mottling of the plant's leaves. Remove affected leaves and spray with insecticide.

Aphids (Greenfly): brown, grey or green insects that suck the sap, leaving sticky honeydew that causes leaves to wither. Remove with alcohol-impregnated swabs, and spray with pesticide.

Powdery Mildew: coats the leaves with a white powdery deposit. Remove and destroy affected leaves and spray with a systemic fungicide. Improve the ventilation.

Black Leg (Black Stem Rot): affects stem cuttings, turning the bases black. Destroy affected cuttings. Use a well-draining medium and dip cuttings in a fungicide hormone-rooting powder.

Sooty Mould (Black Mold): fungus that grows on honeydew left by aphids and mealy bugs. Wipe off the mould using diluted soapy water.

Botrytis (Grey Mold): caused by a cool, damp atmosphere with poor air circulation. Remove affected parts and spray with a systemic fungicide.

Above: If whitefly or aphid infestation is mild you may be able to reduce the population by swishing the plant in water.

A–Z of Houseplants

Most of the houseplants in the following pages can be found in garden centres and shops. The selection covers flowering, foliage and scented varieties.

ACALYPHA HISPIDA

Tall and quick-growing foliage plant with long red tassel-like flowers, in autumn. 'Alba': white flowers.

Temperature: winter 15°C (59°F).
Humidity: high humidity. Mist frequently if room is centrally heated.
Position: good light, not direct sun.
Watering and feeding: never let soil dry out. Feed from spring to autumn.
Care: deadhead. Prune by half in early spring or late summer. Repot in spring or topdress if in large pot.
Propagation: cuttings.

ACHIMENES HYBRIDS

Short-lived flowers, in pink, purple, yellow, red or white, through summer. Dormant over winter.

Temperature: undemanding when dormant; minimum 13°C (55°F) while it is growing.
Humidity: mist developing flower buds then provide humidity without spraying by standing plant on a tray of wet pebbles.
Position: good light, not direct sun.
Watering and feeding: water with tepid, soft water during growing season, keeping soil moist. Feed regularly.
Care: support the stems or grow in a hanging pot. Stop watering when leaves begin to drop. Leave rhizomes in pot or store in peat or sand in frost-free place. Start into growth or replant in late winter or early spring.
Propagation: division of rhizomes; cuttings; seed (not named varieties).

AECHMEA FASCIATA

Bromeliad with banded foliage. Long-lasting, spiky blue flowers fading to lilac with pink bracts, mid-summer to early winter.

Temperature: winter minimum 15°C (59°F).

Humidity: undemanding.

Position: good light, not direct sun.

Watering and feeding: keep roots moist. Top up water in funnel in summer, but empty it in winter. Feed with weak fertilizer in summer.

Care: mist only on hot days. To stimulate mature plant into flower, enclose in plastic bag with two ripe apples for a few days. Main plant will die after flowering, but produces offsets.

Propagation: offsets (remove when about half height of parent).

AGLAONEMA HYBRIDS

Tolerant clump-forming foliage plants with silvery-grey variegations.

Temperature: winter minimum 15°C (59°F).

Humidity: high humidity. Mist regularly.

Position: Light shade, not direct sun.

Watering and feeding: water freely from spring to autumn, sparingly in winter. Feed from spring to autumn.

Care: repot only when necessary.

Propagation: cuttings; division.

ALOE VARIEGATA

Trouble-free succulents with thick fleshy, banded leaves, occasionally red flowers.

Temperature: cool but frost-free in winter, 5°C (41°F).

Humidity: will tolerate dry air.

Position: full sun.

Watering and feeding: water twice a week in summer. Feed occasionally in summer.

Care: repot in spring every second year.

Propagation: offsets; seed in spring.

ANANAS BRACTEATUS STRIATUS

Foliage bromeliads with spiky, brightly striped, cream-and-pink leaves.

Temperature: winter 15–18°C (59–64°F).

Humidity: undemanding, but mist in very hot weather.

Position: good light. Variegation often better in sun.

Watering and feeding: water freely in summer, cautiously in winter. Feed from spring to autumn.

Care: in summer, occasionally add a little water to the leaf "vase". Encourage mature plants to flower by placing in a plastic bag with ripe apples or bananas.

Propagation: leaf crown on top of fruit.

ANTHURIUM SCHERZERIANUM

Distinctive foliage plant with exotic red blooms spring to late summer.

Temperature: winter minimum 16°C (60°F).

Humidity: high humidity. Mist frequently, avoiding flowers.

Position: good light, not direct summer sun.

Watering and feeding: water freely in summer, sparingly in winter. Soft water if possible. Feed with weak fertilizer in summer.

Care: repot every second year, in spring, using fibrous potting mixture.

Propagation: division.

ASPARAGUS DENSIFLORUS 'SPRENGERI'

Fern-like foliage on arching to pendulous, thread-like stems.

Temperature: winter minimum 7°C (45°F).

Humidity: mist occasionally, especially in centrally heated room.

Position: good light or partial shade, not direct sun.

Watering and feeding: water from spring to autumn, sparingly in winter. Feed from spring to early autumn.

Care: cut back by half if turns yellow or grows too large. Repot young plants every spring, older ones every second spring.

Propagation: division; seed.

ASPIDISTRA ELATIOR

Evergreen herbaceous plant with large dark green leaves growing directly from soil. Tough constitution. 'Variegata': creamy white longitudinal stripes.

Temperature: keep cool, 7–10°C (45–50°F) is ideal.

Humidity: tolerates dry air.

Position: light or shade, but avoid exposing to direct sun.

Watering and feeding: water moderately from spring to autumn, sparingly in winter. Feed from spring to early autumn.

Care: wash or sponge leaves occasionally to remove dust and improve light penetration. Repot when necessary – every three or four years.

Propagation: division.

ASPLENIUM
Useful ferns. *A. bulbiferum*: ferny fronds, small plantlets on mature leaves. *A. nidus*: glossy, undivided leaves forming vase-like rosette, very tolerant.

Temperature: winter minimum: *A. bulbiferum* 13°C (55°F); *A. nidus* 16°C (60°F)
Humidity: high humidity.
Position: shade.
Watering and feeding: water freely from spring to autumn, moderately in winter. Soft water if possible.
Care: dust *A. nidus* periodically. Trim off any brown edges.
Propagation: division; pot up plantlets of *A. bulbiferum*.

BEGONIA ELATIOR HYBRIDS
Single or double flowers mainly red, pink, yellow, orange and white, all seasons, especially winter.

Temperature: winter minimum 13–21°C (55–70°F) while growing.
Humidity: high humidity is beneficial.
Position: good light, not direct summer sun. Best possible light in winter.
Watering and feeding: water freely while in flower. Feed with weak fertilizer while in bud and flowering.
Care: deadhead regularly. Discard after flowering.
Propagation: propagate from leaf or tip cuttings.

BEGONIA FOLIAGE
Foliage begonias are attractive all year. Several species, all compact, with hairy or puckered leaves in brightly variegated colours.

Temperature: winter minimum 16°C (60°F).
Humidity: require high humidity, but avoid spraying leaves.
Position: good light, not direct sun.
Watering and feeding: water freely from spring to autumn, sparingly in winter.
Care: repot annually in spring.
Propagation: division; leaf cuttings.

599

BILLBERGIA NUTANS

Bromeliad with yellow-and-green, blue-edged flowers with pink bracts, in spring.

Temperature: winter minimum 13°C (55°F).

Humidity: tolerates dry air if necessary.

Position: good light, not direct sun.

Watering and feeding: water freely from spring to autumn, sparingly in winter. In summer pour some water into the leaf rosettes. Feed from spring to autumn.

Care: allow offsets around base to grow into a large clump – they will soon flower. Repot when clump fills the pot.

Propagation: offsets (separate when new shoots are half as tall as parent plant).

BROWALLIA SPECIOSA

Bushy herbaceous plant with blue, purple or white flowers. Many varieties. Regular sowing ensures year-round colour.

Temperature: 10–15°C (50–59°F) for longer flowering.

Humidity: undemanding, but mist leaves occasionally.

Position: good light. Tolerates some direct sun, but not through glass at hottest part of the day.

Watering and feeding: water freely at all times. Feed regularly.

Care: grow one plant in a 10 cm (4 in) pot, or three in a 15 cm (6 in) pot. Pinch out growing tips for bushiness. Deadhead regularly. Discard plant after flowering.

Propagation: seed, in late winter or early spring.

CAMPANULA ISOPHYLLA

Trailing stems with soft blue, star-like flowers in mid and late summer.

Temperature: winter minimum 7°C (45°F) for longer flowering.

Humidity: undemanding, but mist leaves occasionally.

Position: good light, avoid direct summer sun.

Watering and feeding: water freely from spring to autumn, sparingly in winter. Feed regularly.

Care: deadhead regularly. Cut stems back to 5–7.5 cm (2–3 in) at end of growing season.

Propagation: seed; or can take cuttings.

CELOSIA CRISTATA

Deeply ruffled flowers in red, yellow, orange and pink, in summer and early autumn. The Plumosa group has feathery flower plumes.

Temperature: 10–15°C (50–59°F) if possible.
Humidity: moderate humidity.
Position: good light, avoid direct summer sun through glass.
Watering and feeding: water moderately; vulnerable to under- and overwatering. Feed regularly but cautiously – too much leads to poor flowers.
Care: raise in greenhouse or buy as young plants. Discard after flowering.
Propagation: seed.

CEROPEGIA WOODII

Succulent trailer with heart-shaped leaves, with silver mottling.

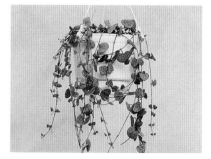

Temperature: winter minimum 10°C (50°F).
Humidity: tolerates dry air.
Position: good light, tolerates full sun and partial shade.
Watering and feeding: water sparingly at all times. Feed regularly with weak fertilizer in summer.
Care: shorten bare spindly stems in spring.
Propagation: Seed; layering; stem tuber cuttings.

CHAMAEDOREA ELEGANS

Compact palm with arching leaves growing from base, and tiny yellow ball flowers.

Temperature: winter 12–15°C (53–59°F).
Humidity: mist occasionally, even in winter if the room is centrally heated.
Position: good light, avoid direct summer sun.
Watering and feeding: water generously from spring to autumn, keep just moist in winter. Feed regularly in spring and summer with weak fertilizer.
Care: repot when roots grow through bottom of pot.
Propagation: seed; division.

601

CHLOROPHYTUM COMOSUM 'VITTATUM'
Arching, linear white-and-green variegated
leaves, 30–60 cm (12–24 in) long. Long
stalks bear small white flowers and
leaf plantlets.

Temperature: winter minimum 7°C (45°F).
Humidity: mist leaves occasionally.
Position: good light, not direct sun.
Watering and feeding: water generously
spring to autumn, sparingly in winter.
Feed regularly from spring to autumn.
Care: repot young plants each spring,
mature ones when roots push the plant
out of pot.
Propagation: stem plantlets; division.

CHRYSANTHEMUM YEAR-ROUND
Compact plants for year-round colour, in
red, pink, purple, yellow and white.

Temperature: 10–15°C (50–59°F).
Tolerates a warm room, but flowers will
be shorter-lived.
Humidity: undemanding; mist leaves from
time to time.
Position: undemanding.
Watering and feeding: keep moist.
Care: deadhead regularly. Discard after
flowering or transfer to garden.
Propagation: None.

CISSUS RHOMBIFOLIA
Vigorous climber with dark green leaves.

Temperature: winter 7–13°C (45–55°F).
Humidity: undemanding, but mist leaves
occasionally, especially in summer.
Position: good light, avoid direct
summer sun.
Watering and feeding: water generously
from spring to autumn, but sparingly
in winter.
Care: pinch out growing tips on young
plants; tie new shoots to the support. Thin
overcrowded shoots in spring.
Propagation: cuttings.

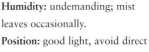

x *CITROFORTUNELLA MICROCARPA*

Glossy, dark green evergreen plant up to 1.2 m (4 ft) high. Clusters of fragrant white flowers, usually in summer, followed by miniature orange fruits.

Temperature: winter minimum 10°C (50°F).

Humidity: undemanding, but mist leaves occasionally.

Position: good light, avoid direct summer sun through glass.

Watering and feeding: water freely in summer, sparingly in winter. Feed regularly in summer, perhaps including magnesium and iron.

Care: pollinate flowers using cotton wool.

Propagation: cuttings.

CLIVIA MINIATA

Evergreen perennial with strap-shaped leaves. Large flower head of orange or yellow funnel-shaped flowers, in early spring.

Temperature: winter minimum 10°C (50°F). Avoid warm winter temperatures.

Humidity: undemanding; mist leaves occasionally.

Position: good light, avoid direct summer sun.

Watering and feeding: water moderately from spring to autumn, sparingly in winter until flower stalk is 15 cm (6 in). Feed from flowering to early autumn.

Care: sponge leaves occasionally. Repot when roots push plant from pot, after flowering. Winter in unheated room.

Propagation: division (after flowering).

COCOS NUCIFERA

Tall and slow-growing palm with visible coconut. Grows to 3 m (10 ft) indoors.

Temperature: winter minimum 18°C (64°F).

Humidity: high humidity.

Position: good light, some full sun, but avoid direct sun through glass during hottest part of day.

Watering and feeding: water freely in summer, moderately in winter. Feed with weak fertilizer in summer.

Care: sponge leaves occasionally; never use leaf shine. Repot young plants in the spring.

Propagation: seed (difficult at home, can be done by a professional plantsman).

CODIAEUM VARIEGATUM VAR. PICTUM

Many varieties with colourful or variegated, glossy, evergreen leaves, many colours.

Temperature: winter minimum 16°C (60°F).
Humidity: high humidity. Mist leaves regularly.
Position: good light, avoid direct summer sun.
Watering and feeding: water generously from spring to autumn, sparingly in winter. Feed regularly in spring and summer.
Care: avoid cold draughts. Repot when outgrown pot.
Propagation: cuttings.

COLCHICUM AUTUMNALE

Corms producing large crocus-shaped, pink flowers in early autumn.
Temperature: undemanding and hardy.
Humidity: undemanding.

Position: light windowsill, preferably out of strong direct sunlight.
Watering and feeding: none required.
Care: place dry corms in saucer of sand or tray of dry pebbles, set in light position and leave to flower. After flowering plant in garden in light shade.
Propagation: buy new corms.

COLEUS BLUMEI (SOLENOSTEMON) HYBRIDS

Perennial sub-shrubs treated as annuals. Variegated leaves in a range of pattern and colour – reds, yellows and greens.
Temperature: winter minimum 10°C (50°F).
Humidity: high humidity. Mist leaves frequently.
Position: good light, avoid direct summer sun.
Watering and feeding: water freely from spring to autumn, keep roots just moist in winter. Use soft water. Feed from spring to autumn.
Care: pinch out growing tips of young plants, several times to obtain really bushy plants. Cut back hard old overwintered plants and repot in spring. If grown from seed, retain most appealing and discard the rest.
Propagation: seed in spring; stem cuttings in spring or summer.

COLUMNEA

Trailing evergreen perennials with red or orange-red flowers, winter or early spring.

Temperature: winter minimum 13°C (55°F).
Humidity: high humidity. Mist regularly.
Position: good light, but avoid direct summer sun.
Watering and feeding: water freely from spring to autumn, sparingly in winter. Feed regularly in spring and summer.
Care: shorten stems after flowering. Repot every second or third year, in humus-rich, fibrous potting mixture.
Propagation: cuttings.

CROCUS

Mainly spring-flowering corms. Plant in autumn for late winter to early spring colour.
Temperature: keep cool.
Humidity: undemanding.
Position: good light indoors.

Watering and feeding: water cautiously.
Care: leave in garden until mid-winter, but protect from excessive freezing and waterlogging. Maintain cool conditions in house until at least a third of developing flower bud is visible. After flowering plant in garden.
Propagation: new corms; offset corms; and seed.

CYCLAMEN

Tuber for autumn to spring colour, in pinks, red, purples, salmon and white.

Temperature: 10–15°C (50–59°F) in winter.
Humidity: moderate humidity. Stand pot on tray of wet pebbles. Mist leaves only.
Position: Good light, not direct sun.
Watering and feeding: water freely while actively growing, gradually reduce after flowering. Feed regularly during active growing and flowering periods.
Care: deadhead regularly, removing entire stalk. When leaves have died, keep cool (perhaps outside) and almost dry until mid-summer. Start watering, repot if necessary (burying tuber to half its depth) and bring indoors if outside.
Propagation: seed.

CYPERUS

Rush-like plants, with leaves radiating from stiff stalks. Tolerates overwatering.

Temperature: winter minimum 7°C (45°F).

Humidity: mist regularly.

Position: good light, avoid direct summer sun.

Watering and feeding: water

freely at all times, keeping roots moist. Feed from mid-spring to early autumn.

Care: cut off yellowing stems. Repot in spring.

Propagation: division.

DIEFFENBACHIA MACULATA

Bold oval leaves with ivory or cream markings. Poisonous or irritant sap.

Temperature: winter minimum 16°C (60°F).

Humidity: mist leaves regularly.

Position: partial shade and good light, avoid direct summer sun.

Watering and feeding: water freely from spring to autumn, sparingly in winter. Feed regularly in spring and summer.

Care: wash leaves occasionally. Repot each spring.

Propagation: cane or stem cuttings.

DIZYGOTHECA ELEGANTISSIMA

Graceful evergreen with dark green, almost black, elongated, serrated leaves. Grows up to 1.2 m (4 ft) tall.

Temperature: winter minimum 13°C (55°F).

Humidity: mist regularly.

Position: good light, avoid direct summer sun at hottest part of day.

Watering and feeding: water moderately from spring to autumn, sparingly in winter.

Care: repot every second spring.

Propagation: seed or air layering in spring; tip cuttings in summer.

DRACAENA

Tough, palm-like foliage plants with striking variegation and bold outline.

Temperature: winter minimum 13°C (55°F).
Humidity: mist leaves regularly.
Position: good light, not direct sun.
Watering and feeding: water freely from spring to autumn, sparingly in winter. Never let roots dry out. Feed regularly in spring and summer.
Care: sponge leaves occasionally. Repot in spring if necessary.
Propagation: tip cuttings; air layering; cane cuttings.

ECHEVERIA

Rosette-forming succulents grown for shape and bluish-grey colouring. Yellow, pink or red flowers, from spring through to mid-summer.
Temperature: winter 5–10°C (41–50°F).
Humidity: tolerates dry air.
Position: best possible light. Will tolerate full sun.

Watering and feeding: water moderately from spring to autumn, practically dry in winter. Feed with weak fertilizer in spring and summer.
Care: avoid getting water on leaves. Can use winter-fallen tips as cuttings.
Propagation: tip cuttings; leaf cuttings; offsets; seed.

ECHINOCACTUS GRUSONII

Slow-growing spherical cactus, more cylindrical with age.
Temperature: winter 5–10°C (41–50°F).

Humidity: tolerates dry air.
Position: best possible light. Tolerates full sun.
Watering and feeding: water moderately from spring to autumn, practically dry in winter. Feed with weak fertilizer in spring and summer.
Care: repot only as necessary, using cactus mixture.
Propagation: seed.

EPIPREMNUM AUREUM

Climber or trailer with heart-shaped glossy leaves, blotched or streaked with yellow.

Temperature: winter minimum 13°C (55°F).
Humidity: undemanding, but benefits from occasional misting.
Position: good light, not direct sun.
Watering and feeding: water freely from spring to autumn, sparingly in winter. Feed in spring and summer.
Care: repot in spring if necessary. To keep plant compact, shorten long shoots.
Propagation: leaf bud cuttings; stem tip cuttings; layering.

ERICA

Two species provide indoor winter colour.
E. gracilis: white-tipped, pink urn-shaped flowers;
E. hyemalis: white, pink or reddish bell-shaped flowers.

Temperature: 5–13°C (41–55°F) when flowering.
Humidity: mist leaves regularly.
Position: good light. Benefits from winter sun.
Watering and feeding: water freely at all times. Never allow roots to dry out. Soft water if possible.
Care: buy when in flower, then discard.
Propagation: cuttings.

EUSTOMA GRANDIFLORUM

Short-term, compact plant with blue, pink and white poppy flowers, in summer.

Temperature: winter minimum 7°C (45°F).
Humidity: Mist occasionally.
Position: good light, but avoid direct summer sun.
Watering and feeding: water with care. Do not overwater but keep compost moist. Feed regularly once nutrients in potting soil are depleted.
Care: discard when flowering finished.
Propagation: seeds.

EXACUM AFFINE

Masses of small, pale purple or white flowers, from mid-summer to late autumn.

Temperature: 10–21°C (50–70°F).

Humidity: mist leaves regularly.

Position: good light, avoid direct summer sun.

Watering and feeding: water freely. Feed regularly once nutrients in potting soil are depleted.

Care: deadhead regularly. Discard after flowering.

Propagation: seed.

X FATSHEDERA LIZEI

Tall-growing foliage plant with shiny, five-fingered leaves. Attractive variegations.

Temperature: winter minimum 3°C (37°F).

Humidity: undemanding in a cool position, but mist occasionally in a warm room.

Position: good light, avoid direct summer sun. Best possible light in winter.

Watering and feeding: water freely from spring to autumn, sparingly in winter. Tepid water if possible. Feed in spring and summer.

Care: repot each spring. Provide support to grow tall, or pinch growing tips each spring for bushy plant.

Propagation: cuttings.

FATSIA JAPONICA

Large, deeply lobed, glossy dark green leaves. Also variegated varieties.

Temperature: winter minimum 3°C (37°F), 13°C (55°F) for variegated types. Keep below 21°C (70°F) if possible.

Humidity: moderate humidity.

Position: good light, avoid direct summer sun. Tolerates shade.

Watering and feeding: water freely from spring to autumn, sparingly in winter. Never let roots dry out. Feed in spring and summer.

Care: sponge leaves monthly. Repot in spring if necessary.

Propagation: cuttings; air layering; seed.

FICUS BENJAMINA

Pendulous shoots with green leaves, up to 2.4 m (8 ft) indoors, useful for focal plant. 'Starlight': variegated leaves.

Temperature: winter minimum 13°C (55°F).

Humidity: mist the leaves occasionally.

Position: good light, avoid direct summer sun during hottest part of day.

Watering and feeding: water freely from spring to autumn, sparingly in winter, using tepid water. Feed in spring and summer.

Care: repot young plants every second year.

Propagation: cuttings; air layering.

FITTONIA VERSCHAFFELTII

Creeping plant with pink-veined, olive-green leaves, about 5 cm (2 in) long.

Temperature: winter minimum 16°C (60°F).

Humidity: high humidity.

Position: partial shade, not direct sun.

Watering and feeding: water freely from spring to autumn, sparingly in winter. Tepid water if possible. Feed from spring to autumn with weak fertilizer.

Care: pinch back straggly shoots. Repot each spring. Does best in a bottle garden.

Propagation: division; cuttings; pot up where rooted.

FUCHSIA HYBRIDS

Compact deciduous shrubs grown for their bell-shaped flowers with flared "skirts", in a range of colours. Grows to 45–60 cm (18–24 in).

Temperature: winter 10–16°C (50–60°F).

Humidity: mist leaves occasionally.

Position: good light, not direct summer sun.

Watering and feeding: water freely from spring to autumn while plant is growing vigorously, otherwise sparingly, and very sparingly in winter if plants are dormant. Feed from late spring through summer.

Care: shorten old shoots just before or as new growth starts; pruning can be severe. Repot every second or third year in humus-rich, fibrous potting mixture.

Propagation: cuttings.

GARDENIA JASMINOIDES

Glossy evergreen shrub. Large, fragrant, white flowers, in summer. 45 cm (18 in) houseplant or 1.5 m (5 ft) in conservatory.

Temperature: winter minimum 16°C (60°F).
Humidity: mist leaves regularly.
Position: good light, but avoid direct summer sun during hottest part of day.
Watering and feeding: water freely from spring to autumn, sparingly in winter, never let roots become dry. Soft water if possible. Feed from spring to autumn.
Care: avoid widely fluctuating temperatures when buds forming. Repot every second or third year with ericaceous potting soil.
Propagation: cuttings.

HEDERA

Self-clinging climbers or trailers, many varieties, including variegated ones.
H. canariensis: large lobed leaves.
H. helix: small leaves.

Temperature: cool but frost-free.
Humidity: mist leaves occasionally, regularly in summer.
Position: good light or some shade, avoid direct summer sun.
Watering and feeding: water freely in warm weather, moderately in cool temperatures, never let roots become dry. Soft water if possible. Feed regularly from spring to autumn.
Care: repot each spring, unless in a large pot. Pinch out growing tips periodically for a bushy plant.
Propagation: cuttings.

HIBISCUS ROSA-SINENSIS

Large-flowered evergreen in many colours, spring to autumn. Up to 75 cm (2½ ft). 'Cooperi': variegated foliage and red flowers.
Temperature: winter minimum 13°C (55°F).
Humidity: mist leaves occasionally.
Position: good light, avoid direct summer sun during hottest part of day.
Watering and feeding: water freely from spring to autumn, sparingly in winter, but never allow roots to dry out. Feed regularly in summer.
Care: deadhead regularly. Shorten long shoots after flowering or in late winter. Once buds form do not turn plant. Repot each spring.
Propagation: cuttings; seed.

HOWEA BELMOREANA

Evergreen palms with thin green stems and arching, pinnate foliage. Can grow to ceiling height.

Temperature: winter minimum 16°C (60°F).

Humidity: mist leaves regularly.

Position: good light, avoid direct summer sun during hottest part of day.

Watering and feeding: water moderately in summer, sparingly in winter. Keep soil just moist. Feed in summer.

Care: sponge leaves occasionally. Don't use leaf shine.

Propagation: seed (difficult).

HOYA BELLA

Fleshy-leaved evergreen climber or trailer. Pendulous clusters of fragrant, white star-shaped flowers, through summer.

Temperature: winter minimum of 18°C (64°F).

Humidity: mist leaves regularly, except when in bloom.

Position: good light, avoid summer sun through glass during hottest part of day.

Watering and feeding: water freely from spring to autumn, sparingly in winter, but never allow roots to dry out.
Feed sparingly when in flower.

Care: provide support if grown as climber. Repot only when necessary and never once flower buds formed.

Propagation: semi-ripe cuttings; also eye cuttings.

HYACINTHUS ORIENTALIS

Indoor bulbs for winter and early spring colour and fragrance, in many colours.

Temperature: hardy. Keep as cool as possible unless advancing flowering.

Humidity: undemanding.

Position: good light once buds begin to show colour. Anywhere once in full flower.

Watering and feeding: Ensure roots do not dry out. Feed only if planting bulbs in garden.

Care: discard after flowering, or plant in garden.

Propagation: buy fresh bulbs each year.

Hydrangea macrophylla

Deciduous shrubs with ball-shaped flower heads in blue, pink or white, usually in spring, but sometimes at other times.

Temperature: winter minimum 7°C (45°F). Move to warm bright position in mid-winter, when you can increase watering.
Humidity: mist occasionally.
Position: good light or light shade. Avoid direct summer sun.
Watering and feeding: water freely from spring to autumn, sparingly in early winter. Soft water if possible. Feed regularly during active growth.
Care: flower colour is affected by the type of potting soil: use ericaceous for blue flowers. Never allow roots to dry out during growing season. Stand outside after flowering. Repot every second or third year with ericaceous potting soil.
Propagation: semi-ripe cuttings.

Hypoestes phyllostachya

Evergreen with pointed oval leaves covered with red or pink spots or blotches.
Temperature: winter minimum 13°C (55°F).
Humidity: mist leaves regularly.
Position: good light, avoid direct summer sun during hottest part of day.
Watering and feeding: water freely from spring to autumn, sparingly in winter, soil just moist. Feed regularly in summer; spindly growth results from overfeeding.

Care: pinch out leaf tips and cut back straggly shoots. Pinch out flowers – these spoil compact shape.
Propagation: cuttings; seed.

Impatiens hybrids

Compact plants with masses of flat flowers in red, orange, pink or white, year-round.

Temperature: winter minimum 13°C (55°F), or 16°C (60°F) if flowering.
Humidity: mist leaves occasionally, avoiding flowers.
Position: good light, avoid direct summer sun.
Watering and feeding: water freely from spring to autumn, sparingly in winter.
Care: pinch out tips of young plants. Cut back lanky old plants, or discard.
Propagation: seed; cuttings.

JASMINUM

Woody climbers with very fragrant flowers, suitable for conservatory, usually deciduous.

J. officinale: white summer flowers. *J. polyanthum*: white winter flowers.

Temperature: winter minimum 7°C (45°F).
Humidity: mist leaves regularly.
Position: good light with some direct sun.
Watering and feeding: water freely from spring to autumn, in winter keep soil barely moist. Feed regularly during active growth.
Care: large pot with support. Prune to contain size if necessary. Avoid high winter temperatures.
Propagation: cuttings.

JUSTICIA BRANDEGEEANA

Evergreen grown for long-lasting reddish-brown bracts, available all year. Rarely reaches its potential 90 cm (3 ft).

Temperature: winter 10–16°C (50–60°F).
Humidity: mist occasionally.
Position: good light with some direct sun, but not through glass in summer.
Watering and feeding: water freely from spring to autumn, sparingly in winter. Feed regularly from spring to autumn.
Care: repot each spring, and prune back shoots by one-third.
Propagation: cuttings.

KALANCHOE BLOSSFELDIANA

Fleshy-leaved succulent. Flowers in various colours, year-round.

Temperature: winter minimum 10°C (50°F).
Humidity: tolerates dry air
Position: good light with some direct sun, but avoid direct summer sun during hottest part of day.
Watering and feeding: water freely from spring to autumn, sparingly in winter. Feed regularly from spring to autumn.
Care: discard after flowering.
Propagation: cuttings; seed.

LILIUM HYBRIDS

Indoor bulbs for spring colour and fragrance, in many colours, usually mottled.

Temperature: 3–10°C (37–50°F), avoid high temperatures.
Humidity: mist occasionally.
Position: good light, but avoid direct summer sun.
Watering and feeding: keep soil moist during active growth. Feed regularly.
Care: pot bulb in autumn or winter when bought, with at least 5 cm (2 in) soil beneath and 10 cm (4 in) above. Keep in cool place with soil just moist, ensuring good light once shoots appear. Move in to house when buds show colour. Plant in garden after flowering.
Propagation: buy fresh bulbs each year.

LITHOPS

Prostrate succulents with pairs of fused swollen leaves resembling pebbles.

Temperature: winter minimum 7°C (45°F).
Humidity: tolerates dry air.
Position: good light with plenty of sun.
Watering and feeding: water moderately in summer. Keep dry in winter. Recommence when old leaves split to reveal new ones. Only feed after many years in same pot, with cactus fertilizer.
Care: repot only when the pot filled with leaves.
Propagation: seed.

MARANTA LEUCONEURA ERYTHRONEURA

Squat foliage plants with strikingly marked round oval leaves.

Temperature: winter minimum 10°C (50°F).
Humidity: high humidity. Mist the leaves regularly.
Position: good light, avoid direct summer sun. Best possible light in winter.
Watering and feeding: water freely from spring to summer. Soft water if possible. Feed regularly in summer.
Care: repot every second spring.
Propagation: division.

Monstera deliciosa

Thick-stemmed climber with very large leaves, perforated with age. Can grow to reach the ceiling.

Temperature: winter minimum 10°C (50°F).
Humidity: mist leaves regularly.
Position: good light or shade, not direct sun. Best possible light in winter.
Watering and feeding: water freely from spring to autumn, sparingly in winter. Feed regularly in summer.
Care: provide support. Lightly sponge leaves occasionally.
Propagation: cuttings; air layering.

Narcissus hybrids

Bulbs for late winter and early spring colour. White, fragrant 'Paperwhite' and yellow 'Soleil d'Or' are suitable for forcing.

Temperature: 15–21°C (59–70°F).
Humidity: undemanding.
Position: good light.
Watering and feeding: water moderately while bulbs growing.
Care: grow in pots or in bowls of water supported by pebbles, keeping base of bulb above water.
Propagation: buy fresh bulbs each year.

Nephrolepsis exaltata

Evergreen fern forming a dense clump of pinnate leaves, varying according to the variety.

Temperature: winter minimum 18°C (64°F).
Humidity: mist leaves regularly.
Position: partial shade, not direct sun.
Watering and feeding: water freely in summer, cautiously in winter, keeping roots moist without being wet. Use soft water if possible.
Care: repot in spring if becomes too large for pot. Avoid draughts.
Propagation: plantlets; spores (species only).

NERTERA GRANADENSIS

Mound-forming, creeping perennial grown for bright orange berries, in autumn.

Temperature: winter minimum 7°C (45°F).
Humidity: mist leaves occasionally.
Position: good light, with some direct sun.
Watering and feeding: water freely from spring to autumn, sparingly in winter. Never allow roots to dry out completely.
Care: can leave outdoors all summer until berries form. Discard after berries finished.
Propagation: division; seed.

OPUNTIA

Branching cacti, some cylindrical, some with flat pads. Red or yellow flowers.
Temperature: winter minimum 7°C (45°F).
Humidity: tolerates dry air as it is a desert plant.

Position: Best possible light, benefits from direct sun.
Watering and feeding: water moderately from spring to autumn, very sparingly in winter. Feed in summer with weak fertilizer or cactus food.
Care: repot in spring if necessary. Flat pad types do well in ordinary loam-based potting soil, others prefer cactus mixture.
Propagation: cuttings or detach pads; seed.

PARODIA

Rounded to cylindrical cacti with bristly spines. Yellow flowers in spring.

Temperature: winter 7–12°C (45–53°F).
Humidity: tolerates dry air as it is a desert plant.
Position: Best possible light, benefits from full sun.
Watering and feeding: water moderately from spring to autumn, leave practically dry in winter. Use soft water if possible. Feed in summer with weak fertilizer or cactus food.
Care: Plants are slow-growing, but if they need repotting use a special cactus mixture if possible.
Propagation: seed.

617

PELARGONIUM, REGAL OR MARTHA WASHINGTON

Scalloped leaves and showy, often bicoloured blooms from early spring to late summer.

Temperature: winter minimum 7°C (45°F).

Humidity: tolerates dry air.

Position: good light with some sun. Tolerates full sun.

Watering and feeding: water moderately between spring and autumn. Feed regularly from spring to autumn.

Care: can be kept in leaf if given sufficient warmth. Repot in spring if necessary. Deadhead regularly. Shorten long shoots in autumn. Pinch out growing tip for bushy growth.

Propagation: cuttings; seed.

PELLAEA

Ferns with feathery fronds. Tolerate dry conditions, humidity improves growth.

Temperature: winter 13–16°C (55–60°F).

Humidity: mist leaves occasionally.

Position: good light, not direct sun.

Watering and feeding: water moderately at all times, with care. Feed with weak fertilizer in summer.

Care: if repotting, use shallow container or hanging basket.

Propagation: division; spores.

PEPEROMIA

Undemanding compact, slow-growing foliage plants with wide variety of leaf shapes, colouring and size.

Temperature: winter minimum 10°C (50°F).

Humidity: mist leaves occasionally with warm water, not in winter.

Position: semi-shade or good light, avoid direct summer sun.

Watering and feeding: water moderately from spring to autumn, cautiously in winter. Soft water if possible. Feed from spring to autumn.

Care: repot only when necessary to slightly larger pot, in spring, with peat-based mix.

Propagation: cuttings; leaf cuttings.

PHILODENDRON SCANDENS

Climber or trailer
with heart-
shaped, glossy
green leaves. Can
reach ceiling.
Temperature:
winter minimum
13°C (55°F).
Humidity: mist
leaves regularly.
Position: good
light, avoid direct
summer sun.
Tolerates low
light levels well.

Watering and feeding: water freely from
spring to autumn. Soft water if possible.
Feed from spring to autumn; to limit
growth avoid nitrogen feeds.
Care: provide suitable support.
Propagation: cuttings; air layering.

PHOENIX CANARIENSIS

Palm with feathery fronds, stiff at first,
arching later.

Temperature: winter minimum 7°C (45°F).
Humidity: tolerates dry air.
Position: good light, especially direct sun.
Watering and feeding: water moderately
from spring to autumn, sparingly in
winter. Feed regularly from spring
to autumn.
Care: repot only when becomes
pot-bound, in deep container.
Propagation: seed.

PILEA

Bushy or trailing foliage plants. Many textured and with silver or bronze markings.

Temperature: winter minimum
10°C (50°F).
Humidity: mist leaves regularly.
Position: good light or partial shade, avoid
direct summer sun.
Watering and feeding: water freely while
in active growth. Feed regularly from
spring to autumn.
Care: pinch out growing tips of young
plants and again a month or two later.
Repot in spring.
Propagation: cuttings.

PRIMULA OBCONICA

Rounded, fragrant flowers, in winter and spring. Leaves can cause allergic reaction.

Temperature: winter minimum 13°C (55°F).
Humidity: mist leaves occasionally.
Position: good light, not direct sun.
Watering and feeding: water moderately from autumn to spring, sparingly in summer. Feed regularly during flowering with weak fertilizer.
Care: keep cool during summer.
Propagation: seed.

PTERIS

Ferns with deeply divided fronds. Several variegated varieties.
Temperature: winter minimum: 13°C (55°F) for pale green forms; 16°C (60°F) for variegated ones.
Humidity: mist leaves regularly.
Position: good

light, not direct sun. Plain green forms will tolerate poorer light than variegated varieties.
Watering and feeding: water freely from spring to autumn, sparingly in winter. Soft water if possible. Feed regularly with weak fertilizer from spring to autumn.
Care: never allow roots to become dry.
Propagation: division; spores.

RADERMACHERA SINICA

Vigorous, evergreen, bushy foliage plant with individual leaflets, about 60 cm (24 in) tall.

Temperature: winter minimum 13°C (55°F).
Humidity: undemanding.
Position: good light, avoid direct summer sun during hottest part of day.
Watering and feeding: water freely from spring to autumn, moderately in winter.
Care: Pinch out growing tips of young plants.
Propagation: cuttings.

REBUTIA

Rounded or oval cacti with bristly spines. Flowers in spring or early summer.

Temperature: winter minimum 5°C (41°F).
Humidity: tolerates dry air, but appreciates humid atmosphere in spring and summer.
Position: good light, full sun.
Watering and feeding: water moderately from spring to autumn, almost dry in winter. Feed in summer with cactus food.
Care: repot in spring if necessary, using cactus mixture.
Propagation: cuttings from offshoots; seed.

RHODODENDRON

R. x *obtusum* (range of colours) and *R. simsii* (pinks and reds) are good for winter and spring colour. Known as azaleas.

Temperature: winter 10–16°C (50–60°F).
Humidity: mist leaves regularly.
Position: good light, not direct sun.
Watering and feeding: water freely at all times, using soft water if possible. Feed regularly in summer.
Care: repot in ericaceous mixture one month after flowering. Place in garden in sheltered shady spot after all danger of frost is past. Keep watered and fed. *R. simsii* must be brought indoors in early autumn.
Propagation: cuttings.

ROSA, MINIATURE HYBRIDS

Miniature bushes or standards make short-term houseplants in various colours.

Temperature: frost hardy. 10–21°C (50–70°F) when plants growing actively.
Humidity: undemanding, but advisable to mist occasionally.
Position: best possible light. Tolerates full sun.
Watering and feeding: water freely from spring to autumn, while in leaf. Feed regularly in summer.
Care: place outdoors when not in flower. Repot in autumn if necessary. Prune in spring. Bring indoors in late spring, or as soon as flowering starts.
Propagation: cuttings.

SAINTPAULIA

Rosette-forming, hairy-leaved perennials with large colour range. Long-flowering with appropriate light intensities.

Temperature: winter minimum 16°C (60°F).

Humidity: high humidity, stand on tray of wet pebbles; misting is unsuitable.

Position: good light, avoid direct summer sun during hottest part of day. Artificial light at least 5,000 lux.

Watering and feeding: water freely from spring to autumn, moderately in winter, allowing surface to dry out a little. Soft water if possible. Don't wet leaves. Feed during active growth, but stop if lots of leaves and few flowers.

Care: will continue flowering with supplemental light, but needs at least one month's rest; lower temperature to minimum, reduce watering and shorten day length. Place the plant in good light to restart growth.

Propagation: leaf cuttings; seed.

SANSEVIERIA TRIFASCIATA 'LAURENTII'

Tough, fleshy, sword-like leaves, dull green with paler cross-banding and yellow edges.

Temperature: winter minimum 10°C (50°F).

Humidity: tolerates dry air.

Position: bright, indirect light, but it tolerates direct sun and some shade.

Watering and feeding: water moderately from spring to autumn, very sparingly in winter. Always allow the soil to dry out slightly before watering. Feed regularly in summer.

Care: repotting is seldom required.

Propagation: division.

SAXIFRAGA STOLONIFERA

Trailing alpine with rounded, broadly toothed leaves, olive green with veining.

Temperature: winter minimum 7°C (45°F).

Humidity: mist occasionally.

Position: good light, not direct sun.

Watering and feeding: water freely from spring to autumn, sparingly in winter. Feed regularly in summer.

Care: trim off long runners if untidy.

Propagation: plantlets (peg down in pots).

SCHEFFLERA ARBORICOLA 'AUREA'

Erect, branched, variegated evergreen with oval leaflets radiating from each leaf stalk.

Temperature: winter minimum of 13°C (55°F).
Humidity: mist regularly.
Position: good light, avoid direct sun.
Watering and feeding: water freely from spring to autumn, sparingly in winter. Feed regularly in summer.
Care: either train as upright, unbranching plant by staking, or remove growing tip to make bushy. Repot annually in spring.

SEDUM

Small, fleshy, branching succulents, some with white, pink or yellow flowers.
Temperature: winter minimum 5°C (41°F).
Humidity: tolerates dry air.

Position: best possible light.
Watering and feeding: water sparingly from spring to autumn, keep nearly dry during winter.
Care: repot in spring, using free-draining potting soil such as cactus mixture.
Propagation: leaf cuttings (for large fleshy leaves); stem cuttings.

SINNINGIA SPECIOSA

Tuberous perennials with large, hairy leaves and bell-shaped flowers in various colours, in summer. It is often sold as *Gloxinia*.

Temperature: minimum 16°C (60°F) during growing season.
Humidity: mist around plant regularly, but avoid wetting leaves or flowers. Provide as much humidity as possible.
Position: good light, not direct sun.
Watering and feeding: water freely once tubers have rooted well. Decrease at end of growing season. Feed regularly in the summer months.
Care: store tubers in the pot in frost-free place, ideally at 10°C (50°F). Repot in the spring.
Propagation: leaf cuttings; seed.

SOLANUM CAPSICASTRUM

Sub-shrubs grown for their autumn to winter fruit (green turning red). Poisonous fruit.

Temperature: winter 10–16°C (50–60°F).
Humidity: mist leaves regularly.
Position: best possible light. Tolerates some direct sun.
Watering and feeding: water freely through growing period. Feed regularly in summer.
Care: buy in fruit or raise in greenhouse until fruit formed.
Propagation: seed; cuttings.

SOLEIROLIA SOLEIROLII

Compact, mounded plant, with tiny leaves, 5 cm (2 in) high. Silver and gold varieties.

Temperature: frost hardy, but 7°C (45°F) is ideal.
Humidity: mist regularly.
Position: good light, not direct sun.
Watering and feeding: water freely.
Care: repot in spring in low, wide container.
Propagation: division.

SPARRMANNIA AFRICANA

Tall and fast-growing ever-green with pale green, downy leaves. White spring flowers.
Temperature: winter minimum 7°C (45°F).
Humidity: mist occasionally.
Position: good light, but not direct summer sun during the hottest part of the day.
Watering and feeding: water freely from spring through to autumn, sparingly in the winter. Feed regularly in spring and summer.
Care: cut back stems after flowering. When repotting, cut back to 30 cm (12 in) if necessary. Young plants may need repotting seveal times a year to accommodate its fast growth. Pinch out growing tips of young plants for a bushy shape.
Propagation: cuttings.

STEPHANOTIS FLORIBUNDA

Climber with glossy, oval leaves. Clusters of fragrant white flowers in summer.

Temperature: winter 13–16°C (55–60°F).
Humidity: mist occasionally.
Position: good light, avoid direct summer sun during hottest part of day.
Watering and feeding: water freely from spring to autumn, sparingly in winter. Feed regularly in summer, in moderation if plant is large.
Care: train to a support. Shorten overlong shoots and cut out overcrowded stems in spring.
Propagation: cuttings.

STREPTOCARPUS HYBRIDS

Perennial with horizontal, stemless leaves and large trumpet-shaped flowers in pink, red and blue, late spring through summer. Leaf sap can cause an irritating rash.

Temperature: winter minimum 13°C (55°F).
Humidity: lightly mist leaves occasionally.
Position: good light, avoid direct summer sun.
Watering and feeding: water freely from spring to autumn, sparingly in winter. Feed regularly in summer.
Care: benefits from dormant winter season, with soil only slightly moist and temperature close to winter minimum. Repot early spring.
Propagation: leaf cuttings; seed.

SYNGONIUM PODOPHYLLUM

Evergreen climber with foot-shaped leaves, arrow-shaped on young plants. Variegated varieties. Will grow to 1.8 m (6 ft).

Temperature: winter minimum 16°C (60°F).
Humidity: mist leaves regularly.
Position: good light, not direct sun. Tolerates low light levels.
Watering and feeding: water freely from spring to autumn, sparingly in winter but do not allow it to dry out completely. Feed regularly in spring and summer.
Care: to retain juvenile leaves, cut off climbing stems at the base. Repot the plant every second spring.
Propagation: cuttings; air layering.

TILLANDSIA CYNEA

Rosette of narrow, striped grass-like leaves. Summer flower spike has pink or red bract and purple-blue flowers.

Temperature: winter minimum 18°C (64°F).
Humidity: mist regularly.
Position: good light, not direct summer sun.
Watering and feeding: water freely from spring to autumn, sparingly in winter. Soft water if possible. Apply weak fertilizer to leaves, using mister, or to soil.
Care: can pot in spring.
Propagation: offsets.

TOLMIEA MENZIESII

Bright green foliage plant with heart-shaped leaves. Plantlets develop on base of each leaf blade. Variegated varieties are available.

Temperature: winter minimum 5°C (41°F). Avoid high winter temperature.
Humidity: mist occasionally.
Position: good light or semi-shade, not direct sun.
Watering and feeding: water freely from spring to autumn, sparingly in winter. Feed regularly in summer.
Care: if plant too large and stems congested, cut back in spring. Repot each spring.
Propagation: division; pot up plantlets.

TRADESCANTIA

Trailing foliage houseplants. Several variegated varieties with white or purple tinges.

Temperature: winter minimum 7°C (45°F).
Humidity: mist occasionally.
Position: good light, with some direct sun.
Watering and feeding: water freely from spring to autumn, sparingly in winter. Feed regularly from spring through to the autumn months.
Care: pinch out any unattractive shoots.
Propagation: cuttings.

TULIPA

Some tulips can be forced for winter colour.

Temperature: hardy. Once in flower, the cooler the room, the longer the flowers will last.

Humidity: undemanding.

Position: can be placed anywhere if brought indoors just as flowers open.

Watering and feeding: water moderately while in the home.

Care: in early or mid-autumn, plant bulbs with necks just below soil. Place in sheltered place outdoors and cover with fine gravel or other suitable mulch at least 5 cm (2 in) deep. Keep soil in pots moist but not overwatered. When shoots are 4–5 cm (1½–2 in) tall, place in light at about 15°C (59°F) until buds show colour. Bring into the home. Discard or plant in garden after flowering.

Propagation: buy fresh bulbs each year.

VRIESEA SPLENDENS

Bromeliad with rosette of arching, strap-shaped, banded leaves. Bright red flower bract in summer and autumn.

Temperature: winter minimum 15°C (59°F).

Humidity: mist leaves regularly.

Position: light shade or good light out of direct sun.

Watering and feeding: water freely from spring to autumn, sparingly in winter. Keep "vase" of leaves topped up with water from mid-spring to mid-autumn. Soft water if possible. Feed a weak fertilizer in summer.

Care: discard after flowering, or pot up offsets in ericaceous soil.

Propagation: offsets.

YUCCA ELEPHANTIPES

Rosettes with long pointed leaves growing from a trunk section. Can grow to ceiling.

Temperature: winter minimum 7°C (45°F).

Humidity: tolerates dry air.

Position: prefers good light with some sun but avoid full sun.

Watering and feeding: water freely from spring to autumn, sparingly in winter.

Care: repot small plants as necessary, large ones can remain in same container for many years, but replace top 5 cm (2 in) of potting soil.

Propagation: use sideshoots from the plant as cuttings.

Common Names of Plants

aconite *Aconitum*
African daisy *Arctotis*
African lily *Agapanthus*
African marigold
   Tagetes erecta
Algerian iris
   Iris unguicularis
alyssum
   Lobularia maritima
annual pepper
   Capsicum annuum
auricula *Primula auricula*
   hybrids
autumn crocus
   Colchicum autumnale,
   Crocus nudiflorus
arum lily *Zantedeschia*
   aethiopica
avens *Geum*

baby blue-eyes
   Nemophila menziesii
baby's breath
   Gypsophila paniculata
balsam poplar
   Populus balsamifera
Barberry
   Berberis sargentiana
basil *Ocimum basilicum*
bay *Laurus nobilis*
bear's breeches *Acanthus*
beauty bush
   Kolkwitzia amabilis
bedding geranium
   Pelargonium
beech *Fagus sylvatica*
bellflower *Campanula*
bells of Ireland
   Moluccella laevis
bergamot *Monarda*

betony *Stachys*
black-eyed Susan
   Rudbeckia
bladder senna *Colutea*
blazing star *Liatris*
bleeding heart
   Dicentra spectabilis
blue daisy *Felicia*
blue fescue *Festuca glauca*
bluebell *Hyacinthoides*
borage *Borago officinalis*
Boston ivy *Parthenocissus*
   tricuspidata
box *Buxus sempervirens*
bridal wreath *Francoa*
broom *Cytisus, Genista*
bulrush *Typha latifolia*
burnet *Sanguisorba*
busy Lizzie *Impatiens*
buttercup *Ranunculus*
butterfly bush *Buddleja*
   davidii

calamint *Calamintha*
calico bush *Kalmia*
   latifolia
California lilac
   Ceanothus
Californian poppy
   Eschscholzia

campion *Silene*
candytuft *Iberis*
Canterbury bells
   Campanula medium
Cape figwort *Phygelius*
cardoon *Cynara*
   cardunculus
carnation *Dianthus*
castor oil plant *Ricinus*
catchfly *Lychnis*
catmint *Nepeta* x *faasseni*
chamomile
   Chamaemelum nobile
cherry *Prunus*
cherry pie *Heliotropum*
China aster *Callistephus*
   chinensis
Chinese pink *Dianthus*
   chinensis
chives *Allium*
   schoenoprasum
Christmas box
   Sarcococca
Christmas cactus
   Schlumbergera
cineraria
   Senecio cineraria
cinquefoil *Potentilla*
climbing hydrangea
   Hydrangea petiolaris
coleus *Solenostemon*
columbine *Aquilegia*
comfrey *Symphytum*
common bugle
   Ajuga reptans
coneflower *Echinacea,*
   Rudbeckia
contorted or corkscrew
   hazel *Corylus avellana*
   'Contorta'

coral flower *Heuchera*
cornflower *Centaurea cinerea*
cotton lavender *Santolina chamaecyparissus*
cowslip *Primula veris*
crab apple *Malus*
cranesbill *Geranium*
creeping Jenny *Lysimachia nummularia*
creeping zinnia *Sanvitalia*
cuckoo flower *Cardamine pratensis*
Cupid's dart *Catanache*
curry plant *Helichrysum italicum*

daffodil *Narcissus*
daisy *Bellis perennis*
daisy bush *Olearia*
dame's violet *Hesperis matronalis*
daylily *Hemerocallis*
deadnettle *Lamium*
dittany *Dictamnus*
dogwood *Cornus*
dog's tooth violet *Erythronium*
Dutchman's pipe *Aristolochia*

elder *Sambucus*
elephant ears *Bergenia*
evening primrose *Oenothera speciosa*

false castor oil plant *Fatsia japonica*
feather grass *Stipa*

fennel *Foeniculum vulgare*
feverfew *Tanacetum parthenium*
firethorn *Pyracantha*
flag *Iris germanica*
fleabane *Erigeron*
floss flower *Ageratum*
flowering currant *Ribes sanguineum*
flowering flax *Linum grandiflorum*
flowering quince *Chaenomeles*
forget-me-not *Myosotis*
foxglove *Digitalis purpurea*
French marigold *Tagetes patula*
fritillary *Fritillaria*
furze *Ulex*

garlic *Allium sativum*
gay feather *Liatris*
gentian *Gentiana*
geranium *Pelargonium*
giant thistle *Onopordum*
ginger mint *Mentha* x *gracilis* 'Variegata'
globe amaranth *Gomphrena globosa*
globe thistle *Echinops*
globeflower *Ranunculus ficaria*
godetia *Clarkia*
golden privet *Ligustrum ovalifolium* 'Aureum'
golden rod *Solidago*
gorse *Ulex*
grape hyacinth *Muscari*
guelder rose *Viburnum opulus*
gum *Eucalyptus*

harebell *Campanula rotundifolia*
Harry Lauder's walking stick *Corylus avellana* 'Contorta'
hart's tongue fern *Asplenium scolopendrium*
hawthorn *Crataegus*
hazel *Corylus*
heartsease *Viola tricolor*
heath *Erica carnea*
heather *Calluna vulgaris*
heliotrope *Heliotropium*
hellebore *Helleborus*
hemp agrimony *Eupatorium*
Himalayan poppy *Meconopsis*
holly *Ilex aquifolium*
hollyhock *Alcea rosea*
honesty *Lunaria annua*
honey bush *Melianthus*
honeysuckle *Lonicera*
honeywort *Cerinthe major*
hop *Humulus lupulus*
hornbeam *Carpinus betulus*
houseleek *Sempervivum*
hyacinth *Hyacinthus orientalis*

iceplant *Sedum spectabile*
Indian bean tree *Catalpa bignonioides*
ironweed *Vernonia*
ivy *Hedera*

Jacob's ladder *Polemonium*
Japanese anemone *Anemone x hybrida*
Japanese quince *Chaenomeles*
Japanese maple *Acer palmatum*
japonica *Chaenomeles*
jasmine *Jasminum*
Jerusalem cross *Lychnis chalcedonica*
jessamine *Jasminum*
Jew's mallow *Kerria japonica*

kaffir lily *Schizolstylis coccinea*
katsura tree *Cercidiphyllum*
king fern *Dryopteris pseudomas* 'Cristata'
kingcup *Caltha*
knapweed *Centaurea*
knotweed *Persicaria*
kolomikta vine *Actinidia kolomikta*

lad's love *Artemisia abrotanum*
lady fern *Athyrium*
lady's mantle *Alchemilla mollis*
larkspur *Consolida ambigua*
lavender *Lavandula*
lemon balm *Melissa officinalis*
lemon verbena *Aloysa triphylla*
leopard's bane *Doronicum*
lesser celandine *Ranunculus ficaria*
lesser stitchwort *Stellaria graminea*
Leyland cypress *x Cupressocyparis leylandii*
lilac *Syringa*
lily *Lilium*
lily-of-the-valley *Convallaria majalis*
lilyturf *Liriope muscari*
lime tree *Tilia*
loosestrife *Lysimachia*
love-in-a-mist *Nigella*
love-lies-bleeding *Amaranthus*
lungwort *Pulmonaria*
lupin *Lupinus*

Madonna lily *Lilium candidum*
mallow *Lavatera, Malva*
maple *Acer*
marguerite *Argyranthemum frutescens*

marjoram *see* pot marjoram, sweet marjoram
marigold *Calendula*
marsh marigold *Caltha palustris*
mask flower *Alonsoa*
masterwort *Astrantia*
meadowsweet *Filipendula*
medlar *Mespilus germanica*
Mexican orange blossom *Choisya ternata*
Mexican sunflower *Tithonia*
Michaelmas daisy *Aster*
mignonette *Reseda odorata*
mile-a-minute plant *Fallopia baldschuanica*
milk thistle *Silybum marianum*
mint *Mentha*
mock orange *Philadelphus*
money flower *Mimulus*
monkshood *Aconitum*
montbretia *Crocosmia*
morning glory *Ipomoea*
Mount Etna broom *Genista aetnensis*
moutan *Paeonia*
mullein *Verbascum*
meadow buttercup *Ranunculus acris*
meadow cranesbill *Geranium pratense*
milfoil *Achillea millefolium*
myrtle *Myrtus*

nasturtium *Tropaeolum majus*

New England aster *Aster novae-angliae*
New Zealand flax *Phormium*
night-scented stock *Matthiola longipetala*

old man *Artemisia abrotanum*
Oregon grape *Mahonia*
oregano *Origanum vulgare*
ornamental onion *Allium*
ornamental rhubarb *Rheum*
ornamental vine *Vitis*
ox eye *Heliopsis*

pampas grass *Cortaderia selloana*
pansy *Viola* x *wittrockiana* cultivars
parsley *Petroselinum crispum*
passion flower *Passiflora caerulea*
pennyroyal *Mentha pulegium*
peony *Paeonia*
periwinkle *Vinca major, V. minor*
Peruvian lily *Alstroemeria*
pimpernel *Anagallis*
pineapple broom *Cytisus battandieri*
pink *Dianthus*
plantain lily *Hosta*
plumbago *Ceratostigma willmottianum*
poached-egg flower *Limnanthes douglasii*
polyanthus *Primula*

poppy, field *Papaver rhoeas*
poppy, opium *Papaver somniferum*
Portugal laurel *Prunus lusitanica*
potato vine *Solanum crispum*
pot marigold *Calendula*
pot marjoram *Origanum*
prickly poppy *Argemone*
primrose *Primula vulgaris*
privet *Ligustrum*
purple coneflower *Echinacea purpurea*
purple loosestrife *Lythrum salicaria*
purple velvet plant *Gynura aurantiaca*
purslane *Portulaca*

quince *Cydonia oblonga*

red-hot poker *Kniphofia*
red orache *Atriplex*
red valerian *Centranthus ruber*
rock cress *Aubrieta deltoidea*
rock rose *Cistus, Helianthemum*
rose *Rosa*

rose of Sharon *Hypericum calycinum*
rosemary *Rosmarinus officinalis*
rue *Ruta graveolens*
Russian sage *Perovskia*

sage *Salvia officinalis*
saxifrage *Saxifraga*
scabious *Scabiosa*
scented geranium *Pelargonium fragrans*
scorpion weed *Phacelia*
sea buckthorn *Hippophäe rhamnoides*
sea holly *Eryngium*

shoo-fly flower *Nicandra physalodes*
Siberian wallflower *Erysimum* x *allioni*
silk tassel bush *Garrya elliptica*
slipper flower *Calceolaria*
smoke bush *Cotinus coggygria*
snake's-head fritillary *Fritillaria meleagris*
snapdragon *Antirrhinum*
sneezeweed *Helenium*
snowberry *Symphoricarpos*
snowdrop *Galanthus nivalis*
snowflake *Leucojum*
Solomon's seal *Polygonatum*
sorrel *Rumex acetosa*
southernwood *Artemisia abrotanum*
Spanish broom *Spartium junceum*
speedwell *Veronica*

spider plant *Chlorophytum comosum*

spiderflower *Cleome*

spindle *Euonymus*

spotted laurel *Aucuba japonica*

spurge *Euphorbia*

squirrel tail grass *Hordeum jubatum*

St John's wort *Hypericum*

stag's horn sumach *Rhus typhina*

star jasmine *Trachelospermum jasminoides*

statice *Limonium*

stock *Matthiola*

stonecrop *Sedum*

sun rose *Cistus, Helianthemum*

sunflower *Helianthus annuus*

Swan river daisy *Brachyscome iberidifolia*

sweet alyssum *Lobularia maritima*

sweet bay *Laurus nobilis*

sweet briar *Rosa eglanteria*

sweet box *Sarcococca*

sweet marjoram *Origanum majorana*

sweet pea *Lathyrus odoratus*

sweet rocket *Hesperis matronalis*

sweet rush *Acorus calamus*

sweet violet *Viola odorata*

sweet William *Dianthus barbatus*

tamarisk *Tamarix*

Texan bluebell *Eustoma grandiflorus*

thyme *Thymus vulgaris*

tickseed *Coreopsis tinctoria*

toadflax *Linaria*

tobacco plant *Nicotiana alata*

Torbay palm *Cordyline*

torch lily *Kniphofia*

tree mallow *Lavatera*

tree peony *Paeonia*

tulip *Tulipa*

turflily *Liriope*

turtle's head *Chelone*

velvet sumach *Rhus typhina*

Venus' navelwort *Omphalodes linifolia*

violet *Viola*

viper's bugloss *Echium vulgare*

Virginia creeper *Parthenocissus quinquefolia*

virgin's bower *Clematis flammula*

wake robin *Trillium grandiflorum*

wallflower *Erysimum cheiri*

wandering Jew *Tradescantia*

wattle *Acacia*

whitewash bramble *Rubus cockburnianus*

wild bergamot *Monarda fistulosa*

willow *Salix*

willow-leaved jessamine *Cestrum parqui*

windflower *Anemone*

winter aconite *Eranthis hyemalis*

winter cherry *Solanum pseudocapsicum*

winter green *Gaultheria procumbens*

winter heath *Erica carnea*

winter jasmine *Jasminum nudiflorum*

winter-sweet *Chimonanthus*

witch hazel *Hamamelis mollis*

woad *Isatis tinctoria*

wood anemone *Anemone nemorosa*

wood lily *Trillium*

wormwood *Artemisia*

yarrow *Achillea*

yew *Taxus baccata*

Index

Index

Index

Index